Somalia:

Diaspora and State Reconstitution In The Horn Of Africa

Published by
Adonis & Abbey Publishers Ltd
P.O. Box 43418
London
SE11 4XZ
http://www.adonis-abbey.com
Email: editor@adonis-abbey.com

First Edition, April 2007

British Library Cataloguing-in-Publication Data
A catalogue record for this book is available from the British Library

ISBN: 9781905068838 (PB)

Printed and bound in Great Britain

Somalia:

Diaspora and State Reconstitution In The Horn Of Africa

Edited by

Abdulkadir Osman Farah, Mammo Muchie & Joakim Gundel

CONTENTS

Section 2: Conflict, reconciliation and state formation

Acknowledgements

The editors of this book express appreciation to associate Professor Johannes D. Schmidt, DIR, Aalborg University, who took the decision to host a major Horn of African conference and invited scholars from the region to contribute to the academic debate and presentations. We also express our thanks to researcher Bjørn Møller, DIIS, who supported us immensely, particularly with the attraction of funds to the project. There are numerous people who one way or the other positively contributed to this project, which stretched to more than two years of constant hard work and engagement. The following persons did more than more than a fair share to ensure that this project succeeds and attracts the necessary international attention:

Professor Mohamed Hadji Mukhtar, Susanne Lilius, *Independent researcher*, Dr. Mohamed Harakow Mohamed, *Chair of Somali academics and researchers in Denmark*, Drs. Sirad Sidow Roble, Ali Abdi Yusuf (Hussein Dubow), *Agronomist*, Aweys Sheikh Yonis, *Educationist*, Abdulkadir Aden, *Educationist*, Abdullahi Ali Ahmed, *Student*, Abdulkadir Mohamed Harakow, *Student*, Kambiz Kalantar Hormoozi, *researcher & consultant*, Maryan Mursal Essa, Abdiaziz M. Hassan, *Mentor*, Emil Gundel, Sejr Gundel, Zeinab M. Ali, *Social health worker*, Redwan Abdulkadir Osman, Rakiya Abdulkadir Osman, Abdulaziz Abdulkadir Osman, Maryan Abdulle, *Somali Women Organisation Aalborg*, Abdi Adde & Somali Online TV, Hiiraan Online, Abdisalaan Hareeri of BBC, Amun Ali, Radio Sweden.

Preface

The dispersal of Somalis throughout the world is one of the consequences of the end of the Cold War. Two years after the fall of the Berlin Wall in 1991, the Somali dictator Siad Barre fell and left no consequential authority behind. His dictatorial rule forced public conversation into the safe haven of the home and the clan, where any form of inter- Somali level trust seems to have been on retreat ever since. It appears politics migrated into the hands of clans and society appeared to be a sum total of self-defining, self-acting, self-ruling clans. The Somalia post colonial state broke down with the ensuing insecurity in public and private lives. It led to the era of warlordism and Somalia became even more of a victim of various types of regional and international interventions than under the earlier regimes.

The reconstitution of public political authority has been a paramount concern for all who wish stability and security to be above all else a priority for normalising public and private lives in Somalia. But stability and security have become rare commodities to this day. Reconciling the warlords to join a new transitional authority has not gone well despite the fact that the international community recognised this authority to help it succeed and even move into the capital Mogadishu. As the transitional authority slowly made its long journey from Nairobi to the Somali city of Baidoa, the Union of Islamic Courts (IUC) came on the scene, backed by the business community and a significant portion of the Somali Diaspora. They seem to provide a new model of re-building the state through a combination of religion, grass roots mobilisation and business support. Whilst the world (with reservations from Western Governments) that puts a premium on stability that has been a rare commodity in Somali, welcomed their swift ability to control Mogadishu, the capital of Somalia and extend their influence in the Southern part of Somalia, they too came soon between a rock and hard place. They began to espouse crude and indigestible 'holy war' or Jihad-type rhetoric, which turned into reservation by those who fear the rise of Islamic ideology led movements into outright hostility against them. This inflaming and ill-timed rhetoric attracted the further animosity of the neighbouring powers as well as the current US administration. Allegations that they are providing safe haven to Al-Qaeda operatives continued to pour in the press. The ray of hope that stability and security may come through the Islamic Union Courts soon was dashed by the ensuing hostility between the transitional authority in Baidoa and the IUCs in Mogadishu. The negotiations between the Transitional Government and the IUCs failed, providing the pre-text for the intervention by the Meles regime against the IUCs. The leaders of the Islamic Union Courts are now in disarray. Some are said to have melted into the populace. Others are regrouping. Still others have left Somalia. Whether this is an orderly retreat or a hasty and unplanned retreat is not very clear. This will be known in the next few months, whether a resistance is born or the exhaustion of over a decade of un-relentless chaos has taken its toll and people are ready to follow any Government whatever it may be: good, bad or tasteless. If the Somali can accept without protest a Meles-backed regime, it can only mean they are exhausted by the years of chaos and destruction and wish to be ruled by anyone as long as there is some semblance of public and private security. However, one doubts very much that this is the case with the Somali situation.

The project of creating a state issued from grassroots mobilisation and from below at least through the agency of the Islamic Union Courts seems in tatters now. If the Islamic Union Courts are defeated, and the Transitional Government succeeds, Somalia would have to embark on a post-colonial state formation just like in many other African countries driven by the constellation and overlapping interests of internal and domestic elites and forces. A historical opportunity of a made- in-Somalia state would have been lost. Whilst that larger composition of political authority and legitimacy from below is very novel and a rare opportunity were it to unfold, the more urgent issue for Somalis is restoring relative peace, security and stability in Somalia.

It remains to be seen whether the UN and EU-recognised transitional government, supported by the USA and the Meles regime, can constitute a political authority that can restore peace, stability and security in Somalia. The recomposition of Somalia from its clan fragments into a united Somali entity is critically important. Without such recomposition, Somali will continue to be a hazard to itself primarily, but also to the wider Horn of Africa region, Middle East and Africa generally and the world. Thus the most important issue is to bring back stability. It would have been helpful were this stability to be constituted with negotiation, conversation, debate, freedom and argument. But that may not be available now especially if the yet untested Transitional Government becomes exclusionist, unrepresentative and undemocratic. The route to an entirely Somali-generated state has been closed now by the use of force, invasion and external intervention.

The issue is whether this external intervention will bring about the constitution of a stable political order in Somalia. The odds seem heavily against it if the remnants of the Courts and the un-accommodated warlords pursue guerrilla actions against the transitional Government headed by Mr. Abdullahi Yusuf Ahmed and Mr. Ali Mohamed Ghedi. If this guerrilla action cannot take off, there may be a chance that a relatively stable Somalia regime may ensue. But there is a big "if" to this scenario.

The collection of articles here are bound by the common tragedy of a nation that should not have been broken into inter clan conflicts, and its state failing to keep rudimentary authority. Together they tell a story, convey a message, articulate hope and inspire the possibility that Somalis carry on life in Denmark as well as in Minneapolis, in a refugee camp in Kenya to a metropole in London, even as they fight also to recompose their nation.

As an Ethiopian who desperately wishes Somali to re-emerge as a stable, democratic, peaceful and prosperous nation, I can only wish the agony would be over soon and life for the people will shine with hope and possibility. In the end, it will only be the Somalis who should know what is best for them. Others cannot tell them by killing them that what they do for them is the best. Thus securing and composing internal legitimacy is far more important than the external support that the current Transitional Federal Somali Government led by Mr. Yusuf and Mr. Ghedi seem to enjoy.

Mammo Muchie
Professor & Director
www.ihis.aau.dk/development

Introduction

A. Osman Farah, Mammo Muchie & Joakim Gundel

Since the final collapse of the centralised and suppressive government of Somalia in 1991, Somalia has presented the world with not only the most profound case of state collapse witnessed during the modern historical era, but also with one of the most intriguing cases of social complexity stemming from clan-related political fragmentation, armed conflict, lawlessness and statelessness, and the impacts of the worldwide dispersal of Somalis who fled the Somali quagmire.

Needless to add that the last 20 years of conflict, state collapse and destruction has left the Somali economy destitute, being ranked among the five lowest countries in the United Nations Human Development Index.

However, the developments within the territory of the former Republic of Somalia since the state collapse have by no means been uniform. Indeed, while there have been, and still are many negative features within the last 14 years such as the anarchy and terror people in Mogadishu endured due to the domination of warlords and intimidation and robbery by lawless militias (known as *Mooryan*), and violent conflicts between clans in the rural areas. There are also positive stories to tell such as the evolution and development of relatively stable and secure state formations in North-western Somalia (known as Somaliland) and North-eastern Somalia (known as Puntland). These two areas are the prime examples of how Somalis have struggled to survive and build a future under the difficult circumstances following the state collapse and the centrifugal tendencies of clannist conflicts. But, it also is possible to find another positive and strong Somalia in the Central and South. Indeed, civil society groups, traditional structures, and Diaspora groups, assert major influence in improving the socio-political and economic situation of the Somalis. The traveller to present-day Somalia cannot avoid being impressed by 'booming' businesses such as trade of goods, telecommunications, airlines, money remittance systems (*Xawilaad*), transport and real estate construction. Somali business entrepreneurs have direct global commercial links.

Interestingly, since the state collapse, the ensuing processes of state-formation in the Somali regions have been transboundary in character, amongst other things, because of these factors: 1) the impact and interrelations with the Somali Diaspora; 2) the refugee flows across borders to the neighbouring countries and the Somali refugee populations there; 3) the internationalisation of the conflict following the international interventions in the form humanitarian assistance and military intervention during UNOSOM (1992-1995), and the low-scale humanitarian aid since 1995; 4) the influence from political and military interventions from the regional powers and 5) international peace mediations led by the Inter-Governmental Authority on Development (IGAD) and UN representatives.

It is to these intriguing linkages between the processes of state-formation following total state collapse, and the hardships, aspirations and entrepreneurships of the global Somali Diaspora following the refugee migration, during and after the civil war, which is the adjoining focus of the chapters in this book. The chapters are based on papers presented at the 9th Congress of the Somali Studies International Association, which was hosted by the Centre for Development and International Relations, Aalborg University, Denmark in September 2004. The main theme of the congress was *Diaspora and State Formation in the Horn of Africa.* It was the aim of the organisers of the congress that the papers would contribute to a better understanding of the links and dynamics between the pursuit of developing a new state formation(s) in Somalia and the roles that the Diaspora and civil society groups play in this process. Hence, the point of departure for the 9th Congress was the dispersal of Somalis beyond the boundaries of the Republic of Somalia that collapsed as a state in 1991. Somalis have always lived beyond the territory of the Republic of Somalia, especially in the neighbouring states of Kenya, Ethiopia and Djibouti. Additionally, the Ogaden war (1977-1979), and the Civil Wars from 1988 and up till today caused millions of Somalis to flee and migrate throughout the region of the Horn of Africa - and further abroad to Europe, North America and other destinations (Gundel 2003). The dispersal of Somalis has been intimately linked to the still ongoing conflicts in the Horn of Africa, and is related to the complex processes of reconciliation and state formation there. The scope of the Congress therefore included all of the Horn of Africa as well as Somalis of the global Diaspora. Two parallel themes were set up for the congress:

> 1) The linkages between Diaspora and Development: This theme focused on the large numbers of Somalis, both in the region and further abroad and their potential importance for the political, social, cultural and economic development of Somalis 'away' as well as at 'home'.
>
> 2) Regionalism, Reconciliation and State Formation: This theme approached the issues of state formation from a regional perspective, which is not necessarily confined to the existing structure of so-called 'nation-states', but which investigates the processes that may result in

the formation of political authorities or states, even if they are regional, transboundary or non-territorial.

The Congress-papers selected for this book contribute to the ongoing debate on the future of the post-colonial state with relevance for Africa generally and Somalis particularly. With a long history and old traditions, the Somalis continue to apply customary laws and their own practices to build trust, reconcile and create social structures with relative peace and coexistence. For instance, Somaliland and Puntland were successful in their systematic application of a social and political contract based on traditional consensus and bottom-up approach.

Diaspora and Development

Although worldwide interest in the theme of Diaspora re-emerged during the last decades, Diaspora is an old concept. In simple terms, Diaspora could be defined as a distinct community with an identity linking members to their geographical area of origin. These communities could have similar physical attributes and derivative cultural traditions. With regard to the role Diaspora plays, earlier focus appeared to be on the patterns and processes of immigrants adopting or assimilating into their host societies. More recently however, the debate has moved to stress trans-nationalism and trans-border communities where immigrants and refugees are considered global actors. For instance, increasingly Diasporas are playing an increasingly important role in contributing to their home country economies through remittances and by acquiring education and skills that are later transferred to their home countries.

The legendary Somali poet and educator, Mohamed Ibrahim Hadrawi, visiting Denmark in November 2003 in connection with his International Peace Journey, told a gathering of Danish public officials that Somalis were learning to act as refugees in the Diaspora. They could be described as nomads but to be a refugee in a large scale is relatively new experience for them. Never in the history of this nation, he added, had so many ordinary Somali people moved and settled in far away places where their cultures were estranged and subordinated. For the Europeans like the Danes the experiences were opposite because they experienced expansion during the slavery period and subsequent colonialism and also during the poverty-induced great migrations across the Atlantic, including the migrations during, and after the two major world wars.

Reconstructing the Somali polity

The state is an abstract concept that refers to an umbrella that includes the whole range of offices and institutions that enforce collective decisions for the society. With this approach, the state should monopolise power, meaning violence and major collective decisions must be implemented within the state framework. In post independent Africa, where the post colonial state was challenged by the society, the military and the personal ruler largely represented the state. The previous Somali state was a personalised state that ultimately collapsed and left behind destruction and underdevelopment.

Various ideas and suggestions have been presented to find alternatives to the wilderness Somalia is currently undergoing. These ideas vary from the notion of a stateless society, to the creation of hybrid forms of state combining the Somali clan-based political structures with modern democratic governmental institutions, and finally to the reference to the potential importance of building a state upon Islamic principles, because it believed Islam can unite the disunited Somalis, and provide an important basis for the basic founding idea of new formations of States in the Somali socio-cultural and religious fabric. Although Somalis are considered one of the most homogeneous people in the world with a single language and ethnicity, their clan factions and fault lines complicate any endeavour to stabilise the country and introduce and sustain the rule of law.

An important stumbling factor for building a centralised state in the Somali social fabric is essentially the very notion of the government and presidency of the state being centralised, in a society that is socially organised along vertical clan lines, with nearly no historical traditions of political centralisation. How to solve this feature has been central to many analyses of the Somali polity during the last decade. Two lines of thought, and practice, seem to have emerged. One idea builds upon the incorporation of the elder-institution into the formal political system, where their main role is to ensure political stability and be the ultimate conflict resolution mechanism. The other emphasises the ideationally unifying potentials of Islam, especially Islamic values and law. However, the main limitation to the application of Islamic values and law is that most Somalis in fact rather cherish their traditional Somali practices in their daily life. In addition, practising and implementing Islamic moral code requires that people have a certain knowledge and understanding of the holy scripts.

Rather than building modern political institutions, other scholars on Somalia have stressed the primacy of the economy and the significance of regional trader networks and global markets, hence advocating the potentials of the Somali stateless society. Somalis have in the last decade managed to engage in economic activities that created an environment where private enterprises flourished; they have cooperated and prospered within a stateless setting. However, this is not without negative side effects because this does produce an uncontrolled capitalist structure where the fittest survives and the vulnerable groups are left behind. Nevertheless, evidence shows that a significant number of economic activities increased during 'stateless' Somalia as compared to the previous centralised regime, leading to a discussion of whether the establishment of a viable state that can protect people's properties and investments for the common good is possible or not.

Numerous major obstacles confront the attempts to obtain a proper functioning Somali state. Firstly, although Somalis are described as democratic, pragmatic and consensus seeking people, many reconciliation efforts (14 of them at the last count) failed to construct a viable state that will address national and international challenges. Major obstacles include the local political culture. For instance political allegiances are not based on ideology but on group identity. Ideas are not valued or debated on their own terms, but only in terms of who is proposing them. Formulas for power-sharing take precedence over formulas for problem-solving (the "legitimacy" of any government depends on the inclusion in it of every sub and sub sub-clan, rather than on its adherence to law and democratic procedures, its efficacy in solving problems, or its fairness in distributing the benefits of its solutions). Somalis tend to identify politics with individuals, not institutions.

Second, the international situation after 9/11 and specifically the "war on terrorism," have also diverted energy and resources away from development and local peace-making initiatives. Additionally, there is the international involvement and interference, which complicates the process of creating peace and a stable state in Somalia. In the reconciliation and peace process, there are layers of external actors who took an interest in the conflict or in its management acting out of security, geopolitical, cultural, economic and humanitarian concerns. The relationship between the conflicting parties and their sponsors abroad, colonial relations, weapons, aid resources, the issue of terrorism are, among other things, identified as some of the factors that internationalised, exacerbated and prolonged the conflict.

The contributors to this volume reflect on the issues and problems that are tied to the failure of the Somali state and its consequences for the people who migrated outside Somalia, and went all over the world.

In Chapter one, Cassanelli discusses and analysis how to develop the Somali state through the participation and contribution of Diaspora communities. He tries to develop a thesis on how the Diasporic communities are involved in economic, politics and developmental activities. Often it is assumed that political stability is necessary to develop the state. But Cassanelli argues that the economic dynamics may be spearheading political stability.

In chapter two, Kusow provides a preliminary conceptualisation of the contemporary African Diaspora in which he distinguishes between the universality of the diasporas' social phenomenon and the specificity of the African Diasporic condition. Dr. Kusow uses his distinction to reflect the transformation of the Somali Diaspora in their new environment.

In chapter three, Lulling talks about the difficulties of refugee settlement by introducing concrete empirical case in the UK concerning Somali asylum seekers and their application.

In chapter four, Fangen, using exploratory empirical methods of Somali Diaspora in Norway, examines the homogeneity of Somalis and their fragmentation into clan segments. Fangen argues that clan identities are accentuated and aggravated in relation to stereotypes, stigmatisation and racial discrimination confronted in the host environment.

In chapter five, Richard Ford investigates whether methods of peace building and cooperation among communities that have proven success in some parts of Somalia could be applied to Somali Diaspora communities in the US.

In Chapter six, Horst emphasises the importance of taking a holistic view that combines an analysis of migration, remittances and information exchanges by conducting empirical research in Dadaab refugee camp and Diasporic communities in Minneapolis.

In Chapter seven, Bjork, using ethnographic field work, participant observation and in-depth interviews distinguishes the concept of clan from its highly sensitive political connotation. In addition, she nuances the concept of clan, which in some cases is stigmatised but celebrated in other cases. She also shows how clan identity is socially constructed in the everyday interaction of the lives of the Diasporic Somalis. She argues that the social context and the environment influence the clan dynamics

In Chapter eight, Kleist and Hansen analyse the Diaspora Somalis not as a nostalgic and static community or sociologically with status linked to economic responsibilities and expectations but as a moral community involved in translational political struggle.

In chapter nine, Abdulkadir Yahya and Jabril Ibrahim Abdulle, in two separate sections, introduce two important and contrasting features of current Somalia: the negative destructive impact of violence, crime and insecurity, and at the middle of this destruction the role of women in the Somali fabric, which increasingly represents a positive and constructive future for Somalia.

In Chapter ten, Hill discusses the Somali peace process, using a human rights perspective, by raising problems of post conflict reconstruction and the production of justice and reconciliation in Somalia.

In Chapter eleven, Farah discusses the main political actors in the Somali debacle by introducing the role of civil society and Diaspora communities in reconstituting a viable political system.

In chapter twelve, Abdullahi introduces proposals to reconsider the structure and the legitimacy of the Somali state which he states will be more accountable and progressive if it is built upon indigenous institutions such as the Islamic principles and the traditional customary livelihood of the Somalis.

In Chapter thirteen, Ibrahim introduced the political and democratisation processes in Somaliland and how they are related to the conduct and transformation of main political actors in Somaliland.

In Chapter fourteen, Höhne argues that in post civil war Somalia, some new political identities based on regional territories emerged. He analyses the clash of political identities between regional authorities such as Puntland and Somaliland and also discusses the inconsistencies and contradictions of identities that are fenced with what he refers to as 'territorial and mental' borders.

In chapter fifteen, Fowsia Abdulkadir, highlights the issue and relevance of empowering women and promoting educational opportunities for the eventual transformation of the society and the provision of sustainable security and development.

In Chapter sixteen, Saggiomo analyses the impact of international aid on the identity formation processes in Somalia.

In Chapter seventeen, Salmio describes the kind of challenges and obstacles of voluntary repatriation and resettlement the Somali refugees confront in their desire to return home.

In Chapter eighteen, Gundel and Osman Farah discuss the process of state formation in Somalia.

In conclusion papers included in this volume specifically deal with the themes of state reconfiguration, the role of Diaspora and civil society. In an increasingly complex global world, the ongoing debate on the sustainability and promotion of democratic governance with regard to the African state, particularly the attempt to reconfigure a viable Somali state, as discussed above, suggest that it is important to consider and include further dimensions such as the role of Diaspora and civil society groups. In the case of Somalia there is a need for the recognition of the growing importance of the dispersed Somali communities that are now more or less global. The willingness to respond to their wishes and priorities is necessary as part of the process of creating a just and comprehensive state and society. The Diaspora communities also belong to the most capable, in economic and professional terms, among the Somalis. It is interesting, therefore, to explore how civil society groups, whether traditional or professional, play important roles in the processes of creating institutions of governance within the processes of state-formation in the Horn of Africa. In an international political system where the state still remains the primary actor in enforcing internal and external power and sovereignty, it is also interesting to see how the Somali Diaspora and civil society engage and cooperate in the process of state-formation in their efforts not to recreate the flawed centralised and neo-patrimonial state structures of the past regimes in Somalia.

Section 1:
Diaspora, Identity and Development

Chapter 1

Somali Diaspora and the Reconstruction of Somalia: Obstacles and Opportunities

Lee Cassanelli

Introduction and brief history of SSIA

It is a great honour to be invited as one of the keynote speakers at this Congress, here in the presence of so many Somali friends and friends of Somalia. This is the Ninth International Congress of Somali Studies. It is truly remarkable that the SSIA has continued to hold an international Congress every three years, even after the collapse of the Somali state and the tragic civil war. Friends of Somalia around the world—in Italy, Germany, the U.S.A., Canada, Somaliland, and now Denmark—have been willing to step forward and host the meetings, to raise funds to support the participants, and to publish the proceedings, so that every three years new generations of Somalis and Somali experts can come together with old ones. We owe a great debt of gratitude to our hosts here in Aalborg for keeping this tradition alive. We can thank them best, I believe, by working diligently, positively, and cooperatively throughout these next three days to confront the challenges that face us. We all know how much work needs to be done.

The first Congress met in Mogadishu in 1979. Much of the work of organizing that first Congress was done by Hussein Adam "Tanzania", and he has been the Association's guiding light for more than two decades since that time. Because his wife remains, sadly, in a persistent coma, Hussein rarely travels away from home and cannot be with us at this year's Congress in Aalborg. But I spoke with him last week and he sends his greetings to all. He was confident that we would carry on in the spirit of the previous Congresses, to which he gave so much of his energy. Let me just remind you of the objectives of the SSIA, as stated in its constitution and by-laws at its founding in 1978.

- to promote scholarly research, both within and outside Somalia, in all areas and disciplines within the social sciences, natural sciences and humanities
- to encourage international cooperation and to facilitate the exchange of ideas among scholars engaged in research on Somalia and the Horn

of Africa
- to organize international congresses on Somali studies and periodic panels at meetings of national and international associations and organizations
- to provide the general public with information on historical, cultural, and contemporary issues in the Horn of Africa

I have been involved in Somali studies for more than thirty years, ever since I went to Somalia in 1971 to carry out research for my Ph.D. dissertation at the University of Wisconsin. Because I am an historian, I usually try to look back and see what the past can teach us. Every nation, even one which includes a large Diaspora living far from the homeland, needs to know its history and confront it, even if it is painful sometimes to do so. I will do a little bit of historical reflection in my remarks today. But mainly, I want to look at the present and the future, and to challenge all of us to think both critically and creatively about what roles we might play in the reconstruction of Somalia. This is YOUR conference. I might have the first word, but you should have the last word; and hopefully, more than simply words, you will speak with your actions. You can make this an historic Congress, one that will be remembered years from now when Somalis look back at the intellectual landmarks on their country's road to recovery and renewal.

Development and State Formation: which path to follow?

When I learned that I was to be the first speaker on the program, I resolved to try and do three things. First was to provide a brief history of the SSIA, which I've done. Second was to say a few words about the dual themes that our conference organizers proposed. And third was to discuss some of the "obstacles and opportunities" in our ongoing efforts to renew Somalia.

Let me try to link the two broad themes of this conference. Those themes are Diaspora and Development on the one hand, and Reconciliation and State Formation, or Institution Building, on the other. The first theme emphasizes economic and social development, the second political reconstruction. Now we know the organizers are right to bring the two themes together. To have sustainable economic development, Somalia requires a legitimate political authority that can uphold the law for all Somali citizens domestically, and that can represent the entire nation internationally. But to sustain a governing system, one needs institutions that have the capacity to provide for the economic and social well being of the people being governed. So what should experts address first: security and sovereignty, or economic and social needs?

Now if we look at history (which is always my first inclination), it seems to me that we can find plenty of examples of Somali success at economic recovery, even after prolonged periods of war, or drought, or dictatorship (see, e.g., Cassanelli 2002, Jamal 1988, Reusse 1982). Peter Little advises us that the history of Somalia since 1991 gives observers grounds for both "economic optimism" and "political pessimism." Little's recent (2003) book, *Somalia: Economy without State,* describes how Somali livestock traders, particularly those in the Lower Jubba region, have managed not only to survive but in some cases even to prosper despite the absence of a functioning government. He concludes that it is possible to have some degree of economic recovery without a strong state. The recent example of Somaliland is also instructive here. Wherever one stands on the sovereignty issue, most would agree that the modest economic gains in the north have occurred in spite of the fact (or maybe because of the fact) that the Somaliland state has not had the capacity to intrude very heavily into the private sector. Moreover, even without formal diplomatic recognition or substantial bilateral foreign aid, Somaliland has succeeded in attracting valuable contributions of money, skills, and professional expertise from members of its own Diaspora and from a number of NGOs. What is striking to me is the fact that in several regions of Somalia, economic recovery appears to be leading political recovery, despite our intuitive sense that political stability and order ought to come first.

The examples provided by Little and by the Somaliland case suggest to me that the international community, along with many Somali politicians, may have their priorities wrong. They have put their intellects and their energies and their resources (including those contributed by NGOs and friendly foreign governments) into finding political solutions first, which is always the most difficult thing for Somalis to achieve; and not enough energy and resources into building on what Somalis do best—that is, responding to economic opportunities. Maybe we should be concentrating on finding ways to build political consensus on the foundations of economic security, rather than vice versa.

I realize that many experts may not agree with this formulation. My good friends and colleagues, Ahmed and Abdi Samatar, argue strongly that Somalia's recovery and future development require the existence of a strong state— not a repressive one, but one with competent leadership committed to the rule of law and to justice for all its citizens. They argue that a legitimate state with effective institutions is essential 1) to establish and uphold general security and enforce the law; 2) to invest in basic services and infrastructure; 3) to protect the weak (and minorities) in the society; 4) to safeguard the environment;

and 5) to fashion out of the diverse and partisan interest groups found in every society a national development agenda that serves all of the nation's citizens, not just a favoured few (Samatar and Samatar, 2002).

The livestock traders and entrepreneurs that Peter Little describes in his book are too busy trying to survive to pursue the objectives that the Samatars see as critical for state building. As Little himself acknowledges, Somalia's post-1991 economic recovery has benefited some, but by no means all Somalis; it has produced some winners, but has also left many, many losers—including women and children (Little, p.5). Little also reminds us that those aspects of development we call "social" (e.g., health, education, welfare), tend to take second place when businessmen and entrepreneurs lead the way (156 ff). As Little notes, a legitimate government of some sort is necessary to deal with such long-term issues as regulating water from the Ethiopian highlands, defending Somalia's forests and fisheries from opportunistic exploitation, working to counter bans imposed by competing nations on Somalia's livestock exports, not to mention investing in social services (Little 2003a 173-74; see also Little 2003b). A viable state is also necessary to reverse the "retreat of global capital from Somalia" (Toggia 2000). Moreover, a "stateless economy" like Somalia's cannot easily control illicit trafficking in arms and drugs, which some Somalis have taken up in collaboration with criminal elements in neighbouring countries (see. e.g. Muranga 2003). Such activities only add to the reputation of Somalis in some quarters as lawless bandits.

I suspect there is no one in this audience who would disagree that some kind of efficient and representative Somali state is the most desirable long-term goal for Somalis both inside and outside the Horn. Somalis and their international friends must continue to work for political reconstruction and a stable constitutional order. I am only saying that if we wait until all Somalis agree on the form that a new government should take before we begin rebuilding social and economic institutions, we will have a long wait. Events following the Mbagathi agreement suggest that there are no political leaders today who enjoy nation-wide support in Somalia, and there are few, as far as I can tell, on the immediate horizon. As a result, we are faced with a situation where fragmentation and narrow self-interest still dominate the political process. But they need not dominate the process of capacity building. And it is here, I believe, that members of the Somali diaspora, working together with community leaders, NGOs, and civic-minded politicians in Somalia, can have a real impact. I am not saying it will be easy; there are, as you well know, many obstacles. But there are also opportunities.

Obstacles and opportunities

We will talk about many of these obstacles and opportunities, I am certain, over the next three days. But let me give you my list of the major ones. The obstacles fall into three categories, which we can separate for purposes of discussion but which are clearly interrelated. These obstacles are both internal and external, and it is important to recognize that Somalia is not the only country that faces them. They are 1) what we can call the local political culture, a set of ideas and practices about governance that are rooted in the historical experience of a given country; 2) the international situation after 9/11 and specifically the "war on terrorism," which has diverted energy and resources away from local development and peace-making initiatives; and 3) what development experts call "donor fatigue," which prevents the international community from doing all it can to assist Somalia in rebuilding its economy and government. My purpose in outlining these obstacles is not to point fingers of blame—there has been enough of that already over the past fifteen years—but to clarify what barriers we face and to help us make wise choices about how to navigate them.

Let us begin with the most visible obstacle.

Somali politics and political culture

You all know how Somali politics work. "Traditional" Somali political culture has been described as democratic, pragmatic, and consensus-driven. But as we have seen from the thirteen reconciliation conferences since 1991, consensus is hard to come by and even harder to sustain. We have all heard the characterizations of Somali politics:

- Political allegiances are not based on ideology but on group identity.
- Ideas are not valued/debated on their own merits, but only in terms of who is proposing them. Many Somalis judge a proposal as "good" or "bad" depending on who advances it. If it comes from our side, it is a good idea; if the same idea comes from the other side, it should be rejected—a bit like American politics these days!
- Formulas for power-sharing take precedence over formulas for problem-solving. This means that the "legitimacy" of any government depends on the inclusion in it of someone from every clan, sub-clan, and sub sub-clan, rather than on its adherence to law and democratic procedures, its efficacy in solving problems, or its fairness in distributing the benefits of its solutions.
- Somalis tend to identify politics with individuals, not institutions.

These aspects of Somali political culture have largely proven to be dysfunctional in recent efforts to restore a national government.

Over the years, many dedicated Somali professionals and civil servants have served their nation without regard to clan or regional affiliations. Today, many Somalis in the Diaspora continue to reject attitudes which put group loyalty ahead of long-term national solutions; but they have not been able to infuse their approach toward problem solving into the political processes in their homeland. So one of our challenges is how to transmit professional and associational identities and attitudes from the Diaspora to the homeland.

I am not sure that it can be done in the political arena for the time being. Even during the optimistic years of the 1960s, when Somalia's national leaders recognized the need to recruit skilled managers and engineers for the newly independent state, ministerial portfolios were shared out largely to satisfy political interests. The Samatars, who have been doing research on the early independence period, note how many well-intentioned Somali parliamentarians were pressured by their constituents to hire relatives for government posts and to provide special favours to their own home regions. The result was that many Somalis appointed to office had very little administrative experience or technical expertise, which "set very low professional standards for ministerial posts, a terrible precedent that continues to bedevil Somali leadership" (Samatar and Samatar 2002).

To overcome the obstacle of this deeply rooted political outlook, some observers have sought to find system of governance that ensures clan representation while insulating planners and administrators from excessive political pressure. A few years ago, Roland Marchal and Michel del Buono (2002) proposed a model for an interim government in Somalia that included both technical ministries staffed by the most competent professionals <u>and</u> political bodies representing regional and clan constituencies. This approach to institution building presumed that the Somali delegates at Mbagathi would be as concerned with solving problems as with ensuring the proper numerical representation of their constituencies. Unfortunately, this has not proven to be the case and the new government appears to be facing a political stalemate. As a result, Somali professionals abroad may have to work for the time being in parallel with the political reconstruction process, striving to build problem-solving teams that eventually can be incorporated into an interim or permanent government.

Impact of 9/11

A second major factor that obstructs the road to reconstruction is the international "war on terrorism." In the aftermath of 9/11, the notion of "development"—both economic and political—-has been redefined by international aid agencies as a "security" issue rather than as a technical/economic one. Whether we are speaking of Afghanistan, Iraq, the Congo, Sierra Leone, or Somalia, the prevailing view in international circles is that there can be no development without security. This emphasis on military security as a precondition for economic reform serves to reduce the importance, relatively speaking, of the technical, legal, and organizational skills that emigrant communities have to offer, while putting a premium on arming and training police forces and private security personnel to combat terrorists, insurgents, jihadists, or youth militias.

The "war on terrorism" has also made it more difficult for those who favour various pluralistic or decentralized models of political reconstruction to make their case. Western governments engaged in fighting terrorism have tended to lend their financial and diplomatic support to strong central authorities (even undemocratic ones) whom they regard as more effective partners in combating international terror networks. This tendency has served to derail or sideline other potentially creative solutions to long-standing problems of governance and law and order in war-torn societies like Somalia.

Finally, the "war on terrorism" has made it more difficult for (moderate) Western NGOs and (moderate) Islamic service organizations to cooperate. Even where such organizations share basic goals, such as delivery of basic health services, food and shelter for displaced persons, and primary education, there have been few efforts to coordinate actions. The reluctance to coordinate (much less to cooperate) comes from both sides, as old suspicions and new fears of being too closely identified with the other party keeps these agencies at arms length. My own view is that serious educational development cannot happen in Somalia without improved dialogue between Islamic charities and NGOs, and their Western counterparts. Both Islamic and Western charitable organizations represent large, non-violent constituencies that can be mobilized for civic improvement, and I suspect Diaspora leaders could take more initiatives in this area of cross-confessional coordination, even if cooperation or collaboration are not at this moment a realistic prospect.

Donor fatigue

The third obstacle is what has been called "donor fatigue," which I am using as shorthand for the frustration of Western governments, NGOs, and relief agencies in dealing not only with the continued turmoil in the Horn of Africa but also with the growing "backlash" of their own citizens against immigrants from Somalia and elsewhere who draw upon the social and medical services of their host countries. I think this is one area where members of the Somali Diaspora can have an immediate and important impact. If overseas Somalis cannot yet do much to transform the political culture of Somalia or to shape attitudes toward the war on terrorism, I think they can do something to help relieve the fatigue of their supporters here in Denmark and elsewhere around the world. It is clear from the list of presentations on our program that members of the Diaspora are already thinking about these challenges. One reason we are all together here is to draw ideas and inspiration from what others are doing, and maybe turn this conference into a catalyst for more systematic and cooperative initiatives. I will just give you a short list of some strategies that I have heard or read about, to help prompt discussion as our Congress proceeds.

Reversing the brain drain

As everyone knows, many countries in Africa continue to lose their most talented professionals to jobs overseas, leading to critical shortages in the health professions, the sciences, engineering, and law. For Africa as a whole, it has been estimated that 1/3 of the most highly qualified African nationals live outside their country—and their continent—of origin (Ammassari and Black, 2001). The crisis is even more acute for countries like Somalia where economic uncertainty and political instability discourage skilled émigrés from returning to offer even short-term assistance to their home countries. Just recently (August 2004), the Somalia office of the UNDP announced that it had launched a project to encourage Somali professionals living abroad to employ their skills back home. The project is called QUESTS (Qualified Expatriate Somali Technical Support), modelled after the UNDP's global initiative known as TOKTEN (Transfer of Knowledge Through Expatriate Nationals). The project requests authorities in Somalia, NGOs, and concerned Somalis overseas to identify high-priority development projects that could benefit from the skills of Somali expatriates. Health, education, and agriculture are among the initial priorities suggested in the appeal. The stated goals are to reverse the brain drain, support lasting peace, and give the Diaspora an increased role in creating an environment for sustainable human development (IRINNEWS 2004).

Supporting the families of Somali professionals who return to Somalia

To encourage Somali émigrés to acquire professional skills and take them back home, Western host governments should explore (along with NGOs) ways of supplementing the local (African) salaries of Somali professionals who return to Somalia for a year or more to work on designated projects. Part of the supplement would be retained by the host country to help subsidize the costs of housing, schooling, and job training for members of the professionals' families who stay behind in Europe or the U.S. or Canada. By integrating "foreign" technical assistance with "domestic" social benefits, this arrangement would assist Somalia while reducing émigré families' dependence on the social welfare system of the host country.

Somali Peace Corps

This is a young adult's version of the project described above. Somali youth can be given training in teaching, computer and communications, engineering, etc. and apprenticed to projects in Somalia. Ideally, Somalis returning to the Horn will be encouraged to live and in work in regions other than their clan homelands, to reduce pressures of local clan politics and bring some of the new civic attitudes to their homeland.

Setting priorities and planning action

Who takes the initiative here is important. One idea is to have workshops in different countries where there is a critical mass of professionally-trained Somalis and foreigners with Somali experience to design actual projects and identify counterpart organizations in Somalia with which the technical teams can work. Institution-building projects can be designed in Higher Education, Agriculture, Housing, Legal Education, Nursing, Communications, Environmental Planning, Engineering, etc. SACD (Somalia Aid Coordinating Body) might take some organizational initiatives in this area.

Creating more space for women's participation in planning and implementation

In setting priorities and planning action, institution builders should follow the lead of women's groups both in Somalia and in the Diaspora. As we know, women have borne much of the brunt of the war and have assumed new roles in family life, the workplace, and the service professions. Studies have shown that women in the Diaspora generally believe that Somali energies should be put first into solving the problems that face them and their families in the host societies, whereas men in the Diaspora still appear to direct much of their intellectual and financial resources to the homeland, often to support political factions. Even inside Somalia, it appears that the majority of women are very committed to improving the immediate circumstances in which they and their children live while leaving political affairs to the men. We need not romanticize the role of women, nor overstate their capacity to effect fundamental change, to urge that international donors and service agencies pay more attention to the strategies women have been employing for the past fifteen years in all spheres of public and private life. A very important new book should be required reading for all: *Somalia: The Untold Story. The War Through the Eyes of Somali Women,* edited by Judith Gardner and Judy El Bushra.

Building professional associations

Models for professional groups among Somalis already exist. With USAID funding and the support of Somaliland authorities, a Somaliland Lawyers Association was established and a public legal clinic was set up at the Hargiesa Faculty of Law, to offer low cost legal representation to poor individuals. In Mogadishu, SOJON (Somali Journalists Network) monitors human rights violations against journalists. Somali think tanks have been set up to provide Somalis in the homeland with civic education, computer training, and business management and planning skills. The results of these projects should be studied so that success stories can be replicated elsewhere in the country.

Remittances: learning from the experiences of other African Diasporas

We know that economic remittances are the most common way that overseas emigrants from every country contribute to the well-being of their homeland (Cassanelli 2004; Guarnizio 2003; Van Hear 2001). On a worldwide level, emigrant remittances are officially estimated at around $70 billion, and many experts believe the real figure to be double that. Either way, the amount far surpasses the total amount of development aid sent by the wealthier countries to the developing ones. For Somalia, estimates of the value of remittances sent back home by members of the Diaspora range from $250m annually to two or three times that amount. The important point about remittances is that while they assist families to meet economic and social needs, they do not necessarily contribute to the building of institutions or infrastructure in the home country (see. e.g., Gundel 2002). They are private rather than national assets, and so do not contribute directly to the restoration of state structures or public institutions like schools and hospitals.

A few African countries have found ways of addressing institutional development through emigrant associations which raise funds for particular public services in their home towns or districts. Ghanaians, with a large professional population in the U.S., have been able to fund eye clinics, maternity wards, and medical testing centres in their home regions. In Ghana, local and regional authorities are often authorized to deal directly with foreign donors, as long as their projects serve the larger national interest—a model that might be appropriate for regional administrations in a transitional decentralized Somali state. In the Eritrean case, overseas nationals are asked to contribute two percent of their annual income (even if it comes from welfare payments) to the Eritrean government to promote national development. While this model is clearly not feasible in the current circumstances of Somalia, regional administrations or technical ministries in a Somali transitional government might be responsive to creative proposals funded by Somali associations abroad. These might include the willingness to hire Somali expatriate consultants from lists of experts drawn up by associations of professionals in the Diaspora; to issue bonds to overseas nationals to fund public works in Somalia; or to explore private-public partnerships as a way of channelling a portion of the remittance pool into development projects that serve the public good (Koser 2002)

Conclusion

While examples from the comparative literature caution us not to overestimate the impact that Diaspora communities can have on political negotiations or political institution building in their home countries (see, e.g., Ostergaard:2002), overseas Somalis have the capacity to be more than passive spectators in the process of economic and social development. They can use their financial resources—however limited—and their skills, which are limitless, in a variety of creative ways. We need only think of the underutilized expertise that Somalis have demonstrated in learning foreign languages, in implementing telecommunications and transportation networks across the most difficult of terrains, in veterinary medicine and animal husbandry—to imagine how professional teams might serve not only Somalis but other peoples in the Horn of Africa and beyond. Somali professional associations can work with their counterparts in host countries on projects that will assist the homeland and also integrate their members more fully into the educational and economic life of their host societies.

Part of the challenge is to begin to think differently about today's world and Somalia's potential place in it—even if a positive Somali role in world affairs seems like a distant dream at this point in time. If, for example, we think in terms of "professional building blocks," rather than political building blocks (a notion which upsets Somali nationalists who fear that regionalization might become permanent), we can conceive of a corps of Somali experts in various professions who can be deployed to deal with common problems across the entire country. If we think of a "Greater Somalia" not in geo-political terms (which scares Somalia's neighbours and gives hesitation to its friends), but in terms of what Little calls a "greater Somalia" of trade and finance networks (and I would add professional associations and think tanks), then we have a resource with potential far greater than any warlord's war chest. (For some comparative examples from other developing countries, see Portes et al, 2002; Nyberg-Sorensen et al, 2002).

Let me end where I started, by saying that this Aalborg Congress of Somali Studies has the potential to contribute to the process of Somalia's reconstruction. Somalis, as we know, are excellent critics of other peoples' ideas, so I look forward to lots of discussion and debate on the topics I have outlined. We also know that Somalis have very good memories and like to argue about history, and about who or what was responsible for the predicament the Somali nation finds itself in today. But I do hope at this Congress that we can be creative as well as critical. I hope that we can use our panel sessions to explore future possibilities and not simply rehearse the failures of the past. As the proverb says, *Dagaal waa gelin dambe* (it's the second half of the war that matters, i.e., how it ends rather than how it begins).

For the next three days, I trust that all of us here will be fully engaged in the second half of that struggle to heal Somalia, the half that matters.

References

Ammassari, S. and R. Black (2001) *Harnessing the Potential of Migration and Return to Promote Development.* IOM Migration Research Series (Geneva: IOM)

Cassanelli, Lee (2004) "The Role of Diaspora Communities in Homeland Development," in Richard Ford, Hussein M. Adam, and Edna Aden Ismail, eds., *War Destroys, Peace Nurtures* (Lawrenceville, NJ: Red Sea Press, Inc.)

_____________ (2001). "An Historian's View of the Prospects for Somali Reconstruction," in Jorg Janzen, ed., *What are Somalia's*

Development Perspectives? Proceedings of the Sixth International Congress of Somali Studies (Berlin: Das Arabische Buch)

Gardner, Judith and Judy El-Bushra, eds. (2004) *Somalia, The Untold Story. The War Through the Eyes of Somali Women* (London: Pluto Press)

Guarnizo, Luis Eduardo (2003) "The Economics of Transnational Living," *International Migration Review,* vol 37, no 3.

Gundel, Joakim (2002) "The Migration-Development Nexus: Somalia Case Study."Prepared for the Centre for Development Research Study: *Migration-Development Links: Evidence and Policy Options.*

Koser, Khalid (2002)"Long-Distance Nationalism and the Responsible State: The Case of Eritrea," in Eva Ostergaard-Nielsen, ed., *International Migration and Sending Countries* (New York: Palgrave Macmillan)

Litte, Peter D (2003a) *Somalia: Economy without State* (Oxford: James Currey)

____________ (2003b) "Reflections on Somalia, or How to Conclude an Inconclusive Story," *Bildhaan. An International Journal of Somali Studies,* vol. 3. pp. 61-74.

Marchal, Roland and Michel del Buono (*NORD-SÜD aktuell 04/2002*) "Elements for a debate: A Tentative Description of Government Institutions and Program for Somalia's Recovery."

Murunga, Godwin Rapando (2003) "Refugees at Home? Crime and the Somalia Refugee in Nairobi, Kenya. Paper presented at the 46th Meeting of the African Studies Association, Boston, Massachusetts.

Nyberg-Sorensen, N., Nicholas Van Hear and P. Engberg-Pedersen (2002) *The Migration-Development Nexus. Evidence and Policy Options.* IOM Migration Research Series (Geneva. http://www.iom.int)

Ostergaard-Nielsen, Eva, ed. (2002) International *Migration and Sending Countries. Perceptions, Policies and Transnational Relations* (New York: Palgrave Macmillan)

Portes, A., I. E. Guarnizo, and P. Landolt (2002) "Transnational entrepreneurs: an alternative form of immigrant economic adaptation," *American Sociological Review* 67 (April): 278-98

Reusse, E. (1982) "Somalia's Nomadic Livestock Economy: Its Response to Profitable Export Opportunity," *World Animal Review* 43, pp. 2-11.

Samatar, Abdi Ismail and Ahmed I. Samatar (2002) "Somalis as Africa's First Democrats: Premier Abdirizak H. Hussein and President Aden A. Osman," *Bildhaan. An International Journal of Somali Studies,* vol. 2, pp. 1-64.

Toggia, Pietro (2000) "Civil Society and State Crisis in Somalia," in P. Toggia, Pat Lauderdale, and Abebe Zegeye, eds., *Crisis and Terror in the Horn of Africa* (Burlington, VT: Ashgate)

Van Hear, Nicholas (2001) "Sustaining societies under strain: remittances as a form of transnational exchange in Sri Lanka and Ghana," in N. Al-Ali and K. Koser, eds., *New Approaches to Migration? Transnational Communities and the Transformation of Home* (London: Routledge)

Chapter 2

From Mogadishu to Dixon: Conceptualising the Somali Diaspora

Abdi M. Kusow

Introduction

The recent proliferation of scholarship on Diaspora and transnational migration marks a revisionist scholarly turn. This turn embodies an important epistemological and paradigmatic - to borrow from Kuhn- a social scientific revolution, which promises to replace the received hegemony of the nation-state dividing line with borderlands of shifting and increasingly contested and blurred social and spatial boundaries. Emblematic of this trend is the appearance of new journals: *Diaspora, Public Culture, Journal of Black Studies,* and the newly revived *Transitions,* and a host of books and scholarly articles, all but devoted to understanding how the production, reproduction, and the circulation of diasporic cultural identities transcend the limits of the nation-state.

By using Somalia, the first post-cold war nation to fall into the vacuum created by the sudden disappearance of the geopolitics of two supper power arrangements; and the appearance of a spatially and temporally compressed world; as a case study, the purpose of this essay is to provide a preliminary conceptualization of the contemporary African Diaspora. One way to delimit the conceptual parameters of the contemporary African Diaspora is to distinguish it from general migration. According to Palmer (1988), migration refers to the movement of people from one point to another within or outside a political entity (a nation-state). Diaspora (Safran, 1991; Clifford, 1994; Cohen, 1996; Tololian, 1996; Palmer, 1998) on the other hand, refers to the dispersal of an entire population or a segment of it to multiple destinations at once or over a period of time.

Beyond this distinction, however, there is no consensus on how to define Diaspora, or the African Diaspora to which the present study is concerned. William Safran (1991) defines the African Diaspora on the basis of a six point criteria that can be summarized as: (1) dispersal from a single original homeland to multiple destination; (2) a collective memory, real or imagined about an original homeland; (3) a sense of otherness, a feeling of partial alienation from a host society; (4) a myth of an eventual return; (5) active participation in the maintenance and restoration of their original homeland; (6) a collective identity defined by the existence of an original homeland. Robin Cohen (1996) defines Diaspora on the basis of several sociological attributes. Using this process, he identifies the following: victim diasporas (Jewish, African, and Armenian), labour diasporas (Indians), imperial diasporas (British), trade diasporas (Chinese and Lebanese), or cultural diasporas (Caribbean). Palmer (1998) defines the African Diaspora on the basis of periodical and chronological schema. With this scheme, he identifies the first African Diaspora with the origin and dispersal of the human kind from the African continent and proceeds to the transatlantic, and ends with the ongoing post slavery and post-colonial African Diasporas.

The problem with the basic characteristics/checklist or features based definition is that it lacks the methodological language necessary to study the African Diaspora as a social phenomenon. Butler (2000), for example, rightly suggests that an application of a diasporan methodology, one that can articulate the social, economic, and cultural dynamics is needed. She specifically suggests that the definition of a Diaspora must not be based on the characteristics of the group, but rather by the type of research questions asked. Butler provides five dimensions or research questions: (1) the reasons and the conditions of dispersal; (2) the dynamics of relationship with a homeland; (3) relations with the host society; (4) relations within a Diaspora group; and (5) comparative studies of different Diasporas. Darlene Clark Hine suggests that a Black Diaspora Studies must have three features: a transatlantic framework, an interdisciplinary methodology, and a global framework.

For the purpose of this essay, Diaspora will be used to refer to the *social transformations* that result from the movement and subsequent settlement of a cultural group from an original homeland to multiple destinations while attempting to assimilate into their new host societies; and without at the same time severing social, political, and economic ties to an original, imagined or real homeland. The noble thing about the *social transformations* concept is that it de-emphasized the characteristic/features based, or methodological definitions and concentrates on the nature and dynamics of the *social transformations* that diasporic populations experience in their host societies and how, they in turn, relate those transformation to those they left behind. The Somali Diaspora, to which the present work is concerned, will be conceptualized under this rubric. It will be used as a generic concept to describe the nature of the social transformations that members of the Somali Diaspora undergo as a result of their existence in western societies, and how they, in turn, modify the social dynamics of the society they left behind. It captures how the proliferation of Somali political, social, economic activities, and cultural identities across boundaries as informed by globalization and the recent advances in technology, truly turned Somalia into a transnational entity from the ground up. Such transformations have, in essence, created a situation in which members of the Somalia Diaspora lead simultaneous lives-one that socially and politically locates them in a socially and politically fractured homeland and multiple host societies at the same time.

Brief historical background

Today, Somali communities are literally found in most countries and cities of the world, ranging from small rural towns like Lewiston, Maine in the United States to Sydney Australia. They speak most languages of the world from Dutch to Danish. Their multiple existences have no doubt made significant impacts on both their original homeland and host communities. Despite tentative oral evidence indicating historical traces of the presence of Somali cultural elements in parts of the Middle East and South India, and the small communities that formed in Eden, Yemen, and Birmingham, England, as a result of the British colonisation of Somalia, the history of the Somali Diaspora is a recent phenomenon. The first significant and identifiable wave consisted of young male migrant workers to Saudi Arabia and the Gulf States of the Middle East, or what Somalis endearingly call *Khalijka,* a Somalised Arabic term meaning the Gulf. Initially, the oil boom of the 1970s and early 1980s in the Middle East pulled many of these immigrants as temporary workers with the intention of saving enough money to start a decent life in Somalia. As the political and economic condition of the country deteriorated, coupled in the late 1980s by the slowing of Saudi economy, many stayed put. By the eve of the Somali civil war, hundreds of thousands, many of them, with families lived in the Middle East without much prospects in their host societies, and no home to return.

The largest and the most significant wave started in the early 1990s and continue unabated. They have now established small, but significant Diasporas in many parts of the world from Aalborg, Denmark to Sydney Australia. They speak most languages of the world from English to Danish such that first cousins can no longer communicate with each other. Recently, a friend of mine who took his two young boys born in Toronto to Italy to visit with his brother, sisters, and their children related to me the difficulties him and his siblings faced about how to broker communication between his English speaking children and the Italian speaking children of siblings. He said,

> "...one of my nephews will ask my son something pertaining to Canada, and my son will come running to me, saying what is he talking about Papa? I will go to my nephew and ask him what he said in Italian, and then translate it to my son. We kept doing this back and forth for twenty days until I was exhausted and gave up. Many times, I tried to encourage them to communicate in Somali, but none spoke any meaningful Somali either."

The social transformations that resulted from the interaction between this flourishing Diaspora with their host societies, on the one hand, and those they left behind in the homeland, will be the primary concern of what I have to say in the coming paragraphs. Because of space, I will, confine my discussion to the following dimensions, but it is important to note that other transformation can be equally incorporated into the *social transformations model*. First, I will discuss issues pertaining to gender transformations and consequences. I do this because the nature of gender relations has both sociological and economic implication. Specifically, the nature of gender relations informs family cohesion, which in turn, informs the social, political, and economic lives of the Somali community in the Diaspora. What I have in mind here is the well known tension between men and women in the Diaspora and the potential sociological effects it may have on the community as a whole, and specifically the success of the second generation. Second, I will discuss the social and political impact of the Somali Diaspora on the homeland over the past decade. I will conclude with a brief discussion of the internally displaced, or what I will call the unacknowledged Diaspora within.

Gender transformations

It is by no means an exaggeration to say that the social and cultural values that the Somali Diaspora emerged from are radically different from those found in western societies. One dimension in which the cultural differences between the Somali Diaspora and their host societies can be readily revealed is how gender, and in general, family relations are organized. The relationship between men and women in Somalia is more clearly demarcated, less egalitarian, and less fluid than those found in Europe and North America. In Somalia, women operate in the private/domestic, while men run the public sphere of society with boundary maintenance carried by the social society as whole and not individual men. Women who attempt to cross the boundary are socially stigmatized through rumours and other forms of social policing. Even the female population participates in the social policing of gender boundaries. Of course, the economic, and property structure of the society lends a big hand to the process of policing the borderland between the female and male worlds.

Once in the west, however, Somalis face a different social structure, one where the relationship between the sexes is at least nominally more egalitarian with less boundary demarcation. This is so because women participate more in the economic sphere, and are therefore able to assert themselves in predominantly male designated social worlds. The contact between the two systems of social understanding creates a social and gender schizophrenia, one where the male and female social bodies are in a constant social confrontation, not unlike what Karl Marx characterized as the capitalist dilemma of nurturing the seeds of its own destruction. Somali men and women in the Diaspora are nurturing the seeds of their social and communal destruction. Divorce rates and father absenteeism is becoming a chronic ailment for Somalis in the Diaspora. This process is particularly revealed among low income and those who rely on government social assistance, which a majority are, whether in Denmark or Toronto. Here, women, particularly those who have children are the primary recipients of *Shabta* or *Cayrta*, a Somali term for social assistance payments. The consequence of designating women as the primary recipients of social assistance is a complete reversal of who has economic power over the household. Unlike in Somalia, women now became the economic heads of the household and the power to have the final word over household issues, and men are left in the cold, so to speak, and nothing to do but resign from family affairs.

The following auto-ethnographic anecdote, its comic nature not withstanding, reveals the resulting tensions between Somali men and women in the Diaspora. In the mid 1990s, I visited the apartment of a family friend in the now famous Dixon high rise building in Toronto. Few minutes into our conversation, I realized that the television was tuned to the security camera of the main entrance showing residents coming and leaving. When I asked my friend's wife why they were watching the security camera, and not other programs, she said, "Oh, you mean *Channel 15?"* to which I responded in the affirmative. With a bit of a mischievous giggle, she continued, and said, "You see, this is the biggest entertainment in the neighbourhood. We watch which man/men in the building are let go by their wives during that day". "How you know whose being let go?" I asked. "By the brown bag they carry and their clothing, on their way out", she responded. "Also, any woman who is putting her husband out calls her women friends in advance so they can tune to the channel and enjoy the sight of the latest male victim being thrown out".

Few days later, I went to a *Coffee time*, one of the popular coffee shop hangouts of Somali men in Toronto in the mid 1990s. There, I related the anecdote that my friend's wife told me, and they all laughed. One of them, said, "Well, I can tell you they are not going to enjoy on our expenses from now on". "How so?" I asked. He responded by saying, "you know, we have now decided to take the delivery exit, the door the maintenance personnel of the building use. There, there are not security cameras and they cannot see us leave the building". We all laughed again, but with a grin of sadness this time.

When I presented this anecdote to the conference audience in Aalborg, the reaction was laughter again. In fact, a Somali radio commentator from Sweden taped my comments and, as I understood broadcast it later with, I assume, similar reactions. But the reality is that the anecdote informs the culture shock and the consequent gender role reversals that the Somali Diaspora is experiencing. In the Diaspora, thanks to *Shabta,* women are now the economic warlords. Off course, I assume one can raise the question, why aren't men working and taking control of their lives and that of their families? The answer is not as simple as it may seem on the surface. The majority of the early Somali immigrant men in Toronto have had a professional or a business career in Somalia prior to the civil war. A significant number were already in their late 30s or mid 40s, which made the process of assimilating to a new and alien culture a bit more difficult, particularly, accepting the downward professional mobility that educated immigrants and refugees normally face in West. The Canadian system, like the American, and European economic systems, does not allow easy transfer of educational and professional credentials. As a result, the only option open to the majority of the early Somali immigrant men was unskilled low wage jobs. The irony is that, in most cases, income from these low wage jobs pays less than what the social welfare system provides. The impact of this dual social calamities, downward professional mobility, and women's newly found economic and social power leaves men with no option but to, as I said earlier, disengage from active participation in the affairs of their families. They find solace in chewing *Chat,* a mild narcotic substance that provides just the right amount of hallucination and momentary mental escapism from the reality on the ground. More specifically, this dual calamity speaks to the breakdown of the family structure in the Diaspora.

The social disorganization that bedevils the Somali family in the Diaspora is not confined to gender problems alone, but extends to parent-child relations. One Somali mother's complaint to me about her sons barrage of "Chill mother, Chill" speaks to the tension between first and second generation Somalis in the Diaspora. To the second generation, parents are out of touch with realities in the West, while parents think their children have gone wild. In the mid 1990s, I remember a Somali parent whose sixteen year old daughter started dressing like her classmates in Toronto. The father and mother's reaction was to device a plan to take all the children back to Somalia. They told the children that they were going to visit relatives in Europe. From there, they told the children that they would go to Dubai for few weeks to visit other relatives. After few weeks in Dubai, they boarded a plane bound for Somalia. I later heard that the daughter was married to a Somali man in a rural town in southern Somalia. Of course, this is a bit radical example, but Somalis in the Diaspora, who cannot go to Mogadishu, continue to exile their children in other Muslim countries. There is, in fact, an increasing number of Somali families from Australia, Europe, and North America settling in Egypt and other countries so as to counter the "Chill Mom, Chill" effect. This is not to say that this phenomenon is unique to Somalis, but rather, something that most Diasporas from developing countries experience in the West. It is in fact something that has crossed the mind of this author many a time. The question, however, is whether exiling children will ameliorate the problem.

Another dimension pertains to the social, political, and economic effects that the Somali Diaspora has had on the homeland. The genesis of the interaction between Somalis in the Diaspora and those left behind started with the desire of the Diaspora to help relatives in the homeland as a result of the economic disorganization that resulted from the Somali civil war. In fact, one can make the argument that there is no single family or individual in the Diaspora that does not send remittance. Single mothers who are economically dependent on social welfare continue to send money to relatives. Diaspora Somalis are reconstructing the economic, and education infrastructure of the country. They have opened schools, brought technology, and created transnational economic links between the Diaspora and the homeland. As a result of this economic upper hand, the Diaspora is also influencing the political dynamics of the homeland. Different Diaspora Somalis side with different warlords, thus, in many ways, extending the political conflict that led to their exile in the first place. In fact, a significant number of what is nominally known as the Transitional Parliament of the Federal Government constituted recently in Nairobi consist of Somalis who have citizenship and permanent residence in one or other western country. Recently, when the transitional president and speaker of the parliament visited the United States separately, those in Minnesota welcomed the president and not the speaker, while those in Toronto welcomed the speaker and not the president. Or maybe the president chose to visit Minneapolis and not Toronto by choice, and the speaker did the same thing by choice. Either way, there are sociological and political implications.

What is not commonly discussed within Somali scholarship, however, is internal displacement, the hundreds of thousands of individuals and families who were unable to leave the country after the civil war and who are scattered around the fringes of warlord zones. Who was able to leave and who is displaced internally is an important part of any discussion pertaining to Somali Diaspora. For the elites who were already better off in Mogadishu, and to a certain degree those who had clan connections, and whose relatives left in the early days of the civil war, the exit was easy. They either had the means to leave on their own, or they received assistance from those who preceded them in the Diaspora. But, for the poor and non-clan connected populations, it was and remains internal permanent displacement or even internal bondage. This later group is triply marginalized by 1) Somali clan chauvinists, 2) by international refugees policies, and 3) by Somali scholars who do not acknowledge their existence altogether. They have been driven out of their land by more powerful clans; and unrecognized by the international community and sociology as legitimate refugees in need of assistance.

My final comment pertains to methodological issues. How does one study the Somali Diaspora? Since the social and spatial boundaries between Somalia and the Somali Diaspora cannot be empirically separated, any methodology that attempts to do so will not capture the empirical realities on the ground. How does one talk about the persistence of the Somali civil war without at the same time talking about the role of the Diaspora. What is needed is methodology that can also blur the social and spatial boundaries between Somalia as a geographical entity and the multiple centres that Somali Diaspora populations are constituted. Such a methodology will also concentrate on the consequences of the two-way traffic transformations that are taking place between Somali and the Somali Diaspora.

References

Akyeampong, E. (2000) "Africans in the Diaspora: The Diaspora and Africa." *African Affairs* 99:183-215.

Alpers, E. (2000) "Recollecting Africa: Diasporic Memory in the Indian Ocean World." *African Studies Review* 43:83-100.

Butler, K. (2000) "From Black History to Diasporan History: Brazilian Abolition in Afro-Atlantic Context." *African Studies Review* 43:

125-140.

Byfield, J. (2000) "Introduction: Rethinking the African Diaspora." *African Studies Review* 43: 1-10.

Clifford, J. (1994) "Diasporas." *Cultural Anthropology* 9:302-338

Cohen, Robin. (1996) "Diaspora and the Nation-State: From Victims to Challengers." *International Affairs* 72:507-520.

Gilroy, P. (1993) *The Black Atlantic: Modernity and Double-Consciousness*. Cambridge: Harvard University Press.

Hanchard, M. (1990) "Identity, Meaning, and the African America." *Social Text* 24:31-42

Hanchard, M. (1999) "Afro-Modernity: Temporality, Politics, and the African Diaspora." *Public Culture* 11:245-68.

Hine, D. (2001) Frontiers in Black Studies and Comparative History: Enhanced Knowledge of Our Complex Past." *The Negro Educational Review* 52:101-108

Kearney, M. (1995) "The Local and the Global: The Anthropology of Globalization and Transnationalism." *Annual Review of Anthropology* 24:547-567.

Mintz, S., and R. Price (1992) *The Birth of the African American Culture: An Anthropological Perspective*. Boston: Beacon Press

Odim, C. 2000. 'Unfinished Migrations: Commentary and Response', *African Studies Review* 43: 51-53.

Palmer, Colin. (1998) "Defining and Studying the Modern African Diaspora." *Perspectives* Paterson, T., and R. Kelly (2000) "Unfinished Migrations: Reflections on the African Diaspora and the Making of the Modern World." *African Studies Review* 43:11-45.

Safran, W. (1991) "Diasporas in Modern Societies: Myths of Homeland and Return." *Diaspora* 1:83-84. Tololyan, K. (1996) "Rethinking Diaspora (s): Stateless Power in Transnational Moment." *Diaspora* 5:3-36 Zeleza, P. (2005) "Rewriting the African Diaspora: Beyond the Black Atlantic." *African Affairs* 104:35-68.

Chapter 3

A Game of Chance: Somali Asylum Applicants in the UK

Virginia Lulling

The background

Any consideration of the Somali Diaspora must include some examination of the ways by which Somalis have reached their present locations abroad. The majority of those in Europe today have arrived as refugees seeking political asylum, and this fact is fundamental to both the process of entry into their new countries and the way in which they are treated once there. We all know so well that Somalis arrive abroad via this route that we are in danger of treating it as something self-evident. But it is worth taking a closer look at the actual process by which Somalis reach or fail to reach their goal of finding a more or less stable home in a foreign country – in this case the United Kingdom.

This paper, which draws on the writer's experience as an 'expert witness' in Somali asylum cases, examines the process by which the British authorities attempt to establish whether the applicant is a 'genuine' asylum seeker, and the results of this process, for the asylum seekers themselves.

Since 1980 the number of Somalis in Britain has grown from a few small communities of former seamen in port cities and a handful of students, to a population of hundreds of thousands.[i] When I moved to London at the beginning of the 1980s, one virtually never saw Somalis in the streets; now one sees them all the time, and every suburban high street has its Somali café, and one or more *xawaalado.* The significant fact is that virtually all these people have arrived as asylum seekers, since other paths of immigration are almost totally closed.

Among the asylum-seekers arriving in the UK since 1985, Somalis form one of the largest groups. Somalia was the highest applicant nationality in 1997 and 2003, and the second highest in 1995, 1998 and 1999 (Harris 2004: 25) though in 2004 Iran and China appear to be overtaking it (Home Office 2004). The first influx began with the war in the north and the bombing of Hargeisa, with numbers rising from 305 in 1988 to 1,850 in 1989. In the 1990s with the spread of the civil war the numbers continued to climb, reaching a peak of about 7,500 in 1999. Since then they have declined to 5,090 in 2003 (Home Office 2004), a fact undoubtedly related to the increasing difficulty of gaining permission to remain in the country. These are the numbers of applications for asylum, excluding dependants. The numbers of actual people must be quite a lot higher, since many women arrive with children.

When I was first asked to prepare reports on asylum seekers in the mid 1990s (and at that time I was asked for only two or three times a year) it was enough to ascertain that the person was really a Somali - not a Kenyan, for instance. It was in 2000 that the regulations changed: in order for a Somali to establish a 'well founded fear of persecution', as the 1951 International Convention relating to the Status of Refugees stipulates, it is now necessary to show that he or she belongs to a minority group, that is to say a group that has been systematically targeted for human rights abuses, or is especially vulnerable. It is not enough simply to have been living in a lawless environment where anyone might be robbed or caught in crossfire. This fact is reflected by this quotation: 'Somalia is a country torn apart by civil war over a number of years. Where such a state exists, it is not enough for the appellant to show that she would be at risk on return simply for that reason. She must be able to show a differential impact; a fear of persecution for a conventional reason over and above the ordinary risks of a civil war.' (Adjudicators decision, Appeal no HX/01540/2004, 16 March 2004)

The natural and inevitable result is that now everyone claims to belong to a 'minority'; generally to one of the groups who are nowadays placed under the umbrella term 'Benadiri', though other possibilities are the Sheikhaal, the Ashraf, or – a very different sort of minority – the Midgaan and other low status castes. (People claiming to be Bajuni, if they are not really so, will be not Somalis but Kenyans). This means that the idea of 'clan' has become an important factor in Somali asylum claims, and British Home Office interviewers and assessors are required to wrestle with this - to them - strange idea and its implications.

Who are the refugees?

Somali asylum applicants come to the attention of the authorities (and generally to mine) when they arrive in the UK or soon after. An important question, but one which I cannot tackle here, is what has happened to them before they arrive at that point? How many Somali asylum seekers are brought by 'agents' and how many arrive by them selves? From where do they come?

New arrivals generally say that they have come directly from Somalia, or have stayed only a short while in Kenya or Ethiopia, and this is no doubt true for many. It is however a fairly open secret that some have actually been living for years in other European countries – a fact they cannot admit because they would simply be returned there. As to why they do so, the relative ease of obtaining state benefit in the UK may be one factor but it is not the only one, though some elements in the British press may insist that it is.

There are other pull factors: rejoining relatives, a more tolerant and less regulated society, greater business opportunities, and of course a preference for operating in a world language rather than one with only a national base (Harris 2004: 24). The Somalis who reach Britain are not, of course those most in need, but the relatively privileged, those able to raise the money for the fare, and in some cases to pay an 'agent' to arrange a forged passport as well as a ticket. Most of the inhabitants of refugee and displaced persons camps do not have this opportunity.

As far as gender and age is concerned, Somalis are not necessary typical of all the UK asylum seekers. According to Sergeant (2001: 47), drawing on the statistics, '... the majority of asylum seekers are single young men...often educated, ambitious and resourceful.' This is not true of the Somalis. Though they do include the kind of enterprising young men Sergeant refers to, there are at least as many women, generally with children, and quite a lot of elderly people, as well as a worrying number of very young people of both sexes. This is from my own observation; the official figures on Somali asylum applicants do not provide a breakdown by gender or age, except that they record unaccompanied children, of whom there were 55 in the third quarter of 2004.

The game of chance

I have chosen to present the asylum process metaphorically as a game of chance, a board game of the kind where the players make their way from one square to another by throwing dice. I apply approach, simply as a technique for explaining the stages of the process, and partly because I hope it conveys something of its quality: a journey towards a goal, through stages, which are arbitrary but unavoidable.

Here then is 'Asylum', the game for all the family – even if some of the family members are still in Somalia, or in a refugee camp, or in some other location.

On this board, the final HOME Square is Refugee Status. A new arrival is an 'asylum seeker'; it is not until you are granted asylum, that you can be officially described as a refugee. If you get there, you may take a job, draw state benefits if unemployed, and above all you have the right to ask for 'family reunion' for a spouse and dependent children – though not for other relatives except in special cases.

Let us assume that Square 1 is the PORT OF ENTRY (in the case of Somalis this is generally an airport). From this point you can go to either 2 or 3.

Square 3: You apply for asylum at the port of entry. Gain ten points (it will help your case later). On claiming asylum the immigrant must fill in a 20-page "statement of evidence" form optimistically entitled 'for self completion' but which in fact require the services of both a lawyer and a translator. The form must be completed and returned to the Immigration and Nationality Department within two weeks or the claim is invalidated. This is a difficult task for a stranger (Sergeant: 21)

or

Square 4: You somehow enter the country without applying: This will count against you as you are suspected of having been in the country previously as an illegal immigrant. However the great majority of Somalis do this - in 2003 out of 5,090 Somali applications 4,430 were 'in country' (Home Office 2004).

Square 5: If you throw the dice right and land on this square you will now get a legal representative. Gain twenty points.

Your next throw will land you on either 6 or 7.

Square 6: HOME OFFICE INTERVIEW. You return your self-completion form and present yourself for interview by the Home Office. Interviews are conducted mainly at the central office in Croydon near London, Lunar House. This is known to its habitués as 'Loony House' and everyone agrees that conditions there are chaotic. If you have a legal representative they may accompany you, but most people are without such support. You are grilled for an hour or so about the details of your journey, your history and background. Depending on your next throw, go to square 8, 9 or 10.

Square 7: You did not complete your questionnaire or you did not manage to get to the interview within the compulsory two weeks. Your claim is rejected for 'NON-COMPLIANCE'. Wait two turns, lose twenty points and then go to square 11.

In 2003, 465 Somali asylum applications were refused on the grounds of non-compliance. This constituted 12% of the total number of refusals and 8% of the total number of decisions made during that year (Harris 2004: 29). Immigration lawyers complain that even when they have sent the papers on time, the claim is rejected because of non-compliance.

"This is the case despite providing proof of reception by the HO" said one exasperated immigration lawyer. "....they just lose the papers". He accused the HO of using non-compliance to massage the rejection figures into something more acceptable for the last General Election.... A massive 33% of refusals are on the grounds of non-compliance.'

(Sergeant 2001: 21) [The entire quote is by Sergeant]

Square 8. They believe your story - go straight to HOME = REFUGEE STATUS.

This is nowadays an unlikely outcome. In 2003 out of a total of 6,050 Home Office decisions in Somali cases, only 1,665 were granted the right of asylum.

It was not always so – up to the early 1990s, most Somali asylum seekers received status almost as a matter of course. One result of this was that large numbers of people gained status as Somalis who were not Somali at all. Perhaps because this was realised, as well as because of the pressure of public prejudice and fear of asylum seekers, the criteria for granting refugee status have become progressively more restrictive, and the process of convincing the authorities that one is (a) a Somali, and (b) in danger of persecution, more difficult. In the first quarter of 2002, three out of every five Somali applicants were accepted as genuine refugees or in need of other forms of protection, at the initial Home Office decision. In the last quarter of 2003, only one in four was accepted (Kundnani 2004).

This is part of a broader process which applies to all asylum seekers. Before the 1993 (Asylum) act was brought in, about three quarters of those who sought asylum were either recognised as refugees under the Convention or were given exceptional leave to remain. In 1993 the proportions were quite suddenly reversed; three quarters of all asylum applicants were refused, and the refusal rate continued to grow (Pirouet 2001: 46-47)

Square 9. Your claim is rejected, but you are given some form of TEMPORARY LEAVE TO REMAIN. In 2003, this happened to 555 applicants out of 6,050. Wait one year and then go back to square 6. During this time you may take employment, but not get your family to join you. In 2004, a large number of those applying for asylum were repeating their claim after a year or more of temporary residence. This is likely to go on for several years.

Square 10. REFUSAL. Your claim is rejected outright. This is now the most usual outcome (3,835 out of 6,151 in 2003). You get a 'Reasons for Refusal Letter'. It informs you that you have the right to appeal and recommends you take legal advice. While many "reasons" are given for refusing asylum, the Home Office gives no hint what yardstick it applies when refugee status is granted. ... asylum seekers often comment that they do not know why one among them gets refugee status, while another is refused (Asylum Aid 1999: 11).

This is where you get a legal advisor if you had not done so before. Generally this is a private solicitor, though funding comes from the state in the form of 'legal aid'. Others are advised by NGOs such as the

Refugee Legal Service or Asylum Aid.

You can now land on either

Square 11. A GOOD SOLICITOR, who specialises in Somali cases and has a grasp of the issues. Gain ten points.

or

Square 12. AN INADEQUATE SOLICITOR, who has never or seldom dealt with Somali clients and knows nothing about them (or worse - thinks he knows but does not) and does not give enough attention to your case. Lose ten points.

This is where the 'country expert' may be called in. In Somali cases this is generally in order to testify – so the solicitor hopes – both that the client belongs to the minority they claim to, and that that minority is indeed a persecuted one.

By now I could write an ethnography of British (mainly London) immigration solicitors. Those solicitors whom I see are by definition the better ones, since they have taken the trouble to get an 'expert witness' report. Nevertheless they vary widely. Their diverse ethnic origins would be a study in themselves; none of them, so far, are Somalis, though a few employ Somali case workers. Their premises range from large and well-appointed offices to a few ramshackle rooms so full of piles of documents that one can hardly move around. A firm may move from the one condition to the other; I have seen several firms grow rapidly in the last three or four years, taking over neighbouring buildings and smartening up amazingly between one visit and the next. Immigration law is a growth industry, even though compared with other forms of legal work it is not well paid. However recent changes in the law may cause it to shrink again.

Square 13. You are 'DISPERSED' from London to Glasgow, as part of the government effort to spread asylum seekers around the country rather than concentrating them in the capital. You find a new solicitor, but your former solicitor loses your file and fails to send it on. Miss three turns.

Square 14. Your case goes to APPEAL and is heard by an immigration adjudicator. Because of the deficiencies of the initial Home Office decisions the appeal is all too often the first and only substantive hearing (Asylum Aid 1999: 74)

The setup is similar to that of a court of law, though less formal: the applicant and his or her representative on one side, the Home Office representative on the other, and the adjudicator, who has already been presented with the evidence in written form, acting as judge. The expert witness's report, if any, will have been submitted to the adjudicator in writing in advance. Only rarely is the expert witness asked to actually attend the hearing.

Asylum cases require the applicant to prove their eligibility for refugee status. However the standard of proof is not as high as it would be in a normal court of law – the applicant has to show only that there is a 'reasonable likelihood' that they will face persecution if they return to their home country.

Square 15. The Adjudicator ALLOWS your appeal and overturns the Home Office decision - go to HOME. Somalis are the largest group of asylum seekers in Britain to have decisions overturned on appeal (Good 2004: 117). In 2003, out of 5, 365 appeals by Somali asylum seekers, 2015 (38%) were allowed (Home Office 2004).

Square 16. The Adjudicator allows your appeal but in their turn the HOME OFFICE APPEAL against the decision. Miss two turns, and then go to 21 (APPEALS TRIBUNAL).

Square 17. The Adjudicator DISMISSES your appeal. In 2003, 2,960 appeals, 55% of the total, were dismissed (and 7% withdrawn - Home Office 2004).

Square 18. You apply to the Immigration Appeals Authority for PERMISSION TO APPEAL against the Adjudicator's decision.

Square 19. Leave to appeal is GRANTED. Go to 21 (APPEALS TRIBUNAL).

Square 20. Leave to appeal is NOT GRANTED – go to 25 (LIMBO).

Square 21. IMMIGRATION APPEALS TRIBUNAL (IAT). Your case is heard by the Tribunal - generally a three person panel. But tribunals '...rarely overturn adjudicators' findings on fact or credibility, so appeals tend to turn on the legal safety of the adjudicator's decision rather than reconsideration of evidence.' (Good 2004: 116-117)

Square 22. The Tribunal finds the former decision unsound and your case is 'REMITTED' to be heard by a different Adjudicator - go back to 14.

Square 23. The tribunal UPHOLDS the Adjudicator's decision - go to 25 = LIMBO.

Square 24. The Tribunal overturns the Adjudicator's decision and ALLOWS your appeal - go to HOME.

Square 25. LIMBO. Once you are here you are legally a non-person. According to the Home Office rules you ought to be deported back to Somalia. However because of the state of the country this has hardly ever been done until recently. About 100 Somalis were forcibly deported at the end of 2003 and the beginning of 2004, it is not clear to where. The policy has apparently been suspended and its future is uncertain (The Observer, London, Sunday October 24, 2004). Though you have not been deported, the public body which provides subsistence to refugees, will no longer maintain you.

You now have to be supported by relatives - close or distant - and are probably moving from one person's house or flat to another.

If a case is dismissed by the IAT there are in the last resort two further possibilities, if you can persuade a solicitor it is worthwhile.

Square 26. It may to be taken to the COURT OF APPEAL, or

Square 27. The asylum seeker (that is to say their lawyer) may apply for permission to move a JUDICIAL REVIEW of any decision taken during the process.

Permission is rarely granted for either of these steps, and neither of these processes looks at any new evidence; they will consider whether the decision was correctly taken on the basis of the evidence already presented.

Square 29. Permission is not sought or not granted - the most likely outcome. Remain in LIMBO

Square 30. One of these procedures succeeds - go to HOME.

Square 31. Your case fails yet again. Go back to LIMBO.

Where you are stuck, unless you remove yourself from the board by, for instance going (back?) to some other country. Another way is to commit suicide and I have heard of one such case.

This is a simplified account of what is a very involved and long-drawn-out process. Months elapse between each stage - though things are not as bad as they were in the mid-1990s, when people often waited for years to have their cases heard. Asylum and immigration law is highly complex and has changed repeatedly in recent years, so that it is confusing even to its professionals.

New regulations now under consideration may shorten this process, removing the right to appeal to the Tribunal.

So much for the general outline of the game. I will now look in more detail at some aspects of it. I am particularly concerned with the way in which the process which is supposed to sort out the 'genuine'

from the 'bogus' refugee can go wrong in the Somali context, and how throughout, an asylum seeker has to face '...a well established, officially sanctioned culture of disbelief' (Pirouet 2001: 61).

How it goes wrong: the Home Office

The interviewers and assessors of the Home Office are not very highly qualified people, and they know nothing of Somalia. (The same people have to deal with asylum seekers from Kosovo, Sri Lanka, China and every part of the world.) The Reasons for Refusal letters sent out by the Home Office are notoriously of poor quality, and considered rather a bad joke by solicitors and others working in the field. They have been analysed by Amnesty International (2004) and Asylum Aid (1999) among others (and see Good 2004: 116). All agree that the faults of these letters are inadequate knowledge about the country concerned, and a desire to 'catch applicants out' rather than assess their case in a sympathetic way, together with excessive reliance on standard paragraphs, which can even lead to the inclusion of paragraphs that obviously refer to a different case.

One cannot avoid concluding when dealing with these documents that the aim is to reject the applicant. As Louise Pirouet (2001: 24) says, 'If governments wish to keep numbers down, but are unable or unwilling to act through their foreign policy, then all they can do is try to reduce the numbers admitted, and refuse as many of those who apply for asylum as they dare.' The issue is the 'credibility' of the person, and the assessor is clearly trying to discredit them by finding as many contradictions, real or imagined, as possible in their narrative.

The main criterion in Somali cases nowadays is whether the applicant belongs to one of the minority groups or not, since it is agreed that these minorities have been particularly targeted for persecution. Time and again people who are quite clearly members of minority clans are refused and told that they do not belong to these clans, and indeed are not Somalis at all. At the same time applicants are accepted as minority members who are not. Those who do belong to minorities, especially what are now called the 'Benadiri' clans, feel extremely bitter when they see that their own people, many of whom have suffered severely, are excluded, while members of the very groups who have persecuted them are believed and admitted.

There are specific reasons for these mistakes which have to do with the character and situation of the 'Benadiri' people. Firstly, they (especially the women) tend to be retiring and lack the self-confidence in interview that many majority Somalis have. Secondly, they are often asked inappropriate questions. The whole point about these people is that they are in many ways different from majority Somalis in their culture. Some of them have lived in their enclaves with little knowledge of the national scene. This is the very reason why they have been persecuted, for 'not being real Somalis'. Hence they are often unable to answer questions about the subjects (geography or clan structure) which according to the Home Office 'all Somalis should know'. For instance knowledge of one's genealogy up to thirty generations, and a grasp of the broader clan system, is part of the culture of the majority clans, particularly in the north. Benadiri do not have this sort of knowledge. At the same time the real knowledge which they do show is often not recognised, because it is special to them, and not found in the sources consulted by the Home Office.

On the other hand a good deal of information about the Benadiri minority is publicly available, either on the internet or by word of mouth. People also have come to know the sort of information the Home Office asks for. Hence it may be possible for a person from the Somali majority clans to present him or herself plausibly as Benadiri. There are inappropriate conclusions that are typical of Home Office Reasons for Refusal letters on Somali cases. For instance: Supposed 'contradictions', which may amount to no more than different spellings of the same name.

Arguing that because the applicant does not show the sort of knowledge of the clan system that the interviewer expects (this, as I have pointed out, is particularly likely in Benadiri applicants) they do not come from Somalia at all - though knowledge or ignorance about clan affairs has nothing to do with whether a person comes from inside the former Republic of Somalia or outside it.

Demanding to know exact dates - by the European calendar, of course: 'Absolute accuracy over dates is demanded, and when people cannot remember clearly the temptation is to invent a date'(Pirouet 2001 p 50). It is not realised that most Somalis do not know their 'birthdays'. Hence the large number of Somali applicants who state that they were born on January 1.

Concluding that the person does not come from the clan they say they do, on the basis of their general lack of 'credibility', rather than eliciting relevant information about that clan, in other words saying e.g. 'We do not believe your story of your journey, therefore we do not believe you belong to the Reer Xamar.

Demanding an 'address' i.e. street name and number, and concluding that because the applicant cannot supply one, they did not live in the town where they claimed to. I have spent years pointing out that this does not make sense in the context of Mogadishu or Somalia generally.

Making assumptions about what individuals might or might not have done and experienced, e.g. 'Your father would have done x or 'the militia would not have done y.' I certainly do not have the insight into the mental processes of the mooryaan which the Home Office employees apparently suppose they have. One very common version of this is: 'We do not believe a Hawiye man befriended you, because it was the Hawiye who were persecuting you.' This shows both a failure to understand that there is more than one lot of Hawiye, and a refusal to allow that individuals may sometimes behave in untypical ways.

Arguing that because 'statistics show that Somalia is one of the world's poorest countries', the applicant could not possibly have raised the funds for their journey.

The following are actual extracts from Reasons for Refusal letters. They are not exceptional, but are taken from cases I have recently worked on:

> '...it is noted that you claim upon your release after two months you were only given some basic medicine and an injection by your husband's friend. It is considered that had you been detained and beaten as you claim for a period of two months you would have required urgent medical attention, consequently it is not accepted that you were detained and beaten as you claim.' In other words because you did not get medical attention you cannot have needed it.'
>
> '...it is noted that when asked who the current president of Somalia was, you claimed 'There is no president in Somalia.' However, country information tells us...the first ever multiparty elections were held on 14 April 2003. Somaliland President Dahir Riyale Kahin... It is reasonable to conclude that had you been living in Mogadishu until 2004 as you have claimed, you would have known this.' The writer apparently does not know the difference between Somalia and Somaliland.'

How it goes wrong: the courts

Adjudicators generally take a more perceptive view, but how far this is so depends very much on the individual. 'The result of an appeal can depend on which adjudicator you get '(Pirouet 2001: 75). They often show the same ignorance of Somali realities as do the Home Office assessors; much time may be spent in argument about 'what must have happened' - in situations which the adjudicator must find it very hard to visualise.

Often other Somalis - kin or former neighbours are called as witnesses to the identity of the applicant.

However it is fatally easy for these to be trapped into more supposed 'contradictions' and therefore held to be 'not credible'. Here too, a degree of accuracy about dates may be expected which is quite unrealistic. In one case a woman appeared as witness in her sister's case; it was found that according to their statements they had been born in January and May of the same year. The adjudicator – logically from his point of view – concluded they could not be sisters, and that hence the witness was not credible.

To quote from a recent determination, 'She was initially adamant that the appellant was born in 1986, when she was 8 years old, but after it had been pointed out that she would have been nine years old at the time of his birth if (as she claimed) she was born in 1977 and he was born in 1986, she changed her position to saying that her father had told her that the appellant was 8 years younger than her (which if she was born in 1977 would mean that he was born in 1985, as he originally claimed) and concluded by saying that she was guessing her age at the time of his birth. She also misnamed his brother and only corrected herself in re-examination, saying that she had originally given his nickname, even though she mentioned his other forename and his surname in full.' (This also shows ignorance of the Somali naming system). No wonder one Somali legal advisor I know avoids calling Somali witnesses at all.

The three-person Appeals Tribunals generally have a more balanced and careful approach than either Home Office assessors or adjudicators. However if the original case was badly prepared, and no further evidence is produced, then the tribunal can only rehash the existing arguments. The same applies to the further stages of Judicial Review and the Court of Appeal, which are specifically not empowered to look at new evidence. The result can often be described by the old computer adage: garbage in - garbage out. I think of one woman I have encountered who, to anyone who knows Somalia, is quite obviously a genuine member of a minority clan, and in fact belongs to a well-known family in that clan, who has been rejected by both an adjudicator and the IAT.

This is not to say, of course, that the system never gets it right. Many decisions, whether taken by Home Office assessors, adjudicators or the IAT, are well founded. Nor would it be reasonable to expect those involved to have much knowledge of Somali culture without being told. What is disturbing however is the failure even to ask about possible relevant cultural differences, or to realise that they may exist, apart from some oversimplified ideas about 'clans'.

The role of the interpreter

One person who is of great significance in all this is the Somali interpreter. These work for the Home Office, the solicitors and legal aid organisations, and in the courts; it is one way that Somalis in Britain can get a living. Often the interpreter can tell perfectly well what the truth of the case is, but their role forbids them to say it.

A good interpreter is an enormous help. On the other hand, where the interpreter comes from a different area and clan background from the asylum seeker, they can misunderstand what is being said, and this can be yet another source of error. I have more than once interviewed an asylum seeker who was from the Reer Xamar or some other southern clan, and understood perfectly what they were talking about, while the interpreter - who was from the north - did not.

On being an 'expert witness'

At this point let me give my own definition of an 'expert': one who is less ignorant on a given subject than the other people present. By this definition it is rather easy in most places to be an expert on Somalia.

I do not know whether the main criterion adopted by the British Home Office in admitting Somalis, that they must be shown to belong to an endangered minority, is the most appropriate one. Probably if there has to be a rule it is as sensible as any. At all events, as an 'expert witness' this is the criterion I have to work with, and in nearly all cases what I am asked by the solicitor to do, is to confirm that this person really does belong to a minority group, and that that group really is an endangered one. I am not asked to say whether the person is in general 'credible' or whether their whole story is true. Indeed I would be reprimanded by the adjudicator or the tribunal if I tried to do so. 'An expert witness cannot decide that an asylum seeker is or is not "genuine" nor decide that someone should or should not be recognised as a Convention refugee; that is the task of the IAA (Immigration Appeals Authority). The expert's task is to throw light on the evidence' (Pirouet: 78).

After I have agreed to look at a case the solicitor sends me copies of the applicant's own statement in support of their claim, the Home Office interview, and the Reasons for Refusal letter. I may be able to reach a decision on the basis of these alone, but generally I prefer to meet the person before making up my mind.

In some cases, after interviewing him or her, I am quite sure one way or the other, in others I am uncertain - and I would always rather lean towards saying 'yes' than 'no'. I am sure I have made not a few mistakes, but always in that direction. In many cases I simply have to refuse to do a report since I do not know any way of telling whether the individual belongs to the group they claim - this is generally true for instance of people claiming to be Midgaan.

In many cases it is all too clear that the person is not from the clan they claim to be. It must be galling for people who belong, for instance, to one of the Isaaq or Daarood clans, who a few years ago would have gained refugee status without difficulty, to find that now they are excluded from it, and it is not surprising if they invent new identities for themselves. I do not blame them at all for trying, but professionally I will not knowingly help them to do it. However, if I have to inform the solicitor that, sorry, I cannot say that Mr Farah Abshir Guleed is a member of the Reer Xamar, the solicitor is not legally obliged to pass on this information to the court. It does not necessarily follow that Farah will be refused - merely that he will have to take his chance without any help from me (Occasionally however a solicitor will drop a case).

This points up the ambiguity of my situation as an 'expert witness': as I am obliged to state in every report, 'I understand that my duty is to the court, to provide an impartial expert opinion and to assist the court in reaching a decision.' But, the people who actually hire me are not the court but the asylum seeker and their legal representative.

In the process of preparing these reports over the last few years, I have learnt a great deal. In order to check people's statements I have had, in effect, to do research; since published sources about minorities are few, this has been mainly first hand enquiry among members of the Somali community in Britain. Also, the asylum applicants' own accounts have been an important source of information, since what one person tells me about the subdivisions of clans, and about the history and leading members of clans or lineages, can be used to check what another person says, and the various accounts supplement and confirm one another. So I am still learning - while ever more conscious of how much more there is to know.

Conclusion

Attitudes in Britain – and in the rest of Europe – to asylum seekers tend to polarise into 'right wing' and 'left wing'. The first sees asylum seekers as 'bogus', people who face no real danger at all in their home countries, but are simply here to get more money and an easier life. The second sees them as real victims of persecution and fears their being excluded or sent back into the hands of their tormentors. This of course sets up too simple a dichotomy between victims of persecution on the one hand and 'purely economic' migrants on the other. In reality there is a large grey area in between, where there is both a degree of danger, and a desire for economic opportunity; I believe that most Somali asylum seekers fall in this area. Some - the 'Benadiri' particularly - are persecuted by any standards; others are not 'bogus' but simply people who, as Pirouet (2001: 46) puts it, 'have not suffered quite sufficiently' to satisfy the criteria set up by those who control the asylum process.

I hope that my description of the asylum seeking process as a game of chance will not be taken as making light of asylum seekers and their struggle.

What I mean to emphasise is that the process is not, as the British authorities and their counterparts in other countries would like to suppose, a wise and fair-minded sifting of 'genuine' from 'bogus' claims, but to a very large extent a matter of chance. The Somali applicants themselves can see this quite well, and no doubt word gets back. The result may be that, while some people with a very good case for asylum may be frightened off from applying, others with a less good claim but more confidence may be encouraged to take a gamble.

I feel – to change the metaphor – that I am witnessing a contest with one side trying to get through a door and the other side trying to prevent them – but a contest fought in the dark. Neither side really understands what the other is doing. Each has its own aims, part overt, part hidden. One side is vastly more powerful, but it is hampered by its interior divisions and its contradictory aims. So they dodge and blunder, and from time to time a lucky contestant manages to get through the door.

The prize is real enough, in terms of security and opportunity – even though the attainment of refugee status is no 'happy ever after'. As one young man said to me recently, subverting my cynicism, 'I am so glad now; I am safe, I have a flat and now, I have job, and I can begin to pay back what I owe this country.' Or to quote an older woman: 'What problems? There is no shooting in the street here.' Yet real too are the stress and anxiety, the heartache of separation from children and other family, and the toll which this takes on people's mental and physical health. For in the end this is a game played with human lives.

References

Amnesty International (2004) Get *It Right: How Home Office Decision Making Fails Refugees*. London: UK

Asylum Aid (1999) *Still No Reason At All; Home Office Decisions on Asylum Claims*. London: UK

Good, A. (2004) 'Undoubtedly an Expert'; Anthropologists in British Asylum Courts. *Journal of the Royal Anthropological Institute,* Vol. 10 No.1 pp 113-133.

Harris, H. (2004) *The Somali Community in the UK, What we know and how we know it*. ICAR (Information Centre about Asylum and Refugees in the UK): London

Home Office Asylum Statistics (2004) *Third Quarter 2004* (www.homeoffice.gov.uk).

ICAR (Information Centre about Asylum and Refugees) (2004) *Navigation guide: UK asylum law and process: legal aspects.* London: UK

Kundnani, A (2004) *Somali asylum seekers: Home Office gets it wrong two times out of five*. Independent race and refugee news network (Institute of Race Relations) http://www.irr.org.uk/

Pirouet, L. (2001) *Whatever Happened to Asylum in Britain; a Tale of Two Walls.* Berghahn Books, NY/Oxford

Sergeant,H. (2001) *Welcome to the Asylum; Immigration and Asylum in the UK*, Centre for Policy Studies, London

UNHCR (2002) *Annual Statistical Report*: Somalia

Chapter 4

Somali Pastoralists in Lewiston, Maine: Searching with Participatory Tools for a New Life

Richard Ford

(with Laura Hammond, Abdirizak Mahboub, & Shukri O. Abdillahi)[1]

Whereas the Somali culture is among the most resilient in the world, the legacy of two decades of clan-based conflict has left deep scars among the people. These hostilities have followed the global Somali diaspora and entered into the refugee communities, including Lewiston, Maine where 1100 Somalis from multiple clans have descended on an aging and economically declining New England factory town of about 37,000 people. Creating an environment in which Somalis can access services and jobs while maintaining good relationships with the existing Lewiston community has posed many challenges.

This chapter seeks to explore whether tools that have worked effectively to build peace and generate cooperation and community development in Somalia can work equally well among Somali refugees who have settled in Lewiston, Maine.

Background

Since the early 1990s, Somali refugees have been settled in several US cities including Minneapolis, Atlanta, Pittsburgh, Portland (Maine), and several cities in Texas. Once government subsidies run out, the refugees are unable to afford housing in safe neighborhoods so they move into less expensive housing. They soon encounter difficulties in schools, unsafe streets, drug traffic, and poor health services. Some seek alternatives. One such search found Lewiston – a mostly white, French-Canadian mill town that was losing residents and therefore had inexpensive and generally safe housing readily available.

The first Somali residents arrived in January 2001. Within a year the ranks had swelled to 800 or 900 and by the middle of the second year had reached about 1100 – some say as many as 2000, but the official count is 1100. City services were, to say the least, unprepared. There was no English as a Second Language (ESL) for Somali speakers in the schools; the local health services had never encountered some of the particular needs associated with Somalis – *e.g.* male health providers and Somali female patients; local employers were reluctant to hire Somalis, in part because of language limitations and in part because of dress codes – *e.g.* L.L. Bean prohibits head scarves for personnel working on sewing machines or other forms of power knitting or fabric processing equipment.

Lewiston's transportation system was organized on the assumption that everyone owned a car, as in much of small town America. Yet most Somalis did not own cars and those who did were experiencing difficulty passing the written portion of the Maine driver's test. Refugees who held professional credentials such as physicians, university professors, and lawyers could not obtain professional positions in Maine because either their credentials were not accepted by US licensing boards or because all of their certificates were destroyed when the records of the Somali Institute for Development Administration and Management (SIDAM), La Foole, or the Somali National University were destroyed in looting and the collapse of the Somali government.

Finally the experience that many of the men brought with them – civil service in the Somali government, pastoral or agricultural production, or export marketing – had little carryover to Maine employment opportunities. The women found it far easier to find work in Maine than did the men. The result was heavy unemployment among the Somalis, especially the men, and substantial social and cultural distance between the three percent Somali population and the majority French-Canadian population who themselves had been newcomers about a century earlier. In their generation they had worked their way through the social hierarchy of small-town Maine and believed that hard work and self help were the traits required to make it in America.

The City of Lewiston worked vigorously to deal with the new "Somali problem." The City Administrator's office frantically began writing proposals to provide more relevant health services, new teachers in the public schools, special ESL programs for all interested Somalis, special housing assistance, job-training programs, and special counselling and conflict mediation support. As these services expanded the refugees began to receive assistance. However, the programs also created some resentment because almost all of the employment opportunities created by the new funding were linked to professional qualifications. Most Somalis could not qualify.

But there was another, more deeply rooted issue. While the refugees brought only small amounts of personal baggage in their journey from every region of Somalia, they all brought volumes of their cultural and political baggage. The most visible item in their cultural-political suitcases was their previous decade of clan hostility that Siyad[2] had played upon, exploited, and exacerbated. This political luggage destroyed any chance of unity or cooperation among the Somali refugees and made provision of Lewiston's social and human services a quagmire.

In a moment of frustration and anger – and political short-sightedness – the Mayor of Lewiston wrote, in the fall of 2002, an open letter to the Somali community, stating:

This large number of new arrivals cannot continue without negative results for all. The Somali community must exercise some discipline and reduce the stress on our limited finances and our generosity. I am well aware of the legal right of a U.S. resident to move anywhere he/she pleases, but it is time for the Somali community to exercise this discipline in view of the effort that has been made on its behalf. Our city is maxed-out financially, physically and emotionally.

The letter had at least three impacts:

1. It angered many in the Somali community and attracted journalists and the media in unprecedented numbers. As a result of the letter, the City has documented more than 400 news items and articles about the Lewiston Somalis, including the national TV and press as well as international coverage from as far away as Denmark. The letter itself and the publicity that followed brought a sensational tone to the situation and tended to exaggerate, even polarize, what had previously been a sticky but not confrontational situation.
2. It attracted the attention of racist and fascist hate groups in America who came to Lewiston under the instigation of the World Church of the Creator to "preserve American values." They organized a rally that threatened to attract extremists of many perspectives from all over the country. The City and the State of Maine anticipated the potentially volatile situation of such a rally and mobilized every available state and local law enforcement officer to be on hand for the rally.
3. The letter also energized the moderates of Lewiston including church, educational, social service, and public interest groups of Lewiston and surrounding towns. They organized a counter rally to inform the Lewiston Somalis that they were welcome residents of their community and that they would all work together to make the Somalis' adjustment to America as gentle as possible.

While the general reaction to the letter was that it was inappropriate and fully unacceptable, one prominent leader of the Somali community commented that without the letter the Somalis would have stumbled along with often unhelpful programs and services. With the letter, he noted, there was a dramatically heightened awareness that something out of the ordinary had to be done to avoid future tensions. While the counter rally and the police had succeeded in getting through the crisis of the extremists, it did little to change the direction of social services and did even less to quell the divisiveness within Lewiston's Somali refugee community.

The City and a small group of Somali leaders opened a new style of discussion. What next steps could move them beyond the provision of services and create a different environment in which Somali needs could be addressed more effectively and training/community organizing established that was more directly linked to Somali needs? Their talks opened a search that eventually identified case studies that described tools for conflict mediation and development planning that researchers from Clark University had created and used in two communities in Somaliland[3]. The Assistant City Administrator and the Director of Somali Community Services travelled to Clark to meet with appropriate faculty and graduate students. In particular they were interested in the case study describing the impact of community-based conflict mediation used in Dararweyne (near Hargeisa) and described in *Nabad iyo Caano*.

The case study describes how a cluster of participatory tools helped Dararweyne to solve its leadership problems and, as a result, to transform Dararweyne from a conflict-ridden and dysfunctional community, filled with discord among three sub-clans, into an energetic and productive community. In the three years since creating their action plan, the people of Dararweyne have found partners to join with them to:

- Renovate their clinic and hire a health assistant
- Construct a subsurface dam to increase the storage capacity in the village's seasonal riverbed (*tog*)
- Renovate existing and construct new shallow wells to increase water supply for irrigating market crops
- Attract 15 new families to the village who have built sturdy stone houses
- Extend the water pipe for the village's drinking water supply
- Rebuild the village school.

Perhaps more important, Dararweyne's assessment has helped the community to rethink its leadership arrangement so that discord is now the exception and consensus the rule.

The Lewiston Somali community discussed whether the approach might be helpful to meet their needs and agreed to invite a Clark team to spend three weekends (it eventually became four) to conduct a participatory needs assessment to enable Lewiston's Somalis to analyze their needs and reach consensus on their highest priority concerns and how to solve them. The assessment would focus on a residential housing complex, called Hill view, in which 60 of the 90 households were Somalis.

Analysis

The participatory exercises in Lewiston began slowly. While many women and young people came to the meetings, the men held back. Of the 40 to 45 residents at the first meeting, only two or three were men over 30. There were several explanations offered – a competing meeting of the mosque committee pulled the men away; the men had to go to work and could not spare time to come to community meetings; a married couple was having a major dispute and all the elders had been called to an emergency meeting to hear their complaints. While all of these explanations were accurate, it was not clear that they were the reasons why there were so few men present.

Even without the men, the exercises produced good results. A sketch map (Figure 1) revealed that transportation was a problem for shopping, getting to work or school, obtaining medical services, and visiting friends. The map also showed that travel to ESL classes was difficult, so many who would benefit from ESL did not go. Finally the map illustrated that few employment opportunities were available close to where Somalis lived. The list of needs began to emerge as improved transport, more jobs, more accessible ESL classes, better access to health services, and larger housing units for some of the extended Somali families.

The afternoon of the first day focused on institutions within the Lewiston Somali community as well as Lewiston's institutions. The institutional exercises are presented as Figures 2A and 2B. The first (2A) shows the Somali community's view of institutions within their community. It identifies the mosque as the dominant institution, working closely with the Council of Elders as well as with a local NGO, Somali Community Services. It portrays the women's organization as separate from the mosque and elders as well as removed from a local self-help group known as Daryeel. The diagram indicates a small number of Somali organizations and rather considerable isolation among them.

Figure 1
Sketch Map of Hillview Housing Community, Lewiston, Maine

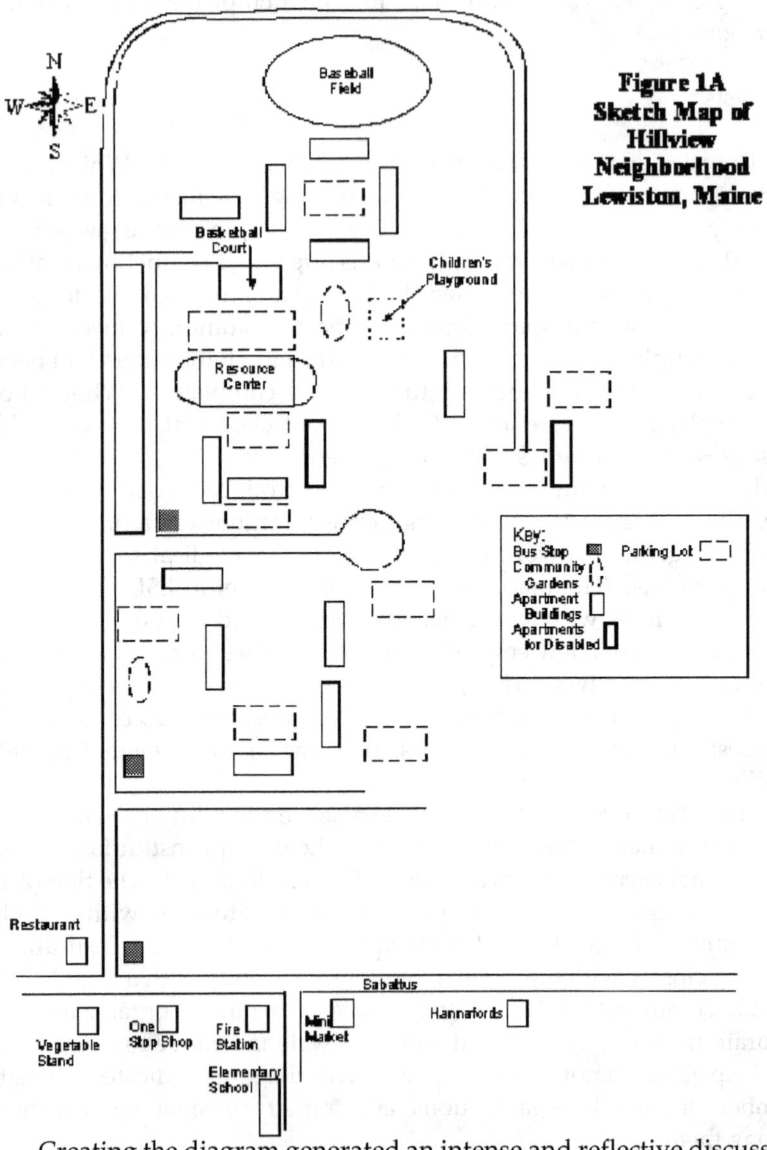

Creating the diagram generated an intense and reflective discussion among those present. It is of interest to note that a message must have been spreading into the community, stating that the discussion was heavy, important, and opening up many issues relevant to Somali needs. Some of the adult men began drifting into the meeting.

Comments emerged about why there were so few Somali institutions. Others asked whether the mosque might be a good institution to take a more active role in solving some of the community's problems. Still others wondered whether the existing institutions were doing as much as they could and whether they were fully accountable to the Somali community. Finally and perhaps most telling, participants began to wonder how accountable these institutions were and what might be done to make them more transparent. There was much soul searching and considerable introspection during the institutional analysis.

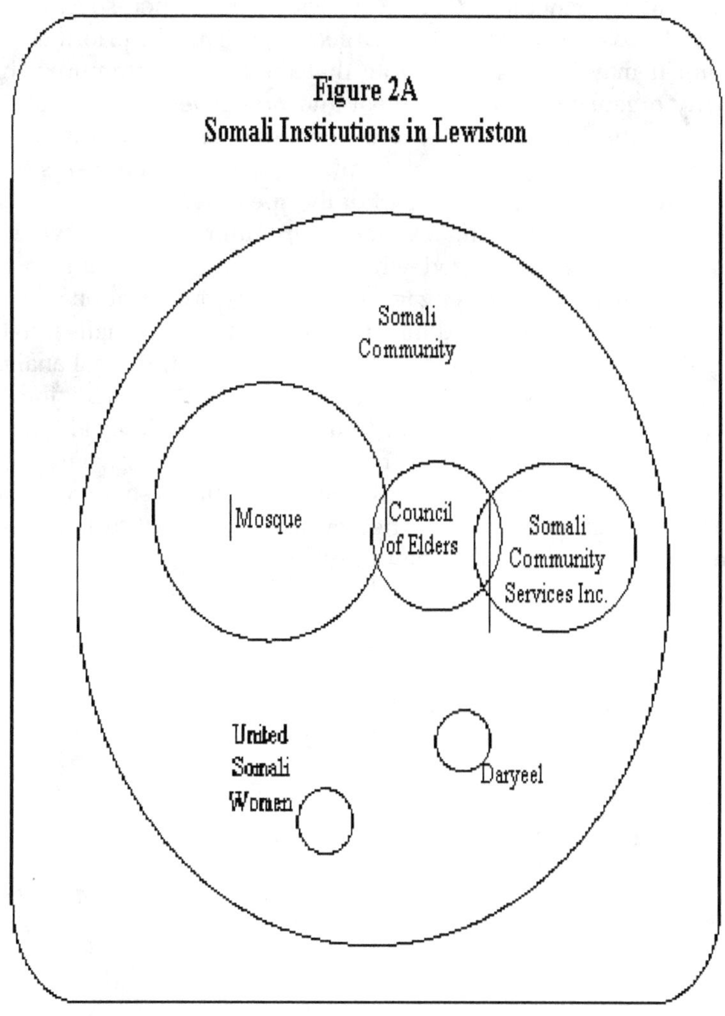

The discussion then turned to the Lewiston institutions external to the Somali community (Figure 2B). The resulting diagram is fascinating and reveals how the Somali community perceives the city's institutions. It shows many institutions but virtually all are represented as marginal to the Somalis. They are located along the fringe of the community with very little overlap or interaction with Somali individuals or institutions. Whether this is an accurate representation is less important than the point that it is how many in the Somali community feel. While the Somalis were unanimous in their praise and thanks for the hard work Lewiston residents were doing, they stated that these organizations were providing generalized services designed for non-specific and loosely defined needs rather than targeted and specific priorities. At this point it may be helpful to note that the Somali community had asked city organizations (government and non-government) to absent them from the needs assessment discussions. In addition, all conversation was conducted in Somali. As a result, comments were candid, direct, and close to the heart of the speakers.

By this time, adult males and community leaders were in abundance. Several wondered whether there were other and better ways in which they might engage the external organizations. How could there be more direct and meaningful input from Somalis into the City's planning and implementation process. The institutional analysis concluded on a highly reflective note, especially in internalizing the institutional dilemma in which they found themselves. They also noted that this discussion was perhaps the first time that men, women, and youth as well as members of several clans were able to share open and trusting conversations about whether and how institutions were meeting needs of the Somali community.

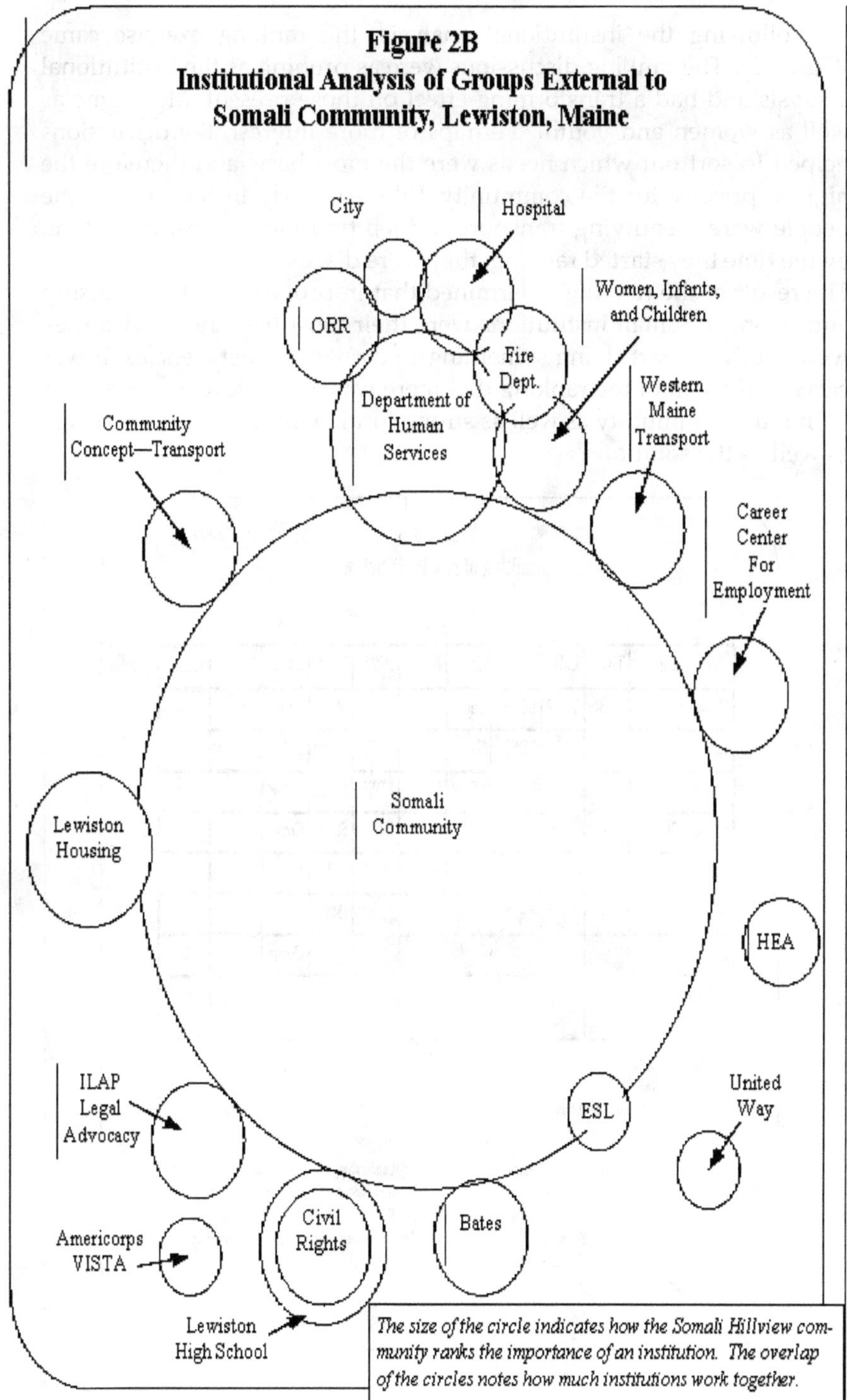

The size of the circle indicates how the Somali Hillview community ranks the importance of an institution. The overlap of the circles notes how much institutions work together.

Following the institutional analysis, the ranking exercise came (Figure 3). The ranking discussions were as probing as the institutional analysis and had a transforming effect on those present. Men came as well as women and youth. Perhaps of more interest, the discussions helped to sort out which needs were the most basic and therefore the highest priority for the community. Whereas early in the process the people were identifying transport and job training as most important, by the time they started ranking, they were discussing far deeper issues. The result of the ranking determined that improved Somali leadership and stronger Somali institutions were their most basic needs and they were ready to start doing something to correct the deficiencies. It was clear by the end of the ranking that there was a high level of consensus within the community as well as strong local ownership of the problem as well as the solutions.

Figure 3
Ranking of Needs: Hillview

Topic/Need	TRSP	EMP	LDSP	Gap	ESL	INST	SServ	Comm	Score	Rank
Transport		TRSP	LDSP	Gap	ESL	INST	SServ	Comm	1	5b
Employment			LDSP	Gap	ESL	INST	SServ	EMP	1	5a
Leadership				LDSP	LDSP	LDSP	LDSP	LDSP	7	1
Cultural Gap					Gap	INST	SServ	Comm	3	4c
ESL						INST	ESL	ESL	4	3
Institutions							INST	INST	6	2
Social Services								Comm	3	4b
Communication With City Hall									3	4a

Key to Abbreviations

1. TRSP = Transport
2. EMP = Employment
3. LDSP = Leadership
4. Gap = Cultural Gap
5. ESL = English as a Second Language
6. INST = Community Institutions
7. SServ = Social Services
8. Comm = Communication with City Hall

Final Ranked Order

1. Leadership
2. Institutions
3. ESL

4.a Communications with City Hall
4.b. Social Services
4.c. Cultural Gap
5.a. Employment
5.b. Transport

These two exercises (institutional analysis and ranking) marked a breakthrough for the Lewiston assessment. It was exploration of the relative weight and importance of local institutions that changed the entire emotional and political environment. When word began to spread that the discussions were dealing with issues that the community felt were the most important — *e.g.* leadership and institutions — even more men joined in. In the earlier exercises, the men had observed the process but did not play an active role. The institutional analysis established a threshold, indicating that this was a serious planning activity and that the men should be part of it. A similar threshold crossing took place in Dararweyne, Somaliland (see *Nabad iyo Caano*) while conducting the pairwise ranking. Institutional analysis did for Hill view what the ranking accomplished for Dararweyne; it cemented the community's engagement. It marked the formal passing of ownership from the Clark team to the Somali community. The Clark team knew by the end of the ranking discussions that Hill view would benefit from the exercises. It is of interest that since the conclusion of the Hill view assessment other Lewiston Somali groups have expressed interest in learning more about the Clark group and whether an assessment might be possible for their neighbourhood or community. This is a significant indicator of the importance the Somalis have attached to the approach.

Subsequent to the assessment, still another measure of engagement has emerged. The Somali community in Portland Maine — about 40 miles from Lewiston — has asked if some of Lewiston's Somalis experienced in community assessment will come to help them to get organized. Although the Portland mission has not yet taken place, it is of interest to ponder how the approach is taking hold in the region.

Figure 4 (opposite page) presents the first part of the Community Action Plan, noting what the community was going to do and how they would do it. While the total action plan represents responses to all eight priorities (see Figure 3), the action related only to the highest priority (leadership) is presented here. For a full discussion of the entire process in Lewiston, including the full action plan, see *Somali Families in Hill view* as identified in footnote 1 on page 1.

Figure 4
Lewiston Action Plan (partial)

Rank	Problem	Suggested Activity	First Step	Labor, Materials, Money	Who Will Act and/or Follow up	When	Indicators
1	Build Leadership Within the Somali Community	- Identify leaders to speak for community	- Organize community for electing working committee	- Meeting space - Volunteers to mobilize - Collecting money - Transport	- Elected committee of elders, youth, women	- During Eid celebration - After Ramadan	- When community elects official leader
		- Encourage youth leadership	- Organize youth for discussion	- Space - Volunteers to mobilize - Raise money	- Elected committee and youth	- One month after Ramadan	- When they organize tasks and activities
		- Leadership and organizational training	- Request organization to support training - Somali experts to help Clark U and other institutions offering training	- Time - Money - Space - Experts	- Elected committee - Universities of Maine, Clark, and Bates - City Hall	- Within two months	- Improved skills available

Fig 4 present planned action, as established in a community forum to deal with the eight ranked priorities (fig 6). The columns set out the activity(ies) that community groups think will help ease or solve the problem, how to get started, what materials or resources are needed (including both resources from within the community as well as assistance that external partners may provide), who will do it, when, and how they can tell if their actions are working.

To strengthen their leadership for example, they have designed a three-pronged attack, including a process to identify and select leaders, efforts to place particular priority on working with the youth and means to organize leadership training. It is important to note that these suggestions came from the community. In this way, the eventual leaders and community institutions (Ranked needs #1 and #2) will belong to the Lewiston Somalis, not to the City or Clark or other external groups. The action plan continues on the next few pages, noting strategies for strengthening community institutions and enhancing English language training.

Initial Follow-up

Over the last 12 months, several steps have been taken to implement the Hill view action plan.

- A course offered at Clark University in project management and program design was expanded to include about half a dozen Lewiston Somalis. The course met two or three times in

Lewiston and on one occasion the Somali participants came to Clark to join with a discussion of the Lewiston experience. While no formal registration took place and while no academic credit was given, the course worked out to be a very positive experience for both the Somalis and the Clark graduate students. It has stimulated plans for additional course opportunities for Lewiston Somalis.

- The City of Lewiston has endorsed the priorities of leadership and institution building as important in their program as well. They have printed and distributed 300 copies of the case study (*Somali Families of Hill view*) and posted it on their webpage as a sign of their endorsement as well as demonstrating their interest in helping the Hill view community to follow up on the assessment goals.
- Lewiston's Somali leadership is presently negotiating with the Portland Somali community about a Portland assessment. There are several levels to the discussion, including whether to bring non-Somali refugees/immigrants with the Somali team and whether to include non-Somalis in the Portland community. No decision has been made at this point but interest from Sudanese, Nigerian, and Rwanda/Burundi individuals in Lewiston is stimulating conversations about broadening the numbers and types of participants in the process. The city endorses this expansion.
- A new community college has recently opened in Lewiston. One of its goals is to provide courses and degree programs in community and social services. They are now engaged in talks with Somali Community Services (SCS) to determine whether and how they may be able to establish links between the Hill view Somali leadership and their new curriculum. Because the community college also has a branch in Portland, there may be another dimension of collaboration between community groups and the new college and Lewiston and Portland.
- Clark is working with SCS in two modes. The first is to sponsor a periodic seminar on leadership, drawing from resources in Lewiston and Portland as well as from Clark. The shape of the course is evolving and will be introduced in October/November 2004. Second, Clark will provide faculty and graduate student support for the Portland assessment.

All of these activities are designed to increase the experience, knowledge, and skills of Somali leadership in Maine and to create ways for them to become more self-sufficient in forming partnerships with external government and non-government organizations.

Findings

What does all of this data gathering, analysis, ranking, and planning mean for Lewiston's Somali Hill view community? Will it move them forward in resolving and maintaining internal harmony? Will it result in strengthening their leadership and community institutions? Will Somalis be able to increase their economic well-being and social development as a result? And perhaps most important, will the new generation of young Somalis be able to advance in their educational achievement and skill acquisition because of increased educational and employment opportunities?

The response is a tentative yes. All agree that three "process goals" were achieved as a result of the assessment.

Good Local Support

The Somali community is positive about and enthusiastic for the effort. Abundant information emerged from the discussions, especially conversations about institutional strengths within the Somali community as well as institutional relationships that might be crafted through liaisons with groups external to the community. Questions of whether there were now Somali institutions available to implement a local action plan were discussed. While nothing was decided, there is no question that levels of interest in the process of setting one's own priorities caught the attention of many in the community.

Meaningful and Probing Discussions

Even though people in Hill view see and speak to each other many times a week, the conversations are not necessarily focused on how to solve needs of the community. At the conclusion of the needs assessment, several people described how helpful the charts and diagrams had been to get people thinking and talking about solving their own problems. On the first Saturday evening, SCS arranged for a resident who is a gifted poet to recite some of his original poetry, mostly about peace, justice, and equity. The Somali women had cooked a meal for 50 people and the entire group ate together. The food and poetry were another opportunity for everyone to think deeply about why we had come together and what could be accomplished as a result. While it is much too early to say that the discussions were "successful," it is possible to say that all took the meetings seriously and thoughtfully.

Local Ownership

Another goal of the participatory method is for the residents to take over the action plan and make it their own. While we are only beginning the process, it is clear that many of the Hill view residents already see the needs, the institutional discussions, the action plan, and the responsibility for implementation as something they are ready to take over. The key to sustaining action plans is local ownership. The Hill view Somalis are off to a splendid start.

Beyond the process accomplishments at least five "products" were created.

The assessment achieved consensus

While fragile and tentative on a number of occasions (due to lack of information about the process, busy work schedules, and childcare responsibilities), the concluding sessions were fulfilling. The participatory tools drew out many views and attitudes that became central to the final list of priority needs. Levels of commitment at this initial stage are substantial because of the participatory nature of the discussions. The mechanics of implementation are now being worked out. Not only is there accord among all residents, Clark has received requests from two additional Lewiston Somali groups to conduct similar needs assessments for their groups.

The Community Action Plan is profound

While several "needs" of a short-term nature were discussed during the initial meetings – *e.g.* transportation, employment, English language training – the two issues ranked as the highest priority needs were strengthening leadership and building community institutions. Discussion during the ranking noted that the core problem of the recently settled Somalis was one of building cohesiveness and cooperation amongst themselves. With good leadership and smoothly functioning institutions, the Somalis noted, they would be able to create their own solutions for transportation, employment, and many other needs.

The Action Committee

The Action Committee has strong backing from the community at the present time. The new and highly energized group represents most elements of Hillview Somalis and is already meeting to work out its plan of action. The community has tentatively nominated eight people who are well respected and who understand and are committed to the process of action plan implementation. These nominations have been approved by the entire Hillview community.

Somali Community Services, Inc.

Somali Community Services, Inc. a small non-governmental organization recently founded and run entirely by Somalis to focus on Somali needs in Lewiston, is prepared to assist in facilitating the creation of partnerships between Hillview and external agencies (both Somali and non-Somali). If the model of community-generated plans and a locally-based facilitating group can make a dent on the needs of leadership and community institution building, there may be lessons learned that will benefit other Somalis in the Lewiston-Auburn area and perhaps in other parts of the US and Canada.

Partnerships

Partnerships are the final ingredient that will make the process work. At an initial stakeholders meeting held in early September, approximately 65 people came to hear about the tools of analysis to be used in the needs assessment and how their institution might help out. The December Stakeholders' meeting, held on a Saturday, drew approximately 45 participants. It should be noted that a partnership is not simply an agency funding one or more "projects" of the Hillview Somalis. Rather, the partnership is defined as a joint enterprise in which Somali institutions join with external groups to define and implement actions that are of benefit to all partners. While partners may invest some money, the purpose of the partnership transcends money. The details of individual partnerships will vary, depending on circumstances, yet at the core of the partnership is an understanding that all parties have things to contribute and benefits to receive.

Achieving consensus in December 2003 does not mean that harmony and consensus will last for many years. There will be challenges to conclusions and recommendations. People will differ on precisely how to implement particular action. Skilled leaders will move away or take new jobs. Partnerships will rise and fall, depending on many circumstances. Yet the CAP belongs to the entire community, not just to the leaders of the Action Committee. Regular meetings, periodic monitoring, continuous updates on the action plan, and frequent consultations with the City, NGOs, and other partner agencies will form the ingredients that assure sustained energy and ownership.

The Lewiston needs assessment worked, not because it is a miracle methodology. Rather, it was effective for three reasons:

The data gathering was an **inclusive and public process**. Young and old, male and female, multiple clan groups, and the Clark team came ready to listen to one another in meaningful and serious ways. The visual nature of the documents helped transcend language and cultural barriers. The participatory tools helped all members of the group to express their ideas and attitudes.

The ranking worked effectively.

It provided a public arena in which all members of the community had opportunity to express views, listen to others, and decide for themselves. There was no voting, no caucusing, and no politicizing. Rather it was a genuine sharing of views and a process of give and take to achieve consensus.

The **Community Action Plan (CAP) will guide the Somali community** as it embarks on **implementing solutions** as well as **attracting partners**. The Hillview residents have organized their information and mobilized their resources. These are reflected in the CAP. These steps greatly increase the possibility of development partners joining with the community and substantially assure that both parties to the partnership will achieve their goals.

These ingredients – inclusiveness, public group process, transparent ranking, listening to others, visual data gathering techniques, building consensus rather than voting, creating a Community Action Plan, organizing information, mobilizing resources, and building partnerships – are the foundation upon which sustainable actions will be achieved. They are the qualities that will enable the Hillview Somali community to continue listening to each other as well as to become the managers of their own community. The next move, implementing the Action Plan, belongs to the Somalis. If they can solve their leadership needs, it is because they have learned how to do it during the needs assessment. If they create effective community institutions, it will be based on their efforts implementing the Action Plan. Community-based planning builds upon the strengths of the community, not on the funds of outside helpers. For the many stakeholders who have been working with the Lewiston Somalis and for the City of Lewiston, the key for the next few years is listening to the new leadership and collaborating with the new institutions. The resulting partnerships hold the answer to the long term and sustainable well-being for Lewiston's newest citizens.

References

Ahmed, A. (eds.) (1995) The *Invention of Somalia*. (Trenton, NJ: Red Sea Press).

Cassanelli, L. (1982) *The Shaping of Somali Society: Reconstruction of the History of a Pastoral People, 1600-1900*. (Philadelphia: University of Pennsylvania Press).

Chambers, Robert. (1997) *Whose Reality Counts: Putting the First Last* (Intermediate Technology Press, London).

Clark University, Egerton University, National Environment Secretariat, World Resources Institute (1990) *Participatory Rural Appraisal Handbook: Doing PRAs in Kenya.*

Ford, Richard, Hussein Adam, Adan Yusuf Abokor, Ahmed Farah, Osman Hirad Barre (1994) *PRA with Somali Pastoralists: Building Community Institutions for Africa's Twenty-First Century,* Clark Program for International Development and GTZ, 1994 (also translated into Russian and Somali).

Ford, Richard, Francis Lelo and Harlys Rabarison. March, (1998) Linking *Governance and Effective Resource Management: A Guidebook for Community-Based Monitoring and Evaluation, Clark* Program for International Development, Egerton University, and APAM/Madagascar.

Ford, Richard, and B. Thomas-Slayter. (2001) "Alternatives to Anarchy: Africa's Transition from Agricultural to Industrial Societies" in *Progress in Planning:* Vol. 56 Part 2, 2001 (Elsevier, London).

Ford, Richard, Adan Abokor and Shukri Abdullahi. (2002) *Nabad iyo Caano (Peace and Milk): Linking Peace Building and Community-Based Development for a Decentralized Somaliland* (Program for International Development, Clark University).

Korten, David, and Rudi Klauss. (eds.) (1984) *People-Centered Development: Contributions Toward Theory and Planning Frameworks* (Kumarian Press, Hartford).

Thomas-Slayter, Barbara, Andrea Lee Esser, M. Dale Shields. July (1993) Tools *of Gender Analysis: A Guide to Field Methods for Bringing Gender into Sustainable Resource Management,* USAID and Clark University Program for International Development. (an ECOGEN Publication).

Thomas-Slayter, Barbara, and Genese Sodikoff. (2000) "Sustainable Investment: Women's Contributions to Natural Resource Management Projects in Africa," *Development in Practice*.

Thomas-Slayter, Barbara, Rachel Polestico, Andrea Lee Esser, Octavia Taylor, Elvina Mutua. (1995) *A Manual for Socio-Economic and*

Gender Analysis: Responding to the Development Challenge. (Clark University ECOGEN Project, 1995).

---

1. This chapter is based on a case study prepared in April 2004 by Laura Hammond, Richard Ford, Abdirizak Mahboub, and Shukri Abdillahi entitled, Somali Families in Hillview: Assessing Needs, Setting Priorities, Building Consensus. Copies of that case study can be viewed and downloaded from the website of the City of Lewiston Maine. The web address is: http://ci.lewiston.me.us/cultures/index.htm

2. Siyad Barre, President of Somalia from 1969 to 1991, was deposed during a long and bitter civil war.

3. Ford, R.B. Adan Abokor and Shukri Abdullahi, Nabad iyo Caano (Peace and Milk): Linking Peace Building and Community-Based Development for a Decentralized Somaliland (Program for International Development, Clark University; International Cooperation for Development, Hargeisa, 2002); Ford, R.B., Hussein Adam, Adan Abokor, Ahmed Farah, Osman Hirad Barre, PRA with Somali Pastoralists: Building Community Institutions for Africa's Twenty First Century, Clark Program for International Development and GTZ, 1994 (also translated into Russian and Somali).

Chapter 5

The need to belong and the need to distance oneself: Contra-identification among Somali refugees in Norway

Katrine Fangen

"The tens and thousands of Somali refugees in the U.S., Canada, Sweden, Germany, Italy, etc. are divided and frustrated, unable to unite to help each other and to overcome their problems (health, education, language, etc.). ... Can the Somali intellectual live in peace with the Western media which every day presents a distorted image and an exotic interpretation of his/her country?" (Ahmed Quassim Ali, 1995)

Statements such as the above are common among Somali refugees in Norway as well. Since the late 1990s the stigmatization of Somalis in Norway has increased as a result of a very one-sided, negative focus on Somalis in the media[1]. As a result, for many Norwegians the term "Somali" has become equivalent with violence, with the use of *khat,* female genital circumcision, polygamy, and a stereotype of worst-case immigrants who do not want to integrate. The result is a public image of the dangerous, the criminal or the non-integrated Somali. The many resourceful Somalis, who do have an important job in the municipalities or in various public offices, are seldom portrayed in the media.

Common to almost all of the Somalis I have interviewed, is that they in one way or another define themselves in opposition to the negative public image that has been created. In this article I will analyse Somalis' identification/contra-identification with their own group[2].

The need to belong and the need to distance oneself

Identification might be seen as an ongoing negotiation process, formed by media images, positive and negative experiences and the reactions we meet in school, in the family, among peers and other parts of society. For immigrants, identification processes might go hand in hand with the social process of gradually becoming a part of the new society. For some, this process takes a long time, and perhaps they will never be able to, or will never want to become an integrated part of this new society; for others, the integration process goes quickly, and their identifications with others will also change accordingly.

Despite the conflicts between different clans, Somalis are often portrayed as a very homogenous people; all Somalis – with the exception of a few minority clans – share the same language and the same religion (Sunni-Islam). The colonisation of Somalia contributed to fictive borders which separated many ethnic Somalis from the territory defined as Somalia. As a result, there are many people who have lived all their lives in Ethiopia, Kenya and Djibouti, but who still consider themselves as Somalis. Although ethnicity is an important entity of identification for most Somalis, it varies whether or not my Somali respondents identify with all other Somalis, or only with their own clan or with some category of Somalis (for example those with further education). Ethnic identity is one of the many identities of my respondents, and the way they define themselves in ethnic terms is clearly related to how they define themselves according to gender differences, class differences and other structuring factors in society, as will be seen in the following section on contra-identifications.

Identities are, as Stuart Hall (1996) argues, constructed through difference, through the relation to what it is not. Contra-identification might be defined as defining oneself in contrast with, or opposition to some particular group or characteristic. When my Somali respondents' contra-identify with distinct other groups of Somalis in Norway, they see themselves clearly as different from these, and also view these negatively. Contra-identification often takes the form of dichotomisation (Eriksen 1995:434), which means the establishment of a distinct identity through contrasts vis-à-vis the other (Østberg, 2003:86). Many of these dichotomies might be overlapping, and some might diverge with each other.

The public debate contributes to the definition among Somalis of which categories are central. Somalis with different backgrounds from Somalia and with different aspirations in Norwegian society, have different ways of identifying themselves. Overall, there seems to be general agreement of what the central categories of identification are, but great variation in the interpretation of positive and negative aspects.

Identifications and contra-identifications with other Somalis

Common for almost all of the Somalis I have interviewed, is that they in some way or another define themselves in opposition to the negative public image of the Somalis. When I as a white middle-class woman interview Somali refugees in Norway, their need to take a stand against those Somalis who contribute to the stigma becomes activated. However, my impression is that some Somalis' contra-identifications in relation to some distinct groups of other Somalis are activated also in all-Somali settings. In Somali interest and welfare organisations, there is a lot of discussion about the need to take a stand against *khat,* against female genital mutilation, and the need to motivate Somalis to educate themselves and to help Somalis get a job. These are issues that interest and activate Somalis living in Norway.

However, not all the issues were as important for these Somalis when living in Somalia. Then there were other more urgent issues to be concerned about, such as the need to remain safe. Following Harun Hassan (2004), Somalia is a country in ruins. With 70% of the population living below the poverty level and international relief largely cut-off by civil war, it is a place where survival is a full-time occupation. In Norway, however, there is peace and social benefits provide a stable and safe income. Here issues other than survival become important, such as ways of making one's living in the new country. In the following sections I present how different Somalis contra-identify themselves to other Somalis living in Norway.

Arriving early vs. arriving later

Among those Somalis I have interviewed and who work in the Norwegian public or local government systems, the contra-identity to the public image of Somalis is most explicitly expressed. Osman, who worked in a Norwegian municipality, maintained that one should distinguish between those Somalis who came in the late 1980s and early 1990s, and those who came later. Those who came first integrated better than those who came after the mid 1990s, he maintained. He is frustrated by some of those who came later, who are very religious, and who he thinks prevent the integration process, in the way they want to lead the local mosque.

Many Somalis tell me that they see people becoming very actively religious, after coming to Norway, whereas in Somalia they never visited a mosque. The community with other Somalis in the mosque becomes a way to feel safe, if one does not manage to find a way of living as part of the new society. Hawa Haji Mohamed (2004) writes of Somali women in Finland that they feel that the Islamic identity is stronger than it was in Somalia. In exile, she writes, Islam is used to maintain a sense of identity and belonging.

Some of the early-arrived Somalis see the degree to which one joins all-Somali or all-Muslim encounters like the Somali café or the mosque, as typical of those Somalis who came during the latter years. They report the same feature of different backgrounds and different abilities to integrate among people who came to Norway in different periods. They think those who have come during the later years[6] have less education prior to arrival, and they have had greater problems and/or less interest in finding their way into the Norwegian society.

Such contra-identification among first-arrived refugees from those coming later is also a well-known mode of identity-strategy among other refugee groups. Those coming later might threaten the positive self-ascription of those who have been in the host country for many years, as they have managed to learn the new language and get employment and/or formal education[3]. Those who come later and start anew on the integration process might be perceived as threatening as they might contribute to the negative picture of people from their own ethnic group, as is often seen in media representations of this group.

Spending time in the street and the café vs. spending time with the family

Some Somali women, but also some men, distance themselves from Somali men who use their time in cafés, chewing *khat*. They argue that this extended chewing of *khat* causes many problems. It contributes to the breaking up of families, because the wives do not want to continue to live with a man who spends his money on *khat* and who does not take responsibility for the children. *Khat* is thus an issue which causes conflicts between the sexes. Some of my male Somali respondents know many of them. They say that it is common for these men to feel their status as family provider threatened after coming to Norway, as their wives suddenly become economically independent because of social benefits from the state. These men feel threatened by this new feeling of loss of power within the family, and they also feel useless in society. My respondents state that seeking comfort in the company of other men, and chewing *khat* in order to forget their daily frustrations are some of these men's ways of coping with their new situation.

Very much the same picture is reported by Hassan (2002) in his article about Somali women in the Diaspora in UK: He writes that most Somali women in the UK receive state benefits and housing allowances. Many of them want to study, to work if possible, to socialise and join in with the new culture. Men, he argues, often feel differently. Most of them firmly believe that women should remain at home, provide meals and raise the children. By conducting a survey of 78 Somalis, he found that 28% blamed *khat* for being the cause of the many divorces between Somali men and women living in the UK. He quotes a Somali woman who divorced her husband. She claims that he refused to contribute to housework and the family income and he had a weakness for *khat*. 'He chewed with other people and came home to sleep,' she remarks. 'He never spent time with me…a lot of single mothers would agree with me.'

For both women and some men the category of men who use a lot of time and money on *khat* is a symbol of men who do not take the responsibility for their families and who have a negative orientation to Norwegian society. It seems that particularly those Somalis who see Norway as a country of future residence distance themselves from such a lifestyle. Abdalla, in his early 40s, knew several of these men, and from time to time went to the cafés in order to chat and share the latest news from the development in Somalia, but he did not like the negative attitude the other men took towards the Norwegian system, and all the rumours they shared of their bad experiences with different authorities. Abdalla, who had no education beyond elementary school level, had been working as a cleaner in a hotel for three out of the total of four years he has been living in Norway. He maintains that he wants to adopt what he calls "the Norwegian way".

He says he identifies with those Somalis who want to integrate. However, he does not want his wife to participate in the introduction programme for refugees (including Norwegian language training), because he thinks (and she says she thinks the same) that she should stay home and take care of the children and make food. He himself has not tried to get a new job after he was fired from his previous job at the hotel. He thought the dismissal was unfair, and now he thinks he is better off with various social benefits. But he tries to remain active, by attending new courses such as job training courses etc. He sends his children to the Qu'ran-school on Saturdays, and his oldest daughter must wear a *hijab.* Also the two younger daughters wear *hijabs* when going to the Qu'ran school. They are however allowed to take it off at home and when going to ordinary school. There are many ways in which neither he nor his wife and children go "the Norwegian way".

There are, however, various aspects which seem to be included in his sense of identification with "the Norwegian way". He contrasts himself with Muslim fundamentalists, and also with Somali men who spend their time in the cafés instead of taking their task of guiding their children and helping within the family. Probably, there are many like Abdalla, who want to take the responsibility by spending time with their family and helping with the children, but who still choose not to work, and who now and then join the men in the street in order to chat. According to Søholt (2001), many Somali men have difficulties getting a job, and choose to live on the dole instead of taking low status jobs which would lead to a loss of social status. Abdullah's position might be seen as a very rational one: He takes advantage of the social benefit system in the way that it offers him and his wife an opportunity to spend time with the children, and at the same time prevent them from being discriminated on the job market. Then he spends some time with the male-dominated Somali milieu downtown to socialise and share some frustrations of living in Norway, at the same time as it gives a needed sense of Somali life.

Drifting around / being illiterate vs. taking education

Having a job and a formal education is highly valued, both among those who are educated and among those who are not. According to my respondents, the continuum ranging from those without formal education to those with long-term education, has become more important for Somalis living in Norway than it was in Somalia, where many other entities gave status as well, such as membership in a dominant clan, one's knowledge of Islam, etc. The degree to which one has formal education or not becomes important for Somalis when coming to Norway, as this factor is an important structuring factor in Norwegian society at large.

The distinction between educated and illiterate individuals functions as a major symbolic distinction in regard to how internal boundaries in the Somali minority are conceptualised, as it also did for Pakistanis studied by Andersson (2000:163), and as is the case in Norwegian society in general. For immigrants education might be experienced as the road to becoming equal to the majority. Thus, many of my Somali respondents verbalise the goal of education as the path to salvation with regard to the future of the second generation refugees, as did many of Anderson's (2000) Pakistani respondents. For immigrants the need to take advantage of the education system is important in order to obtain social mobility and improve the reputation of ethnic minority members (ibid.). For Somalis, this need can thus be seen as a contra-reaction to the stigmatisation of Somalis in the public, but in addition, this need is clearly related to their expectations for "good lives" irrespective of where they find themselves.

Misra, a college-student in her 20s, defines herself in contrast to those Somalis who are too occupied with clan membership. Somalis are strange people, she states. They judge other people by their clan membership and by how they dress. Nonetheless, she thinks there is a big difference between Somalis living in villages and having no formal education, and Somalis who come from the big cities. The first category has much greater difficulties integrating than the latter, she states. If you know the language and have gone to school in Norway, and know how the society works, there is no problem, she says. Then you contribute to society. According to her impression, the young Somalis are also oriented towards the clan system. Still, most of her own friends are from the south, even though she is from North-Somalia. For this young woman, it is important to make friends with other Somalis, without regard to which clan they come from. However, she contra-identifies with Somalis who lack formal education and come from the villages. Her main identification is with those Somalis coming from the big cities, and who seek formal education.

Some Somalis, like Misra, stress the same distinction as Andersson found among her Pakistani respondents: an urban background represents a better condition, by drawing connotations of illiterate, rural background and less enlightened as opposed to educated, urban background and more civilised. Similar dichotomies are surely also seen in the Norwegian population, people from the cities regard themselves as better educated and more sophisticated than people from rural areas. For immigrants, the construction of illiterates and people with rural background as negative reference groups can be seen as a strategy to be recognised as individuals of equal worth and with equal capacities as ethnic Norwegians (cp. Andersson, 2000:164).

The problem for many Somalis, however, is that even though they idealise formal education, they have been in Norway for so short a time that the road to this goal is more difficult than it is for many second generation Pakistanis, whose parents have lived here for many years. One Somali male who strives to master the road to education and employment, is Jimale, 20-years-old, who was previously into gangs and dope. Now he wants to be a good father to his three-year old son, with whom he lost contact. He came to Norway alone as a young boy, and has been drifting around for years. But now he no longer wants to interact with other Somalis who use drugs and disturb people. Earlier he often experienced fellow Somalis coming to his shared flat during the night, so that he woke up and could not get any sleep. He had to sleep during the day in order to get enough sleep. He reports that he feels good now, because now he is on his way to attaining his goal, which is to have a stable job and to get some further education. He lost the trainee job he had received through the employment office because he did not manage to come to work regularly. He says he likes those Somalis who help each other. He does not like those who do not follow the rules any more and who steal from people. He likes those who are calm and "who walk up the stairs, not down".

The story of this young man might illustrate how hard it is to make a life for oneself in Norway. He came to Norway on his own, and his parents are in Somalia and do not know how he is getting on with his life. He is fortunate in that he gets a lot of help from a Somali man who works in the municipality, and more than before, he is filled with hope that he will attain his goals, even though the road ahead is still long and probably difficult. Jimale thus has a need to contra-identify with those

Somalis who led him in the wrong direction in the past, and on the other hand in identifying with "those who go up the stairs", who get an education, who help other people, and who stay calm.

Because of prejudices against Somalis as a result of the stigmatised representation of Somalis in the media, there is reason to believe that Somalis are more subjected to employers' discrimination than for example Pakistanis. Resignation and anger become for many one possible reaction to long periods where they have worked hard to succeed in the educational system, or with training in the labour market, without finding any open door.

Discussion

The vulnerable position in which many Somalis in Norway find themselves - as a result of processes of segregation, discrimination and stigmatization - leads to an identity navigation centred around the need to distance oneself from those Somalis who fit in with the negative public image, and a need to be able to define one's own picture of what it means being a Somali, as a contrast. We can relate this to what David Griffiths (2002) found among Somalis in London, that the collapse of the post-colonial state leads to fragmentation.

Examples of different dichotomies that the Somalis I interviewed use in order to attribute negative vs. positive characteristics are:

men who do not care for their family	women who take all the responsibility
men who gather in cafés, chewing *khat*	men who want to integrate in Norwegian society
people who spend a lot of time in the mosque	people who are more secular
youths with problems	youths who manage both cultures
people who work	people who choose not to work
girls who wear *hijab*	girls who do not wear *hijab*
those who arrived first	those who have newly arrived
those from the cities	those from rural areas in Somalia
people occupied with clan	people who do not regard clan as important
people who only associate themselves with Somalis	people who interact a lot with Norwegians

We often see that the poles rural, *khat*-chewing, occupied with clan, *hijab*, unemployed, no education, occur simultaneously; and as opposed to from the cities, immigrated first, not interested in clans, interacting with Norwegians, getting a formal education, having a job, etc. The first axis is often linked to a stronger Somali identity than the latter. But there are many cross-versions, such as women who dress in traditional Muslim clothes but are very integrated because they know many Norwegians, have a formal education and a stable job. Some of the categories might be actively chosen, whereas others are categories that the individual cannot choose, or eventually tries to change but are hindered by marginalising mechanisms in Norwegian society, as when Ahmed tries to get the kind of job he is educated for without succeeding, or when Jimale tries to deal with keeping a stable job or getting an education, but again and again experiences that he does not succeed in this. Some, such as Ahmed and Jimale, identify with having stable jobs, and fixing life, even though they have problems achieving this goal. For some, several such experiences might lead to a re-identification, for example into more all-Somali settings, for others it might lead to new alternative routes of obtaining the goal. That is, some change into a renewed focus on roots (understood as association with an all-Somali community and rejecting the Norwegian society), others try to find new routes.

In Norway, what it means to be a Somali is constructed by the use of 'us-them' dichotomies, between Somalis as contrasted to Norwegians, but also between their own ways of being a Somali in Norway versus other Somalis' ways of behaving in Norway. The differences have to do with *formal education:* those who aspire to become educated versus those who do not, or those who have a formal education versus those who do not. The *religious dimension* goes both ways; those who are religious identify negatively in relation to those who are more secular, and those who are more secular identify negatively in relation to those most religious.

Many Somalis I have talked with say that the traditional Somali clan networks which provide help for those in need are weakened here in Norway. Instead of providing understanding and guidance, condemnation and gossip is often reported as a problem among Somalis. The interaction between Somalis in Norway occurs within a context of Norwegian discrimination, their own minority position, Diaspora etc. which so to say leads many Somalis to take a position against each other instead of standing together in consolation and safety, with more positive role models for the young ones as a result.

This leads again to Ahmed Quassim Jimale's statement in the beginning of this article. For some Somalis, the breaking up of networks and the one-sided picture of Somalis in the media might not cause big problems. They have their own network of other resourceful individuals. For others, however, the breaking up or lack of traditional networks leads to loneliness and deep frustration. Several new forms of identity might grow out of such a situation. Politicised, creolised, transnational or renewed traditional identities in the form of symbolic ethnicity may all be the consequent identities which have been formed by frustration in the exile situation.

References

Ali, Ahmed Qassim. (1995) The predicament of the Somali Studies. In: Ali Jimale Ahmed (ed.) (1995) The Invention of Somalia Lawrenceville: The Red Sea Press.

Andersson, Mette. (2000) All five fingers are not the same. Identity work among ethnic minority youth in an urban Norwegian context, PhD thesis, University of Bergen.

Eriksen, Thomas Hylland. (1995) We and us: Two modes of group identification. In: Journal of Peace Research, vol. 32, no. 4, 427-36.

Griffiths, David. (2002) Somali and Kurdish Refugees in London: New Identities in the Diaspora, Aldershot: Ashgate.

Hall, Stuart. (1996) Introduction: Who needs 'identity'? In: Hall, Stuart and Paul du Gay (eds.) (1996) Questions of cultural identity London: Sage.

Hassan, Harun. (2002) 'Not housekeepers any more': Somali women of the Diaspora http://www.mafhoum.com/press4/120S66.htm

Hassan, Harun. (2004) The Phones Keep Ringing In World's Poorest Country http://www.globalenvision.org/library/3/526/

Klepp, Ingun. (2002) Ein diskursiv analyse av relasjonar mellom somaliske familiar og lokalbefolkninga i ein vestnorsk bygdeby, MA-thesis in social anthropology, University of Bergen.

Mohamed, Hawa Haji. (2004) Somali immigrants in Finland. Somali women between two cultures, paper for the 9th Somali Studies International Conference, Aalborg, Denmark.

Rotheram, Mary Jane and Jean S. Phinney (eds.) 1987. Children's ethnic socialization: pluralism and development. Newbury Park: Sage.

Søholt, Susanne. (2001) Etniske minoriteter og strategier på boligmarkedet i Oslo. En undersøkelse blant innbyggere med pakistansk, tamilsk og somalisk opprinnelse. Prosjektrapport, Oslo: Byggforsk.

Østberg, Sissel. (2003) Pakistani children in Norway: Islamic nurture in a Norwegian context, Leeds: Department of Theology and Religious Studies, University of Leeds.

1. Ingun Klepp (2002:1) analyses the turn in media's portrayal of Somalis after the UN's intervention in the Somalia war in 1993. She argues that there was a sudden turn in how the war was being reported. During the first years of the war, the media focused on the Somali victims, but after 1993, the focus was on the killing of UN soldiers, supported by a cheering crowd of people.
2.. I have conducted semi-structured interviews with about 25 Somalis, and in addition written down casual conversations with some 20 more. Furthermore, my material consists of participant observation in two families and participation in a casual conversation with a group of young Somalis and repeated participation in a focus group for Somali women. In order to grasp how different Somalis experience their current situation in Norway, and how they construe their own identities, my interviewees have different positions in society, ranging from those with full college or university education and/or stable jobs, to those who are unemployed and even a few with a criminal background. I have interviewed both young and old, both deeply religious and more secular persons. My goal is to attempt to grasp the whole picture, while using in- depth interviews. I have given my respondents fictive names, mainly inspired by the characters in the novel Maps by the Somali author Nuruddin Farah.
6. 62% of Somali first generation immigrants have lived in Norway less than five years (Lie 2004). Only a minor number of Somalis came to Norway before 1987.
3. Somalis are more often hit by unemployment than any other immigrant groups in Norway, and more often receive social welfare. Some 25.8 % of Somalis in Norway in 2001 had a job (cf. Lie 2004). 19% of the women had work, whereas 31.1% of the men were working. The total income for Somali households in Norway is very low compared to other immigrant groups (ibid.).

Chapter 6

Connected Lives: Somalis in Minneapolis dealing with family responsibilities and migration dreams of relatives

Cindy Horst

Introduction

Somalis have migrated and dispersed globally for centuries, but especially since the civil war, they can be found in almost every country. A lot of research has been done on Somalis across the world, focusing on Internally Displaced People (IDPs), returnees, urban refugees, refugees in regional camps and resettled refugees. Yet, there are many connections between the lives and livelihoods of these people in different positions. As such, a more integrated approach that studies their connectedness from the point of view of Somalis in different places is vital; both for an increased understanding of their situation as well as in order to improve the policies that affect their lives.

Research has shown how transnational networks and flows of remittances, goods and information are essential for the livelihoods of Somalis in the Dadaab refugee camps of Kenya (Horst Forthcoming). Dadaab lies in one of Kenya's most marginal provinces, in an area that is unsuitable for agricultural production. The province has a very poor infrastructure and on top of that is insecure due to frequent attacks by *shifta;* Somali 'bandits' (Crisp 1999). Refugees are able to survive in the camps despite these limited regional livelihood opportunities and insufficient and decreasing international assistance, due to remittances that are sent by their relatives elsewhere. About fifteen percent of the refugees receive remittances, enabling a much larger part of the camp population to survive in the camps. As a consequence of the monetary flows into the camps and the accompanying images of life in, for example, North America and Europe, many of the refugees in the camps dream of migration to the West. After the civil war, a term was invented to describe this 'dream of going for resettlement': *buufis*. *Buufis* is caused on the one hand by the lack of regional opportunities, and on the other by the opportunity of people around the world, created by technological developments in global communication and transportation, to imagine their lives elsewhere.

Because an important part of the financial and communicational interactions take place between the camps and resettlement countries, the question arises: How do resettled Somalis view these connections? In order to understand this, research was carried out amongst Somalis in the USA, and more specifically in Minneapolis. The focus is on three types of connections. In the first place, what kind of *material assistance* is provided, what are the capacities and constraints that Somalis in the West face in this respect, and does their current position change their willingness to remit (see also Al-Ali et al. 2001)? Secondly, what *information exchanges* take place, and how does this affect images of lives in the West and the migration dreams that are termed 'buufis' in Kenya? Also, does the exchange of such information lead to shared decision making on livelihood strategies in general and migration options in particular by family members, across borders? And thirdly, what *migration processes* are taking place, related to historical patterns as well as current opportunities? This chapter will explore these issues in order to determine how Somalis in Diaspora deal with their transnational family obligations and the migration dreams of relatives living in the Horn

The Somali community in Minneapolis

Minnesota is amongst the top destinations for Somalis, and in recent years, Minneapolis is said to host the largest number of Somalis in the US. The problem however is that there is no precise figures on the Somali population here or anywhere else. Consequently, estimates of exact numbers vary widely. The 2000 Census data for the state of Minnesota indicated that 11,164 Somalis live in Minnesota; 0.2 percent of the total state population (United States Census 2000). Many choose to live in the Twin Cities, because of the urban setting and Somali economy available. Others stay in regional small towns with large concentrations of Somalis, because life is cheaper there and the environment is more safe and less threatening e.g. in terms of upbringing of children. It is likely that official census figures greatly underestimate actual numbers, as many extended Somali families live in one house with larger numbers than allowed, so they underreport their numbers. Public school enrolment and welfare statistics suggest a range of 15,000 to 30,000 Somalis in Minnesota; a number that is still growing.

Thus, the Somali community in Minneapolis may well be larger than other towns with major concentrations of Somalis such as Columbus, Seattle and San Diego. Somalis began to arrive in Minnesota in the mid to late 90s (Layman and Basnyat 2003). In 1994 and 1995, groups of Somalis (amongst whom mainly Benadiri) were officially resettled in Minneapolis. But the large majority of Somalis currently residing in Minneapolis, at least sixty percent, came from other states (Mattessich 2000). Secondary movement within the US largely took place in recent years, from 1998 – 1999 onwards. When asked for the reason for the steady increase of the Somali population in Minneapolis, a number of factors are usually mentioned. Minnesota has a healthy economy with low unemployment rates, so job opportunities are quite good. Somalis work in the Twin Cities in various low-skilled jobs in assembly plants and meat factories, or as security guards, parking attendants, cleaners and taxi drivers. These jobs require little knowledge of English and often give the possibility of working many over-hours. Furthermore, higher educated Somalis with excellent English skills work as teachers, social workers, lawyers, managers, professors or doctors.

A second reason mentioned for the mass migration to Minneapolis is its more open, welcoming climate towards migrants and better social welfare system in general. Minnesota is a state with a large population of Scandinavian origin, which is reflected by relatively good social security arrangements and services provided for example in education and health care. Its history of dealing with large groups of migrants also assists in the creation of a welcoming attitude. A further, very important reason for the migration flows, is the fact that the word about the virtues of Minnesota spread and a Somali community established itself there. A parallel economy was created that enables Somalis nowadays to do everything 'the Somali way': there are Somali shops, malls, NGOs, travel agents, hairdressers, restaurants, Quranic schools, mosques etc. For businessmen and women, providing goods and services to the now well-established Somali community in the area may be a good alternative or addition to having a regular job. And as the community grows, more Somalis move to Minnesota to be near their families.

In order to understand how Somalis are doing in Minneapolis, it is important to realize that the Somali community is not a homogeneous mass. There are single students, young men and women in their twenties who have at least one but more often two or even three jobs besides their studies and / or operate a business. While working very hard, most of them are settling well in town and live a rather comfortable life. There are single mothers with three to six children, who do not speak English and have to work twenty hours and go to school twenty hours in order to be eligible for, often insufficient, social benefits. Most of the lower income group in Minneapolis live in the Riverside-Cedar area, in large, run-down flats with cheap rents that are mainly occupied by Somalis. Others, like professionals or successful businessmen and women, live in the suburbs in nicely decorated mansions, driving comfortable family cars. Then, I also met men and women working in poultry factories in small Minnesota towns, single or with families that were left behind in the region or came with them. Most of these men and women spoke highly insufficient English for other types of jobs and often also did not have the required education. They worked many over-hours, doing very filthy jobs, and lived extremely sober lives in empty flats.

Sending of remittances

Whether someone was successful in Minneapolis depended on age, gender, education, English proficiency, length of stay, type of employment, social network and number of dependants. In general, only a small percentage of Somali professionals and top businessmen formed a highly successful elite; then, a reasonably large middle class was formed by social workers, teachers, university students etc.; the group of (non-English speaking) Somalis with low-skilled jobs leading sober lives was similar in size; and finally, a small percentage of the Somali community, mainly consisting of single mothers and some elderly without relatives, were really struggling to make ends meet. Yet, financially stable or not, almost all Somalis in Minneapolis at least send some money to their relatives left behind. Dahabo Abdulahi, a single mother of four, told me: 'We have to send. We know that life in Somalia and Kenya and those regions is very difficult. So if my mother calls and tells me that she does not have food on the table that night, I will have to send something. I know their difficulties. But it is not easy for me, having four daughters to take care of. At times, I send 50 dollars, at times 100, at times nothing; it depends on the expenses I had that month'.

Others are able to send much more, with amounts ranging from 200 up to even 1,000 dollars a month; larger amounts being sent to a number of families. Sending large amounts of money home does not necessarily indicate the wealth of the sender. One case that provides good insight into this is a small village close to Minneapolis, where a large group of Somalis had migrated to work in a turkey factory. A tour through the factory gave an impression of the monotone and filthy jobs people had. Afterwards, we visited a number of men who worked there at their home; an empty apartment decorated with a huge flag of Somalia. They all sent 400 dollars home monthly, but people 'back home' often did not know where the money came from. Hassan told me that he had visited relatives in Kenya recently, telling them he sold mobiles and cars for a living. The contrast between the image being created and the actual life these people lived was huge. I imagined that on the one hand these young men created dreams to deal with reality and add to their status as successful migrants, but on the other hand these dreams made the reality of life in 'turkey town' much more difficult.

Somalis in Minneapolis make decisions about their lives that are not only determined by local factors, but also by transnational ones. Khadija Osman for example explains how the money she sends to relatives in Somalia is often part of her monthly bill and she always pays them before even paying the rent: 'If I cannot pay the rent, I will still manage. But if those people do not get the money I send them, life will be too tough for them'. Besides affecting patterns of expenditure, family obligations affect migration decisions. I met quite a number of Somalis who had moved from the Netherlands, and one of the reasons they mentioned for their migration was the difficulty of sending remittances from the Netherlands[1]. Others rather indicate how family responsibilities restricted their movements: even if they wanted to, they could not go back to some of the African cities they lived before. Rashid Kasim told me: 'I cannot go back to Cairo, because my family is there and I have to take care of them. No matter how difficult life may be here, at least I can provide for my family. In Cairo, I could not send them anything, now I send money to my sister in Cairo and my parents and siblings in Somalia every month.

Family obligations can cause great pressures in the personal lives of Somalis in Minneapolis, as some decide not to get married as long as they have pressing responsibilities towards their relatives elsewhere, and others may divorce because of disagreements related to remittance sending. Many Somalis in Minneapolis feel that these stresses are not sufficiently understood by their relatives. Yusuf Abdinoor arrived in Minneapolis only one year ago and is very disappointed with his inability to find an appropriate job. Still, he sends a total of about 1,000 dollars a month to a number of relatives in various places. Yet, as Yusuf says, 'I cannot assist all of them all the time, and they do not understand. They will comment "he is gone, he is in America now", which means that I no longer care for them. They do not understand my position'. Moxamed Hussein similarly sighs: 'I wish I was alone. I have worked all my life to assist others, and they are never satisfied. Everybody thinks that life is good here, and that I am rich'.

A further frustration in some instances is caused by the fact that remittances do not appear to be used wisely and may cause dependency. Remittances are mainly sent to families and used for daily survival. At times, the money can be used to start up a small business or send people to school, but others use it to buy *qat* or stop working altogether because of remittances sent. Dhofa Abdi told me how she recently went to Mudug to visit her relatives, and stopped sending 800 dollars a month after that. Now, she only sends 200 dollars to her father, who is taking care of her epileptic brother, and 200 dollars to a cousin of her father who is a sheikh:

'I used to send that money to the ex-wife of my brother, but realized the lady is a spender. Some of the children did not even have a bed to sleep in, so I bought them beds while I was there and no longer send the money through their mother. Also, I no longer send money to some of my brothers. The three who stay in Galgacayo chew *qat* and leave their wives behind. I used to be very sensitive when they call and work on my conscience, saying their condition is so bad. But at least since I went, feelings of guilt have really reduced: They do not work hard like me, having many responsibilities. The problem is that they have become dependent on the money I sent. What if I am no longer around, or am no longer able? I asked them what they did with all the money I had sent them throughout the years. Where did it go? They could not answer me'.

Migration patterns from and to Minneapolis

In Minneapolis, the lives of Somalis are intertwined across borders, with Somalis there having many options of keeping in touch with relatives and friends, engaging in various social, economic and information-sharing ties. At the same time, the level of actual physical mobility as well as discussions or dreams about migration amongst Somalis is very high. The *buufis* I observed in Dadaab is part of a much wider pattern, both in geographical and historical terms, where migration plays a vital role in Somali lives and livelihoods. In this respect, travel documents are very valuable possessions for Somalis. Since Somalia is no longer a functioning nation-state and Somali documents are not accepted for travelling, Somalis are restrained in their movements practically. The main goal to be reached while living in the USA or Europe for a number of years, is to obtain travel documents, preferably those that do not need extra visas for most countries. Once such a document has been obtained, free travel becomes possible and shifts in residence can also be envisioned. At the same time, obtaining a passport provides the holder with more rights to assist others to migrate, for example through family reunion programs.

Very complex patterns of back and forth migration from and to Minneapolis in all directions, for short-term and long-term stay, can be discerned. Movements include family visits during weddings and holidays, as well as gatherings for religious occasions like *Idh*. During these instances, Somalis move to and from Minneapolis for shorter periods to be together with relatives and friends. This may also lead to longer-term settlement, as in the case of Abdulkadir Warsame, who visited his brother in Rochester, Minnesota, on his Dutch passport: 'Life seemed very OK here, with my brother operating his own grocery shop. In the Netherlands, Somalis live more spread-out and setting up a business is very hard. Besides, many are unemployed and receive welfare. I realized it is easy to find a job in the US, even if you do not speak English. So I went back to the Netherlands only to wait for an opportunity to move to the USA. In 2000, I was given a chance to go'. But like other 'Dutch Somalis', Abdulkadir does maintain a link with the Netherlands, occasionally visiting his relatives and friends there.

The majority of Somalis have lived in another state before coming to Minnesota, some even have lived in three or four other states before ending up there. Even within Minneapolis, it is not uncommon for Somalis to move frequently. As Omar Shire semi-jokingly explained to me: 'We do not have beds in our house, because we move so much. I now live in Minneapolis for two years, and have moved three times already'. Over the last couple of years, there has also been quite a lot of movement between places in Canada and the Minnesota area. Originally, Toronto was a city with a very high population of Somalis, but many of them moved to Minneapolis when a large community established itself there and it seemed job opportunities and services were better. When the US economy went down, a number of them returned to Canada. Others are engaged in transnational households, where parts of the family live in Minneapolis and parts in Toronto[2].

All these examples and many more, confirm that Somalis can be described as transnational nomads, like earlier research suggested (Horst Forthcoming). As Aden Yusuf, who now lives in the Washington D.C. with his family, remarked in support of this thesis,

> 'Somalis treat the US – Canadian border the same as they would treat the Ethiopian – Somali border: "If it rains better today, we move there". They are always on the move and changing their residency and they often do not like to be constrained by rules and regulations'.

In my opinion, this also means that Minneapolis will not necessarily be the final destination of the many Somalis who live there. And indeed, a number of Somalis had moved from Minneapolis already or were thinking about moving from there soon or eventually. A survey amongst Somalis in Minneapolis and Saint Paul indicated that 71 percent were hopeful of returning to their native country someday (Mattessich 2000). Some people had already returned and especially in safer areas like Somaliland, groups of Somalis are returning from all over the world and carefully preparing the return of others (Fink-

Nielsen et al. 2001). And return did not only occur to the home country, but also for example to Egypt. Rashid Kasim's aunt is considering moving back to Cairo, wanting to buy a house there and take the children: 'Their main concerns are that Cairo has a better educational system and a better religious system. They want to be able to give their children an Islamic upbringing'.

Dealing with *buufis*

Those who now live in Minneapolis are frequently confronted with the fact that many others would want to follow their example. These dreams to move to a Western country from Africa or the Middle East are not called *buufis* by all. In fact, when I started asking questions about *buufis*, I realized that many Somalis in the USA used the word differently. Only those who had come from Kenya or Cairo more recently were familiar with the way in which I used it. As Yusuf Abdinoor told me:

> 'In Mogadishu the word was used amongst young people, as a kind of slang, meaning "suspect". I then heard it being used in Egypt and realized the person did not mean suspect, so I asked what it meant. I was informed that *buufis* was related to resettlement'.

Yet in the US, *buufis* is far more often used to indicate mental health problems of all kinds. It is fascinating to see the various uses of the term in different places, although there does seem to be a link between the use of the word in Dadaab and Minneapolis. Those who really dream of going for resettlement badly, suffering from serious *buufis* in the Dadaab sense, are often seen to have mental problems that can only be solved by enabling them to go for resettlement.

Rashid Kasim's brother for example was a serious *buufis* case. His mother was really worried about her 20-year old son, as at times he would not talk to anybody, behaving strangely. Rashid realized he really had to help him to move from Mogadishu, as the 'symptoms' were getting increasingly worse:

> 'My brother just finished High school and has extreme *buufis* because all around him, all people of his age, like neighbours and classmates, have gone or are going. There are simply no opportunities for them in Somalia, and he says that he cannot be in Mogadishu in 2004. His mind is focused on Western countries. I guess it used to be the same for me as well; we used to talk about streets and places in the UK or Canada, about people who went, or as we formulated it *'wuu galay'* (he has entered), as if it was paradise they were entering'.

Just before I left, Rashid's brother attempted to go to London through Dubai with an uncle who would move there with his family. Rashid bought the ticket of 2,500 dollars for him, and there was no one to assist him: 'Everybody is in the same position; if you do not have your family here, you will have to work towards bringing them over. We tried before and I spent 5,000 dollars on him, but the attempt failed'. Unfortunately, I was informed that the second attempt also failed, but they would try again.

This possible loss of money was not the only risk that people were taking while attempting to reach Western countries. Sacadiyo Muse showed me a book that she kept with pictures and stories from and about friends and relatives who stayed with her in Cairo. They were all young people, some living in European countries, some staying in the US, Canada or Australia, some who went back to Somalia, but also three who had died while trying to cross from Libya to Italy by boat; independent from each other. I was informed that on Internet, one could find the names and clans of those who died there. Somalis take great risks when trying to 'enter', and one may wonder whether their relatives in Minneapolis are always ready to assist them in such dangerous attempts. Besides, there are other reasons why some may not be ready to sponsor their relatives. Dhofa Abdi clearly explained this to me:

> 'My brothers all want me to sponsor them, but how can I sponsor them when they are so irresponsible? How can I sponsor my brother who left his wife with four children? If he behaves so irresponsible in Somalia, what can I expect of his behaviour here? I will be responsible for their misbehaviour here. What if one of my brothers marries a new wife here? How will my sister-in-law accept that I have assisted him to come to the US?'

A further dilemma that Somalis in Minneapolis face is caused by the fact that their relatives have dreams of coming to the US, but as Sacadiyo formulated it, 'the America that is there in Africa is not here'. Almost everybody arriving in the US has much higher expectations of his or her life there than reality can offer. Suleiman Hashi, the director of one of the Somali NGOs in Minnepolis, tells me: 'When they come to the USA, people expect plenty of money, work, no responsibility and easy access to everything. Then, the reality is that they have to look for a job, some live on welfare and life is very hard. Many people cannot deal with that reality'. Positive images are based on media and communication with relatives and friends already in the USA. Khadija Osman remarks: 'They watch TV there and think that life in America is like the Hollywood movies'. Then, pictures that relatives send distort reality, but also the fact that large amounts of money are being sent from the US and people seemingly obtain everything that those 'left behind' can only dream of. Abdulhakim Axmed had very clear ideas in this respect:

> 'We tell horrible stories about life in America, but when they see we have a car, we have housing, we have education and we have an income, all things that they do not have and that thus seem like a dream, it is difficult to make them change their views. A friend of mine is going back to Galgacayo and asked me whether he can do anything for me there. I told him to show people "Bowling for Columbine", just to make them understand that in the US, guns are freely available and cause as much problems as in the places they are running from'.

So on the one hand, some Somalis in Minneapolis try to explain to their relatives and friends what their lives are really like, but it seems they are not listened to. Yet on the other hand, others do not provide correct information. Yusuf Abdinoor admits that he does not inform most of his relatives of the fact that he has nothing. He simply gives them what he can, and tries to explain his situation only if they complain that he does not send enough. He tells me: 'Somalis are very proud people, and they will not tell the truth. If someone was a manager in Somalia and now works as a loader, he will not confess that. He will hide the reality and send money'. At the same time, when going to Africa many Somalis engage in a lifestyle that also portrays a different image, while their relatives will not realize that the life styles they display there for a short period are the result of a hard and difficult life for the rest of the year (compare Salih 2001: 58). For those who are seen to 'have made it', keeping up appearances may be just as vital as the dream of a better future is for those in difficult circumstances like in the Dadaab refugee camps.

Conclusion

How do Somalis in Minneapolis and other places in the West deal both with the responsibilities they have towards their families and others 'remaining behind' in Africa, as well as with the migration dreams they are confronted with, based on images of a life that does not exist? I began this chapter by distinguishing three types of connections that are of importance in this respect: The flows of 1) people, 2) money and goods as well as 3) ideas, all of which characterize transnationalism, and transgresses national boundaries and thereby connects different physical, social, economic and political spaces (Mazzucato et al. 2004). The livelihoods that people engage in, the choices they have and the decisions they make in one place, may very well be influenced by the way their lives are connected with those of relatives and friends elsewhere. When studying such processes, it is important to take a holistic view that combines an analysis of migration, remittances and information exchanges; as these fields are very clearly influencing one another.

Somalis in Dadaab, as well as in Minneapolis, engage in transnational livelihoods both financially and in terms of decision-making. In Dadaab, research indicated that the Somali refugees would not have been able to survive the limited regional opportunities and insufficient handouts provided, without the assistance of remittances sent to the camps. Monthly or occasional amounts of dollars were vital in enabling daily survival as well as dealing with contingencies. Somalis in Minneapolis were very aware of the vital role they played in the survival of relatives living in the region, and almost everybody was sending the little or much he or she could send. There were some concerns about the endurance of remittance sending over generations. As Abdulhakim Axmed indicated:

> "Generations change and the children might not send money to the extent that their parents did. They have to be taught, like I do with my five-year old daughter. I take her to the hawala and tell her to give the money to the owner, and my daughter can even ask me 'father, when are we going to send them money again?' But many parents do not teach their children, saying that they are working hard for their pensions so that their children do not need to send them money."

Another threat to the continuity of transnational networks is the fact that the pressures are often very high. Somalis in Minneapolis feel an obligation to send money to relatives in Kenya or Somalia who might otherwise not be able to survive there. But, this obligation is often a real burden to their own livelihoods. In many cases, this burden is managed with an idea of temporality: eventually, sending remittances may no longer be necessary or at least the amount can be lessened considerably. In order to achieve that, Somalis in Minneapolis for example try to assist those who are dependent on them to migrate from the region. Alternatively, they try to encourage investments that enable people's self-sufficiency. In some cases, Somalis in Minneapolis have actually already reduced the amount of dollars they were sending because they were dissatisfied with how their money was used. This may threaten the durability of remittance incomes to relatives. There are initiatives that try to combine the funds of a number of Somalis in the Diaspora to contribute to longer-term development initiatives that may encourage self-sufficiency, like building schools or setting up water projects. Still, in many places self-sufficiency can only be envisioned in the long-term and might not be possible without large-scale political-economic changes.

A final problem is that those 'left behind' do not understand the extent to which they burden those who 'have entered' places like Minneapolis. Images of life in resettlement countries are still highly unrealistic, leading to extreme expectations of the role of the Somali Diaspora. As such, an important step towards a more balanced division of responsibilities, and thus possibly greater endurance, could be a communal attempt amongst the Somali Diaspora to provide more realistic images of their lives 'overseas'. On the one hand, this may remain extremely difficult as material realities do differ greatly and it may be hard to understand for those who were never there in what sense life could be difficult in places like Minneapolis. As Abdulhakim illustrated: 'It is like trying to explain to my mother what snow is. You cannot make people understand exactly how cold it is'. On the other hand, there is also still reluctance to give up the status and relative power that comes with living in the USA. Some find it unnecessary to burden their relatives with the problems they are facing in Minneapolis. Others are embarrassed to admit to the humble lives they lead. Many would not easily give up their position as wealthy, successful migrants, no matter the difficulties they find in keeping up this image.

References

Al-Ali, N., R. Black, and K. Koser (2001) Refugees and transnationalism: the experience of Bosnians and Eritreans in Europe. *Journal of Ethnic and Migration Studies* 27(4): 615-634.

Bang Nielsen, K. (2004) Next stop Britain: The influence of transnational networks on the secondary movement of Danish Somalis. Working Paper No. 22. Sussex , Centre for Migration Research.

Crisp, J. (1999) A state of insecurity: The political economy of violence in refugee-populated areas of Kenya. Working Paper No. 16, *New issues in refugee research.* Geneva, UNHCR.

Fink-Nielsen, M., Hansen, P., and Kleist, N. (2001) Roots, rights and responsibilities: Place-making and repatriation among Somalis in Denmark and Somaliland, *Paper presented at the conference 'Living on the edge: Migration, conflict and state in the backyards of globalisation'.* Copenhagen, University of Copenhagen.

Horst, C. (2006) *Transnational Nomads. How Somalis cope with refugee life in the Dadaab camps of Kenya.* Oxford & New York: Berghahn Books.

Layman, A. and Basnyat, A. (2003) Social capital of the Somali and Hmong Communities in Minneapolis - Saint Paul, *Minnesota Social Capital Research Project.*

Mattessich, P. (2000) Speaking for themselves. A survey of Hispanic, Hmong, Russian and Somali immigrants in Minneapolis-Saint Paul. Saint Paul, Wilder Research Center.

Mazzucato, V., R. v. Dijk, C. Horst, and P. d. Vries (2004) Transcending the nation. Explorations of transnationalism as a concept and phenomenon. In *Globalization and development. Themes and concepts in current research.* D. Kalb, W. Pansters, and H. Siebers, eds. Dordrecht/Boston/London: Kluwer Academic Publishers.

Reek, E. van den and Hussein, A. Igeh (2003) Somaliers op doorreis. Verhuisgedrag van Nederlandse Somaliers naar Engeland. Tilburg, Wetenschapswinkel Universiteit van Tilburg.

Salih, R. 2001 Shifting meanings of 'home'. Consumption and identity in Moroccan women's transnational practices between Italy and Morocco. In *New approaches to migration? Transnational communities and the transformation of home.* K. Koser and N. Al-Ali, eds. Pp. 51-67. London: Routledge.

United States Census (2000) American Fact finder, Quick Tables: P13 Ancestry. www.census.gov, Accessed at August 13, 2004

---

1. Somalis also move from the Netherlands and Denmark to the UK in very large numbers for similar reasons (see also Bang Nielsen 2004; Reek and Hussein 2003).

2.. Research has indicated that at least 18 percent of married Somalis in the Twin Cities are geographically separated from their spouse (Mattessich 2000).

Chapter 7

Clan Identities in Practice: The Somali Diaspora in Finland

Stephanie R. Bjork

Introduction

Today clan is a highly politicized and sensitive issue for Somalis at home and for those dispersed throughout the world. Clan divisions have been especially significant during inter-clan struggles in Somalia throughout its civil war and continue to affect Somalis at home and abroad. Yet, researchers have ignored the notable role clan plays for diasporic Somalis. Ethnographic research among Somali immigrants in Finland reveals it is clan that organizes Somalis 'on the ground' and is the basis for networks extending beyond the Finnish borders. While Somalis in Finland claim that clan is less important than it was in the early to mid-1990s, clan is nonetheless ubiquitous in everyday life for Somalis abroad. Perhaps because 'clan' is associated with the barbarity of the warlords, and seems antithetical to modernity, Diaspora Somalis deny significance of their clan affiliations even as they point out their and their associates' clans. The anthropologist observer sees clan networks to be the structure and instrument of Somali life abroad, in spite of attitudes that clan recognitions are to be glossed over.

This research project was carried out over a period of sixteen months (2003-2004) in Finland's capital city, Helsinki, and the surrounding cities of Espoo and Vantaa. The primary data collection technique used in this study was ethnographic fieldwork. Participant observation was conducted in private spaces such as households and wedding celebrations, and in public spaces such as schools, discos, multicultural centres, Somali-owned businesses, shopping centres, cafes, and transportation stations. Participant observation allowed me to observe clan in its everyday use and practice. Socio-demographic surveys were conducted with 186 men and women eighteen years and over. From the surveyed individuals, I selected ten key respondents for in-depth interviews. In-depth interviews allowed respondent to reflect upon their position within the Somali clan system and the meanings attached to these groupings in Finland and prior to migration. In this paper, I substitute pseudonyms for real names and remove or alter all identifying information to ensure confidentiality for respondents. The Somali community in Finland is relatively small and the respondents' identity would be easy to discern otherwise. Additionally, I refer to clans in a neutral way; I substitute clan names with pseudonyms.

Clan in the 1990s

According to most respondents, clan is less important today for Somalis in Finland than it was ten to fifteen years ago. Most respondents told me that they knew little about their clan until after they arrived in Finland. This was especially evident among persons raised in the former capital city of Mogadishu, the most diverse city in the former Somali Democratic Republic (Bhoola 1989). Respondents from Mogadishu, Baidoa, and Kismayo commonly reported in interviews that they lived in mixed clan neighbourhoods. In this context, inter-clan social interaction was an everyday experience prior to the outbreak of the Somali civil war. In contrast, respondents from the Northern region (i.e. Somaliland and Puntland) and rural areas, reported that inter-clan interaction was rare. Moreover, persons residing outside of Somalia prior to the civil war, particularly in the Middle East and Arabian Peninsula, reportedly utilized clan networks to find jobs and housing due to the discrimination they faced as immigrants.

The Somali civil war brought clan to the forefront for Somalis worldwide. Knowing 'where a person is from' was vital for early arrivals seeking to align themselves with persons they could trust. Findings from in-depth interviews suggest that the first large groups of Somalis who arrived in Finland in the early 1990s organized themselves according to clan affiliation. In some cases, each floor of refugee reception centres became the domain of one clan. Respondents also reported fighting mirroring a clan conflict in Somalia erupted between two clans at a reception centre. The following quotes from in-depth interviews provide a glimpse into the complex clan dynamics that many Somalis faced upon arrival in Finland:

How did you first learn about your tribe?

> "Mother taught me about clan. I was some four or five years old. Maybe. I don't remember. Father's and her's. It is important to know the general clan and who are your closest relatives and not. If you go visit, but I never remembered it. Somalis asked me my clan for three years but I would not tell. I told everyone that I did not know. People were calling me Clan A until a guy I went to high school with in Somalia told the other people that I was Clan B. I don't know much about clan things" (Mohamed, 2004).

Recall the first time someone asked you 'where you are from' in Finland?

> "Yeah, when I came to Finland you had to say your tribe. Everyone was asking. Everyone was looking for their own tribe. They were all suspicious. Not even once, too much!" (Hodan, 2004).
>
> "When I went to Finnish course, it was 1994. Who am I? Who is my tribe? They told me what tribe I belong. I did not know. I had to call my father to ask. It was very stupid. These are painful questions for me" (Nur, 2004).
>
> *When you first arrived in Finland, how did Somalis relate to one another?*
> "Most of them know each other already; they were in Russia long time and they live by tribes. I asked people right away if there were any Sub-clan A there. They said no but there was one guy who was from my tribe but he lied and told them that he belonged to another tribe. He was afraid" (Abdi, 2004).
>
> *When you first arrived in Finland, how did Somalis relate to one another?*
> "We people from Mogadishu did not care about clan. We, from South, speak same language; we act as Mogadishu" (Xassan, 2004).
>
> *Tell me about the first time you met another Somali in Finland?*
> "People were friendly, but if we came to another clan they were afraid because he thinks that we tell something from them to another clan." Did they ask you about your clan? "They didn't say, but I was going to school to learn Finnish language, to town, to disco. I made myself Finnish friends and went out from them. I just came to sleep. I did not depend on them for anything. They were always talking clan and they lost a lot of time to these things" (Amina, 2004).

Clan was the focal point of these early encounters in refugee reception centres. Newcomers were directed to self-identify by clan. Each claim tested by an individual's ability to exhibit cultural competence. By cultural competence, I mean "knowledge of genealogical relationships and of real connections and skill at using them" (Bourdieu 1986:250). This "specific cultural competence," a form of cultural capital, in its embodied state, is transmitted through socialization (Bourdieu 1986:245). It was vital for newcomers to 'know where they were from', to legitimize their claim to others; however, many respondents lacked cultural competence of clan relationships. Parents or other relatives were contacted to teach clan genealogy. This personal investment in clan competence (i.e. cultural capital) paved the way for individuals to build clan-based social networks, a form of social capital.

During the 1990s, Somalis in Finland formed over forty separate associations. The vast majority of these groups are organized according to clan affiliation; thus, membership in these groups is a seemingly overt sign of clan affiliation. Irmeli Tuomarla (1998) notes that Finnish authorities anticipated uniformity among Somali immigrants; authorities were perplexed by Somalis' inability to unite in an effort to represent their community. As asylum seekers or quota refugees, Somalis were assumed to embody little more than the label of refugee, a generic and essentialised figure (Malkki 1992). I refused several invitations to visit Somali associations because I did not want to appear to favour one clan over another. Despite this, several respondents told me that they heard a rumour that I had visited one such association. Finnish researcher, Alitolppa-Niitamo (2000), notes that a history of inter-clan conflict has disabled Somalis' ability to act as a cohesive interest group. Thirty-nine surveyed individuals reported membership in Somali associations. The other 147 respondents sited clannism and related mistrust as reasons for avoiding Somali associations.

Methodological Considerations

In order to identify participants for the surveys, I built upon my existing network of respondents from research conducted from 2000-2001, and accessed additional respondents through the social networks of surveyed individuals. I utilized the same signs Somalis use to decipher clan to access Somalis through their own social networks. In Finland, Somalis commonly access other Somalis through people they trust, clan relatives. Thus, when I encountered a new person in the field, I often used names of their relatives in order to establish trust. On most occasions, I could ascertain clan affiliation utilizing the same signs Somalis use to read clan. While conducting a survey with Jama, a male in his early thirties, I used this very method to establish rapport. Realizing what I had done, Jama said to me, "You are smart. You meet Somalis through relatives; this is the way Somalis meet each other."

Key respondents such as Ayaan regularly helped me access other Somalis. While Ayaan and I took a bus from Itäkeskus, a shopping centre in Eastern Helsinki, to pick-up her child from school, we came across two middle-aged women. Ayaan greeted the two women in a customary fashion of hugging one another and kissing each other on their cheeks. Then, Ayaan introduced me to the two women, and told them about my project. We visited them on the bus until our destinations separated us. They agreed to the interview and invited us to their Finnish class the following day. As Ayaan and I stepped off the bus, she said to me, "They are my clan. That's why they said yes [to participate in the research]. They will answer. I don't like clan, but Somalis are like that." This strategy of accessing repondents while accompanying friends of different clans as they carried out daily activities enabled me to map social networks by situating myself in the various social spaces where interaction between Somalis occur. Nevertheless, other networks formed in the Diaspora: networks with classmates, co-workers, neighbours, friends, and in fewer cases, Finns, facilitated access to respondents.

Reading Clan in the Field

Because Somalis abroad consider clan a sensitive, if not taboo topic for public discourse, they use an array of tactics within conventional social practice to tell clan. According to fieldwork data gathered in the Helsinki metropolitan area[1] (2000-2001; 2003-2004), Somalis distinguish clan affiliation through telling signs: gestures, language, names (e.g. given names, family names, and nicknames), physical appearance, place of birth, and social networks. For example, upon encountering an unfamiliar Somali, Xassan knowingly introduces himself with his second name[2] rather than his given name which lacks any recognizable clan significance. Xassan's second name is recognizably *Sub-clan A* to other Somalis. "I like to tell my clan. I tell my second name. They know its *Sub-clan A*. If I meet someone on the train, I introduce myself using my second name. Then, they will know who I am. Then, we are free to speak. My clan and his clan are put aside and we are free to talk about other clans."

The signs Somalis use to tell clan are based on stereotypes, a mixture of myth and reality. Consequently, these signs are not foolproof indicators of clan affiliation. Weddings or *aroos*, a community-wide event for Somalis, are perhaps the most important occasion for maintaining clan networks in the Diaspora (Bjork 2001). After attending a wedding celebration in Vantaa, a female respondent, Shukri, told me that she was surprised to discover the rightful clan affiliation of Fatima, who like Shukri, arrived in Finland as an asylum seeker in the early 1990s. Over the years, Shukri had falsely assumed Fatima's clan affiliation to be *Sub-clan A*. Shukri based her false assumption on a series of markers such as Fatima's Somali dialect, place of birth, and social networks. During the wedding celebration, Shukri deciphered Fatima's rightful clan affiliation by Fatima's close association with women from her paternal clan. After the wedding, Shukri explained why Fatima's clan affiliation is not easy to decipher: "Fatima is *Clan B*, but raised in *Sub-clan A*". Fatima's mother and father are from different

clans, but she was raised with her mother's clan, *Sub-clan A*, meaning that Fatima did not grow-up in the territory traditionally associated with her paternal clan, and did not learn to speak like people from her clan. In Somali terms, Fatima does not speak '*Clan B* language'.
The uncertainty of Fatima's clan affiliation is just one of many examples in which an individual's clan affiliation was open to negotiation; these situations indicate the difficulties in determining clan on the basis of observational strategies alone. Throughout the research period, the clan affiliation of certain individuals was regularly debated among respondents. In fact, several respondents asked me to disclose the clan affiliation of other surveyed respondents on the basis of physical appearance alone. Fortunately, I could direct individuals to the informed consent form that all persons read and signed before partaking in the research that ensured confidentiality to all participants.

Clan Today

During surveys, I directly asked respondents to identity their clan. The response to this question varied. Many were taken aback by my frankness, surprised that an outsider was familiar with Somali kinship. Others responded to my inquiry by outwardly expressing their contempt for clan. In spite of this, the majority of respondents responded to my question without hesitation. Many respondents had already seen or met me with other Somalis. Somalis viewed me as an unbiased observer: void of clan affiliation and ethnic Finnish heritage. Most importantly, many Somalis knew that I was interested in, and familiar with the clan system (relationships between different clans and sub-clans - especially clan hierarchy) and were perhaps more willing to respond to my inquiry because of this. Because Somalis were aware that I used the same signs Somalis use to read clan, and utilized clan as reference markers in everyday speech, my social intimacy in the field compensated for my cultural distance.

Individuals who responded to my inquiry, 175 of the 186 respondents, knew where they belonged in the Somali clan system. But, the extent of their understanding was relative to their cultural competence (i.e. clan competence). Individuals who arrived in the early to mid 1990s legitimized their clan to each other by exhibiting a certain degree of clan competence. These respondents were skilled at reciting the names of their clan ancestors and the relationship of their clan to other clan families. Whereas persons reared in rural areas tended to exhibit a high degree of clan competence, they were less familiar with clan families outside their home regions. Conversely, young adults[3], particularly those born in Finland or recent arrivals, tended to be familiar only with the name of their clan family or sub-clan grouping. Young adults who first learned about Somali kinship in Finland tended to identify with their sub-clan grouping during surveys. Some of these individuals were unable to name the larger clan family to which their sub-clan belongs.

Today, Somalis are concerned with locating each other's sub-clan. Sub-clan identity is inherently tied to the current political tensions and territorial divisions in Somalia and other parts of the Horn of Africa where Somalis reside. Participant observation indicates that sub-clan affiliation shapes social networks 'on the ground'. When I asked informants who identified themselves by sub-clan during surveys why they did so, they commonly told me that in order to know where a person is really from, you need to know the small clan, not the big clan; clans are too big. A male respondent exclaimed, "Clan is like an address." Surely his statement pointed to the current territorial or spatial organization of ancestral clan territories in the Horn of Africa. Correspondingly, Lewis notes from his fieldwork in British Somaliland, "As Somalis themselves put it, what a person's address is in Europe, his genealogy is in Somaliland" (Lewis 1961:2).

Sub-clan divisions reflect ancestral clan territories. In some cases, sub-clan affiliation determines where an individual may safely travel. Surveys also reveal that persons tend to return to their ancestral homelands rather than the place they may have been born and/or raised because they may have no clan protection in these areas. In these situations, it is common for an individual to travel to the birthplace of parents or grandparents because they are given protection by their clan. Sub-clan networks are formed and maintained in the Diaspora, and it is through these networks that many of the goods sold in the Somali informal economy originate and are later consumed by clan relatives in Finland. More importantly, sub-clan divisions are evident in social networks, in everyday "speech", and in the discourse of return. For example, one respondent who was born and raised outside of Somalia is planning to move with her husband and children to the ancestral territory of their clan. Nearly 25% of surveyed individuals have returned to Somalia or other areas in the Horn of Africa where Somalis reside. Surveys also reveal that 5% of the sample population plans to visit Somalia within the next year. Thus, the importance of sub-clan identity and relationships that result from it are of particular significance as clan identity is conveyed to younger generations.

Eleven respondents in total chose not to report their clan to me. One young male respondent chose not to report his clan because, "All Somalis ask this. I don't want to." Most Somalis tend to reveal clan in socially appropriate ways to appear not to be 'into clan'; however, some individuals prefer to ask strangers to identify their clan or sub-clan by name. A female respondent did not reveal her clan affiliation because; "Clan does not make sense to me." Another young woman responded, "Ei hyvää kysymys"[4] (Not a good question) before revealing her clan. One forty-year-old male's initial response to my question was, "I know where I belong. I do not identify with my clan but my nation." Then, with a clever smile on his face, he casually remarked that since I had already interviewed his cousin, I could easily determine his clan affiliation.

Clan in Everyday Use and Practice

Today, most Somalis regularly interact with persons outside of their clan. Throughout the research period, I observed respondents greeting other Somalis in public spaces, and visiting neighbours and friends from other clans. Women from different clans meet for conversation, sewing and exercise, and to sell goods at various meeting place throughout Helsinki, Espoo, and Vantaa. Men often meet at restaurants, cafes, and the central railway station to discuss current events. However, some public places are commonly known as meeting places for men of particular clans even though other Somalis frequent the same establishments. One male respondent reported that, "Now people go to the Internet to check what is going on and when they meet together they defend their own tribe, but they do talk to each other". Despite the increased interaction among Somalis from different clans, some men and women choose to limit their interaction with other Somalis. Persons working as civil servants who regularly provide services to other Somalis commonly expressed the importance of maintaining a neutral position within the Somali community. These individuals tend to avoid Somali associations and keep to themselves, preferring the company and friendship of Finns or other immigrants.

How do Somalis in Finland relate to each other now?

"Yeah, it changed, I think. I was young when I came here. The tribe didn't mean anything and still it doesn't. I think for other people it has changed now. People are, I don't know, they are not like before. Is he your classmate? Are you working in the same place? How long have you known each other? Not, what tribe is he from?" (Hodan, 2004).

Yet, in another conversation with the same respondent she told me that,

"Tribe, people need tribe when something is happening, for wedding or sorrow, when someone died. Actually, it's like you have to. I have to may be, if there is a *Clan A* who died, I don't have to go. If he is from my clan and his father died, I have to go and say that I am sorry. It's tribe things" (Hodan, 2004).

How do Somalis in Finland relate to each other now?
"I think the same clan. Some people are just friends, they don't think clan. Some people religion and some people drinking. A young girl might have a friend of the same hobby, not clan together" (Ayaan, 2004).

How do Somalis in Finland relate to each other now?

"Very difficult because most are nomad from countryside. It's difficult to understand them. They say they are from Mogadishu, but they are not. Physically they are in Finland, but mentally they are in another place. They have no interest to be in Finland. There is no community here. Everyone is thinking about tribe [clan], and everyone thinking about himself. There is no self confidence" (Nur, 2004).

What do you mean by self confidence?

"If you do something, they think what does *masjid*[5] [mosque] say? What does tribe [clan] say? What does family say? They talk about bullshit. How this country [Finland] is racist. That's why I don't want to do anything for them. It makes me sick" (Nur, 2004).

In everyday speech, Somalis use clan names as reference markers to set apart individuals and groups. For example, after conducting a survey with Ahmed, a civil servant, he asked me if I had interviewed his colleague Abdi. "Who, Abdi?" our friend, Hawa, inquired. Ahmed responded, "Abdi, *Clan A*" explaining: "There are too many Abdi…then, we know which Abdi." Since Abdi is a common Somali name and the individual in question is without a well-known nickname[6], Ahmed utilized Abdi's clan as a reference marker. Clan names are also used to refer to individuals when discussing upcoming weddings. While accompanying some friends to a shopping mall, we came across a group of other women. One of the women interjected to the group, "A girl, Raxima, is getting married. Are you going?" Another woman inquired, "Who, Raxima?" The woman responded, "Raxima-*Sub-clan B*-Koivukylä.[7]" In this example, a series of three words are strategically strung together to help the other women ascertain the rightful identity of the girl to be married. Raxima, the girl's first name, is strung together with two reference markers: her sub-clan and the area in the city of Vantaa she resides, Koivukylä.

Other common references to clan in everyday speech are found in clan stereotypes as well as stereotypes of North (*Waqooyi*) and South (*Koonfur*). Broader categories of North and South tactfully point to groupings of clans rather than individual clans. Hence, clan stereotypes are achievable without naming names (i.e. clan names). In mixed groups, between friends and spouses, clan and related stereotypes are often talked about in jest. For example, during a household visit with two female friends from different clans, I asked Hodan if she could tell me about a situation in which she was discriminated against because of her tribe. Hodan initially responded, "No, I don't think so." Then, after a few seconds, Hodan pointed to her friend Ayaan and exclaimed, "They [the South] will say I am *khaldaan.* She will say that I am *khaldaan* (*khaldaan* is a Somali term meaning mistake/wrong. In everyday speech, persons from the South refer to individuals from the North as *khaldaan*). She's wrong. Everything is wrong: the language, the culture, and the clock." Conversely, the term *hamaraawi* is used by northern Somalis to refer to southern Somalis. *Hamaraawi* refers to persons from Mogadishu, the former capital city. Mogadishu was previously the Banaadir port city of Hamar. Both terms are viewed as negative labels for what is considered as paradoxical: North and South.

Clan names are often heard during household visits while watching videos. Throughout the research period, videos of welcoming parties and weddings filmed in Finland and in other Diaspora communities around the world were watched in households. While watching a video with my two friends Ayaan and Hodan, Ayaan pointed out a woman dancing during her wedding celebration. "Is she *Clan A*?" "No, *Clan B*," Hodan responded. Then, Hodan continued to tell us that most of the songs sung during *buraanbur*[8] were about her ex-husband's clan, not her clan. Hodan pointed to the television and said, "Look, the women from my tribe are so disappointed that I married Jama." Since children are often present during these conversations, they learn the everyday speech and signs Somalis use to decipher clan. By observing ways in which Somalis distinguish clan, social scientists can use these strategies to look for events potentially involving clans. For example, subtleties of clan networks are physically discernable during women's wedding celebrations. In some cases, families of the bride and groom purchase goods such as clothing, decorations and crafts, gold jewelry, and the services of henna applicators, singers, and DJs from clan members working within the informal economy. During wedding celebrations, dance sequences are performed that visually distinguish clan families and seek to identify them with specific regions of Somalia.

Conclusion

Still, clan is a highly politicized and sensitive issue for Somalis throughout the Diaspora. In some contexts, clan is publicly stigmatized while in other contexts such as wedding celebrations it is celebrated. Yet, throughout the research period, Somalis tended to contest the importance of clan in their lives abroad, and expressed their unwillingness to teach their children about clan. Clans seem barbaric in the cosmopolitan milieu of Diaspora Somalis, but because they work for Somalis, they cannot be jettisoned. Maintaining kin networks opens up the potential for individuals to access clan networks that can be called upon in moments of movement, celebration, crisis, and return. Clan identities are socially constructed in the midst of everyday interaction. Somalis learn about clan through the details of everyday life abroad; Somalis learn about clan through their environment, as the following excerpt from an in-depth interview reveals:

> *How did you first learn about your tribe?*
> "I don't remember the first time. Mother and father did not teach us, only good advice. We learned from the environment" (Xassan, 2004).
>
> *How will you teach your children where they are from?*
> "I don't want to teach them. I don't want them to think it is important. They will learn" (Xassan, 2004).

References

Alitolppa-Niitamo, Anne. (2000) "The Equator to the Arctic Circle: A Portrait of Somali Integration and Diasporic Consciousness in Finland." In *Rethinking Refuge and Displacement*. El?bieta M. Go?dziak and Dianna J. Shandy, eds. 43-65. Arlington, VA: American Anthropological Association.

Bhoola, F. A. (1989) *Household Structure, Decision-making, and the Economic, Social, and Legal Status of Women in Mogadishu, Somalia.* Anthropology. Ann Arbor, Michigan State University.

Bjork, Stephanie R. (2001) *Watched Weddings: Circulating Videos and Transnational Community-Building Amongst Somalis in Finland.* Anthropology. Master's thesis, University of Wisconsin-Milwaukee.

Bourdieu, Pierre. (1986) "The Forms of Capital." In *Handbook of Theory and Research for the Sociology of Education*. John G. Richardson, ed. 241-258. New York: Greenwood Press.

Lewis, Ioan M. (1961) *A Pastoral Democracy: A Study of Pastoralism and Politics Among the Northern Somali of the Horn of Africa*. London: International African Institute/Oxford University Press.

Malkki, Liisa H. (1992) "National Geographic: The Rooting of Peoples and Territorialization of Nationalist Identity among Scholars and Refugees." Cultural Anthropology (7):24-44.

Tuomarla, Irmeli. (2001) "The Somalis in Finland and in Britain. A Comment to Asha-Kin F. Duale." *In* Variations on the Theme of Somaliness. Muddle Suzanne Lillius, ed. Pp. 291-293. Turku, Finland: Centre for Continuing Education, Åbo Akademi University.

1.The Helsinki metropolitan region, inhabited by 1.2 million persons, consists of four municipalities; the capital, Helsinki, and the surrounding cities of Espoo, Vantaa, and Kauniainen.

2. Somalis have three names. The first name is a given name. The second name is the given name of the father, and the third name is the given name of the paternal grandfather. Married women do not change their names after marriage; married women's second and third names retain her patrilineage.

3. The population sample for this study consisted of 186 Somalis: men and women eighteen years and older.

4. The Finnish phrase, Ei hyvää kysymys, translates as "Not a good question" in English.

5. Masjid is a Somali term for mosque.

6. It is not uncommon for Somalis to have nicknames to help distinguish individuals. Nicknames may denote physical characteristics such as body shape, hair, skin colour, and eyes; personality traits; or family names. Some nicknames are revealing of clan affiliation in terms of clan dialect. I developed my own nicknaming strategy in the field to distinguish between individuals. On my mobile phone, I listed individual names followed by their place of residence. For example, I used nicknames like "Abdi Havukoski" for a respondent named Abdi, a common male name, who resides in Havukoski, an area in the city of Vantaa.

7. Koivukylä is an area in the city of Vantaa where the wedding was held

8. Somali women's poetry, buraanbur, is performed at Somali wedding celebrations. Buranbuur poetry praises the bride, groom, and their families.

Chapter 8

Performing Diaspora: The mobilization of a Somaliland transborder citizenry[1]

Nauja Kleist & Peter Hansen

Demonstrating on Parliament Square

In the afternoon on the 17th of March 2004, thousands of Somalilanders were waving their flags and banners and singing Somaliland slogans on Parliament Square in London. The crowd had started gathering outside the Home Office at about 10am, but, as it grew larger and larger during the day, it had to be relocated by the Metropolitan Police to Parliament Square. Not quite familiar with the colours and slogans of the crowd, most of the parliamentarians in Westminster and Portcullis House, and most of the people passing by the square, wondered who they were and what they were demonstrating for or against. To the media in the UK, the 17th of March 2004, was an important day, not because of the demonstration taking place on Parliament Square, but because the budget was presented by the Chancellor of the Exchequer to Parliament and the public. To the demonstrators and Somalilanders all over the world, however, the day was important for reasons that had very little to do with the state of the economy and the public finances in the UK.

On the 17th of March 2004 Somalilanders from all over England, and Scandinavia as well, came to London to protest for the recognition of Somaliland. Demonstrating at the footsteps of Big Ben, the Somalilanders wished to open the eyes and ears of British parliamentarians and the international community to what they saw as a legitimate claim to being accepted as a real nation-state. In this sense, the 17th of March 2004 was meant for the demonstrators to be a milestone in the history of Somaliland, as it aimed at bringing an end to the ignorance and negligence by the international community on the issue of Somaliland. The demonstration was strategically organised to coincide with a visit made by the Somaliland president and his delegation to the United Kingdom. For the first time ever, a president of Somaliland was on a semi-official visit to a western country. Previously the president had visited neighbouring countries like Djibouti and

Ethiopia, but this visit was different as the president and his delegation visited the United Kingdom that is seen as Somaliland's closest ally in their quest for independence. On the 17th of March 2004, Somalilanders came together to show their loyalty towards Somaliland and to honour the visiting Somaliland president and his delegation. The people involved in the demonstration behaved according to a 'diasporic morality' (Werbner 2002) that is directed towards the wellbeing and future of Somaliland.

In this paper we wish to analyse the meaning of the Somaliland Diaspora, not as a nostalgic and aesthetic community or a social position associated with certain financial responsibilities and expectations (Hansen 2004; Kleist 2003) but as a moral community engaged in a transnational political struggle. We will analyse how different meanings of Diaspora are employed and performed before, during and after the demonstration at Parliament Square. We unfold the demonstration at Parliament Square and the events relating to this event and argue that a possible and fruitful way of studying issues relating to Diaspora is by exploring the ways the term is performed and actively used in transnational political mobilisations. The use of the term Diaspora as an analytical concept is not unproblematic as it has the dangers of solidifying or essentialising social phenomena that are in fact fluid and always in the making. Therefore, our understanding and use of Diaspora is ambivalent and similar to James Clifford's understanding of culture as a deeply compromised idea, yet something he cannot do without (Clifford 1988: 10).

Methodologically and analytically we see the 17th of March 2004 as a 'social situation' (Gluckman 1958) and apply the 'extended case method and situational analysis' (Van Velsen 1967) in our attempt to understand the processes of diasporic identity formation and the performance of Diaspora (Werbner 2002). In focusing on one specific event we wish to show how a diasporic event is constructed not only by a shared and publicly performed identity, often anchored in shared symbols and a communal history of suffering and a vision of return, but also by conflicting meanings and practices that exist within diasporas themselves and between diasporas and the host society. In the case of Somaliland, and indeed in relation to Somali politics in general, what is most striking, and what we see as generative and driving social forces in the process of diasporic identity formation, are the conflicting views, frictions and tensions that make up this particular social and political scene.

The paper is not only based on interviewing and participating on the 17th of March 2004 demonstration in London but also draws on ethnographic fieldworks undertaken in Somaliland in 1997, 1998, 2003 and in the greater Copenhagen area in 1999 and 2003. As researchers we wish to stress that we try not to take sides relating to the recognition of Somaliland. As any researcher who undertakes social studies knows, neutrality is a difficult position to claim, yet we do not see the events analysed in this paper as either an argument for or against the legitimacy of the recognition of Somaliland.

The Big Demonstration

Firstly, we will analyse the immediate events taking place before the demonstration. Secondly, we focus on the demonstration in London itself. Thirdly, we describe and analyse events unfolding in Portcullis House, and finally we close our case study by describing a reception held at The Landmark Hotel.

Parliament Square

Prior to the demonstration on the 17th and the president's visit to the UK, the all party Select Committee on International Development of the House of Commons, visited Somaliland on the 24th and 25th of January 2004. Newspapers in Somaliland stressed that the Committee was the largest group of British politicians to visit Somaliland since the days of independence and that the visit signalled a heightened attention and understanding from the international community in general and the UK government in particular towards the predicament and possible recognition of Somaliland.

Following the Committee's visit to Somaliland, a debate on Somaliland was held in the House of Commons. Present at this debate were eight members of the Committee, the Secretary of State for International Development as well as an interested crowd of about twenty Somalilanders living in the UK. During the two hours long debate, the Committee members presented a version of the political history of Somalia and Somaliland that firmly rooted Somaliland in a legitimate claim to independence. In this understanding, Somaliland has done everything right, but is being ignored by the international community. Somaliland is depicted as a place in the Horn of Africa where there is genuine peace, unity and a functioning state, whereas Somalia is depicted as a place where there is war and lack of state. In sum, the Committee members presented a picture of Somaliland as a *de facto* functioning nation-state, complete with its own colonial and political history, state institutions, government policies and a dedicated and concerned citizenry dispersed all over the world. Therefore the strategy pursued by the international community to insist on a solution for all of Somalia, including Somaliland, is getting in the way of a legitimate claim to self-determination and hindering Somaliland from developing into a prosperous and truly democratic state in area of Africa, that is known to be ravaged by war, corruption and destruction.

On the 15th and 16th of March, the president had met with different British politicians, ministers and bureaucrats in the British government. On the 17th of March the president was to continue his line of meetings with British politicians and bureaucrats and later in the afternoon address the House of Commons personally. We had been told that the demonstration was to start at 10 o'clock in the morning in front of the Home Office. When we got there at around 10.30, there were no Somalilanders in sight. After an hour, two women and one man showed up for the demonstration. The man was around fifty years old and had come from Norway. The two women were in their twenties and both from London. One of them was working as a nurse at a hospital in West London. She was born in London and had never actually seen Somaliland. Her parents were from Hargeisa and they were living together with her and her brothers and sisters in London. The other woman was born in Hargeisa. She married a Somali man from London and had come to live with him and their children. She was not working, spoke only a few words of English but was taking English lessons.

Within another hour or so, a few more men and women had joined the demonstration. There were a few men from Cardiff, where there is a large Somaliland community. Before the war and the break-up of Somalia into different political regions, the Somalis living in Cardiff were not explicit Somalilanders but just Somalis. Now that Somaliland was trying to establish a nation state without their brothers and sisters in the south of Somalia, the identity of forming an explicit Somaliland community in Cardiff had grown equally stronger. One of the men from Cardiff was working as a community worker within the Somaliland community. He and some Somaliland friends had an NGO in Cardiff that was helping Somalilanders, as well as other Somalis, with all sorts of legal and practical matters. He told us that he was working on a project of collecting the life histories of the old Somaliland seamen that were living in Cardiff. There are no Somalilanders or Somalis working as seamen any longer. He wanted to document their history and tell the untold story about the legacy of the Somaliland community in Cardiff and the United Kingdom.

As we were waiting for more people to join the demonstration, we were discussing the organisational skills of Somalis with the few who had shown up. They told us that different persons and organisations had organised to meet at different places and at different times during the day. The Somaliland Mission in East London had issued an invitation on the internet that the demonstration would begin at two in the afternoon outside No. 10 Downing Street. The Envoy for the recognition of Somaliland had issued an invitation in the local Somaliland newspaper in the UK for people to meet on the 15th, 16th and 17th of March from 10am to 4pm outside the Home Office. A third group of Somalilanders had distributed an invitation within the community that they would meet on the 17th of March at 3pm opposite No. 10 Downing Street. Jokingly, yet with a touch of insight into own shortcomings, the few demonstrators told us that there was no good coordination within the community in the UK or the Nordic countries. They pointed out that being part of an oral network community, they were good at talking and exchanging information about almost everything, but very poor at getting a job done or organising almost anything. This is reflected in the fact that there is no well-defined centre of political power within the Somaliland community in the Diaspora and that anyone who feels an obligation and urge to do something can do so, they explained. The fact that several different invitations had been distributed within the community was also interpreted among the few arrivals as a political statement by the part of the Somaliland Diaspora that were members of the political opposition to the ruling party in Somaliland. Clearly the Somaliland opposition to the president and his government in Somaliland would try to sabotage the demonstration by distributing different invitations and thereby divide the Somalilanders living in the UK.

During the day the demonstration grew larger and larger and people were beginning to feel more and more optimistic and enthusiastic as Somalilanders from different parts of the UK turned up at the demonstration. Not only Somalilanders from the United Kingdom but also from Scandinavia arrived to take part in the demonstration. At one point the demonstration grew too large for the pavement outside the Home Office and the Metropolitan Police relocated it to Parliament Square. At this stage the initial nervousness of ever being able to form one coherent demonstrating community had been replaced by joy and confidence.

At the demonstration both men and women, young and old presented the colours of Somaliland and waved banners and posters with messages relating to Somaliland's claim to independence. This was the day for Somalilanders to stand united in their joint effort to achieve recognition. The Somaliland flag played an important symbolic role during the demonstration. The demonstrators were of course waving Somaliland flags, as could be expected on an occasion like this, but more than this, many had also wrapped it around their bodies, or made hats and dresses out of the green, white and red colours, or painted the flag on their faces as if to embody their sense of national identity and loyalty towards Somaliland. Furthermore, several persons carried t-shirts with the flag on their stomach and the text *Rebirth of Somaliland* printed on them. Besides the Somaliland flag, many of the demonstrators had also brought Union Jacks as if to show that Somaliland and the UK share an unbreakable colonial past and to highlight that they have developed some form of loyalty and affection for their second motherland. The demonstrators were also waving their homemade posters and banners carrying messages referring to the unrecognised status and democratic achievements of Somaliland. With slogans like: *Somaliland is not prepared to destroy its nation by joining the destroyers, Somaliland fulfils the condition of democracy, Somaliland asks for recognition from the World. We are a democracy; Somaliland is a model for effective nation building in Africa, Free election. Free Society. Free Press. Hallmark of Somaliland* and *No to Somalia. Yes to Somaliland,* the demonstrators aimed at portraying Somaliland as a legitimate and democratic nation state.

Portcullis House

About 5 PM, some of the demonstrators made their way to Portcullis House, House of Common, to listen to the president of Somaliland, Dahir Riyale Kahin, and his delegation. About 200 people filled up the room to the last chair and latecomers had to stand. The majority of the audience consisted of well-dressed Somaliland men, some Somaliland women and a few white researchers, consultants and MPs. The Somaliland delegation included the president, several members of the *Guurti,* the House of Elders, and not the least the minister of foreign affairs, Edna Aden, as the only woman in the delegation.

While the demonstration still continued outside, the meeting in Portcullis House represented a completely different scene. Not only was the audience much smaller, it was selected, seated and co-ordinated along the lines of an ordinary parliamentary dialogue. The feeling of festivity, enthusiasm and the hopeful making of Somaliland history, however, made this more than an ordinary event. Mr. Tony Worthington, MP, who visited Somaliland with the Committee in January 2004 and before that in 1992, chaired the session and welcomed the delegates in this spirit. As an outspoken proponent of the recognition of Somaliland, Worthington fully matched the delegation and the Somaliland-British audience in his celebration and explicit articulation of the achievements of the Diaspora and of the Somaliland nation. Likewise his denouncement of the relationship to Somalia was equally outspoken. Referring to the union between Somalia and Somaliland, Worthington claimed that"*you were not getting a fair deal* and *you regretted it"*. He furthermore expressed his understanding that Somaliland has remained outside the peace negotiations of Somalia *"because you could not co-operate with people such as General Morgan, known as the butcher of Hargeisa."* Concluding his speech with the words, that he would now"*allow your President to speak to you",* Worthington explicitly recognised the Somalilanders present as part of a nation with a president.

The articulations of a nation and a nation-state continued throughout the meeting. President Riyale Kahin, reading up aloud, rehearsed the colonial history of Somaliland as a British colony, arguing that Somaliland – in opposition to Somalia – is not a failed state. *"When Eritrea, Serbia and Bosnia could be recognised – why not Somaliland?"* Kahin asked, receiving a standing applause for his speech. Following the President's speech, Worthington opened the floor for questions, though he underlined that he would prioritise non-Somalilanders to ask questions thereby indicating a division of the audience between white British and black Somalilanders. Apparently the priority of non-Somalilanders was to give the British audience a chance to interrogate the delegation and avoid a discussion of domestic Somaliland affairs. As the session proceeded, however, it became clear, that the definition of the black audience as consisting of Somalilanders only did not hold water.

A further range of questions focused on the role of the Diaspora and on the political relations between Somaliland, Somalia and the neighbouring countries. The answers pointed at the importance of the Somaliland relations to the Diaspora and the UK, and the impossible relations to Somalia. The atmosphere was festive and good questions, answers and one-liners were rewarded with apprehensive applause and laughter from the floor. Videos and photos were taken. Jokes were told. Towards the end of the session, Abdi Ismail Samatar, a Somali-American Professor took the floor. Presenting himself as from the North, but *not* as a Somalilander, Samatar immediately stirred up a fuss. Some of the audience started to shout and complain, and while some insisted that"*only Somalilanders can talk!"* others hissed *"give him a chance"*. After a little while, Samatar was allowed to speak. Stating that he felt threatened, Samatar argued that the whole of Somalia deserved to be at peace from North to South – and then the different parts of Somalia could decide their futures. After this intervention, Samatar left Portcullis House, but later published his version of the meeting on a Somali web page, **www.hornafrik.com** (Samatar 2004).

The meeting was then concluded and the audience slowly left

Portcullis House, joining the demonstration again or heading somewhere else to celebrate the event. Others hurried towards taxis and the Underground. It was time for the reception.

The Landmark Hotel

Even though we had not been officially invited, two young Somali women whom we had met during the session insisted that we could just pop up at the reception anyway. They had not been invited either, but seemed to know some of the organisers and insisted that it was no problem. So we all took the Underground to Marigold Station in a fashionable part of London and walked into The Landmark Hotel, a very posh hotel. After a couple of minutes of negotiation, we were allowed to enter. Passing through an impressive hall with golden chandeliers, marble floor and luxurious furniture, we entered another huge room with small reception tables and an abundant buffet with Somali, Italian and French style food. In one end of this room, chairs were lined up for people to sit comfortably and listen to the speeches before the dinner. The whole place was filled with beautifully dressed Somalilanders in dress suits, evening gowns, high heels, shimmering jewellery and shiny long dresses with a delicate and sweet scent of *ussi*, a special kind of Somali incense. The president, his delegation, the organisers as well as representatives of organisations, models, politicians and reporters, in short, the elite of the Somaliland-British communities were all there - as well as a few British MPs.

The reception was arranged by the *UK Somaliland Communities*, a name for a loosely organised group of patriotic Somalilanders in the UK formed specifically with the purpose of organising the events relating to the visit of the president, the Welsh Somaliland Committee and the Somaliland Mission in the UK. The arrangement hosted several hundred guests and days of work and large amounts of money had gone into the arrangement of the reception, because, as some people said,"*the delegation deserves it*". Celebrating the delegation and the historic moment of the semi-official visit, the reception was also an opportunity to mingle, discuss, make contacts and take photos of each other and maybe of the president and his delegation. The reception could be said to be a celebration of the Somaliland nation and its achievements towards official recognition. It could also be said to be a social event turning the stereotypical image of the marginalised Somalilanders upside down, making a sumptuous reception everybody could be proud of and talk about for days. As such, the reception represented a third stage of the big demonstration, where the extent, presence and political commitment of the Somaliland communities were demonstrated during the day, and now celebrated.

The reception started out with a range of speakers introduced by two Somaliland women. The first speaker was the Emeritus Professor in Social Anthropology, I.M. Lewis from the London School of Economics. Lewis made explicit his support of the recognition of Somaliland, blaming the international society in general and the British government in particular that they continue to ignore the virtues of Somaliland in favour of their support of the ongoing peace negotiations in Somalia. Like Samatar, Lewis later published his speech on **www.hornafrik.com** (Lewis 2004), but without direct reference to the demonstration and the other events2. After a couple of more speakers, Edna Aden, the minister of foreign affairs spoke on behalf of the president. Edna Aden, who is trained as a midwife and who has founded a maternity hospital in Hargeisa, coupled the nationalistic imaginary of the (re)birth of the Somaliland nation with the idea of *difference* in relation to Somalia. She said:

> "I never expected, when I came to UK to study nursing and later midwifery, that I would be a member of a team trying to deliver a nation. Somaliland grew into a nation in spite of the nation who tried to kill them, but not fighting back, respecting human rights. We separated because of basic differences with people from Somalia. We are Somalilanders and they are Somalis. It is not a question of North and South, we are from Somaliland, it has a name and a place on the map. Somaliland is here to stay. You should inform the world of who you are, you should co-ordinate it."

Edna Aden got standing applause in a both enthusiastic and emotional atmosphere. Her employment of the imagery of giving birth to a nation points to a gendering of the nation in which the more masculine practices of Somaliland politics with only very few female politicians is challenged. Or rather, the reproduction of the nation is feminised and familiarised (cf. Eriksen 2002). Going on to address and encourage the audience to *"inform the world about who you are"* in a co-ordinated way, Edna Aden delivered an outspoken example of mobilisation of (long-distance) nationalism, transformed into an at once local and global political responsibility.

Nations and Empires: Political Kinship and Differences

Obviously the events that unfolded on the 17th can be analysed and interpreted in a number of ways. As already indicated, it was as much a social event as a political manifestation. Or in other words, it was both a demonstration in the sense of a public meeting as well as in the sense of showing British politicians and the British public, other Somalis – and maybe even each other as well – that there is such a thing as a Somaliland nation. In this part of the paper, we will focus on the political, cultural, social and historical aspects of the demonstration, the session in Portcullis House and the reception to analyse how these events are part of a larger national and diasporic framework. All four levels are part of the mobilisation and performance of a contested Somaliland nationalist ideology, which highlights issues of sameness as well as difference.

Colonial ties

The strong linkages between Britain and Somaliland had been underlined within the past months, not only by Somalilanders seeking recognition of the country, but also by the British Parliamentarians who, as members of the Select Committee on International Development, visited and debated Somaliland in Parliament. During the debate in Parliament, both Somalilanders and the Committee members shared the notion that the UK has a special moral responsibility to support Somaliland because of their shared colonial past. Also, the Committee members underlined that even today the population of Somaliland displayed loyalty and affection for the UK.

During the debate in Parliament in February 2004, reference was made to a statement made by the Secretary of State for the Colonies on his visit to Hargeisa on the 9th of February 1959. In the statement the Secretary underlined that

> "whatever the eventual destiny of the Protectorate, Her Majesty's Government will continue to take an interest in the welfare of its inhabitants, and will in the light of the circumstances prevailing from time to time, be prepared to give sympathetic consideration to the continuation of financial assistance within the limits of the amount of aid at present being provided to the Protectorate."

Mr. Tony Baldry of the Committee underlined that this statement was reiterated in a Colonial Office report that was submitted to Parliament on independence. The committee members underlined that the closeness between the UK and Somaliland is also found today in the fact that there are many British citizens of Somaliland origin now living in Somaliland, that some of the committee members' constituency live part time in Somaliland and that the UK Somaliland Diaspora has played a vital part in the rebuilding of Somaliland.

Following up on this positive attitude towards recognition, one of the most important messages of the demonstration was to remind the British government of its past as a coloniser. During the demonstration, a large number of posters with a map of Somaliland surrounded by the words *Republic of Somaliland* and *British Somaliland Protectorate* was handed out and taped on the demonstrators' bodies or held in front of them. This focus on the British-Somaliland past is at least two-fold. First of all, should Britain recognise Somaliland, it might very well be the first step in a range of recognitions from other countries – at least, this is what Somaliland politicians seem to hope. Secondly, the British colonial past and thus colonial borders means that the country is in accordance with the principle of the African Union, which maintains that the borders of African nation states must not violate the colonial borders. Thirdly, Somaliland did receive its Independence on the 26th of June 1960, that is four days before it united into the Republic of Somalia and Somaliland politicians therefore claim that since the country has once been recognised as an independent nation state, it could and should obtain this status again.

Somaliland thus re-claims its nationhood along several lines of arguments and strategies. One is to set the date of Somaliland Independence to 1960 and not 1991. Accordingly, when Mr. Tony Worthington welcomed the delegates in Portcullis House and dated independence to 1991, the minister of foreign affairs, Edna Aden, immediately corrected him. Stating the date of international recognition of Somaliland to the year of 1961, the reunion with Somalia is turned into a historical, illegitimate and unhappy parenthesis, which is now over. On a broader level, this strategy of de-legitimisation of the union and thereby the Republic of Somalia, is also related to the failure of Somalia in terms of unifying all the Somali speaking areas in one nation state, of which the union of the British Protectorate and the UN-Trusteeship of Somalia was supposed to be the first step. Furthermore, it is claimed that the treaty of union was never signed by Somaliland and therefore that the Republic of Somalia has been an invalid arrangement the whole time. Returning to the political arguments, which were actually articulated during the big demonstration, the illegitimacy of the Republic of Somalia was however more linked to the arguments of failed states.

As emphasised both by President Riyale Kahin and other members of the delegation, by Worthington and later I.M. Lewis, the union with Somalia turned out unhappily, due to the failure of Somalia and most especially the dictatorship of General Siyad Barre. President Riyale Kahin, not only invoking the past, but also the future, reminded the audience about September 11 2001 and the dangers of terrorism and failed states *"in the fast-shrinking world of ours"*. In contrast to Somalia, where suspected Al-Qaeda terrorists have been detained, Somaliland, Kahin argued, is peaceful, stable, democratic and, most important,*"no building ground for terrorists"*. However, while emphasising that Somaliland is not a failed state, Kahin also seemed to imply that Somaliland has not unfolded its full potential for securing peace and stability in the region, as Somaliland cannot *"co-operate with international trade organisations, does not attract investments or fight the war of terrorism"*.

Later that day, during the reception at night, Lewis also referred to the number of failed peace accords and negotiations as well as the absence of a government in Somalia. In his words, the peace negotiations are more about *"the division of power and economic interest among a squabbling bunch of predatory gangsters"*, who *"should have been arrested in Kenya as suspected war crimes perpetrators"* (Lewis 2004). The legitimacy – and accordingly recognition – of Somaliland is, in other words, linked both to the colonial past of Somaliland as a British Protectorate as well as to the illegitimacy of the failed state of Somalia in its claims to keep Somaliland as a part of the state territory.

The colonial past was also invoked in the question of *difference* both politically and culturally between Somaliland and Somalia, due to differences in the Italian and British colonisation. This argument is often related to the 'Italianisation' of Somalia - the corrupt Mafia culture of the *Somalia Italiana* and the Italian administrated UN-Trusteeship of Somalia - in contrast to the pure and authentic culture in the British Protectorate. This purity, the argument goes, is due to the small number of British officials in the Protectorate during colonisation and the claimed British colonial politics of non-intervention in terms of culture. The politics of non-intervention are said to have been even more pronounced in the Protectorate where local warriors and the resistance movement of Mohamed Abdullah Hassan, the so-called Mad Mullah, forcefully challenged the colonisers from the beginning of colonisation until 1920.

This argument of a pure and authentic culture due to the *distance* between the British colonisers and the Somaliland colonial subjects was not revived during the parliament session or the reception. On the contrary: close colonial ties, loyalty, friendship, bonds of kinship and even allegiance to the Queen was emphasised. Worthington, visibly impressed, told that his recent delegation to Somaliland was received with signs stating *The Queen is our Mother*. President Riyale Kahin expressed his hope that the friendship between Great Britain and Somaliland that existed at the time of Independence in 1960 could continue in the future and be revived between the two nations. The Deputy Speaker of the House of Elders, the *Guurti*, however, was more critical when he reminded the British of the service of the Somalilanders during the two world wars. A British MP asked him about Somaliland's relations towards its neighbouring countries. The Deputy Speaker replied by recounting that Somaliland had not asked Britain about its relations towards other countries when they were called upon to join the British Forces at the outbreak of the Second World War, but had in fact supported its friend without any questions asked. Also, the Deputy Speaker blamed the British for not educating their former colonial subjects while *"the Somalis in Somalia had been taught tricks by Italy for ten years"*. Continuing that the British failed to help the former Protectorate in this situation, he exclaimed, that *"we are British orphans"*, thereby emphasising a mixture of parental bonds and failed responsibility from the side of the British, i.e. the missing parents. As already mentioned, the image of birth and kinship had been a theme throughout the day, printed on t-shirts and banners, invoked by the coupling of both the Somaliland flag and Union Jack and articulated by politicians, most forcefully by foreign minister Edna Aden when she invoked the imagery of delivering a nation. Only this time, the parents were not supposed to be the British, but the Somalilanders themselves – in Diaspora and in Somaliland.

Diaspora, Liminality and Conflict

Looking at the events relating to the demonstration at Parliament Square one first of all sees the shared expression of a Diaspora organised around shared histories, symbols and political agendas. Also Somalilanders living in the Diaspora performed according to what was expected from members of the Somaliland transborder citizenry (Glick Schiller and Fouron 2001: 20) that are more close to the centres of political power than Somalilanders living in Somaliland: they showed up at the demonstration, backed the arguments presented to the international community in general and the British parliamentarians in particular, organised a reception for the visiting delegation and thereby played their role regarding the recognition of Somaliland and towards the visiting homeland politicians and government officials. The demonstrators played their part as good Somaliland citizens living in the Diaspora, caring about the future and wellbeing of their homeland. The notion that the demonstrating Somalilanders were somehow doing what was expected from them as 'good Somalilanders' was highlighted on one of the invitations distributed within the Somaliland community in London a few days before the demonstration took place. The invitation had the design and colours of the Somaliland flag upon which was written: *OFFICIAL UK STATE VISIT: PRESIDENT OF*

SOMALILAND: MR DAHIR RIYAALE, SOMALILANDERS this is it: it is NOW or NEVER, Your country needs your support, take the day off, whatever you are doing!, bring your sirens, drums, flags, etc., Make sure you play your role regarding the recognition of Somaliland!!! and *Tell your mum and dad and everyone else you know!!!*. As exemplified in the invitation, shared symbols like the flag of Somaliland and the image of a community unified in achieving the same goals were used in an effort to mobilise Somalilanders. However, to understand the public ritual at Parliament Square and the relating events and agendas, one needs to look behind the apparent unifying political goal of achieving independence. In other words, one needs to contextualise the demonstration and public expressions of political agendas within a sphere of challenges, conflicts and ambiguities relating to the Somaliland and Somali communities in the UK and the ambiguous status of Somaliland within the international order of nation states.

Within a world of nation states Somaliland remains unrealised as a political community. Following Victor Turner's (1979) theory on liminality and communitas in the performance of public rituals we can arrive at a clearer understanding of what was taking place at Parliament Square. Turner developed his theory of liminality on the basis of Van Gennep's (1909) description of a rite de passage. Rites of passage are rituals marking the passage of one state of life and entry into another, e.g. birth, puberty, marriage, initiation or death. In this sense rites of passage are rites that accompany every change of place, state, social position and age. Van Gennep (ibid) characterised rites of passage as being composed of a phase of separation, margin or limen (signifying 'threshold' in Latin), and aggregation. The liminal phase is characterised by ambiguity as this phase is marked neither by the attributes of the past nor by the coming state. Liminal entities are neither here nor there, they are betwixt and between the positions assigned and arrayed by law, custom and convention (Turner 1979:95). In the liminal phase normal rules and social hierarchies are negated and instead replaced by a heightened sense of solidarity between persons undergoing the ritual (ibid).

In a similar way Somaliland is in a liminal phase within the system of nation states. On the one hand, Somaliland is not ravaged by civil war, lawlessness and general chaos. On the other hand however, Somaliland is not a sovereign nation state. Because of its ambiguous or liminal status Somaliland is subjected to practices by international actors that are not applied towards sovereign nation states. For example, the United Nations are not referring to Somaliland as Somaliland, yet in its daily dealings with the political leadership in Somaliland and in its operation of numerous UN agencies in

Somaliland there is an acknowledgement of the authority of the Somaliland state. Also due to the liminal status, the UNHCR in Somaliland refers directly to UN headquarters in Geneva and not to Nairobi, as other UN agencies in Somaliland do.

The liminal status of Somaliland provides a very powerful base for mobilising solidarity among Somalilanders who identity with the project of achieving independence. At the demonstration in London, Somalilanders formed a visible and existing community. Somalilanders from all over the United Kingdom and Northern Europe were united in London because of their liminal status within the international system of nation states. In this sense what defines the community of Somalilanders as a political categorical identity is their status as a 'non-community' within the international order of nation-states. Turner's observation that liminality is often likened to death and being in the womb (1979:95) corresponds beautifully with the popular image within Somaliland national discourse of a nation that is once again being reborn and given life through delivery. Following Turner, the fact that Somaliland remains unrecognised provides a very powerful base of identity for the abstract community of Somalilanders. The image that Somaliland and the Somaliland transborder citizenry are somehow at present on the move, from somewhere to somewhere else, also resembles the religious pilgrimage analysed by Turner (1974). According to Turner (ibid) pilgrims experience an intensified sense of sacredness and community, referred to by Turner as communitas. The sense of being left out and forgotten by the world, yet still having the possibility of concluding the pilgrimage of moving into the state of being a real internationally recognised nation state, enables people to transcend differences and problems. No one has ever stopped to reflect on what will happen within Somaliland and the Somaliland transborder citizenry if Somaliland is recognised, the pilgrimage comes to an end and the sense of communitas disappears. Will it stir up old antagonism and possibly instigate new fighting within Somaliland? Will the political realization of Somaliland in a paradoxical way lead to its disintegration? Or will the recognition of Somaliland also have some of the imagined positive effects of prosperity and stability that many Somalilanders abroad and at home dream about?

The demonstration in Parliament Square tells us something about the nature of the Somaliland Diaspora and the Somaliland community. These phenomena, identities or positions are not social facts existing without the active ongoing constructions taking place, for example, at a demonstration. In this sense the imagined community of Somalilanders would not exist, or at least have different manifestations, if it was not based in, and causing social interaction. To position the demonstration within its social contexts is also to allow analytical space for all the aspects that are problematic and yet generative for the construction of a shared political ideology and horizon. On several occasions before, during and after the demonstration, the image of a unified and well disciplined and dedicated citizenry was challenged and yet in a more subtle way produced. While waiting for people to show up for the demonstration, the few Somalilanders present were very critical of most things and expressed concerns about the present political leadership in Somaliland. They told us that the president really was not a president, because he was really bad at addressing the people, was not able to govern the country and that he was not only in the UK to discuss development aid and recognition, but also to sign documents allowing the UK to return rejected asylum seekers to Somaliland. Furthermore they told us that people probably would not show up and that the only Somalilanders with discipline were women since all the men were busy chewing *khat* or being unemployed. Moreover they told us that people were too occupied with clan and therefore not really able and ready to form a modern nation-state based on a different way of social organisation. Contrary to the official discourse they told us that people's loyalties were not first and foremost directed at the wellbeing of Somaliland. On the contrary, they stressed, people would think about their family and clan first. Secondly, they would think about their city and local areas. Thirdly, they would think about their reception and only fourthly would they think about Somaliland. We need to stress however, that as the demonstration grew bigger and bigger during the day the frustrations, insecurities and potential conflicts were gradually replaced by a heightened sense of actually forming a united and thriving national community.

These early demonstrators expressed viewpoints that compromise the public ideology of Somaliland and the claims to independence. Our point is precisely that the more difficult it is to realise Somaliland as a functioning political project, the louder the agitators will be shouting at Parliament Square. In this sense Somaliland and the Somaliland community needs to be seen in relation to the challenges it faces. The more ambiguous and liminal it appears, the stronger the solidarity and the more manifest the national rhetoric. The point is that behind the immediate harmony of the demonstration and the coherence of the arguments for recognition, the demonstration displayed disharmony and liminality. For example the disharmony related to two different bases of social organisation: clan and nation. National ideology informs us that Somaliland is a nation based on its own history and culture. In this sense Somaliland is portrayed as a nation that has moved ahead of Somalia and its own past in its defiance of clan as the base of social organisation. However, everyone only vaguely familiar with social realities in Somaliland, and among Somalis and Somalilanders in the West knows that relations between kin, often referred to by westerners and English speaking Somalis as clan, are extremely important. The ambivalence between nation and clan and how to fuse social realities with ideologies of nation and state are not only a problem as such but in a more subtle way also a creative tension having the potential of generating heightened solidarities and new identities.

These challenges and ambivalence were also seen in the fact that not all 'potential Somalilanders' in London had showed up for the demonstration nor found it a particular good idea to pursue the road that perhaps would lead to independence. On the days preceding the demonstration, several Somalis that potentially could claim their Somaliland citizenship, did not wish to join the demonstration because they did not support Somaliland but on the contrary supported the reinstallation of the Somali Republic. One person, who grew up within the boundaries claimed by Somaliland and who, according to the Somaliland constitution, is a possible Somaliland citizen, had committed an act of effective symbolic violence to one of the aforementioned invitations hanging on the wall in a café in Southall. He had cut the invitation designed as the Somaliland flag into pieces because he did not support Somaliland and in no way wished to take part in the demonstration. This 'potential Somalilander' was not alone in his rejection of Somaliland but on the contrary expressed a position taken by several Somalilanders whom we met before the demonstration. The fact that many people from the geographical area known as Somaliland, and genealogically qualifying for Somaliland citizenship are not supporters of Somaliland, is highly sensitive and surrounded by a certain degree of taboo. This was also seen from the reactions from the Somaliland participants in Portcullis House when the Somali-American professor took the floor during the discussion and presented himself as coming from the North but not seeing himself as a Somalilander thereby trespassing the unwritten boundary of what can be expressed in a public forum celebrating the existence of Somaliland.

Cultural notions and practices of community, belonging and solidarity were also being challenged. In London, as in Copenhagen, many Somalilanders and Somalis express how they feel that the values and practices characterising their community are disintegrating and challenged by a western foreign culture. Often people have explained to us that the community is falling apart and that people are just living like individuals. The ideology of solidarity is very manifest and relates to a nomadic history and tradition among Somalis. Often we have been explained that if a nomadic family in need of water or food for themselves or their livestock encounters another family in the nomadic area they will be helped in the best way possible. According to this ideology, Somalis will always help each other and no one can refuse to help another Somali if their help is really needed. In London, the importance and significance of family networks are changed and partly replaced by the welfare system. One respondent explained that in London people are saying goodbye to their clans and joining the welfare community in stead. The notion of 'leaving your clan' or 'community of relations' and joining an abstract 'welfare community' is seen as a threat to 'the Somali culture and community'. Especially to many Somali men living in the west, the welfare system is seen as threatening their position within more traditional Somali family values and practices and thereby Somali values in general. In sum, the fact that notions of community and solidarity are challenged in the West, is an important context for the understanding of the demonstration where people at least for a day formed 'a community'.

Conclusion

The demonstration and the other events unfolding in London point towards a transborder Somaliland citizenry united in its ambitions and orientations towards finding a space for Somaliland within the world of sovereign nation states. The Somaliland Diaspora appears homogeneous, as it stands shoulder to shoulder united through shared symbols of flags, songs, slogans, colonial histories, memories of civil war and oppression. A closer examination, however, reveals the tensions, disagreements and heterogeneity within the Diaspora or transborder citizenry and thereby point to the weakness of these analytical concepts of often highlighting the shared histories, horizons and agendas and neglecting the rifts and cracks behind a public homogenous image. Underneath the image of homogeneity, there appears to be a wealth of dangerous liminal identities not yet certain of what to be, where to go, whom or what to support and how and when to do so. Through detailed ethnographic fieldworks and a sensitive political, cultural and historical contextualisation of the production of a Somaliland political ideology, we have shown how uncertainty and divergent views have both a threatening and creative force within Diasporas.

Moreover, our paper shows the importance of history in arguments for self-determination and how history is not a social fact but the outcome of ongoing arguments and struggles between different actors and institutions. Our study testifies to the important role played by the Diaspora in the making of history and in presenting the arguments for the recognition of Somaliland. Somalilanders in the UK have not only participated in the construction of a national history and arguments for political self determination, but have also worked to facilitate, create and locate a social and political stage, where these arguments can be presented most powerfully. In this sense Somalilanders living in Diaspora have played important roles in spreading the message of Somaliland to an international audience. This shows how the Diaspora has been very important for the ideological and physical construction of a homeland and not primarily the other way round, as has been observed in other similar situations. In the case of Haiti, for example, the Haitian Diaspora was named the *Tenth Department* by the priest politician Aristide when he was inaugurated as president, thereby actively creating a community of Haitians living outside the Haitian nation state. In this way Aristide changed the location of Diaspora from a location of exile into an integral and vital part of Haiti (Schiller and Fouron 2001: 120-121). In the case of Somaliland, there are still many opportunities for actively creating and incorporating the Somaliland Diaspora into the affairs of the Somaliland nation state. Also our study has shown that more than describing specific persons and a geographical location, the Somaliland Diaspora appears to be a social and political position of giving, resourcefulness and agency that can be claimed, wished for and aspired to by different persons in a variety of situations and forms. The complexity of the significance of Diaspora is highlighted in the fact that the word or notion of Diaspora did not play a significant role during the demonstration at Parliament Square as this gathering of people was for all Somalilanders. During the debate at Portcullis House and at the Landmark Hotel, however, there were several references to the Somaliland Diaspora and its importance to Somaliland. This testifies to the elitist connotations associated with the term Diaspora.

Our analysis is based on one specific event and in doing so we go against a strong tradition within anthropology to filter out the freak occurrence, the anomaly, the unrepresentative figure, the non-repeating pattern, and the impermanent and un-remarked cultural form in the finished ethnography. Anthropology has traditionally been concerned with analysing the patterns of culture, the principles of social organisation, customs, and traditions, systems of rules and phenomena that are understood to have withstood the test of time (Malkki 1997: 89-90). The events unfolding in London were unique and transitory, but there can be no doubt that they will not be weak or fleeting in their effects. An interesting path to follow, and a way of extending this case study, would be to follow the intense discussions taking place online where the events in London are being retold, contested and defended by numerous Somalis and Somalilanders around the world. As such the events in London have shaped or influenced notions of being a Somalilander, a Somali, of living in the UK, in the Diaspora, of returning to Somaliland or in other ways engaging oneself in a transnational political struggle.

Finally we would like to repeat that our paper is not an intervention in favour of the political legacy of either Somaliland or a united Somalia, but aims at contributing to a better understanding of the meanings and practices relating to 'the Somaliland Diaspora'.

References

All Party Parliamentary Group on Overseas Development. (2004). *The Challenge of Somaliland*. London, House of Commons. Pamphlet.

Clifford, J. (1988). *The Predicament of Culture. Twentieth-Century Ethnography, Literature, and Art.* Cambridge: Harvard University Press.

Clifford, J. (1994). Diasporas. *Cultural Anthropology*, 9, 302-338.

Danforth, Loring M. (1995). *The Macedonian Conflict. Ethnic Nationalism in a Transnational World.* Princeton: Princeton University Press.

Douglas, Mary (1966). *Purity and Danger. An analysis of concepts of pollution and taboo*. London: Routledge

Eriksen, T. H. (2002). The Sexual Life of Nations. Notes on gender and nationhood. *Kvinder, Køn & Forskning*, 11, 52-65.

Epstein, A. L. (1958). *Politics in an Urban African Community. The Rhodes-Livingstone Institute Northern Rhodesia.* Manchester: Manchester University Press

George, R. M. (1996). *The Politics of Home: Postcolonial relocations and twentieth-century fiction.* Cambridge: Cambridge University Press.

Gluckman, Max (1958). *Analysis of a Social Situation in Modern Zululand*. Manchester: Manchester University Press.

Griffiths, D. (2002). *Somali and Kurdish Refugees in London. New Identities in the Diaspora*. Aldershut: Ashgate.

Hansen, P. (2004). *Migrant Transfers as a Development Tool: The case of Somaliland.*. Copenhagen: DIIS & Geneva: International Organisation for Migration.

House of Commons (2004). *House of Commons Hansard Debates for 4 th of February 2004* (pt 3), http://www.publications.parliament.uk

Kleist, N. (2003). *Somali-Scandinavian Dreaming. The case of Somscan and UK Cooperative Associations.* Paper presented at 'Determinants of Transnational Engagement, Santa Domingo.

Lewis, I. M. (2004). *As the Kenyan Somali 'Peace' Conference falls apart in confusion, Recognition of Somaliland's Independence is overdue.* **www.hornafrik.com** [On-line]. Available: **www.hornafrik.com**

Malkki, Liisa (1997). News and Culture: Transitory Phenomena and the Fieldwork Tradition. In *Anthropological Locations. Boundaries and Grounds of a Field Science.* Akhil Gupta & James Ferguson (ed.) Berkeley: University of California Press.

Samatar, A. I. (2004). *The Secessionist Campaign in London: An Eye-Witness Somali Report.* **www.hornafrik.com** [On-line]. Available: **www.hornafrik.com**

Schiller, G. N. & Fouron, G. (2001). Long-Distance Nationalism Defined. In *Georges Woke Up Laughing. Long-distance Nationalism and the Search for Home* (pp. 17-35). Durham & London: Duke University Press.

Steen, A.-B. (1993). *Varieties of the Tamil Refugee Experience in Denmark and England*. PhD University of Copenhagen.

Turner, S. (2003). *Burundians in Belgium: constructing, performing and contesting Diaspora*. In Paper presented at the workshop, 'Determinants of Transnational Engagement', Santa Domingo.

Turner, V. (1974). Pilgrimage as Social Process, in: *Dramas, Fields, and Metaphors*. Ithaca: Cornell University Press.

Turner, V. (1979). *The Ritual Process. Structure and Anti-Structure.* Ithaca: Cornell University Press.

Van Gennep, Arnold (1909; 1960). *The Rites of Passage.* Chicago: University of Chicago Press.

Van Velsen, J. (1967). The Extended-case Method and Situational Analysis. In: *The Craft of Social Anthropology*, Epstein, A. L., Gluckman, Max (ed.) Oxford: Pergamon Press.

Werbner, Pnina (2002). *Imagined Diasporas among Manchester Muslims*. Oxford: James Curry.

Werbner, Pnina (2001). The Limits of Cultural Hybridity: On Ritual Monsters, Poetic Licence and Contested Postcolonial Purifications. *Journal of the Royal Anthropological Institute*, 7(1): 133-158.
http:///http://:/http://./http://:/

---

1 This is an edited version of an earlier paper entitled "The Big Demonstration - a study of transborder political mobilisation", AMID Working Paper Series 42/2005, published by the Academy for Migration Studies in Denmark.

2.The quotations in our paper are taken from the Internet text (Lewis 2004), where they correspond with our notes taken during his talk at the reception.

Section 2:

Conflict, reconciliation and state formation

Chapter 9

On the Path to Recovery

Jabril Ibrahim Abdulle & Abdulkadir Yahya Ali[1]

War, Crime and Insecurity

For the vast majority of Somalis, insecurity originates from a much more mundane and immediate quarter: their own armed and always recalcitrant political leadership. There are also other interest-based and religious cases that count.

The use of Somali state apparatus as an instrument of repression dates from the early colonial period, although it essentially ceased when the country came under democratic rule (1960-69). However, after the military coup, repression became routine; not only did the Somali government fail to provide security for its citizens, it became the principal agitator of public insecurity — aided and abetted by the many governments who supplied the Barre regime with military and financial assistance[2].

Between 1969 and 1977, the Barre regime embarked on a military build-up entirely incongruous with the needs or capacity of the country. In the context of the Cold War, Barre found the former Soviet Union as a willing partner and built the Somali fighting machine into one of the best-trained and best-equipped in sub-Saharan Africa. However, common interests between the former Soviet Union and Somalia shifted in favour of the United States government and the West after the 1977/78 war in western Somalia. Somalia was forced to withdraw from Ogaden province by the allied forces of Cuba, Ethiopia, East Germany and the former Soviet Union. Subsequent to this, Siyad Barre decreed the immediate expulsion of Russians from Somalia. In the aftermath of Somalia's withdrawal from western Somalia region, the armed Somali opposition groups against the dictatorial military regime were availed a space to wage war and mobilize internal and Diaspora public. Unable to contain the insurgents, the military government resorted to fomenting interclan violence and divide-and-rule tactics. As the violence escalated, many civilians rallied to the armed rebel movements or sought to acquire their own weapons to better defend themselves, their property and their perceived clan interests. When the central government finally collapsed in 1991, its vast store of munitions fell into rebel and civilian hands.

In the ensuing civil war that followed, clan militias used violence against one another, and against the civilian population, with no less ferocity than the military regime had done. In addition to the "collateral damage" wrought by untrained and undisciplined militia, using heavy weapons in urban areas, deliberate, large-scale massacres of civilians were perpetrated in several parts of the country, including Galkayo, Kismayo, Baidoa, Burao and Hargeisa. Other modes of violence, such as torture, and rape — that were virtually unknown in the traditional Somali warfare — were carried out on an unprecedented scale.

Since 1995, much of Somalia has enjoyed relative peace and security. This has come about through the reassertion in some regions of Somalia by the following types of governance authorities: traditional authority, whereby clan elders have taken up the basic functions of governance or invested their authority in local administrations; in other areas, law enforcement and justice have been dispensed by Islamic Shari'a courts. The business community has also played a role, pooling their private security forces to protect common market areas and important economic infrastructure, or by providing street lights free of charge in dangerous neighbourhoods. In parts of Mogadishu, community associations have, at the instigation of women and other civil society groups, set up "neighbourhood watch" arrangements to patrol the streets and respond to security problems.

Nevertheless, much of Somalia is considered to suffering from chronic insecurity. The UN categorized parts of south-central Somalia, including areas of the Jubba Valley and along the south-west Ethiopian/Kenya border as among its most dangerous grade-five duty stations. The absence of a functional central government in Somalia is the single most important contributor to the existing insecurity, but by no means the only one. Proliferation of small arms and light weapons, parochial political rivalries, organized crime, and resource and interest-based conflict are all integral to the volatile environment that threatens the lives and welfare of ordinary Somalis.

Proliferation of Weapons

After the collapse of the Somali state, the military arsenals of the former Somalia Army, Navy and Air Force were either destroyed or looted. Tanks, APCs, mortars, field artillery, anti aircraft batteries, light gunboats, rocket propelled grenades (RPGs), land mines, hand grenades, crew-served machine guns and light weapons (assault rifles, pistols, anti-tank launchers) all fell into the hands of the Somali public and rebel insurgents. Much of these munitions eventually came under the control of various militia groups, some loyal to factions, others to clans and business groups. Some remained with the freebooting armed gangs known throughout south-central Somalia as *"mooryaan"*. A free trade in arms and ammunition ensured that anyone who wanted or needed arms could procure them.

In 1992, the United Nations imposed an arms embargo on Somalia under Security Council Resolution 733 (1992), hoping that it would help to curb violence. But arms shipments to Somalia continued unabated and the cycle of violence continued[3]. In February 2003, an independent Panel of Experts appointed by the UN Secretary General found a clear pattern of "continuous and flagrant violations of the embargo" (UNSC 2003: 6). Faction leaders, self-proclaimed administrations, businessmen and regional governments all continued to traffic weapons and ammunition to Somalia with impunity. Since few factions could pay their fighters in cash, much of the weaponry they received ended up on the market, available to the highest bidder (ICG 2003 10). By 2003, a study commissioned by the European Commission estimated that 64% of Somalis possessed one or more firearms. Unsurprisingly, a high percentage of Somali children have access to weapons. Each year many hundreds of children are caught between warring factions and many more are killed through direct participation in armed conflict (CRD/UNICEF 2003).

Armed Groups

The proliferation of weapons is a contributing factor to insecurity in parts of Somalia but it is by no means the only cause —if it is a cause at all. Several areas, including Somaliland, Puntland and the central regions have known relative peace and security, although their populations are as heavily armed as that elsewhere in the country. A full understanding of the prevailing insecurity therefore demands a study of who possesses weapons and the purposes for which they are used. South-central Somalia is home to a plethora of armed groups, including factional, business and court militias, freelance gunmen and criminal gangs. Each exists for a specific purpose and to defend a particular interest. It is the interaction of these groups, their aims and their interests that defines the security situation in a given area at any given moment.

Factional Militias

These are typically recruited from the clan of the faction leader, although they may also comprise former professional soldiers and freelance fighters from other clans. For most of the period since the government's collapse, these groups have controlled the largest stockpiles of arms and ammunition, much of which remains hidden. When purchasing new arms or replenishing depleted stocks, some factions source their needs on local markets; most, however, either receive them from friendly states or purchase them with funds provided by neighbouring government.

The instability of factional politics is a major source of insecurity and violence. Constantly shifting alliances create an atmosphere of uncertainty and mistrust. Factions often come into conflict with one another or splinter into mutually antagonistic sub groups, only to set aside their differences when new adversaries materialize. When a faction leader is threatened by forces from another clan, his kinsmen may rush to his aid, only to abandon him — or even fight him — when the threat subsides.

Violence between factional militia groups can generally be traced to one of the following causes:

- political rivalry
- and and property disputes
- revenue
- spontaneous violence

The political violence that once fuelled the civil war has by and large subsided. When it does occur, it is usually localized and episodic, as no faction can afford to exert prolonged, large-scale military effort. In recent years, violence of this nature has typically erupted in the lead-up to, or the aftermath of, internationally sponsored peace conferences, when the stakes are perceived to be highest. Political violence is also often associated with external interference, since leadership of a faction can mean access to the financial and military support of a foreign sponsor.

Land and property disputes can take several forms, depending on whether these involve urban real estate, natural resources such as farmland, pasture and water, or traditional clan territories. Mogadishu, the capital, is the town most seriously affected by disputes over urban real estate and property. Public and private property alike has been appropriated by factional militia or their kinsmen – often to secure leverage in political or financial bargaining. Many of the original landowners, especially those from other regions, have fled the capital while retaining a claim to their property. Increasingly, such disputes have been resolved through negotiated settlements, usually involving a pay-off of some kind to those occupying the premises. But a far larger number of these cases remain unresolved, and the landlords are either unwilling or unable to return to reclaim their property. Resolving the inevitable claims and counterclaims will not only be critical for a lasting peace agreement, but also to the re-emergence of Mogadishu as the shared, cosmopolitan capital of the Somali state.

Land disputes are also a key factor in the mass displacement of populations from one region to another across Somalia. Countless Somalis have been uprooted from homes and communities because of their clan affiliation and forced to migrate to safety among their own clan relatives. The dispersal of the Somali population in this fashion has exaggerated the gulf of misunderstanding between members of different clans and minimized opportunities for interclan communication and exchange, thereby adding impetus to demands by some groups that Somalia be reconstituted as a federal state. There is, however, no general correlation between land disputes and federalist sentiment: the inhabitants of *Lower Shabelle*, and *Lower* and *Middle Jubba* are among those worst affected by occupation, dispossession and displacement at the hands of militia from non-resident clans, but many – if not most – of the people in these areas remain unconvinced of the merits of federalism.

Disputes over pasture, water, and other natural resources have recently acquired new importance. Modern firearms and 4-wheel drive vehicles have transformed local feuds into murderous battles in which dozens of people may be killed or injured. Bitter fighting over wells, pasture and other natural resources between clans in *Mudug* and *Galgudud* regions claimed dozens of lives in late 2003, and similar battles erupted in early 2004 between clans in *Hiiraan* region and different parts of *Mudug*. Factional militia, however, rarely become involved in such disputes unless their leaders perceive a direct interest in doing so.

More common are clashes among factional militia over roadblocks, marketplaces or other sources of revenue. Local-level incidents of this nature mirror the broader competition among the interests of both faction leaders and war-economy groups for control of national economic infrastructure such as seaports and airports. Since many factions generate revenue this way, the restoration of state control over such assets directly threatens factional interests and thus represents one of the foremost challenges to a future national Somali government.

The coexistence of young, poorly trained and undisciplined gunmen from different clans and interest groups (factions, business and freelance militias), in close proximity to one another, inevitably generates spontaneous friction and violence — especially in Mogadishu. Most such incidents are rapidly defused and contained, but in some cases they can lead to bloody, tragic feuds. As with other forms of factional violence, the main victims are usually civilians caught in the crossfire rather than militiamen themselves. Years of civil war, in which traditional rules of combat engagement have been repeatedly and willfully contravened, have produced a generation of young fighters with little or no respect for human life and dignity. In particular, traditional respect for non-combatants, known collectively as *birimageydo* ("to be spared from the iron") has lost all meaning: wholesale massacres, burning of houses and villages, the rape of women — sometimes in front of their families, and a multitude of other atrocities have all been committed in this war. Coming to terms with this tragic history of inter-communal cruelty, brutality and humiliation will be a challenge for both local and national reconciliation.

Business Militias

Since the late 1990s, the balance of economic and military power has gradually shifted to the disadvantage of armed factions. The achievement of a UN-brokered ceasefire in 1992, followed by the arrival of an international peacekeeping mission (and the massive infusion of cash it represented) provided a window of opportunity for the private sector to flourish — especially in Mogadishu. As local UN employees and sub-contractors reinvested their newly acquired wealth in homes, hotels, businesses and vehicles, they became increasingly risk averse. Many business leaders who had financed factional militia during the civil war became reluctant to do so and instead begin to work together in defence of their business interests.

These embryonic commercial alliances initially provided much of the impetus for the Islamic Shari'a courts that emerged in parts of Mogadishu and elsewhere in South Central Somalia. Businesses pooled their private security forces under the leadership of the courts, where — unlike the factional militia — they are paid adequate salaries and given medical treatment in case of injury. Most Shari 'a courts retained a distinctive clan character and were unable to pass judgment on members of other clans. Nevertheless, the convergence of commercial, clan and religious agendas permitted road-blocks to be dismantled, and for goods to move freely between regions that had long been cut off from one another. The resumption of informal cross-border trade with Kenya and Ethiopia stimulated the economy even further, adding to the wealth and strength of the new business consortia.

Cooperation between the private sector and the Islamic courts was short lived. Whereas the business community required cross-clan cooperation and loyalty, the Shari' a courts were generally founded along clan lines, limiting the prospects for joint action. At the same time, the religious establishment was becoming increasingly divided among adherents of competing theological movements (*al-ittihad Al-Islami, Al-Islah,* and the *Salafiya,* among others), preventing functional unification of the courts. As relations steadily deteriorated, some of the court militias chose to remain with their business sponsors, while some merged with their clan militia in other regions (notably *Lower Shabelle, Lower* and *Middle Jubba*) and others joined the Transitional National Government (TNG) forces[4].

There is no reliable data on the relative size and strength of the various militia groups in south-central Somalia, but the balance continues to shift steadily in favour of business leaders and away from the armed factions. The relationship between the two groups is complex, and they remain in many respects interdependent. Many of Somalia's *nouveaux riches* class owe their fortunes to the prevailing lawlessness and lack of government no less than do faction leaders. But it is undeniable that this new class of power brokers must play a central role if peace and security are to be restored.

Private Security Guards

A number of militia are engaged as household security guards, small businesses and local and international organizations. Unlike many other armed groups, security guards are traceable as they typically enter into work contracts, and provide background information to employers. Under these circumstances, private security guards provide a necessary and useful function; however, dissatisfaction with work conditions or termination can lead them to become dangerous[5].

Freelance Armed Groups

A growing number of militias in South Central Somalia are guns for hire and owe lasting allegiance to no one at all. It is common for freelance militias to associate in small, autonomous groups of mixed clan composition, for which survival means crime, extortion and violence. Many are habitual drug users, addicted to a combination of stimulants, sedatives and sometimes narcotics[6]. The slang spoken by some members of these groups has evolved into a distinct dialect, virtually unintelligible to outsiders.

The most common activities performed by these groups are:

Assassination: the mercenary nature and mixed clan allegiance make freelance militias well suited to be contracted for killings, for which the instigators and motives often remain undisclosed. Assassinations are also motivated by political rivalry, clan vendettas or business competition. Though uncommon, prominent doctors, engineers, teachers, and military officers have fallen victim to this type of violence. Freelance assassins are suspected of killings several foreigners in Somalia.

Revenge Killing: This is a traditional form of killing that is based on the affiliation of a member of a *diyya* paying clan group to avenge for members killed. During the civil war, the proliferation of weapons into the hands of the clan militia has further exacerbated the extent of such crime and its associated collateral damages.

Kidnappings: Kidnapping is increasingly common. Once a tactic used mainly against expatriates, the victims of kidnapping in recent years have been almost exclusively Somalis —usually for the purpose of ransom or in relation to clan feuds.

Car-jacking: Car-jacking is a common crime throughout Somalia, especially in major cities like Mogadishu, Kismayo, and Galkacyo.

Roadblocks: Factional militia and freelance gunmen often mount roadblocks to collect extortion money from passing traffic.

Rape: A rare occurrence in traditional Somali society in the past, rape of women and abuse of children has become increasingly noticeable since the civil war.

Burglary: This is and was a form of an element of petty crime in the urban areas.

Containment and deterrence of these groups has been tried on many occasions by traditional and religious authorities, Shari 'a courts and neighbourhood committees. A number of civil society initiatives have also attempted to address the dangers they pose. Until the rule of law is restored and alternative livelihoods are available to the members of such groups, freelance militia are likely to remain a pervasive threat to security.

Disarmament, Demobilization and Reintegration

The country faces a major challenge in demobilizing and reintegrating the militias, which are estimated at over 30,000 in Mogadishu alone. Some older fighters have been under arms for over a decade, and are unlikely to adjust easily to a peacetime existence. Others are child soldiers, for whom war and violence have replaced family upbringing and a basic education. Many militiamen across south-central Somalia, are between the ages of fifteen and twenty five, and serve their superiors as informers, roadblock guards, messengers, porters and cooks. Whether or not they have taken a direct part in combat, many have been traumatized by what they have witnessed or the loss of family members, and will require assistance to readjust to normal life.

The demobilization and rehabilitation of Somalia's tens of thousands of militiamen is a prerequisite to recovery, reconstruction and sustainable development. In some parts of the country, notably Somaliland and Puntland, the process of reintegration has made significant progress and militia groups have been replaced with standing military and police establishments. Their success is due in large part to the determination of traditional leaders and the emergence of increasingly effective local authorities. But in South Central Somalia, it appears that these factors alone will be insufficient, and that a more robust approach will be required.

Human Rights and Militarization

During the period of military rule in Somalia (1969-1991), thousands of citizens were persecuted, forced into exile, murdered and tortured. The official lists compiled by human rights organisations report thousands of cases of torture throughout Somalia, particularly in the south-central region, where most state security institutions were headquartered. Torture was employed extensively in detention centres under the Barre government.

Unfortunately, the relatives of victims of human rights abuses have never received justice for their grievances. The government officers that committed these atrocities are frequently among the armed faction leaders that attend reconciliation conferences for Somalia[7]. Since the outbreak of the civil war there have been no indications that the perpetrators of human rights abuses will be brought to justice.

In south-central Somalia, a permanent state of lawlessness and criminality still exists. Young, armed freelance groups have taken advantage of the protracted state collapse by constantly terrorizing defenceless civilians. The civil war, perpetuated by armed political factions, has left behind permanent emotional scars. The traditional Somali respect for human life and dignity has been greatly compromised by years of turmoil. Positive social values based on time-tested kinship ties, both those based on morality, as well as those founded on Islamic principles, have all but been eroded.

Marauding armed gangs have killed tortured and raped innocent civilians. These acts reached frenzy at the height of the civil war. As the war subsided, violations and atrocities continued, albeit to a lesser degree. However, new forms of violence, previously unknown, have, emerged in south-central Somalia, among them, kidnapping (Menkhaus 2003).

The collapse of the powerful Somali Army, and its numerous abandoned arms depot created a huge supply of weapons that the decade long civil war could not exhaust. This enormous supply of weapons went into the hands of the masses, creating a militarized society. Weapons markets flourished in Mogadishu and elsewhere in Somalia and particularly in the south-central regions where the major military weapons depot were situated. The neighbouring countries also provided their share of supply especially after the collapse of subsequent national peace processes.

Although wars subsided and their intensity abated, weapons are in abundant supply in south-central Somalia. Much of these weapons have been transferred into the hands of businessmen, who unlike the warlords, are driven by business ventures rather than military clout. This trend led to the establishment of a crosscutting network that mitigated polarization and tension among clans.

There is irony in that those who have committed human rights abuses, employed armed militias and exploited and manipulated inter-clan warfare for their own political ends in south-central Somalia, are considered by the international community to be the legitimate political leaders of Somalia. Violence committed in the past by individuals and institutions must be linked to current human rights violations, even if motives are significantly different. In south-central Somalia, there are a high number of casualties from politically motivated violence[8].

CRD hosted a forum for the ex-military and police officers in the Banadir region on June 2003, to understand the past and current effects of militarization in Somalia. The forum was intended to explore as well the sense and analysis of the nature of the conflict and security in Somalia and the Banadir region. CRD has captured the discussions and deliberation of this forum in a video film that could be valuable for the future disarmament, demobilization and security of the government and regional/international efforts in this regard.

The Social Position of Women

Background

Traditionally, Somali men and women have occupied different roles and held different responsibilities in society. Women were responsible primarily for the caring of children and managing the household. Men, on the other hand, were expected to be breadwinners and provide physical security to the family. This division of labour found divine sanction in the Islamic faith, which encourages women to seek self-realization and spiritual salvation through the dutiful execution of household obligations.

The tradition-bound civilian regime (1960-69), did not make women's rights a high priority. In the post-colonial administration men held all top political and administrative posts. Although women's right to vote or stand for elections were guaranteed in the constitution, women were *de facto* able only to vote for men and did not run for office. However, during the Barre regime, the rights of Somali women gained wider public acknowledgment. The government introduced a number of laws that brought about significant changes in women's status. As a consequence of this legislation, as well as increasing access to education, Somali women were able, in the 1970s and 1980s, to break down some of the socio-political barriers that inhibited their advancement. New opportunities opened up for women in both private and public sectors. A small but significant number of women rose to executive positions in the government and to mid-level ranks within the armed forces. But the most dramatic change occurred in the number of women employed as clerks, teachers, nurses and veterinarians.

Education for Women

Women in Somalia have historically been denied full access to social services, including education. However, since independence, the gender disparity—especially in primary education—has been reduced. Both the civilian and military administrations strove to broaden and improve education for girls. In 1970, the military regime instituted a co-education policy which significantly boosted the enrolment of female children in public schools. By the early 1980s, girls accounted for about 34 percent of all schoolchildren. The government collapse and civil war ended and even reversed this trend.

Since the fall of the Barre regime many primary schools in south-central Somalia have reopened. However, the education system is at far below capacity. In absolute terms, the enrolment of girls is appallingly low. Relatively speaking, though, the disparity is less significant. A 2002 UNICEF study revealed that girls account for 33 percent of the primary school population, virtually the same as the pre-civil war era. School attendance for girls dramatically decreases with age, and is evident starting from the third grade[9]. In secondary school, enrolment of girls is extremely low. For example at Abu-Bakar Siddiq Secondary School in Marka, *Lower Shabelle*, girls constitute only 5 percent of total high school students, while in the same city, female primary school enrolment is as high as 45 percent.[10]

Adult and Domestic Education for Women

Before the civil war, the Ministry of Education provided adult female education through the Institute of Women's Education (IWE)[11] and the National Institute of Adult Education (NIAE). In 1984, IWE opened several Family Life Centres (FLCs) in different quarters of Mogadishu. The success of the pilot project inspired the establishment of 66 more FLCs in different districts throughout the country. Most of these were in large cities and regional capitals.[12] FLCs taught literacy, numeracy, home economics, basic hygiene, nutrition and skill trainings—i.e., sewing, handicrafts and embroidery. After the fall of the military regime, FLCs, like many other public facilities, were ransacked.

At present, there is an acute shortage of adult and domestic education in south-central Somalia. Recently, a few voluntary women's organizations launched income-generating domestic education projects for women in a number of urban areas. Despite limited resources and experience, these are intended to fulfil some functions previously provided by government education centres. Among the most notable of these are:

IDA and AYUB. These are NGOs based in the city of Marka, *Lower Shabelle*. They provide basic education and skills training, such as domestic science and farming techniques. Both NGOs also feed and care for orphans. Additionally, AYUB provides day care for small children, especially orphans and those of poor families, whose mothers work outside the home. The day care service is extremely important and helpful for working mothers, since their children are fed and looked after while they are at work.

The Ricardo Centre. This centre is located in *Baidoa,* and is named after its Italian benefactor, who was killed in that city. The Ricardo is the only adult education school for women functioning in the *Bay* and *Bakool* regions. It offers short courses in basic education and skills training in sewing, cooking and embroidery. The centre's training program is of extremely short duration because of a shortage of funds and lack of suitable facilities. Therefore, it has not been able to fulfill its income-generation objectives[13].

Samatalis and Salbarwaaqo. These two NGOs operate in *Afgooye* and *Beled Weyne*, respectively. They help poor women by creating for them income-generating activities, such as traditional handicrafts and embroidery. Despite considerable improvement recently, female domestic education in South-Central Somalia is negligible. Many women CRD interviewed expressed keen interest in adult and domestic science education. These women also pointed out that former FLC teachers, as well as facilities, can be found in many towns within the WSP International project area.

Women's Access to Health Care

Women's access to health care in Somalia has always been restricted; war and subsequent lawlessness have only had an exacerbatory effect. The inadequacy of health facilities and paucity of qualified health professionals—gynaecologists, nurses and midwives—has sharply affected women and children. Among major maladies and health conditions that women face include: Anaemia and nutritional problems, caused by insufficient food consumption; pre-natal problems such as preeclampsia; birth complications such as prolonged labour, abnormal child deliveries and internal haemorrhaging; tetanus and infections resulting from the use of unclean equipment during delivery and post-natal complications caused by childhood infibulations[14]. In addition, women are afflicted with other serious diseases that are common to society at large: malaria, jaundice, syphilis and other STDs, TB and cholera, among others. Women also suffer from malnutrition and vitamin deficiencies, which drastically reduce resistance to diseases.

Effects of War on Women

The steady progress of women's rights under the military regime was curtailed by the civil war. Subsequently, the role of women in society underwent many changes. Through necessity, women became breadwinners for their families. Besides shouldering the burden of supporting the family economically, women have endured extraordinary physical and psychological stress, in the form of rape, abuse, murder, kidnapping and robbery. Although frequently the sole breadwinners for their families, women often feel unsafe going about their daily business.

The civil war has had a disruptive effect on family life. In Somalia, marriage is sanctioned not only by social conventions but sanctified by the Islamic faith. Traditionally, parents usually arranged marriages for their children soon after they reached puberty. The marriage of girls, in particular, was a very serious matter in which parents invested much effort and emotion[15]. More recently, marriage like many other aspects of Somali culture, has undergone profound change; non-arranged marriages without family blessing have become as common as arranged ones.[16]

This change represents not only a drastic departure from cultural precedent but a new threat to the welfare and security of women and children. The diminution of parental oversight in marriage has resulted in an increased rate of teenage marriages and consequently a high divorce rate. Usually, when a marriage between teens ends, the care of children and, in some cases, the divorcee herself, reverts to her parents. This puts an undue burden on families and, perhaps, society at large, particularly if the family is destitute.

The Economic Impact of Dual Responsibility

Women in Somalia contribute greatly to the national economy. They are heavily involved in agriculture, livestock, manufacturing, processing, services, petty commerce, and many other income generating activities.[17] In most of these economic sectors, women perform the labour intensive, low profit work.

In agricultural communities, women constitute a high percentage of the workforce and execute such tasks as land preparation, harvesting, threshing grains and rearing livestock. They sell milk products, eggs and meat[18] and perform laborious and menial tasks like collecting water, fuel, wood, farm products and fodder for animals from long distances. Women in retail businesses are usually occupied in low margin enterprises—selling grains, meat, vegetables, fruits, cigarettes, used clothes, charcoal, candy, toiletries, and *Qat,*. Women also run kiosks and neighbourhood shops in every city, town and village in the country. There are a number of drawbacks attendant on the types of businesses women are involved in including a shortage of investment capital; harsh working conditions; lack of day care assistance; an insecure environment; low income potential and stresses of marriage.

Women in Politics

Traditionally, Somali women played a marginal role in politics. Under the old social scheme, they were expected solely to manage household affairs— raise children and comfort husbands. During the clan *"shir"*, the most important political institution in the country, women were barred from direct participation. As a patriarchal society, Somalis felt that only males could represent clan, subclan or other interests and take authoritative political decisions. Accordingly, only males could indulge in politics and entertain the ambition of accreting political power. To women, on the other hand, fell the role of the confidant— to offer advice and encouragement to their politically active husbands.

Despite these traditional barriers, women's involvement in politics has deep roots, dating back to the colonial era. During the Trusteeship period, there was a robust women's independence movement in Somalia. In affiliation with the Somali Youth League (SYL), then the largest nationalist organization in the country, the women's movement played an indispensable role in the mobilization of society for political independence. Using the organizational structure of the SYL, Somali women established and operated many branches throughout the colonial territory. Following independence, with the goal of liberation achieved, the women's movement slowly withered away.

Throughout the sixties, women's involvement in politics was minimal. However as noted previously, women made significant socio-political strides during the Barre regime. The most dramatic shift in women's political involvement occurred in 2000, during the Djibouti-sponsored Arta Peace Conference. At Arta, women took a lead role in resolving local conflicts, grassroots mobilization, promotion of human rights, and advocacy of public health and education. Owing to the tremendous contribution that women made, as well as intense lobbying and pressure from Somali civil society and international NGOs, Somali women gained seats both in the legislative and executive councils of the Transitional National Government (TNG).[19]

Currently, Somali women are heavily involved in the national reconciliation process underway in Mbagathi, Kenya. In keeping with their traditional status as "gentle ladies," women are facilitators and intermediaries among the contending groups—resolving a variety of political impasses and deadlocks. In Mbagathi (and previously in Eldoret, where talks were begun), women have waged political campaigns to pressure men to reach peaceful settlements through consensus. The contribution of Somali women in the ongoing peace conferences is simply remarkable. Somali delegates and members of the international community alike have acknowledged and praised their invaluable contributions.

Somali women are also very much a part of peace building initiatives at home. Currently, a loose coalition of approximately 100 women's groups is active on the *Benadir* Coast. Exerting leverage as mothers, sisters, daughters and wives, the coalition launched a powerful grassroots peace movement three years ago.[20] Since they began to cooperate, these female associations have organized peace rallies, lobbied local leaders to curb and defuse violence, and helped lift road blockades within Mogadishu. These actions undoubtedly undermined war profiteers by reducing tension and armed conflict. Many women use radio and television to urge Somalis in general to engage in the ongoing peace process.[21]

Despite a newfound prominence in post-state affairs, Somali women lack the wherewithal and clout to maintain (let alone advance) their socio-political standing in society. Due to the lack of institutional mechanisms to aid them in capacity building, public relations or fundraising, there is the chance women might be unable to consolidate their gains. With even limited institutional support, Somali women can have a far reaching impact on society. For instance, the Mogadishu-based women's umbrella association, the Coalition for Grassroots Women's Organization (COGWO) was, after receiving modest financial and technical support from CRD/WSP International, able to raise public awareness and promote local peace initiatives to new levels. Currently, the organization is engaged in a grass-roots peace-building project involving over 750 women from all districts of the *Benaadir* region. COGWO plans to achieve sustainable peace through dialogue and social development.[22]

Women and Civil Society

As previously mentioned, women's involvement in civil society dates back to the colonial era. Today, Somali civil society is largely comprised of national NGOs and their local affiliates. Since the collapse of the state in 1991, these types of organizations have proliferated. Many of these organizations are led by visionary women, whose energy and political skill are widely recognized. COGWO is once more a good example: it was formed in 1996 to unite 20 different women organizations under one umbrella; COGWO empowers women through capacity building, raising awareness and advocacy for women's rights. Since its founding, the organization has documented more than 400 cases of violence against women and provided counselling and emotional support to these victims.[23]

The efforts of women's organizations are frequently hampered by negative perceptions. Many Somalis believe that civil-society groups are foreign tools designed to disrupt the Somali way of life. Another view holds that non governmental organizations are nothing more than moneyspinners for their managers and supporting staff.

Conclusion

Through most of Somalia's history, women have been socially, economically and politically marginalized. In general, they had limited access to education, health care and political leadership. Much of this can be blamed on tradition and custom. However, part of the problem lies with economic underdevelopment. As an impoverished country, Somalia lacks minimal amount of resources to handle all necessary social programs. This is most evident in the rural areas, where the majority of the population lives. In these parts of the country, there is a dearth of public investment in education and health care. In situations like these, the most vulnerable section of society is usually overlooked during the distribution of resources.

Despite these cultural and economic limitations, the involvement of Somali women in politics has been increasing for the past three decades. Since the early 1970s, women have been visibly present in most political and social settings in Somalia. Although certain economic and social improvements have occurred, it seems that the principal cause is the changing attitude of women themselves. During the MR, women took a leading role in the political mobilization of society. Again, after the collapse of the government in 1991, they assumed the new role of promoting peace. Because of their bold contributions, both the Somali and non-Somali political operative realize how indispensable women's role is in the on-going political saga in Somalia. There are encouraging signs that women's involvement in politics will increase in the foreseeable future.

References

Maria Brons. (2001) *Society, Security, Sovereignty and the State: Somalia.* Utrecht: International Books.

United Nations Security Council (S/2003/223): (24 February 2003) *Report of the Panel of Experts on Somalia pursuant to Security Council resolution 1425 (2002),*

International Crisis Group (ICG): (6 March 2003) *Negotiating a Blueprint for Peace in Somalia.* Africa Report No. 59, Mogadishu/Brussels,

CRD/UNICEF report: (January 2003) "impact of small arms on children and youth in south-central Somalia"

Menkhaus, Ken. (2003) "*Protracted State Collapse in Somalia: A Rediagnosis* – Review of Africa Political Economy

UNICEF: (1998) Children and Women in Somalia, a situation analysis, UNICEF Somalia.

1. This chapter stems from the book 'Somalia: Path to Recovery Building a Sustainable Peace', Center for Research and Dialogue (an affiliate of WSP International), 2004. The authors of the 'Path to Recovery', were invited to present their recently finished study to the Somali Studies International Association Conference in 2004. But,

because of their important role in the Somali Peace Process, they had to change plans and leave for Nairobi, as the Peace Conference there was entering a crucial stage. We decided to include a part of the Path to Recovery anyway, partly as a tribute to their work and special contribution for peaceful change in Somalia, and especially to commemorate Abdulkadir Yahya Ali, who was assassinated in Mogadishu in July 2005.

2. For an-depth study of the relationship between the state and security in Somalia, see Maria Brons, Society, Security, Sovereignty and the State: Somalia. Utrecht: International Books, 2001.

3. On Dec. 24, 2002 unidentified gunmen opened fire indiscriminately upon a school bus, killing three and injuring 11 in Mogadishu. Similarly, early 1991 75 innocent civilians from minority clans were massacred in north Mogadishu.

4. Upon establishment of the TNG in Mogadishu, its newly armed forces were absorbed into the pre-existing militia of the Shari'a courts in and around Mogadishu. Also, a number of Shari'a court clerics were appointed to the new judicial systems of the TNG.

5.For example, in early 2001, a security guard hired by the French charity ACF in Mogadishu was laid off. He later attacked the ACF compound, looted agency property and kidnapped expatriates with the help of freelance militia.

6.It is inconceivable to talk about simple disarmament schemes without a community-based initiative supported by international and national actors to rehabilitate these uncoordinated armed groups.

7. One-on-one interview, Marka March (2004).

8. Interview by CRD with Human Rights advocates in Mogadishu, March 2004.

9. According to the chairman of FPENS: 'The enrolment of girls in lower primary schools increases and then noticeably decreases as the education level goes higher from grades three onwards.' Similar patterns are discernible in other parts of the country.

10. This was reported by the education Committee of Marka in 14/01/2002,

11.WES (Women Education service) and WED (Women Education Department) are former names of IWE.

12.IEES(Improving the Efficiency of the Educational System), Somalia Education and Human Resource Sector Assessment, Coordinated for the government of the Somali Democratic Republic by the ministry of National Planning with USAID, January 1984, p. 13-6.

13..There are two adult schools in Jowhar and Dinsor, but they are virtually nonfunctioning due to a shortage of funds.

14.Dr. Abdinur Sheikh, a medical doctor interviewed by CRD/WSP

International claimed that he had operated on 38 cases in which birthing complications resulting from female circumcision.

15. Parents paid special attention to, and had the final say in, the selection of a qualified suitor for their daughter.

16. Marriages have the potential to create strong ties or enmity between the families and clans of the betrothed.

17.SWDO, Women in SDR, An Appraisal of progress in the implementation of the World Plan of Action of the United Nations Decade for women-1975-1985, UNICEF Somalia,1985, P. 1V(Hereafter Women in SDR. The number of women engaged in petty commerce and trade was always relatively very small compared to men.

18. UNICEF, Children and Women in Somalia, a situation analysis, UNICEF Somalia, 1998 p.12-5[hereafter, UNICEF Somalia, 1997/1998].

19. Women in south-central Somalia are unfortunately partially absent from the local councils of municipal and traditional authorities established during UNOSOM II in 1993/5. Women are excluded from the decision making-processes at regional and district levels

20. Between 1991-95, some Somali women admittedly took part in the civil war, siding with the armed militiamen of their clan in a show of solidarity. This tendency has virtually vanished and today women are almost unanimously opposed to the continuation of violence and lawlessness.

21. CRD/WSP International organized a capacity-building and advocacy training workshop intended to enhance women's skill base.

22. This initiative has been successful - in part - because of the capacity-building support provided by CRD and the funds provided by Washington DC-based organization, the National Endowment for Democracy.

23. Aini Abukar Ga'al, head of the documentation unit at COGWO, Mogadishu, 2003. Other notable women's organizations include IDA and AYUB in Merka, Lower Shabelle region.

Chapter 10

The Somali Peace Talks and Human Rights

Martin Hill

Introduction

This paper describes and analyses the Somalia peace talks from a human rights perspective. They are just now concluding in Kenya, with the formation of a new Transitional Federal Government apparently imminent. Issues of post-conflict reconstruction, including transitional justice and reconciliation in relation to the abuses of the past, are also addressed.[1].

Soon after state collapse 13 years ago, some Somali scholars considered that the absence of a state was tolerable in view of the existence of Somali cultural institutions of "governance" at non-state level, and that plenty of time was needed to achieve a viable re-institution of state government. This might be characterized as a position of "no government can be good government".

The period of the UN intervention (1992-1995) ended with universal agreement that only Somalis themselves could design an appropriate form of government to end state collapse. It was by then generally accepted by Somalis as well as the international community that "no government is bad government". There were numerous unsuccessful peace talks, continued intermittent warlordism, but some positive experiences at local community level with the development of civil society organizations.

The disadvantages of state collapse and political violence are now seen more starkly. International concern at the risks this poses for international and regional peace and stability has risen, partly as a consequence of the "war against terrorism". The need to resolve the conflicts and achieve reconciliation has become even more apparent. The mood now could be described as having shifted to the current consensus that "bad government would be better than no government". Steps are however being taken to try to ensure that there are adequate protections against the risks of "bad government" or even a collapse of government amid renewed violent conflict and leading to continuation of state collapse, which might take many years to reverse.

The Human Rights Background.[2]

The Siad Barre government in Somalia originated in a military coup in 1969 after nine years of civilian multi-party government following independence in 1960. It ended in 1991 when it was overthrown by armed opposition forces based in Ethiopia. The Siad Barre government was marked by brutal repression of opposition, narrow clannist rule, a military-based one-party system, corruption and economic mismanagement. The government was responsible for a persistent pattern of gross human rights violations, including near-genocide by the army in the northwest, culminating in massacres and bombing in Hargeisa in 1988; systematic torture of political prisoners by the National Security Service; arbitrary and long-term detentions of thousands of prisoners of conscience; grossly unfair trials by National Security Courts; many judicial executions (including executions of prominent sheikhs in 1975); numerous extra-judicial political killings; and harsh treatment of prisoners in special security prisons.

Within months of the Siad Barre forces fleeing Mogadishu in early 1991, the south disintegrated into clan-based political violence and civil war. In the north-west in 1991, the Somali National Movement (SNM) force defeated the Somali army and unilaterally declared independence for Somaliland from the rest of Somalia, within the borders of the former British Somaliland Protectorate. A UN operation began during a horrendous famine in south-western Somalia in 1992, followed by a huge armed UN intervention ("Operation Restore Hope"). UNOSOM withdrew in 1995 with little achieved in terms of re-establishing peace, disarming armed factions or reconstructing a central government, local councils or justice system.

The UN and EU, classifying different areas as "crisis", "transition" and "recovery", tried a "building-block" approach to reconstruction of regional administrations, on models similar to Somaliland (although it was unrecognised) and Puntland (a regional state proclaimed in 1998). They worked to build local administrations, and had some success in Baidoa, subsequently destroyed by General Mohamed Hussein Aideed's military invasion lasting two years. No other such "building block" attained any reality. The whole of the south ("Somalia" excluding Puntland and Somaliland) was regarded as unsafe and hardly even in transition to "recovery" (though with temporary pockets of peace). In early 2004 the UN High Commission for Refugees opposed returns to the south of even rejected Somali asylum-seekers on account of the absence of security.

A peace conference convened at Arta in Djibouti in 2000 by Djibouti's President Ismail Omar Guelleh, mustered civil society but not all the warlords. A transitional parliament was selected from the Arta delegates and a Transitional National Government (TNG) installed in Mogadishu. There was continuous rivalry between, on the one hand, the TNG, which was informally recognized by the UN, Arab League and EU and supported by some southern Somali factions, and, on the other hand, the Ethiopia-backed faction coalition of the Somali Reconciliation and Restoration Council (SRRC). The TNG, with a three-year term, controlled only a fraction of Mogadishu and did not manage to establish national jurisdiction (even in the south), or a central army and police force, or any system of administration of justice. In some areas Islamic courts with armed militias and prisons provided some security but otherwise protection was sought from within the clan system. Those without clan protection – the unarmed minorities – suffered most. Faction militias controlled different territorial areas, with total impunity for their crimes; kidnappings were widespread of anyone with international connections and hence potential ransom money of US$5,000-10,000, and killing, kidnapping, robbery and rape were common, especially against the minorities. Many Somali NGOs developed during this period, working on a wide variety of rights issues, including human rights defenders, as civil society sought to counter-balance the power of the warlords and re-establish basic security and livelihoods[3].

In the northeast, the Puntland Regional State was unilaterally declared in 1998 as a future part of a federal Somalia, but its progress and developing administration were held back by internal armed conflict (although not on a large scale) between forces of Abdullahi Yusuf (hitherto President) and Jama Ali Jama – both former colonels in Siad Barre's army, both former political prisoners of Siad Barre, and from rival Majerten (Darod) subclans. This conflict started with a constitutional and political crisis in 2001. There was a reconciliation accord signed in 2003 between the two forces, although Jama Ali Jama had by then been sidelined politically by the group originally supporting him. Abdullahi Yusuf, despite the question of his government's constitutional legitimacy, became the generally-recognised President of Puntland and also a prime candidate for the presidency of Somalia. Puntland remained autonomous (like Somaliland) and rejected TNG control, though participating in the peace talks. It began a territorial dispute with Somaliland, which led to some fighting in 2003 and continued tension.

The *de facto* independent Somaliland Republic under a civilian government has not yet received international recognition. It is the only part of the former Somalia to have achieved peace and stability, and reconciliation between former supporters and opponents in its territory of the Siad Barre government. Somaliland continues to press its demand for international recognition, and it has complained about being largely excluded from the "peace dividend" policy of the international community and donors - rewarding peaceful areas with development aid as a means of conflict control. Government institutions have developed slowly but steadily in Somaliland, with a peaceful transfer of power to Vice-President Dahir Riyaale Kahin (a former National Security Service commander in the Siad Barre administration, now President) when President Mohamed Ibrahim Egal died in May 2002. There has generally been peace and security, apart from two brief outbreaks of clan-based fighting and a currently difficult security situation; general respect for human rights and an active local NGO community (although there have been recent cases of arbitrary detention, media repression and unfair political trials); and a substantial degree of democratization, with multi-party elections held in December 2002 for local councils and in April 2003 for the presidency, and with parliamentary elections scheduled for 2005. Somaliland has boycotted the Kenya peace talks and has refused to be part of the outcome, or of Somalia.

The Somalia Peace Talks in Kenya

In October 2002 the 14th Somalia peace talks since the 1991 disintegration of the Somali Republic opened in a hotel in Eldoret in western Kenya. The "Somalia National Reconciliation Conference" was sponsored by IGAD.[4]., funded by the EU and Arab States.[5], hosted by the neighbouring Kenya government through its Foreign Minister, and administered by the Nairobi-based European Commission-Somalia Unit.[6]. The aim was to bring together all the relevant actors - the political factions, international partners, and civil society in a three-phase initiative: to attain a cease-fire, agree on the key issues of reconstruction in Somalia., and create a new interim inclusive government to replace the Transitional National Government, whose three-year term of office ended in August 2003.[7]. The government was intended to be for the whole of the former Somalia, as backed by specific statements on the "unity and integrity" of the state, maps posted on UN websites, and the use of the former Somali flag.[8].

The Conference Facilitation Committee consisted of two frontline states, Ethiopia and Djibouti, and the "International Partners Forum" of relevant governments and donors, with a Kenyan chairperson (Foreign

Minister Elijah Mwangale initially). The Ethiopian diplomatic representative was an ethnic Somali, and the Djibouti representative likewise (as is the Djibouti President) – though from different clans to those inside Somalia. Meetings were also followed attended by the UN agencies and international NGOs. There is also a Somalia Aid Coordination Body (SACB), a grouping of donors and international and local NGOs (who also have an NGO Consortium). All are based in Nairobi on account of the security dangers for international staff in Somalia, although most have small locally-staffed offices in Somalia.[9].

The process itself has been open-ended, to the extent that there was no real consensus on expectations, and often no-one really knew what was going to happen from day to day. It took considerable ingenuity on all sides to analyse and handle the constant mini-crises, ranging from the logistical to the political – including trying to settle outbreaks of fighting within Somalia by militias of warlords attending the conference. Deadlines for decisions were constantly breached. At the outset it was not imagined that the process would take two years and cost so much. Previous peace talks which had failed to greater or lesser degrees had taken place in different venues and with different sponsors and participants but this was the most inclusive so far (with all warlords attending out of fear of sanctions – threatened but never imposed). It seemed to be the most politically neutral and realistic at the outset. It was built on general recognition of the failure of the TNG to establish itself and deliver its mandate, and the need for a new solution after the failure of the Arta agreement.[10].

The conference succeeded in obtaining the presence and participation of all the warlords, the TNG (whose President stayed away until nearly the end), and large numbers of "civil society". There were major logistical and political issues over recognition of delegates[11] and funding.[12] of the conference. The agreement reached about delegates (as established at the Arta conference) was for a 4.5 quota system overall for attendance and future parliamentary representation. This consisted of the three pastoralist clans (Darod, Dir and Hawiye), the agricultural/riverine Digil-Mirifle (or Rahenwein), and a half-share for the discriminated minorities.[13].

"Civil society" was a label for all delegates (self-appointed) except the "leaders" (warlords). It thus included "traditional leaders" (from clans and minorities), Muslim religious leaders, prominent civilians from the time of the former government, political figures from the Diaspora or within the country who turned up at the conference, with or without any financial or political backing or representation, and some members of NGOs in Mogadishu, such as the Coalition of

Grassroots Women Organization (COGWO) and the Dr Ismail Jumale Human Rights Organization (DIJHRO), who were not given any status or representation. Many "civil society delegates" were allegedly connected to factions and warlords through their clans.

This arrangement inevitably strengthened "clannism", since the factions were clan-based and it marginalised genuine civil society and effective local NGOs. At the same time it offered a small opportunity for clans (as well as business and religious leaders) to pressure warlords to make peace and consider objectives other than power and war profiteering. The number of civil society delegates was cut down for both financial and political reasons, from over 1,000 who turned up at the start, to 460 and later to 360 at the time of the move to Mbagathi, despite complaints from those excluded.

As expected, Somaliland's government and civil society boycotted the conference, as it denied Somaliland its desired independence. The conference organisers tried to prevent discussions of this issue, so as not to damage the possibility of Somaliland being later invited or drawn back into a unified federal Somalia at some time in the future. There were, however, self-selected delegates from Somaliland (or rather "the northwest", to use the UN and "unity" terminology) who opposed Somaliland's independence and advocated union with the rest of the former Somalia. These "federalists" or "unionists", considered "traitors" by the Somaliland government, had little status at the outset of the conference but eventually became members of the new Transitional National Assembly for Somalia through the clan-based allocation of seats – Somaliland refused to send or allow Dir clan elders to participate.

There was also a delegate problem over the Puntland internal conflict. The conference accepted Abdullahi Yusuf as the Puntland President (backed and reportedly armed by Ethiopia) but his rival Jama Ali Jama (supported by the TNG, and from a different Majerten subclan) managed to remain at the conference, despite attempts to exclude and de-recognise him.

Phase I

A Cessation of Hostilities declaration was achieved in two weeks, on 27 October 2002, and signed by all 13 faction leaders and the TNG. However, ceasefire violations have occurred frequently in inter-faction fighting or fighting between the TNG and opposed factions. The international partners informally threatened to impose "smart sanctions", such as international visa refusals, residence and passport withdrawals and freezing of foreign bank accounts, against cease-fire violators or any leaders who withdrew from the talks, but the threat was never formally made or implemented. In Bay region there was fighting between subclan factions of the Rahenwein Resistance Army (RRA). In Gedo region, Marehan subclans frequently were in conflict. In Kismayu and the southwest there was a tense peace under the Juba Valley Alliance (JVA), threatened by the force of General Mohamed Said Hersi "Morgan", the most dangerous warlord.

Phase II

This commenced in late 2002 with six "technical committees" (civil society getting one-third of committee places) to discuss key policy issues which would be the principles of future government policy:

- Creation of a Charter (interim Constitution), to settle especially the question of adopting a centralised state structure or a variety of federalism.
- Economic recovery, with international donor assistance.
- Land and property rights - recovery of land, arms and houses seized by faction militias, the Siad Barre government and its officials, and pre-independence colonial interests.
- Disarmament and demobilization of faction militias (including child soldiers) and their integration into new trained and accountable state forces.
- Regional and international relations.
- Conflict resolution and reconciliation, including human rights protections and issues of accountability for abuses of the past.

Most committees had an international resource-person designated to assist, but there was no human rights advisor to give human rights a higher profile and assist the sixth committee.

In January 2003 the talks moved from Eldoret to Mbagathi on the outskirts of Nairobi, for a cheaper and more suitable venue and under a more experienced Kenyan peace talks chairperson, Ambassador Bethuel Kiplagat. In April 2003 the UN Commission on Human Rights, which had been engaged with human rights issues in Somalia since the time of the Siad Barre government, and works with an Independent Expert appointed for Somalia, issued a resolution on human rights in Somalia calling for international assistance for human rights reconstruction. Amnesty International also called for human rights commitments from a future interim parliament.[14].

In May 2003 the six committee reports were debated by the conference plenary and adopted. A Somali experts committee worked to harmonise different positions on the "federalism" versus "centralization" issue. Consensus on this was the most difficult element, with several delays, boycotts and walkouts. Only strong pressure from the IGAD foreign ministers – Ethiopia and Djibouti now cooperating to rescue the peace talks from imminent failure - and from the international partners obtained agreement on a Transitional Federal Charter in May 2004, with subsequent minor dissent successfully ignored.

The Charter specifies a decentralized federal government, with regional bodies, and election of parliament by the clans through sub-sub clan levels, rather than by the faction leaders. Its aim is "to foster reconciliation, national unity and good governance". It contains important provisions for human rights and the rule of law, guaranteeing separation of powers and the independence of the judiciary. Chapter Five on "Protection of the Fundamental Rights and Freedoms of the People" proclaims the equality of citizens before the law; the rights to life, personal liberty and security; fair trial rights, including the right to be brought before a court within 48 hours of arrest; the right to form political parties (except for any of "a military character or tribal character"), trade unions and social organizations, including human rights organizations; the rights to assemble, demonstrate and strike; and the right to freedom of opinion and expression, including the freedom of the press.

Phase III

The final phase commenced in May 2004. It was to form a new all-inclusive interim parliament and government of Somalia, with the consensus of the political leaders and civil society, to replace the TNG. The procedure agreed was for selection of an interim Transitional Federal Assembly (TFA - parliament) which would elect a Speaker and Deputy Speakers to organise the election by the TFA of a President of Somalia. The President would then appoint a Prime Minister who would form a Government. The Transitional Federal Government (TFG) would then be formally recognized by the international community and the collapse of the state would then be theoretically ended.[15].

During Phase III there was a decision to bring in traditional clan elders (to assert clan ownership of the conference and thus, in the hopes of many, to sideline the faction leaders) and Muslim religious leaders from Somalia (as advisors) to the conference. This slightly shifted the balance away from the warlords, whose factions and militias were theoretically dissolved by the Charter, although the situation on the ground was unchanged. In accordance with the Charter requirement, the new 275-member parliament was selected on the same 4.5 formula as the conference delegates. Each clan had to be allocated its share of seats - 61 for each clan and half (31) for the minorities, with 12% of seats (33) reserved for women, to be allocated by their fathers' clans. The Charter specified that members of parliament should be selected by the clans at sub-sub clan level (even though these were not numerically or genealogically equal, or regionally or geographically representative) and according to the different minority groups. An Arbitration Committee was set up to resolve disputes arising from each group's selection, consisting of members of each clan, with members of the clan with a dispute withdrawing for that decision.

This arrangement attained general support among the conference delegates, despite many disputes of detail in the selection process. Amnesty International issued a call for human rights to be a priority in the transitional period.

As it became evident that the process would be completed and not break down, Somali businesspeople formally committed themselves to supporting the outcome and the new TFG. At a special meeting in Djibouti arranged by the donors in July 2004, the "moneylords" (a new term in current usage) who had established several profitable and mainly Middle-East-based businesses in Somalia during the collapsed-state conflicts, agreed to accept some central regulation within a private-sector oriented economy in exchange for governmental commercial protections and security. Hitherto their businesses – which provided no revenue for any public services - had been protected by payments to faction militias, but with a trend to setting up their own militias independently. Without their financing, factions had been weakened and unable to pay their militias to fight rivals.[16].

Ambassador Kiplagat announced in late July 2004 that the selection and swearing-in of the new parliament would proceed immediately, even if it was incomplete due to disputes over delegates, and that this would lead as quickly as possible to the establishment of the TFG. Thus by mid-August most of the new parliament had been selected in clan meetings, which were "closed" and far from transparent, and in September the 275 MPs were sworn in at the UN compound in Gigiri near Nairobi. The women's quota was astonishingly one-third short.

Despite the supposed dissolution of factions under the Charter, faction leaders had mostly succeeded in getting their own candidates into parliament, as well as themselves. Thus all the warlords (whose numbers had increased) were in parliament, with one exception – General "Morgan", who had absented himself from Phase III. In August, Ambassador Kiplagat requested IGAD sanctions against him for withdrawing from the peace process - not for human rights abuses. However, a more serious situation arose in early September when General "Morgan" began to launch a new attack on the southern port of

Kismayu, which was loosely controlled by the Juba Valley Alliance.

This was a serious last-minute threat to the outcome of the peace talks.[17].

Update, January 2005

> *In October the Puntland president, Abdullahi Yusuf Ahmed, was elected President. He appointed Ali Mohamed Ghedi, a non-warlord, as Prime Minister. After a faulty start, the TFG named by the Prime Minister was set up in January 2005 with parliamentary assent, and expected to move to Somalia as soon as possible.*

Transitional Justice and Reconciliation

The key issue of justice in the transition from conflict towards peaceful democratic government was whether those who had committed war crimes, crimes against humanity or gross human rights abuses in the past, during the Siad Barre government or the civil conflicts since 1991, would be prosecuted, either during the transitional period or later, or would benefit from impunity.

At first, the warlords were reportedly planning to grant themselves a general and unconditional amnesty -most had been involved in human rights abuses and faction fighting. The international partners were not directly opposing this, with a "peace at all costs" line. The "blanket amnesty" notion, criticized by Amnesty International and unacceptable in international law, has been pulled back, but without any clear idea emerging yet of a way forward which would prevent total impunity and yet still keep all the warlords inside the process.

These issues of transitional justice have been widely discussed in Somali civil society but fearfully, and rarely directly and openly, due to intimidation by warlords, who might visit reprisals on their accusers. Even outspoken media and NGOs campaigning against political killings, abductions and rape by faction militias in Mogadishu have not dared to name the factions or individual commanders or militias responsible, although they are believed to possess such information and evidence which witnesses might give to a future inquiry or prosecution, provided their safety was guaranteed. Faction leaders are reportedly "scared" about talk of war crimes inquiries and ready to take any steps necessary to guarantee their own impunity and safeguard illegally-acquired gains, while pretending to cooperate or even claiming to support human rights.

It is up to the Somali people to decide during the transitional period how to approach the question of past abuses and when. Various possibly acceptable options are available ranging from conditional amnesty to truth-telling mechanisms or criminal prosecutions. For war crimes and crimes against humanity, the International Criminal Court could be the means to try offences committed after the establishment of the court in mid-2002, but not retroactively for offences before then. Prosecutions in Somali courts would only be possible and acceptable when there is a well-established and competent criminal justice system to bring perpetrators to justice and guarantee fair trial – which is not the case now. There would be nothing gained for future protection of rights through unfair trials. Anti-death penalty groups would also demand the non-application of the death penalty so as to prevent another human rights violation. There is no likelihood of a special international tribunal being established for Somalia, as was the case for the former Yugoslavia and Rwanda.

As regards mechanisms of reconciliation, there is no perfect universal model or system providing all the answers for the Somalia case without any disadvantages. What would work in Somalia would depend on cultural and political acceptability and the needs of the situation. Information could be collected on the worst perpetrators and the worst abuses, and eyewitnesses would be available to give evidence. This kind of documentation has not yet started in earnest, apart from materials published by international NGOs at the time, such as Africa Watch.[18], and the newly-trained Somali NGOs, some of which would be useful as background for truth-telling by victims and witnesses, or developed in more precise form for criminal prosecutions.

Some perpetrators were among the leaders or other delegates at the peace talks - a peculiar situation where they were daily in the sight of people whose relatives had been killed by them or their forces, as well as before international observers who would want to see them on trial. They appeared to have the protection of their clans, irrespective of their crimes.

Amnesty International said that it

> "would find it unacceptable for those responsible for such crimes to be included in any new government, which would be expected to be wholeheartedly committed to the rule of law and respect for human rights. Granting total impunity a general amnesty would not bring lasting peace to Somalia. In practice it would open the door to new violations by the same perpetrators, who would make sure they continued to silence their accusers, and it would encourage others to hope to go unpunished. To the extent that it is possible, an interim government should comprise only members with a clean human rights record and non-involvement with abuses."

Human rights during the Transition

The first year of the five-year transition, leading to multi-party elections and a permanent Constitution by 2009/10, will be a critical period for establishment of the TFG, confirmation of the peace agreement, and visible evidence of reconstruction sufficient to generate support for a "New Somalia". Humanitarian action (both on an emergency and a development basis) and human rights protection will need to be closely integrated, as in the UN "livelihoods" approach. Peace and security will be crucial for both.

In terms of human rights protection, this will mean setting up guarantees of all kinds of security - protection of the state, its government institutions and natural resources; establishment of the rule of law and protection of basic human rights; access to sustainable livelihoods for citizens, including the revival of education and health facilities; protection and regulation of commerce so as to end illegal and criminal enterprises and generate state revenue for public services; personal security from attacks by militias or criminal violence, including kidnapping for ransom and rape; humane treatment of prisoners; protection of humanitarian workers, NGOs, human rights defenders; and protection of vulnerable groups, especially women, minorities, children and internally displaced persons.

There are also certain social rights and justice issues for post-conflict reconstruction. Some of these have been raised in the peace talks committees but without being given sufficient weight or reflection in the Charter, particularly as regards gender issues and minority rights.[19].

There is broad agreement that it will be essential in the early stages to familiarise communities throughout Somalia with the Charter and the rights contained in it, and gain their support. This can build on the growing activities of Somali NGOs and CBOs in all areas and across a wide range of rights activism. The involvement of the worldwide Somali refugee Diaspora (closely in contact through websites, internet, phones and travel) will be important. The Diaspora is estimated to remit US$1billion dollars a year in the form of family support, economic investment (both legal and illegal) and support for clan factions.

Particularly important will be cutting off the flow of weapons to warlords. There has been an international UN arms embargo in force since 1992, which has been constantly broken by neighbouring states (especially Ethiopia, Yemen, and Eritrea), by purchase of arms by warlords through private arms dealers, with funding by Diaspora communities living in the west and the Middle East. In 2002 the UN

Security Council set up a Panel of Experts to investigate violations of the arms embargo by land, air and sea, and to propose means of obtaining compliance with the embargo. Its third report in August 2004 led to the extension by the Security Council of the panel's mandate for a further 6 months to refine a confidential "blacklist" of those who violated the embargo and their supporters (including states, faction leaders and businesspeople, both Somalis and non-Somalis), for possible sanctions by the Security Council. It noted links between the arms trade and the drugs trade (*khat* and *hashish* in particular), and possible links with money-laundering and terrorist connections. It expected the report to have a deterrent value for potential arms embargo violators - "to help ensure that opposition groups do not destabilise the new transitional government that may emerge out of the [peace] conference, or [help to] minimise the violence that may erupt if the outcome of the conference is inconclusive".

Donors are preparing for a substantial flow of international development assistance, on a phased and "benchmarked" system linked to conditionalities of peace and human rights, with a rapid assistance program for the first year.

Without speculating whether the first year of the transition will approximate to either the best or worst scenario, it is possible to pick out some of the risks to peace and reconstruction and the protections which might be put in place to prevent them.

Risks

- One or more warlords might stay out of the process and create new armed conflict through un-disbanded militias, and exploiting the power vacuum, possibly with regional support.
- A warlord or grouping might reject some details of the agreement (e.g. on TNA or TFG representation), or new warlords might emerge to claim political influence, or internal differences within a clan might debilitate the TNA and government.
- The presence in the new government of major war criminals and human rights perpetrators would perpetuate the culture of impunity, encourage new abuses and deter international support for reconstruction.
- Conflict might arise between Somalia (claiming national territorial unity and integrity) and Somaliland (claiming independence).
- Conflict might arise between Puntland and Somaliland over the disputed Sool and Sanag regions.
- There might be internal conflict in any of the regions or districts, e.g. revisiting the Puntland civil war, Rahenwein faction-fighting, Gedo subclan fighting, or divisions among Mogadishu factions.
- There could be a new humanitarian disaster setting back development planning.

Protections

•The guarantors of the peace and reconciliation conference – IGAD states, the UN, the EU, African Union, Arab League and the peace talks' international partners – will need to make the outcome effective: in particular, the African Union's proposed 7,500-strong peace-monitoring military force must be put in place quickly, and sanctions should be imposed on any warlord violating or obstructing peace and reconstruction (e.g. by endangering humanitarian assistance), with perpetrators of new war crimes and crimes against humanity being reported to the International Criminal Court for possible prosecution.

•Human rights protection: the UN should provide a Human Rights Advisor, help establish a National Human Rights Commission for Somalia (as has already been drafted for Somaliland), support civil society advocacy groups monitoring human rights abuses, assist the TFG to implement the human rights protections in the Charter and to abide by the international and regional human rights treaties ratified (though not observed) by the Siad Barre government and still binding on subsequent governments.

•Disarmament, Demobilisation and Reintegration (DDR) of faction militias into civilian life: there are said to be 60,000 militias in different regions, probably responsible for much of the criminal violence and kidnapping, who need to be transformed into disciplined national or regional forces; new militia recruiting must be prevented, and child soldiers demobilised, restored to their families and rehabilitated into peaceful civilian life.

•Stopping the flow of arms to the warlords: the UN's investigation into violations of the arms embargo should lead to public reporting and sanctions against named violators.

•Establishing the rule of law: the TFG will need extensive assistance to set an independent and effective national system of administration of justice consistent with international human rights law and standards; this will include guarantees of the right to fair trial, prohibition of torture or cruel, inhuman or degrading treatment or punishment, access to prisoners by humanitarian organizations, and the non-application of the death penalty.

•Finding an appropriate way of achieving a suitable combination of reconciliation and "justice for the victims" so as to ensure that there is acceptance of the principle of accountability and "no impunity", and that perpetrators do not hold or use public office to commit the same abuses again.

•Special measures to protect the rights of women, with particular attention to the participation of women in public decision-making, the elimination of female genital mutilation, and stopping violence against women in the home and community.

•Special measures to protect the rights of minorities, to protect them from violence and guarantee their equal rights according to international standards.

•Reconstruction: generous assistance should be provided by international donors and financial institutions (e.g. through a Donor Appeal Conference) for humanitarian and development assistance to rebuild the infrastructure, with training and resources – including involving the Diaspora, and paying special attention to vulnerable categories of people.

•Diaspora return: creating conditions for safe return and sustainable livelihood for refugees, with no acceptance of forcible return (refoulement) contrary to international protection standards.

In general, there is an important need to promote a "culture of peace".[20] throughout Somalia and ensure that it is supported by all political authorities and communities.

References

Africa Watch. (1990) *A government at war with its own people*: London

Amnesty International (1988) Somalia: *A long-term human rights crisis*.

Amnesty International (2003) Somalia and Somaliland - *Supporting and strengthening the work of Somali human rights defenders*. Report of a workshop

Amnesty International (November 2002) *Somalia – an open letter to the peace talks*.

International Cooperation for Development (ICD) reports on its NGO work in Somaliland, www.ciir.org.

International Crisis Group (2003) *Somaliland – democratization and its discontents*, Nairobi. Amnesty International and International Cooperation for Development (1999) *Human rights in Somaliland - awareness and action*, report of a workshop, London.

International Crisis Group reports (2002) www.icg.org - *Salvaging Somalia's claim for* International Crisis Group reports (2003) *Negotiation a blueprint for peace in Somalia*.

International Crisis Group reports (2004) *Biting the Somali bullet*.

Judith Gardner and Judy El-Bushra (eds.) (2004) Somalia – the untold story, the war through the eyes of Somali women:CIIR/Pluto Press.

Minority Rights Group International (1998) www.minorityrights.org, *including Children in armed conflict [including Somalia]*.

UN Coordination Unit/OCHA (2002) *A study of minority groups in Somalia*.

UN Office for the Coordination of Humanitarian Activities (OCHA) in Somalia (July 2003) *Livelihoods and protection study of IDPs and vulnerable communities in Kismayo*. Nairobi.

Unicef/Academy for Peace and Development (2002) *Women's rights in Islam and Somali culture.*

----

[1]A paper version of this article was also presented at the African Studies Association (UK) biennial conference in London in September 2004. It does not necessarily reflect the position of Amnesty International on all issues, which will be set out in Amnesty International report on Somalia, 2005.

[2]See Amnesty International annual reports and other materials, www.amnesty.org.

[3]See also details and documents of the NOVIB Somali Civil Society Program, www.Somali-civilsociety,org.

[4]IGAD members are Djibouti, Eritrea, Ethiopia, Kenya, Tanzania and Uganda, and notionally Somalia.

[5]Somalia is a member of the Arab League as well as the African Union.

[6]The European Commission is the largest donor, through Lome Convention funding, including funds frozen since state collapse in 1991

[7]The interim parliament extended its own mandate when it expired in August 2003, until the conclusion of the peace talks.

[8]The flag consists of five white stars on a blue background, originally symbolizing the "Greater Somalia" political objective of unifying the five sub-regional Somali-inhabited territories, including Djibouti, northeast Kenya and the Ogaden (Ethiopia's Somali Region).

[9]Somalia is the only country in the world where security considerations prevent the International Committee of the Red Cross (ICRC) from having a resident international delegation, as a result of the kidnappings of its staff in Mogadishu. International NGOs mostly work through local staff (who also have security problems) and hire armed guards to protect staff and properties at exorbitant rates and often ineffectively.

[10]At the Kenya peace talks the TNG was treated as a faction alongside others, despite its claims to be a government and the demands of the TNG President to be treated as a Head of State. Peace talks facilitators were unable to obtain agreement to a compromise and the TNG President, Abdiqasim Salad Hussein (former Minister of the Interior in the Siad Barre government), boycotted the talks, though other TNG officials and some interim parliament members participated.

[11]This was a continual problem as there was no means of ensuring that delegates represented anyone or any group.

[12]A financial scandal over hotel costs charged to the EC has not yet been resolved.

[13]The Somali minorities comprise principally the large Bantu/Jarir group, the Benadiri/Rer Hamar urban traders, and the Midgan, Tumal and Yibro occupational "outcaste" groups, with other smaller minorities such as the Ashraf and Shikhal Muslim religious communities, Bajuni fishing people, and small hunter-gatherer groups. They are customarily prohibited from inter-marrying with the clans and thus have no clan protection. They have no armed militias and have been extremely vulnerable to killing, torture, rape and kidnapping with impunity. The differing minority groups were sometimes misleadingly called the "fifth clan" at the conference.

[14]Amnesty International calls on the UN Commission on Human Rights to support human rights reconstruction in Somalia, April 2003; Call for a human rights committed-parliament, Amnesty International, July 2003.

[15]There is no doubt that Somalia has been a collapsed state but its status has never been formally clarified. The UN seat had been left vacant but there has been a TNG Permanent Representative to the UN in New York (where the embassy never fully closed) and some embassies have been kept open in the Middle East, funded by host governments. Somalia passports (purchasable in Nairobi and elsewhere) are not fully internationally recognized.

[16]The cost of a substantial short battle was said to have risen to over US$200,000, which warlords could not now afford. Militias, only weakly organized and totally unaccountable, otherwise supported themselves and their drug (khat) addictions by extortion and looting.

[17]Postscript: the JVA and other warlords began to mobilize to oppose him. There was some fighting at a distance from Kismayu and the local population fled, but within some days the conference facilitators had persuaded him to return to Nairobi (paying his outstanding hotel debts) and welcomed him back to the process.

[18]Africa Watch, 1990, ibid. The Somaliland government set up a War Crimes Investigation Commission, focusing on crimes by non-Somalilanders, and marked out mass graves in Hargeisa, but the Commission has not published any findings and there have been no trials.

[19]Somali society, while possessing a high degree of cultural unity deriving from the pastoralist economy, is pluralist in essence. It is a

plurality of clans, sub-divided at many genealogical levels, but also a plurality of inequal social groups - pastoralists having traditionally dominated the agricultural groups (Rahenwein) and the minorities. Recognition and acceptance of this plurality, as well as suppressing the destructive elements of clannism and other forms of identity-based discrimination, would go far towards providing equality and freedoms for all groups and individuals.

[20]For example, through expansion of peace activism by Somali NGOs, poets, artists and musicians.

Chapter 11

Interests and Roles of External Actors in the Somali Peace Processes

Khalif Hassan Farah

This chapter examines the interests and roles of the external actors in the Somali peace processes by examining the last two peace processes, Arta and Mbagathi, respectively hosted by Djibouti and Kenya. It makes an attempt to establish the linkages between the competing interests and the persistent failures of the Somali peace initiatives.

The analysis in the chapter suggest that there are layers of external actors who took an interest in the conflict or in its management acting out of security, geopolitical, cultural, economic and humanitarian concerns. The relationship between the conflicting parties and their sponsors abroad, colonial relations, weapons, aid resources, the issue of terrorism are, among other things, identified as some of the factors that internationalized, exacerbated and prolonged the conflict.

The chapter cites three shortcomings in the Somali peace processes: firstly, the Somali factions who have been dominating the Somali peace processes in the last several years posses neither functional hierarchy nor represent a coherent ideological position or political platform. They multiply in number by the day and continue to shift alliances. It is difficult to imagine any solution in such a situation even with the best intentions of the external parties; secondly, the regional competitions within neighbouring states has resulted in proliferation of parallel initiatives which had supplanted rather than supplemented each other. The regional tension has often been replicated by political cleavages inside Somalia and has exacerbated the volatile internal situation; thirdly, Somalia remains very low on the priority of the major world powers. The peace building objectives of the both United States and the European Union, if any, are very weak and heavily reliant on IGAD, despite its inherent weaknesses, as a potential peace maker in Somalia.

The chapter is divided into two sections. The first section examines some theoretical aspects as to how the Somali conflict became internationalized. The second section explores the interests and roles of the various external actors, namely the frontline IGAD member states, Arab countries, United States, and European Union.

Some Theoretical Perspectives: Internationalization of Somali Conflict

This section attempts at providing a theoretical framework for the internationalization of the Somali conflict. It provides a rationale for the involvement of multiple actors with conflicting interests and agendas in the Somali peace process.

The categorisation of conflicts as either internal or international was influenced by the realist school of thinking which legitimised the dichotomy between domestic and international politics. Article 2(7) of the United Nations Charter prohibits interference in the internal affairs of states. Regional organisation such as the AU and League of Arab states copied the UN charter and immunised the states from external interference when dealing with their domestic problems (Shirwa 2000).

Internal conflicts tend to become internationalized due to the economic, political, social and security interdependencies of the contemporary world. Intractable internal conflicts can no longer be contained within the borders of the state. They have the habit of crossing to the neighbouring countries, entangling and bringing together adversaries and strange bedfellows, thereby assuming a complex international character. As a result, it gives national, regional, and global level participants a broad opportunity either to pursue their own interests in the conduct of conflict or to follow their interests in conflict management (Zartman 1993: 325-338). The introduction of external actors in an originally 'internal' conflict as mediators or facilitators and their mere contacts with local actors internationalises the conflict (Mwagiru 1984: 29).

The new perception of security and its expanded definition is particularly important in explaining the internationalization of the internal conflicts. The definition includes not only the internal security of the state, but also how secure systems of food production, health, trade, provision for basic human needs, environmental degradation, small arms, poverty, illiteracy, ethnicity, refugee problems, uncontrolled population growth, drugs, terrorism and bad politics influence the internationalisation of the conflict (Koech 2004). The intermeshing of the economies and the shared interests in regional stability means that security has become collective good for all states which can no longer provide the well-being of their citizens alone nor can insulate themselves from outside influence because of the globalisation of both domestic and international politics.

Following the collapse of Somali state, Somalia became an international commodity (Makinda 1993). Given the fragmentation of Somali institutions and the inability of any group to impose its will on the country, it became vulnerable to the influence of the external actors and competing geopolitical agendas (Johnson 1999). The mere absence of a central state to articulate national interests and priorities is a breeding ground for competing influences within the region which internationalized the conflict. Since external interests entailed contacting one of the parties of the conflict or the other for the purpose of exercising influence, the Somali conflict became internationalised bringing into picture a complex of issues. A pattern of relationships that cross internal borders and enter into the international realm exist in the Somali conflict, and is such internationalised (Mwagiru 2000:58). The relationship between the conflicting parties and their sponsors abroad, colonial relations, weapons, aid resources, and the issue of terrorism are some of the factors that internationalised the Somali conflict.

Lack of progress in Somalia was attributed to the proliferation of parallel initiatives which has encouraged the Somali faction leaders to continue to play one external actor against the other in order to ensure that the status quo is maintained in the country. A number of measures had been taken to bring all the initiatives aiming at Somali reconciliation below one roof and end the competing parallel initiatives which stalemated the peace process. Some forums such as IGAD Partners Forum Committee on Somalia, Standing Committee on Somalia and IGAD Partners Forum Liaison Group were created. However the membership in these forums did not mean every member country has avoided taking measures to exacerbate the situation in Somalia.

External Actors and Interests

The purpose of this section is to analyse the interests of the various actors in the Somali peace process. Before proceeding to the analysis of the interests, let us define the term "actor". It refers to all the participants in the conflict from mediators to the warring parties (Ramsbotham 1999: 158-159). All actors have certain interests in the process which is the reason they become involved in the first place. The interests of the various external stakeholders vary from security to humanitarian and from commercial to geopolitical concerns. Interests also encompass the ambitions of the leaders of the given states for regional leadership and statesmanship.

There are layers of actors, including regional and extra-regional actors, who responded to the Somali conflict for different reasons and interests, and with different levels of commitments and consistencies. This section examines the roles and interests of the notable external state actors in the Somali peace processes in detail. The major players in the process are IGAD frontline states, Arab States, United States of America, EU and its member states.

Although Both United Nations and African Union are actors in their own right mandated to maintain international and regional peace and stability respectively, their contributions to the Somali peace process are minimal. They mainly left their imprints on the process through their resolutions affirming the territorial integrity of Somalia, condemning the violations of arms embargo and threatening to impose sanctions on those who obstruct peace. These have served, to some degree, as deterrent for peace spoilers. Although these resolutions have legal status, they are merely recommendations incumbent upon members to comply with. This is because the two institutions are union of member states and not supranational organisations. They have only limited powers to enforce their resolutions. Both organisations offer platforms where issues concerning the peace process are discussed. The lack of international or regional interested power to guide the efforts of these two organisations with regard to Somalia is a constraining factor for their meaningful engagement. Of particular significance is, however, the mediation and facilitation role of the United Nations Political Office for Somalia (UNPOS) in both Arta and Mbagathi processes[1].

IGAD Frontline States

This section analyses the interests of the IGAD Frontline States- Ethiopia, Djibouti and Kenya- and their roles in the Somali peace process[2]. These are the major external players in the Somali conflict and the peace process. They hosted most of the reconciliation conferences, including the last major Arta and Mbagthi peace initiatives held in Djibouti and Kenya respectively. They also partly fuelled the conflict by supplying arms to the warring parties in Somalia. The security developments inside Somalia has direct bearing on the frontline states in terms of refugee influx, small arms proliferation etc. Thus, they tried to influence the peace process and its outcome in a way or the other.

Ethiopia

The most important of the regional players in the Somali peace process is Ethiopia. Over the years of the Somali conflict, it maintained its hegemonic position in the process by trying to keep other players at bay. The bitter historical relations between Ethiopia and Somalia had not disappeared with the collapse of the Somali state. President Zenawi and Moi who met in Addis Ababa in November 1991- almost a year after the collapse of the Somali state – declared their determinations to protect their territories against any external power's claim with indirect reference to Somalia (Onyango 2000:92). However there was short détente in the relations between Somalia and Ethiopia after the new EPRDF regime came to power in Ethiopia which showed goodwill gestures to Somalia by hosting thousands of Somali refugees and facilitating them to even obtain Ethiopia's citizenship papers, including passports.

According to Ethiopia's policy direction towards Somalia, it pursues three damage limitation objectives in Somalia; 1) to try to help those regions in Somalia which are comparatively stable and do not shelter extremists and terrorists. These are the regions known as Somaliland and Puntland; 2) to create the capability to defend Ethiopia and foil any attack by forces of extremism, terrorism and other anti-peace elements originating in Somalia; 3) and to work in cooperation with the Somali people in the region, and the international community as a whole, to weaken and neutralise those forces coming from any part of Somalia to perpetuate attacks against Ethiopia[3]. Ethiopia has tended not to support the creation of strong Somali state with greater influence in the Horn of Africa, and rather would opt for a weaker one, with more potential for Ethiopian control and influence and with less threat to Zone V borders (Johnson 1999:12). This is informed by the secessionary tendencies in Ethiopia. Many Somalis in region V of Ethiopia are agitating for independence through armed oppositions such as the Ogaden National Liberation Front (ONLF).

Ethiopia claims that its most immediate concern in Somalia is its own national security , hence to disrupt any groups forging alliance with the secessionist groups opposed to its rule (Omar 2003:50). However, one wonders whether the supply of arms to Somali factions and the thwarting of any effort to establish national government in Somalia serves the security interests of Ethiopia. Fragile and instable security situation in Somalia is prone to create more security problems for Ethiopia, and its internal opposition groups are more likely to enjoy more sanctuary in unstable Somalia. It is also ironical that Ethiopia demanded the Somali authorities to fight Islamic extremist groups while undermining the efforts aimed at creating national government that can extend its control over the entire country.

Ethiopia's vulnerability to 'Greater Somalia' ideology has been greatly diminished by the collapse of Somali state, but according to Ethiopia's official point of view, the disintegration of Somalia has in itself brought ever-growing danger to Ethiopia as the crisis in Somalia has allowed religious extremism to take hold. Some hardliners in Ethiopia's ruling elite maintain that the establishment of a viable government in Somalia would once again resuscitate the ideology of

"Greater Somalia" and that peace, democracy and development in Somalia would, in that case, not benefit Ethiopia. Such views have been reinforced by the independence of Eritrea and the subsequent conflict that erupted between the two countries with some nationalist elements advocating for pre-emptive actions to avoid another "appeasement" to secessionist forces within the oppressed communities of Ethiopia .

Since 1996, when it was mandated to mediate the Somali conflict by OAU and IGAD, Ethiopia has been increasingly and continuously coveting a total monopoly of the Somali peace and reconciliation process to enhance its hegemonic interests, and derailed any other peace initiative which did not promise an outcome in favour of its interests (Ghalib 2002:49). It used the mandate to play blurred multiple part of mediator, regional power and spoiler. It sabotaged the Cairo Accord in late 1997. Those who dropped out of the talks headed to Addis Ababa. Other splinter groups from the factions who signed Cairo Accord had also been encouraged and supported by Ethiopia with hefty arms supplies. Another two attempts by the Kenyan government to mediate between the Transitional National Government and SRRC in 2001 had been aborted after the Ethiopian-backed SRRC groups declined to attend the conference apparently at Ethiopia's dictation.

Ethiopia hosted Sodere conference in November 1996 at a time when it was increasingly worried about the Islamic influence in Somalia. It used the conference to cover and legitimize its military incursions inside Somalia to destroy suspected bases of Islamic groups who allegedly carried out destabilising activities inside Ethiopia, including unsuccessful assassination attempt on Abdulmajid Hussein, the then minister of transport in the federal government in mid-1996. Since that time, Ethiopia has made continuous incursions into parts of Somalia to root out groups it suspects are making common cause with its internal opposition groups. These military incursions intensified in 1999 after Ethiopian-Eritrean conflict broke out when the two countries engaged in proxy war inside Somalia, arming their allies and playing one group against another.

In March 2001, Ethiopia hosted a gathering of the factions opposed to the Transitional National Government (TNG) at Awasa in Ethiopia[4]. The creation of Somali Reconciliation and Restoration Council (SRRC) at Awase meeting was orchestrated by Ethiopia to strengthen its influence in Somalia which has been weakened by Arta peace conference and to weaken TNG's ability to extend its control over Somalia.

Ethiopia's proactive engagement in the recently concluded peace talks left little doubt that the outcome would be tilting in favour of Ethiopia and its allies. Despite the IGAD Summit Resolution of January

2002 in Khartoum which called for broadening and deepening of the Arta peace process, Ethiopia strived that everything be started from scratch. According to some observers, Ethiopia manipulated the screening of the delegates at the conference so that it could 'bet on the horse that can come out of the race'.

Ethiopia has been the author of the 'building block' approach which encourages the emergence of polarised regional governments (Gilkes 1999). Cynics note that this approach coincides with Ethiopia's interest in the possible use of the Somali ports as alternative ports to Djibouti and Eritrea. The approach, with all its merits, aims at distancing the possibility of forming strong central government which Ethiopia fears may resume the redemption policy. The idea of creating decentralised governance system is also a countercheck at Arab influence in the region. Ethiopia's apparent support for Somaliland's stability is contrasted with its negative involvement in the south which it views as a breeding ground of the unitarist orientations in Somalia.

Given its military strength and ability to prop up any dissenting groups from any agreement reached, Ethiopia effectively proved it exercises veto power over political developments in Somalia and that it is hard to imagine a workable agreement in Somalia without the Ethiopians (ICG 2002). The Prime Minister of Ethiopia Mr. Meles Zenawi, unequivocally underlined that any peace initiative which is not endowed with Ethiopia's blessing faces the risk of being sabotaged. In an interview with *Al-Hayat* Newspaper, he stated that his country was more experienced in Somali affairs than any other country in the region, and said: 'No Somali government would be realised without Ethiopia's involvement in its foundation' (Omar 2003:54). Indeed, Ethiopia's attempts at restoring the warlords and engaging them in proxy confrontations with those who stand against its influence in Somalia had reinforced the perception that it desires neither a unified nor a stable Somalia. By keeping Somalia in the status quo, Ethiopia believes that it would eliminate a historic enemy.

Djibouti

Djibouti is a member of Arab league and IGAD. It is a founding member of IGAD and hosts its Headquarter. Since independence, the country was ruled by leaders from the Isse clan of the Somali ethnic Isse. It hosted Arta conference apparently to reciprocate Somalia's investment in its independence.

Djibouti's interests in restoring the Somali state are multiple. Since Independence, Djibouti's rule has been in the hands of the Somali ethnic Isse clan, which faces constant threats from the Afar population that are scattered in Djibouti, Ethiopia and Eritrea and are eying the top leadership of the country. Hence, Djibouti leadership of the Somali ethnic Isse has vested interested in a strong Somali state to support their clinging to power. Ethiopia's hegemonic tendencies in the region are also a source of growing concern for Djibouti. Djibouti perceives that the power imbalances in the region put it in a disadvantaged position. This perception was reinforced by the bullying character of the Ethiopian regime and its attempt to dictate the terms of agreement on the use of Djibouti port.

Commercial and financial linkages between Somali and Djiboutian business people partially explain Djibouti's engagement in the Somali peace process. These commercial interests have apparently been reflected in Arta conference. There have been some business ventures between Djiboutian and Somali business men. Djibouti served as conduit for some of Somalia's international trade which brought gains to both parties.

Given these interests, the restoration of the Somali state is a strategic goal for Djibouti to address the power imbalances in the region and consolidate its commercial and security interests in the Horn of Africa. It vigorously pursued the Arta conference and tried to legitimize its outcome through aggressive lobbying at the international and regional forums. It supported and threw its weight behind the Transitional National Government (TNG).

Djibouti remained passively engaged at the onset of the Somali peace talks in Kenya. Its discontent was manifested by the conspicuous absence of its president from the opening ceremony of the Somali peace talks in Eldoret in October 2002. It stressed that the Arta process become the bases of the new reconciliation initiative in Kenya. As the Ethiopian influence in the talks had increased, Djibouti minimised its role in the talks and tacitly encouraged the disaffected Somali parties to walk out. After the passing of Somali Charter by delegates mainly composed of Ethiopian allies in September 2003, Djibouti pulled out from the Technical Committee in protest for alleged mismanagement of the talks by the Kenyan special envoy and lack of inclusivity (ICG 2004). It returned to the talks after the Technical Committee was expanded to include all IGAD member states and renamed Facilitation Committee. After continuous wrangling, which had paralysed the talks for over one and half years, Ethiopia and Djibouti have shown unprecedented cooperation since the 6th IGAD ministerial meeting in Nairobi on 22 May, 2004. In the end, their cooperation had enabled the process to move ahead and make progress within few months. Djibouti abandoned any pretence of defending the Arta outcome and propping the TNG which grew weaker by the day and lost its credibility both inside and outside Somalia. It welcomed the election of Abdullahi Yusuf who is Ethiopia's ally as the president of Somalia.

Kenya

Kenya's engagement in the process should primarily be seen against the former president's ambition to become the sub-regional statesman. Moi initiated the process of "IGAD Revitalisation" and used the IGAD process to make his country and himself internationally presentable again after the withdrawal of IMF and World Bank and work against the alienation of his regime by its Western friends in early 1990s. Moi always stressed that resolution of the sub-regional conflicts should be sought within the confines of the IGAD[5].

Kenya's interest is also related to the security risks emanating from Somalia's statelessness, according to its officials. It had suffered two terrorist attacks in the last six years which it suspects were organised from inside Somalia. Since September 11, Kenya has been exaggerating these security problems to please Americans and mobilize more U.S. support[6]. Kenyan officials argue that Somalia's statelessness is exceptionally threatening to it as there is no authority to deal with on the insecurity that is worrying them[7].

Furthermore, Kenya's interests in Somalia include trade and employment opportunities for Kenyan citizens: Most of the international organisations and UN agencies operating in Somalia have their operational and logistical bases in Kenya since UNOSOM pulled out from Somalia in early 1995, providing employment for Kenyans as local staff and expatriates. The presence of International organisations also benefits Kenya as expatriates working for them spend their time and resources in the country. A number of Kenya-based flight companies are operating lucrative business in Somalia, including ECHO and UNCAS flights which are used by the humanitarian organisations in Somalia, and a large fleet of Kenya-owned light planes which transport Miraa, passengers and other commodities to and from Somalia. There are almost 12 daily flights to Somalia transporting Miraa to different destinations in the country[8].

Kenya's potential for becoming a *de facto* regional diplomatic leader and mediator of conflicts has increased as result of Ethiopia's deteriorating image resulting from its war with Eritrea, and meddling with Somalia's internal conflict. Its improved relations with the West after conducting a successful democratic transition in 2002 added to Kenya's advantage to play a prominent role in the IGAD sub-region. Kenya was the leading mediator in the recently concluded Somali peace talks in Nairobi, but its role has been overshadowed by Djibouti and Ethiopia which were battling to determine the outcome of the conference. Despite Kenya's chairmanship of the Technical Committee and its financial support, Ethiopia's dominance of the conference was apparent[9]. This had produced an increasingly noticeable bias in favour of SRRC and damaged the Kenyan reputation as a neutral player in the Somali problems (ICG 2004). Kenya's credibility as a neutral player in the Somali peace process suffered when its special envoy to the Somali peace process, Ambassador Kiplagat, endorsed a controversial charter which had been passed by the Ethiopian-backed factions on September 15, 2003. Kiplagat called the occasion 'a historic day'. Statement made by former Kenyan president added to the suspicion among the Somalis that Kenya is not a neutral player. The former president implied that Kenya and Ethiopia could not be trusted with the Somali peace process since they "fear that a reunited Somalia and a prosperous nation might resurrect Somalia's territorial claims" (ICG 2004). However, Kenya's Special Envoy to the Somali peace talks, Ambassador Kiplagat, dismissed that any future Somali government will resort to territorial claims on its neighbours arguing that the irredentism had cost Somalia a lot[10].

Arab Countries

Somalia is one of the 22-Arab League member states. It joined the League in 1974. It currently has special status within the Arab fold because it is the only Arab country without a government[11]. The Arabs are tied to Somalis by cultural, political and commercial relations. The Arab countries see a strong, unified Somali state as an essential bulwark against the Ethiopian influence in the region. This is understandable because the Arab world perceives that a decentralised political system in Somalia is prone to Ethiopian influence and Israeli intervention. With the exception of Egypt and Libya, Arab countries are less equipped with any expertise to deal with fragmented political factions and micro-politics of Somalia, thus stressing the formation of unitary national government.

Somalia has particular strategic significance for the Arab world in both strategic and economic sense. Its geographical location at the Red Sea and at the mouth of Babel-Mandeb, the petroleum exporting shipping lanes, is an important determining factor of Arab-Somali relations. Economically, Somalia has become one of the biggest trade partners for United Arab Emirates after the civil war. The Saudi Arabia also imported 90% of its meat from Somalia before it imposed ban on Somali livestock in 1999 due to the alleged Rift Valley fever.

The Arab role to pursue an effective diplomatic engagement of their own is, however, constrained mainly by three factors; firstly, they lack a deep understanding of the Somali conflict; secondly, Arab involvement is resisted by the IGAD member states, most notably Ethiopia, which claims that sub-regional actors have the exclusive preserve and mandate of peacemaking in Somalia. Indeed, Egypt invited the wrath of IGAD member states particularly Ethiopia when it held reconciliation talks for the Somali factions in late 1997; thirdly, the effectiveness of the League of Arab States to respond to crisis in the Arab world including the Somalia conflict has been constrained by the growing divisions within the Arab world and subsequent weakening of the Arab bond due to the crisis in the gulf and relations with Israeli.

The leading Arab heavyweight, Egypt, had maintained close observation of the Somali situation throughout the Somali civil war. It is a member of the IGAD Partners Forum (IPF) sub-committee on Somalia and Sudan and has been increasingly following the peace processes in the two countries. From onset of the Somali civil war, Egypt offered mediation between the Siyad Barre Regime and opposition groups. It also hosted the Cairo conference in 1997 and closely worked with Djibouti to strengthen the Transitional National Government which sprang from Arta conference to counter Ethiopian influence. Egypt's interests favour a centralised Somali state which can balance Ethiopia's hegemony in the Greater Horn of Africa which is the source of the Nile waters. However, despite allegations that Egypt continues to use Somalia as an element in its efforts to influence Ethiopia's policy on Nile, Egyptian diplomats are discounting such allegations pointing out that an agreement had been reached between Egypt, Sudan and Ethiopia on the common use of the Nile water in December 2003. They argue that a strong Somalia is beneficial not only to Egypt, but also to other Horn countries, which do not want to be bulldozed by a dominant and hegemonic power.

Although the Arab countries provided financial support to TNG, the level of support fell far below the expectation of the TNG. The Arab Summit in Amman, Jordan, in 2001 pledged 56 million dollars for the reconstruction of Somalia but that has never materialized. The TNG ambitiously asked for Arab reconstruction assistances equivalent to that of Marshall Plan which United States carried out to help Europe recover from the destruction of the Second World War.

Arab support to TNG gradually declined for a number of reasons. Firstly, Arab resources and attentions had been consumed by the Palestinian upraising (Intifada) which had coincided with the formation of the TNG; secondly, the September 11 attack on the United States and the subsequent allegations that the donations of Arab countries to

Somalia are falling into the terrorist hands discouraged Arabs from continuing their support. As consequence of these allegations, Saudi Arabia closed the biggest Islamic charity organisation in Somalia, Al-Harameyn foundation, which had been sponsoring over 3,000 orphans and had been funding other welfare projects including schools and health care facilities; thirdly, the lack of progress on the part of the TNG to consolidate its power in Somalia and the fact that no other bilateral or multilateral support was forthcoming from members of the international community discouraged Arab countries from continuing to assist the TNG. Despite the declining financial support, the Arab recognition and lobbying had enabled the TNG to occupy the Somali seats in many international forums such as the African Union, The United Nations and the Organisation of the Islamic Conference.

Egypt and representatives from Arab League attended the Somali peace talks in Kenya as members of the IPF observers. At the onset of the process at El-doret, the Arab League envoy and the Egyptian delegation had been given unwelcome treatment and were considered outsiders in the talks by IGAD, fearing that they may influence the process in their favour. Egypt's presence was particularly viewed with suspicion. Egyptian diplomats at the talks had been finger pointed and alleged to be trying to foil the process and were at times barred from observing the talks. According to Arab diplomats at the talks, as time went on, the scepticism gradually faded away as they proved to be constructive and non-partisan player in the process. The Arab League was instrumental in discouraging dualism whereby those dissenting from the process in Kenya looked for Arab support for a parallel initiative. Their financial contribution, though minimal, and diplomatic support, saved the talks from collapse[12].

At one point, Arab diplomats at the Somali peace talks became angry during the writing of the Somali charter when the Arabic language, which was always the second official language of Somalia, was relegated to the third language of the nation. According to the Special Envoy for the Arab League Secretary General, the Arab diplomats who were observing the talks put down their feet and resisted what was described as attempts to change the Somali identity.

Generally, the Arab countries are concerned that Somali leaders can not do without the diplomatic and financial support of the Arab world; hence, they are less likely to favour any certain personalities to take the leadership in Somalia as opposed to Ethiopia which strove to crown one of its favoured faction leaders for Somalia's leadership. This Arab complacency stems from their conviction that Somalia's historical and geographical links with the Arab world can not be eliminated by any other influence.

United States

US has taken a "wait- and- see" stance in the Somali politics after UNOSOM pulled out from Somalia. However, their interest has been revitalised by the September 11 attack. One of the U.S foreign policy priorities in the Horn of Africa after September 11 is to combat the so-called terrorism forces. It realised that failed states [like Somalia] can create a danger to themselves, to their neighbours and to the United States. However, the American war on terrorism lacked any component of nation-building in Somalia. It had not provided any significant political and financial support to the peace process. It shifted its efforts towards intelligence gathering and individualised dealings with warlords in Somalia which, according to some observers, legitimised faction leaders and created some perceptions that the United States is reinforcing the brutal grip of the warlords on the Somalis. The U.S- led war on terrorism lacked any broader international political engagement and led to an already unstable situation deteriorating, thereby creating potential for more violence and lawlessness of the sort that can offer the alleged terrorists greater opportunities (ICG 2002).

The Administration's East African counter-terrorism initiative recognises that there are real threats in Somalia and cooperates with Kenya, Ethiopia and Djibouti in many areas, including patrolling of the Somali coasts and exchange of intelligence. The initiative had increasingly allied itself with Ethiopia and heavily relied on intelligence provided by Ethiopian intelligence services, which claimed there are terrorist training camps in some parts of Somalia. It is on the bases of this faulty intelligence provided by Ethiopia that the United States closed the biggest remittance company in Somalia, Al Barakat, which was providing vital services to the public, alleging that the company supports terrorist activities in Somalia[13]. The U.S. administration also put some Islamic organisations in Somalia on the list of the terrorist organisations which have been described as being linked to Al Qaeda.

Although then U.S. Secretary of State Colin Powell charged in December 2001 that some Bin Laden followers are holed up in Somalia taking advantage of the absence of a functioning government, and despite the exaggerated reports and allegations made by the Ethiopian government and the Somali warlords that several terrorist elements are operating in Somalia, United States did not discover any terrorist bases in Somalia in the last two years. Senior American experts on Somalia warned U.S policy makers to avoid an over-reliance on information from the Ethiopian government, since it has a vested interest in exaggerating terrorist activities in order to receive assistance in combating its opposition groups.

The U.S has reconnaissance missions in the Indian Ocean and Red Sea coasts and created the Combined Joint Task-Force-Horn of Africa (CJTF-HOA) whose mission is to detect, disrupt, defeat and deny terrorist activity in the Horn of Africa[14]. The CJTF-HOA is a joint and combined effort of personnel from all US services and allied forces from numerous other countries. The CJTF-HOA helped the countries in the region in creating counter terrorism units.

In the recently concluded Somali National Reconciliation Process in Kenya, the United States initially gave some political support to the IGAD initiative by encouraging various Somali parties to participate in reconciliation conference. This fits in with American broader policy of helping failed states grapple with governance problems as articulated by Assistant Secretary of the African Affairs Walter Kansteiner in senate testimony in February 2002[15]. It contributed only $350,000 to help finance the talks in contrast to EU countries which had born the burden of financing the peace talks. The US representation at the talks appeared to have been given the task of a "Somali watcher" rather than a full fledged envoy. However, after September 11, the United States increased humanitarian support to Somalia. From 2000 to 2002, it has provided almost $60 million in assistance, mainly food, to Somalia through USAID. In fiscal year 2002, for the first time in recent years, the United States also approved Economic Support Funds (ESF) for use in Somalia including $1.3 million allocated to fund basic education. The U.S humanitarian assistances targets particular areas such as Gedo regions and towns at Kenyan border where the Islamists had influence in the past. This shows that aid is meant to neutralise the areas prone to Islamist influence, and to create a parallel non-Islamic educational programs in Somalia.

The United States reportedly spends about 280 million US dollars on the fight against terrorism every month in the Horn of Africa[16]. This is in marked contrast with its negligible contribution towards the Somali Peace Conference. One wonders why the vast resources devoted to the deployment of military force in the region and investing in anti-terrorist projects were not devoted to peace-making efforts in Somalia. Indeed, some cynics have argued that the United States is not interested to establish Somali state again, but one analyst rightly contends that while in international politics there are humanitarian services to feed starving people there are no humanitarian services to build states. The lack of evidence linking Somalia to any terrorist activities reduces the prospect of enhanced U.S. engagement in Somalia in the near future. As One American official put it, if no serious threat of terrorism is discovered, no one will give a damn about Somalia (ICG 2002).

EU/ European Countries

The EU has been the most important donor for Somalia during the last ten years. It is represented by the EC Somali unit which is hosted by the EC Kenya Delegation. The broader EU objectives towards Somalia as spelled out by the 2447th meeting of EU council of ministers[17] are: 1) the restoration of peace and stability in all parts of the country and respect for sovereignty, territorial integrity, political independence and unity of the country, and the rights of the Somali people to determine their own future consistent with the purpose of the principles of the Charter of the United Nations; 2) the establishment of legitimate and effective governance structures; 3) and the promotion of friendly and cooperative relations with other countries in the horn of Africa. The Overall long-term objective of the EC strategy for Somalia is to contribute to the alleviation of poverty and to the promotion of more peaceful, equitable and democratic society.

Apart from the humanitarian interests, EU engagement in Somalia is informed by two major issues; terrorism and refugees. Europe wants to stem unwanted immigration to its member states by creating decent living conditions and job opportunities in the developing countries. Few hundred thousands of Somali refugees are living in Europe, causing a heavy financial burden on their host countries. The prejudicial influence of alleged terrorists in the failed states like Somalia also motivates the EU to restore Somali state and its social services. According to EU Foreign and Security Policy Chief, Javier Solana, Somalia has not been forgotten by the EU which has been following the reconciliation process and supporting the Kenyan mediation (acting under IGAD Auspices) and maintaining contacts with various parties. Solana announced that Europe was ready to offer financial help to the new Somali government.

Somalia was a member of Lome Convention, later named Cotonou Agreement, which is an arrangement Europe uses to assist its former colonies known as African Caribbean and Pacific countries (ACP) through development and trade. Being without an internationally recognised national government since the beginning of 1990s, Somalia did not ratify the Fourth Lome Convention and Cotonou agreement. The Council of EU ministers adopted a resolution on 18 November 1992 entrusting the Chief Authorising Officer of European Development Fund with the authority of National Authorising Officer, acting on behalf of the Somali government. Hence, EC which is the executive arm of European Union manages funds allocated to Somalia.

EU spectacularly focused on streamlining civil society participation in the institution of good governance and safeguarding space for them. Its support to civil society participation in the process is justified on the basis of the Cotonou agreement's requirement for the engagement of non-state actors at all levels of development including dialogue on policy priorities and through information and capacity building[18]. The Cotonou agreement obliges ACP partners to involve non-state actors (NSAs) in the political dialogue, policy formulation, and monitoring and evaluation of progress. Funding by EU and the EC to Somalia is predicated on these principles.

Apart from direct funding to the recently concluded peace talks in Kenya, the EC financed three other projects connected to the Somali peace process : 1) information dissemination strategy within Somalia which was implemented by NOVIB (OXFAM) and UNDP/IRIN to fill the gap left by IGAD's lack of information strategy to disseminate the details of the conference discussions to the Somali public. IRIN prepared radio news reports and special radio programs transmitted through their partner radio stations in Somalia.; 2) Support to women's participation through Horn Relief to encourage women's input in the constitution drafting process and strengthen and consolidate the participation of women in the peace process; 3) Technical support to two of the six reconciliation committees, namely the Disarmament , Demobilisation and Reintegration Committee, and the Conflict Resolution and Reconciliation Committee implemented by GTZ and War-torn Society Project respectively.

Some European countries with vested interests pursued their agendas outside the framework of EU principles and objectives, which are purely humanitarian. Italy and Britain, both of them being former colonisers of Somalia, are actively involved in the process both at bilateral and EU levels. These two countries are motivated by historical and commercial ties with Somalia. The British government swayed between wanting to give recognition to Somaliland, its former protectorate, and respecting UN and OAU (AU) founding charters which enshrine the territorial integrity of the state borders. Britain, which had assigned a senior official from British High Commission in Nairobi to the peace talks, tended to encourage the writing of Federal Charter to safeguard the autonomy of Somaliland. After the conclusion of the Mbagathi process where Abdullahi Yusuf was elected as president of Somalia, British government dispatched a minister to Somaliland for the first time to allay their fears and assure them of the British support to their cause (BBC 24-10-2004).

As a former colonial power, Italy has an overall strong interest in Somali affairs and is very active within the framework of IGAD and

SACB. Before the civil war, Italy had close relations with Somalia. It had one of the biggest commercial banana plantations in Somalia. Somalia had also been a market for Italian products. The banana export in which Italy had been the greatest beneficiary was revived briefly after the civil war and the profits from the export were alleged of partially financing the war. Since there was no central government in Somalia, Italian companies, most notably Somali Fruit Company, had also benefited for a while from the subsidies given by the European Union to the banana sector in Somalia under the Lome Convention. The agreement offers a number of trade concessions and technical assistance to African, Caribbean and Pacific Countries including Somalia.

Italy is the chair of the IPF and it is the biggest bilateral donor and funds projects carried out mostly by Italian NGOs. Italy provides assistance not only bilaterally, but also through its 1998-2000 Co-financing Framework Agreement with the EC. Under this agreement, the European Commission manages a variety of rehabilitation projects. During the period of the peace conference in Nairobi (2003), Italy was also the rotating president of the EU. Along with Germany, Italy has been a leading financial contributor to the process. Italy is the only European country with special envoy to Somalia, but has not articulated its policies very well.

Italy was often criticised by the Somalis and members of the international community of not acting in good faith with regard to the peace and stability of Somalia. Its policy is often branded as faceless with no clear agenda. The Italian NGOs which benefit the most from both the EU and Italy's financial support to Somalia are not, in the eyes of the Somalis, accountable. One other criticism often raised is that Italy did not provide leadership on the management of the Somali conflict as other former colonials did in their former colonies; French in a number of francophone countries, Australia in East Timor and the British in Sierra Leone, which led to the end of the civil strife in those countries (Omar 2003:64). Instead of shaping world opinion towards Somalia, Italy has been undermining the efforts of other external actors so as to maintain its influence, not only in Somalia, but also in the Horn of Africa sub-region where it colonised Somalia and Eritrea, and briefly occupied Ethiopia. The Italians monopolized Somalia as their sphere of influence in the EU, often objecting to other countries' involvement in Somalia. Sources close to EU told the author that Italy sabotaged EU plan to appoint a senior special envoy to Somalia, insisting that the envoy must be an Italian citizen.

Other important European players in Somalia are the Scandinavian countries which host a large number of Somali refugees with Sweden hosting 26.000, Norway 16.000 and Denmark 14.000. In 2002, the total aid pledges for Norway, Denmark, Norway and Finland was $20m, mainly allocated for peace and governance oriented programs and basic social services (SACB Donor Report 2002). Sweden delegated the deputy of its Kenya mission to support the Somali peace process in Kenya[19]. It has also assigned an undersecretary in the foreign ministry to directly follow the process. Swedish involvement was initially requested by Kenya's special envoy to the Somali peace process when he met the minister of development and international cooperation in late 2003[20].

In general, European Union and European countries have been positive on Somalia's peacemaking efforts. They are spearheading the conceptualisation of Rapid Assistance Program (RAP) for Somalia. The RAP package is meant to avoid the experience of the previous peace initiatives, which failed partly due to lack of proactive international engagement to support and sustain the agreements reached. The essential aim of the RAP is to ensure that the new transitional federal institutions survive and to make time and expertise available for more comprehensive plans to be developed.

Conclusion

This chapter examined the roles and interests of IGAD member states, Arab countries, United States, and European Union which had played some roles in the last two peace initiatives for Somalia - Arta and Mbgathi processes- with varying interests and commitments. The analyses show that security concerns both in the short-term or long term are cross-cutting for all actors in the peace process. The neighbouring countries have been particularly affected by the stateless situation in Somalia; small arms proliferations and refugees are some of these problems. This explains their involvement in the peace process both as facilitators and, to some extent, spoilers. Some of the regional states fear that a strong Somalia will resuscitate its claims over their territories. For others, restoration of the Somali state will redress the power imbalances in the region, and offer an element of stabilization in the region.

Somali is torn between IGAD member states, particularly Ethiopian and Arab influence. The Influences have been played in the peace process to determine the nature of the future Somali state and its leadership. Each interested party wants the outcome to be in its favour. Arab countries, including the neighbouring Djibouti, favour a strong unitary Somali state whereas Ethiopia and the donor community at large, including the European Union, most notably Britain, prefer-sometimes for good reasons - a decentralised governance system with federal structures. Cynics note that despite the merits of the idea of re-creating a Somali state through a process of 'building block', the approach will be a recipe for undermining the Somali unity and polarising Somalia into ungovernable mini-states. The main concern of the Arab countries is to maintain Somalia's Arab identity and restore the unity and territorial integrity of Somalia. However, any meaningful role for the Arab countries in Somalia is often constrained mainly by their insufficient understanding of the micro-politics in Somalia.

The engagement of the European Union is mainly informed by humanitarian concerns. The issues of terrorism and refugees have also motivated Europe to seek peace and stability in Somalia. Europe is the largest donor for humanitarian activities in Somalia. They supported the latest peace process financially to ensure that there is an enabling environment for their assistance to make a real impact. The two former colonial masters of Somalia, Italy and Britain, have been viewed as acting outside the framework of the general objectives and principles of the European engagement in Somalia in pursuit of some vested interests. America's foreign policy in the Horn of Africa is currently geared towards fighting terrorism. Somalia is currently of low priority for United States. The lack of evidence linking Somalia to any terrorist activities reduces the prospect of enhanced U.S. engagement in Somalia in the near future.

Overall, the chapter suggests three major problems which constrain the search for peaceful settlement to the Somali conflict:

Firstly, the factions which dominate the political scene in Somalia lack any coherent political agenda and ideology. They continue to multiply by the day and every peace conference added more players to the political scene. They do not possess a functional hierarchy, represent a coherent ideological position, or political platform, or can claim an exclusive representation of a clan or a geographical area. These factions see themselves as the legitimate authority to make decisions on all issues, and they hope that their participation in the peace process will give them the option to hold political office and gain access to external resources; but ending the war is not their main goal. It is hard to imagine working out a solution in such a situation of confusing political landscape even with the best intentions of the external parties.

Secondly, the regional competitions have exacerbated the volatile internal situation and distanced the attainment of peace in the country. IGAD itself admitted that lack of improvement in the Somali peace process is attributable to the proliferation of parallel initiatives, which had supplanted rather than supplemented each other (Shirwa 2000). In particular, Ethiopia increasingly took on an inscrutable and complex role as mediator, regional power and trouble-maker. It has become more and more of a spoiler since 2001 through its open antagonism to the Transitional National Government. It remains to be seen whether the apparent consensus and unity of approach achieved at the last part of the Somali peace process among the rival regional actors, particularly between Ethiopia and Djibouti, will be sustained to nurture the nascent government institutions that had been created in Nairobi, and move the peace process forward.

Thirdly, Somalia remains very low on the priority of the major world powers. Neither the United States nor the European Union has shown serious political interest and heavy handed commitment towards the Somali peace process, which could have motivated regional states to get their act together. The peace building objectives of both the United States and the European Union in Somalia are heavily reliant on IGAD as potential peacemaker in Somalia. It can hardly be expected that peace agreement can work without the engagement of the Western powers in terms of offering the funds needed for the construction of the country, disarmament and demobilization of the combatants and revitalizing economic, social and political institutions which are vital for sustainable peace.

References

Ghalib, Jama Mohamed (2002) *Who is a Terrorist?* Mogadishu, Mogadishu Printing

Gilkes, P.S. (1999) *Somalia/ Somaliland, Is There a Way Forward*? London.

ICG Africa Report no 79, (4 May 2004). *Biting the Somali Bullet.*

Johnson, Pat. (1999) *Somalia/land: Political, Economic and Social Analysis*. A report for Oxfam GB

Koech, John (2004) Emerging Challenges of Security in IGAD in (eds.) Makumi Mwagiru, *African Regional Security in the Age of Globalization*. Nairobi, Heinrich Boll Foundation

Makinda, Samuel. (1993) *Seeking Peace from Chaos: Humanitarian Intervention in* Somalia (Boulder, Lynne Rienner Publishers.

Mwagiru, Makumi. (1984) *The International Management of Internal Conflicts in Africa: The Ugandan Mediation 1985*, a doctorate Dissertation in International Conflict Analysis, University of Kent.

Omar, Abshir. (2003) *The Impact of external Political Interventions on the Peace Process: The Case of Somalia,* Dissertation for the Degree of Masters of arts.The university of York.

Onyango Odougo Cyprine. (2000) Territorial Claims as the Model of Determinant of Inter-State Conflict between Ethiopia and Somalia, 1960-1991 in *Conflict in Contemporary Africa* (eds.) Okoth and Ogot.

Nairobi, Jomo Kenyatta Foundation.

Ramsbotham et.al. (1999) *Contemporary Conflict Resolution: The Prevention, Management and transformation of Deadly Conflicts.* Cambridge: Polity Press.

Shirwa, Hassan Farah (2001)*The Sub-Regional Management of Internal Conflicts in Africa (May-August, 2000),* M.A. Dissertation , Institute of Diplomacy and International Studies, University of Nairobi.

Zartman, I.W., ' Changing Forms of Conflict Mitigation', in Slater, R.O., Schutz, B.M. and Dorr, S.R. (eds.) (1993) *Global Transformation and the Third world.* Boulder: Lynne Rienner Publishers.

----

[1]UNPOS was established after the demise of United Nations Operations in Somalia (UNOSOM). Its mandate is, inter alia : to monitor developments in Somalia as a whole and keep the Secretary General informed about the situation in the country; to assist the people of Somalia to achieve national reconciliation; and to assist the external actors on Somalia towards a uniformity of approach in the Somali National Reconciliation Process.

[2]The Intergovernmental Authority on Development (IGAD) superseded the Intergovernmental Authority on Draught and Development (IGADD) established in 1986 by the draught afflicted six African countries of Kenya, Ethiopia, Djibouti, Uganda, Sudan and Somalia. The State of Eritrea joined the sub-regional grouping as the seventh member on September 1993 after it gained its independence from Ethiopia. One of the stated objectives of the organisation is to promote peace and stability in the sub-region and create mechanisms within the sub-region for the prevention, management and resolution of inter and intra-state conflicts through dialogue.

[3] Ministry of Information, "Foreign Affairs and National Security Policy and Strategy", Addis Ababa, November 2002 pp.6-7

[4]Ethiopia extended invitations to Somali factions opposing 'Salballaar' government of Hussein Aideed in November 1996 to meet in the resort town of Sodere in Ethiopia. An anti-Aideed coalition of twenty-six factions (26) attended what was called 'High Level Consultations' and established National Salvation Council(NSC). The meeting also agreed to hold a National Reconciliation Conference in Bosaso mid 1997. TNG sprung from Arta conference which was hosted by Djibouti and in which Ethiopia had minimal influence. Ethiopia alleged the leadership of TNG, including president Abduqasim Salat Hassan, of being close allies of terrorist groups operating in Somalia.

[5]In his speech at the first Somali reconciliation conference in Djibouti in 1991, Moi underscored the urgent need to resolve these conflicts peacefully through the region's own efforts and to strengthen peace and cooperation among the states of the sub-region and prevent foreign interferences with all its negative consequences.

[6]Kenya restricted the entry of Somalis into the country and invalidated the Somali passport. It also raided the Somali-inhabited estates in Kenya a number of times and made arrests.

[7]Interview with Ambassador Mohamed Abdi Afey, Nairobi, 28July, 2004.

[8] This is the mild narcotic leave also known as khat which is grown in the Meru province of Kenya. The revenue from this trade is estimated to be worth of 120 million US dollars a year.

[9]According to Kenya's ambassador to Somalia, Mohamed Abdi Afey, Kenya spent $3.6 million to pay for the accommodation of the Somali delegates at the peace talks in Kenya and issued visas to over 3000 delegates, some of them self-sponsoring.

[10]Interview with Ambassador Bethuel Kiplagat, Kenya's special Envoy to Somalia National Reconciliation Process, Mbagathi, Nairobi, 24 July 2004

[11]Interview with Amb. Salim Khusaibi, the Arab League Special Envoy for Somalia, 22 October, 2004

[12]The total contribution of the Arab countries to the conference in Kenya was amounted to $250,000. During the talks, Kenya's minister of foreign affairs visited Egypt, Saudi Arabia and Qatar to mobilize political and financial support of the Arab countries for the process. The involvement of the Arabs gave the peace process more legitimacy.

[13]The reputed International Crisis Group's report on Somalia dated 11 July 2005 "Counter-Terrorism in Somalia: Losing the Hearts and Minds of the People" argues that U.S. has had some success in combating terrorism in Somalia but risks evoking a backlash. It contends that successful counter-terrorism strategy requires more attention to helping Somalia with the twin task of reconciliation and state building.

[14]Report on the IGAD Conference on the Prevention and Combating Terrorism, Addis Ababa, 24-27 June 2003.

[15]Jim Fisher-Thompson and Lindsey Brooks ' Eldoret Conference Could Mean Peace for Somalia,' U.S. Official says, Washington File Staff Writers, 9 October 2002 at

www.somalilandnet.com/warya/2002/somalinews/11289.shtml

visited on 22/11/04

[16]Interview with Prof. Abdi Ismail Samatar, Nairobi, 24 July, 2004

[17] EU Council of Ministers-General Affairs and External Relations-from the 2447th council meeting , Brussels, 2002 at http://www.somali-civilsociety.org/peaceconference/section3_councilconlusion.asp visited on August 15, 2004

[18] Judith Gardner, Final Report on the Evaluation of EC Support to the IGAD-led Somali National Reconciliation Process. August 14, 2003

[19]Sweden funds humanitarian programs, including the largest education project, in Puntland run by Diakonia Sweden, and the activities of Life and Peace Institute which has been working in Somalia since 1992. Swedish donations for Somalia in 2004 amount to 8 million US dollars.

[20]Interview with Per Lingarde, former Deputy Head of the Swedish Embassy in Kenya, 14 October 2004

Chapter 12

Recovering the Somali State: The Islamic Factor

Abdurahman M. Abdullahi

> "Regardless of the subtleties of Islam in Somalia, it is one of the few elements that virtually all Somalis support to some degree. It provides a code of moral and ethical behaviour, it bolsters Somali cultural tradition by offering a system in which rulings of elders are accepted, and it brings a tradition of continuity greatly needed in Somalia's struggle to bring order out of the last decade of chaos. The presence of traditional Islamic ethics, codes, and laws of conduct offer one piece of a foundation upon which the new Somalia can be built (Hussein Adam and Richard Ford, 1998)"

Islam as one of the great religions in the world, and the fastest growing in the West and Islamic movements, has been taking centre stage in the worldwide since the 1980s. This unprecedented world interest in Islam and its new revival has intensified to the highest degree, after the September 11, 2001 terrorist attacks on some vital USA targets and the subsequent explosion of the hitherto continuous global war on terrorism, resulting so far, in strong US military intervention and regime changes in two Muslim states, namely Afghanistan and Iraq[1]. Somalia had been somewhat spared from being included in the targeted countries for US military intervention, although Al-Barakat Group Co., Al-Haramain charity operating in Somalia and Al-Itihaad Movement were listed among terrorist organizations. Somalia therefore remains a hotspot under constant surveillance as a possible hideout for terrorists.

Islamic movements in the world are united in their considering Islam as a source of religious inspiration, solace and fulfilment for life in this world and beyond and as their supreme guidance for all their social, political and economic activities. Nevertheless, they differ from each other when it comes to the modern interpretations of the Islamic text and its practical application programs and strategies for societal change. The core agenda and programs of these movements are dependent, among other things, on the conditions and environment they have grown up and operate in[2]. For instance, movements operating under foreign occupation, and lacking any other avenues to redress their grievances, most likely go for underground activities and armed resistance[3], while, on the other hand, those functioning in a tolerant and democratic environment go for overt social and political expression[4]. Some of these movements have taken even more extreme approaches of directing their wrath and armed defiance against their national governments, whom they consider as deviating from authentic Islam, and their cohorts and perceived supporters in the West[5].

Somalia is located in the periphery of the historical Islamic world and has never been totally incorporated into the successive Islamic political empires. Nevertheless it does not remain isolated from modern developments in the Muslim world in which new waves of Islamic revivalism has been taking great strides since it originated from Egypt, Saudi Arabia and Indian subcontinent in the early years of the 20th century. Therefore, Somalis, as part of the cultural interaction with the wider Islamic world, have been receiving ample printed literature materials and contacting different scholars from different schools of thought since late 1960s. As a result, Somalia, historically proud and boasting homogeneity even in religious matters, and adhering to one school of thought among the four famous law schools in Islam, that is Shafi'i School, had been witnessing tremendous changes and loss of that historic authenticity since the 1960s. During the last four decades, besides Shafi'i school and Hambali School brought from Saudi Arabia by the "Safiya Movement", Hanafi School brought from India and Pakistan by the "Tablig Movement", had been taking roots in the Somali society. Therefore, besides traditional Sufi brotherhoods, new brands of the Islamic groups had been emerging, calling for Islamic revivalism and adopting different perspectives and approaches, and producing movements akin in their interpretation of Islam and socio-political programs to the different Islamic movements in the world.

The collapsed Somali nation-state in early 1991 after 30 years of its birth on the 1st of July 1960, had disintegrated into many warlord-dominated regions or clan-based fiefdoms, shaky local administrations, nominal transitional government and traditionally administered areas. That being said, up to now, scholars of Somalia disagree on what had really collapsed in Somalia in 1991, which makes recovering Somali state even more time consuming because "the starting point is contentious". Obviously, there are three components that any given state must have. First, the idea of the state, which means the political, economic, religious and social ideologies that lay the foundation for the population of the state. Secondly, the physical land mass of the nation-state, including territorial borders, natural resources, and man-made wealth within these boundaries. Thirdly, are the institutional entities of the nation-state, which consists of executive, legislative, administrative and judicial branches of the state. On the issue of recovering the Somali state, there are two schools of thought: first, the extreme opinion, which entertains the view that everything related to the Somali nation-state had collapsed, and thus, it can only be reconstructed from scratch. This opinion also proposes that the best option for Somalis is to re-invent the nation-state anew through bottom-up process of state formation, based on the concept of "building *Blocks*"[6]. The second opinion is a moderate one, which holds the position that the Somali nation-state had only partially collapsed and that it is recoverable. Only national state institutions had collapsed while other two components of the state namely: population and the physical landmass remain unchanged. Therefore, this opinion supports top-down process of *"state recovery"* instead of the *"re-invention of a new state"*.

The complexity of the Somali crisis does not allow a hazy fixture, emotional solution, repetition of the previously known failures, an imposed external solution, and structures tailored to suit specific group and personality's interests. Reconstructing Somali's nation-state requires re-engineering by sincere experts of Somali affairs supported by multilateral studies, including reviewing the shared core values of society and the state, re-examining appropriate state structures of a clan-based society, considering human capacities required to run institutions of the state, and so on. It also requires prudent understanding of the external actors and addressing their concerns without compromising strategic objectives of recovering the Somali state.

This paper does not examine Islam as a faith and a belief system for all Somalis, nor does it focus on what is termed these days "political Islam" as such. The paper rather focuses on how Islamic moral values supersede and dilute clannish values of disunity and disintegration and how these could be invigorated in order to recover the Somali state. Therefore, the paper brings to the fore aspects of Islam, which bring people together and communities closer, uniting their mission and purpose in life. Of course, in doing so, we can't ignore the active role of modern Islamic movements and their impact in calling for Islamic values and their legal aspects into the daily life of Muslims, thus creating trans-clan organizations to reach these goals. Studying the Islamic factor in recovering the Somali state entails examining the role of Islam in tribal societies as well as exploring the active advocates of revivalist (Tajdiid)[7] Islamic movements. In doing so, it is important, first and foremost, to take note of the difference between Islam as the religion of all Somalis, and the modern development of the Islamic movements, which has a political component among other multitude programs. Islam with its authentic sources of the Qur'an and the Sunna of the Prophet Mohammed (PBUH), is sacrosanct among all Muslims, while Islamic movements representing organized groups carry human deficiencies and limitations. Moreover, the reader must be aware that Islamic movements are not one brand, but constitute a mixture of "moderate" (Al-wasadiyah) and "extremist" (Al-guluwu) groups, if classified in a continuum scale. Classical literature about Islam in Somalia mainly focuses on Sufi brotherhoods and modern Islamic development has only received some attention recently. Moreover, the recent literature tends to discriminate against modern movements, stereotyping them in a variety of unfriendly taxonomies[8]. Being the most active trans-clan and ideologically motivated groups of the society, Islamic movements remain an important factor in the future of Somalia; and thus, deserve more scholarly attention.

This paper takes a moderate view of the recoverability of the Somali nation-state and focuses only on one particular factor among many, which needs to be studied. It examines the Islamic factor and the moral factor in reconstructing the collapsed Somali nation-state. First, it explores the idea of tribal society, nation-building and Islam. Secondly, it offers a background on the role of Islam in the society and the state. Thirdly, it traces the nature and the role of the modern Islamic movements in social transformation and political participation.

Tribal society, Nation-building and Islam.

"Bedouins can acquire royal authority only by making use of religious colouring, such as prophethood or sainthood or some great religious event in general" *Ibn-Khaldun, the Arab philosopher*

There are three requirements in any effort to reconstitute the Somali nation-state. These are; (1) certain level of societal cohesion; (2) accepted form of governance; and (3) sufficient support of the international community. The first two prerequisites are internal factors in which even strong international support yields no results. Here, we will be focusing on these internal factors, examining possibilities of their attainment in the society.

To begin with, we will address questions such as how societal cohesion could be materialized in a clan-based social setting and society suffering from scars of the internecine wars of the last two decades? Is there any form of governance, which reassures Somali people that they receive equal treatment as citizens of the state no matter what their clan affiliation is? To answer these questions, we shall explore the existing indigenous ideologies within the Somali society since both societal cohesion and accepted governance require certain level of shared values. In fact, shared values among most Somalis are tribalism, nationalism and Islam, detectable in the psyche of almost every Somali in varying degrees. Among these values, only tribalism carries the virus of divisiveness in society while nationalism and Islam are agents for societal cohesion and nation building. In fact, one divisive factor can't overcome two unifying factors unless they are weak and internally divided. Finally, it has become clear by now that without reconciling nationalism and Islam and offering space for clan attachments, discussions on reconstructing Somalia will be just a mere entertainment[9].

Tribal Society and Divisive Tribalism:

Somali social setting is based on clans finally being accepted by those involved in the reconciliation process after a long period of denial. In post civil war Somalia, it seems that all local administrations and national reconciliation conferences could not find a better formula than clan representation in accordance with agreed upon power sharing formula during the initial stage of institution building[10]. Attempts to create other options for power sharing, at this stage, did not receive enough popular support. Today, the Somali social setting has become so used to this formula of sharing power based on clans that the first chapter of most literature on Somalia begins with clan classification and mapping.

In weak states like Somalia, social divisions generate what is termed "sub-cultures", which create multitude loyalties within the state. Tribalism being a state of mind, an act of consciousness, generates tribal solidarity and strong loyalty to one's own tribe and high propensity among political leaders to invest in the goal of winning power. In the rural areas, tribal solidarity is necessary and is the only viable way of survival where no central authority exists to arbitrate disputes and to provide security

According to Ibnu-Khaldun "only tribes held together by group feeling can live in the desert". Clan solidarity, however, may take destructive role in urban centres if it transgresses social domain and is used widely as a political instrument. Even so, in the social domain, social relations expected to take another form based on neighbourhood and professional group interests. Instead, "urban tribalism", which is the product of rural migration to the urban centres and preserved tribal allegiances, had developed into overtly political tribalism in the 1950s. Rural tribalism based on that fame of the individual is derived from the fame and glory of his ancestors, loyalty to and self–sacrifice for the sake of the clan and the fulfilment of the law of revenge against rival clans. Rural tribalism was instituted in the urban centres, creating negative political implications. In fact, this clan culture, instead of getting weakened with improved education, increased accumulation of wealth and nationalistic programs; the reverse process of *"nomidazation"* of the urban elite was taking place[11].

The founding fathers of the modern Somali nation-state were very much aware of the obstacles of political clan loyalties to the nation-building process. In the early days of the struggle for independence, besides national political parties, smaller clan- based political parties had emerged in the 1950s. The political system adopted also promoted political tribalism. The founding fathers were confronted with the imperatives for nation building based on promoting nationalism on the one hand, and a society, which lacks appropriate organizational skills in modern political participation on the other. Manifestation of this dilemma had become apparent in the clan alignment of the first ever elections and formation of the local administration in the Southern Somalia in 1956. To deal with the issue of political tribalism, successive Somali governments developed the following three strategies: (1) proportional representation[12]; (2) extreme glorification of the Somali nationalism and condemnation of the clans; and (3) legislative measures to strengthen the first strategies[13]. However, all these efforts failed to stop the development of clan-based government and politics as well as the emergence of clan-based armed factions and armed confrontation that finally led to the collapse of the Somali nation-state.

Clan solidarity in Somalia is more robust in the pastoral areas and, of course, their extended families in the urban centres. Since these pastoralists had dominated Somali clan politics, they have coloured "nomadic" culture in the whole political spectrum of Somalia. The "nomadic culture" *vis-a-vis* state formation was well studied by the Arab philosopher Ibn Khaldun, who wrote that

> ".. Savagery has become (the Bedouins) character and nature. They enjoy it, because it means freedom from authority and no subservience to leadership. Such a natural disposition is the negation and antithesis of civilization...the very nature of their existence is the negation of building (urbanization), which is the basis of civilization. Furthermore, since they do not see any value in labour and craftsman and do not appreciate it, the hope for profit vanishes, and no productive work is done. The sedentary population disperses and civilization decays... The Bedouins are not concerned with laws, or with deterring people from misdeeds... they care only for property that they might take away from people through looting .... Under the rule of Bedouins, their subjects live as in s state of anarchy. Anarchy destroys mankind and ruins civilizations..."

Summarizing the above stated notion, nomads follow three

characteristics which cause destruction of urban life and ultimately the state: (1) Anarchy and lawlessness, (2) despising labour and crafts, and (3) transgressing private and public properties. Since nomads and their cultural extension in the urban areas can't produce functional state institutions due to the above stated behaviours, then, the question becomes how these nomads can be transformed or absorbed into a system of modern state institutions? Founding fathers of Somali nationalism had answered this question in two ways: (1) Intensification of modern education and gaining experience of running state institutions from the colonial administration. (2) Raising national consciousness and condemning everything related with the clan culture. However, both approaches were incomplete due to time constraints, which were practically confined into 10 years[14].

Clan divide is neither evil nor good, rather a neutral and natural social setting prevalent in many societies, particularly among Muslims, where family values are very strong. A true genealogy through one's paternity is an indication of family sanctity and compliance with desired Islamic values. This neutral entity could be utilized either in a positive way or in a destructive manner. Unfortunately, in Somalia, clan settings were, in many instances, employed wrongly, even in the highest echelon of the state institutions. In fact, contrary to the make up of clans in many countries where clans don't share much in their ethnicity, clans in Somalia share all the necessary elements of homogeneity. Due to a well publicized put down of the clan system employed by the nationalist party of SYL and the successive Somali governments afterwards, public perceptions was diverted away from grasping the complex root causes of the collapse of the Somali nation-state. Even further, many Somalis consider clannism as the "*Cancer of Somali State*", which implies incurability. The implication of such a notion is very severe and essentially leads either to forge a policy of "eliminating tribalism" "*dabar-goynta*" or to give up nation-building measures. The fact remains that "clan divide as such is not the core factor of the Somali crisis of state formation: it is rather competition over resources and power, which is seen as safeguarding access to these resources that is expressed in competitive clan labels".

Nation building and Nationalism:

Nation-building requires a certain degree of national consciousness, which tames "nomadic culture" and cements segments "clan blocks" into a solid nation. To do so, early Somali nationalists thought that Somalis were already a *nation in search of a state*[15], and that by strengthening the ideology of nationalism and scorning clanism, nation building would be achieved. Therefore, nationalism was focused on, and expressed in the rich poetic heritage of Somalis in poems and modern songs and as a result the national flag and anthem were looked at with great respect.

According to Saadia Tauval, in addition to the common factors underlying the rise of nationalism in the "Third World" countries, three factors in particular contributed to the rise of nationalism in Somalia[16] . First, resentment against colonial governments, which had ruled but never, subjected the Somalis. As a result, Somalis who had never been subjected to an institutionalized government had to bear the burden of heavy taxation, forced labour, and racial policy. Colonial authority applied the policy of appropriation of agricultural land and intervened in traditional authority. Saadia Tauval states that, "the confrontation of the nomadic, individualistic and independent Somalis with organized government inevitably led to resentments and conflict"[17]. The second factor, relates to religious antagonism towards both European powers and Ethiopia. To the Somalis, the colonial powers represented Christianity whereas they considered themselves Muslims. It was exceedingly difficult and humiliating for them as Muslims to accept a non-Muslim rule"[18]. The third factor was a "deliberate encouragement by various governments" to achieve certain goals. Italy with its "la Grande Somalia" program during its invasion of Ethiopia in 1935, The British ambition of "greater Somalia" in 1946, and Egypt's revolutionary influence in the 1950s, had all contributed to the rise of Somali nationalism. All in all, Somali nationalism and its core ideology revolved around the establishment of a united Somali nation-state, including all regions inhabited by Somalis in the greater Horn of Africa region. However, it appears that this Somali vision of nationalism does not take into consideration how to preserve this nation-state after it's been founded[19].

Nationalism was seemingly a very emotional and conscious feeling of the majority of the people and therefore, national consciousness did not supersede tribal solidarity, though all possible efforts were made to realize its nationalistic goals. The reunification of the former British Somaliland and Italian Somalia and the promulgation of the independence of the Somali Republic on July 1st 1960 was the greatest achievement of the Somali nationalists. Yet, clan alignments and clan politics was gradually mounting and Somalia reached the verge of collapse nine years after independence. In October of 1969, the military intervened and recreated new symbols for nationalistic zeal, including the writing of Somali language in Latin scripts and waged war against Ethiopia in 1977/78 to recover Somali territories captured and colonized by Ethiopia in the pinnacle of nationalist fervour. With the defeat of Somalia in the war and the proclamation of the independent Republic of Djibouti, Somali nationalism was in the process of declining. The over stretched goals of Somali nationalism and the low capacity of the state institutions caused the self-destruction of the Somali nation-state itself. The abysmal level of Somali nationalism and its fragility is evident from the absence of national political institutions and the total demise of the former ruling national political parties[20]. In the vacuum of the fading Somali nationalism and the collapsing of the state, radical clan factions and Islamic movements, with both moderate and radical components, emerged. Radical clan factions are the continuation of political tribalism, while modern Islamic movement is a new social and political force, focusing on the Islamic component of indigenous Somali ideologies.

***Islam: a Fountain for Social Cohesion*:**

The early history of Islam shows how clans of the Arabian Peninsula had changed their political culture after their conversion to Islam. After migration to Medina, the established first Islamic state was based on trans-clan brotherhood bonds among Muslims and a sense of belonging to all other citizens of Medina, combining territorial attachment with common faith in a form of social cohesion among all community members[21]. This history records that present Somali clans, having great similarities with these ancient clans, may also be influenced by the revival of Islamic values where behaviour of anarchy and lawlessness, despising labour and crafts, looting private and public properties and internecine wars are abhorred and admonished. Islam teaches its faithful the concept of one nation *"Ummah wahidah"*[22] adhering to the commands of one God, unified under one leadership that is law abiding, and a committed leadership to the values of good governance. Islam is both individual and communal religion. It calls for the individual to live in harmony with his/her self, with his community as well as with the entire creation of God; it calls for an individual to take direct responsibility for his entire actions[23]. Islam teaches an individual to be honest, truthful, patient, content, charitable, cheerful and tolerant. It commands its faithful to control their anger and to forgive when others wrong them.

Besides the earlier community of believers in Medina, the entire Arabian Peninsula had changed drastically because the new faith that had instilled in the mindset of the segmented clans universal values upon which Islamic civilization was built such as the values of supremacy of the law, equality, justice, freedom and fraternity. In the later years, Arab sociologist and philosopher, Ibn Khaldun had recorded that

> "Bedouins can acquire royal authority only by making use of religious colouring, such as prophethood or sainthood or some great religious event in general. The reason is because of their savagery: the Bedouins are the least willing of all nations to subordinate themselves to each other, as they are rude, proud, ambitious and eager to be leaders. Their individual aspirations rarely coincide. But when there is religion {among them}...then they have some restraining influence upon themselves. The quality of haughtiness and jealousy leave them. It is, then, easy to unite them in {a societal organization}".

Islam also emphasizes social cohesion and harmony. Its basic philosophy is "enjoining the right and prohibiting the wrong" and that one should not harm others[24]. Social cohesion begins in the family and community and extends to human beings at large[25]. The law of Islam emphasises justice and fairness prohibits cheating, exploitation, fraud, deception as well as coercive policies. Moreover, it also emphasizes good governance under broad moral principles, and laws divined by God. Furthermore, Islamic moral teachings also emphasize benevolence, charity, and kindness. Having seen the above brief conceptualization of some Islamic values, let's now consider the minimum necessary value needed to restore the Somali nation-state.

Respecting and abiding by the laws:

In the mindset of many Somalis, man-made laws are derived from the colonial code; therefore, breaking them is not seen to be immoral. On the other hand, if that law is Islamic in nature, in a broader sense, one feels that breaking it will have grave consequence not only in this world but also that on the Day of Judgment, it may lead the person entering the hellfire. For instance, many Somalis consider those who break the laws of Allah as "evil" doers while those who break state laws are sometimes considered *"bona fide"*people with good intentions or even "heroes" among its clan members. Therefore, sacrosanct law is necessary to restore the respectability of laws among individuals and communities by invigorating self-restraining moral codes, which maintains some sort of natural order in the society.

Protecting public and private property:

Among many Somalis, the concept of public property is not well entrenched in their culture. In the pastoral society as well as agricultural communities, private property is well entrenched while public property, according to the understanding of many Somalis, is no-man's property. Nothing is shared in the Somali culture except blood wealth, clan wells and common defence during conflicts. *Zakat* and charities, which are Islamic concepts, are not well developed in the Somali culture. What Somalis know most is not pure charity, but returning favours "*abaal ergasho*". Modern states are built with public properties collected in the form taxation and redistributed to the society through allocated budgetary system. This requires transparency and accountability. On the other hand, the culture of nomads, where raiding and looting are common, was transferred to the urban cities in new cultural form. This nomadic culture appears to be taking roots - where every employee of the state loots whatever he/she can. This process of looting of public property occurs in a setting where the higher and lower echelons of government are interconnected in a complex web of kinship. In the opinion of many concerned with the rebuilding of the Somali nation-state, reviving the value of lawful coexistence and the introduction of basic Islamic principles of (*halal and haram*) in a community very much attached to Islam may create additional added value for the protection of public property.

Supreme Loyalty to the state:

The modern state, which has the responsibility of protecting its citizens from internal as well external threats, demands supreme loyalty to itself. This loyalty is divided in clan-based societies where the individual loyalty is pulled in diametrically opposing directions between the state and clan, creating highly explosive polarizations. Pastoral culture of leadership is based on the fact that the clan chief is first among equals, and hierarchical system of the modern state, is not well known. This creates insubordination in the state institutions as well as extra-institutional connections among clan members. In this way, a member of the clan may easily meet with the ministers and the president belonging to his clan and then ruin the hierarchy required for the modern state management. Islam demands its believers to give loyalty to their state and its leadership as long as the leadership abides by the policies and procedures of the state laws[26].

.*Equality and justice*:

The concept of equality and justice is relatively self-centred in the pastoral communities. Paradoxically, equality and justice in a clan family is well respected while the universal equality of members of all clans is not well entrenched in the culture. Modern state shall offer equal rights to all citizens and they shall be equal before the law. It is difficult to understand this concept in the clan culture; however, Sufi brotherhoods in Somalia had proved the supremacy of Islamic brotherhood and members of bigger clans becoming disciples of the sheikhs from the smaller clans or even despised groups.

Islam, Society and State: Historical Interactions

> "Two things are inviolable in Somalia: the clan and Islam".
> *Somali wisdom*

Islam reached Somalia in its early years and it is believed that some versions of it were adopted by the Umayyad Dynasty (685-705)[27]. Nevertheless, Somalia remained in the periphery of the Muslim world for quite sometime. The Somali race is well known for its ardent belief in Islam to the degree that the identity of being *Somali* is often synonymous with being a Muslim since all Somalis are Muslims by "birth". Traditionally, Somalis mainly belong to one of the two Sufi brotherhoods - Qaderiyah_(which has two offshoots - *Uwesiyah* and *Zayli'yah*) and *Ahmadiyah* (which again has two offshoots - *Salihiyah* and *Dadrawiyah*) and adhere to the *Shafi'* school of the Islamic jurisprudence. Prior to colonial rule, clan elders and religious leaders had been running communities and playing important roles in their affairs. Elders with variety of hierarchical levels and roles managed the affairs of their particular communities during peacetime and during conflicts, they played the role of conflict resolution managers in the affairs of the community. On the other hand, religious leaders played the role of religious teachers and administered religion-related affairs like conducting marriage contracts, inheritance and resolving conflict by Islamic legal code.

Moreover, these religious leaders were responsible for all the matters of community education and, therefore, most of their activities were directed to the fields of education and Islamic propagation. This education system was organized in such a way that the basics were founded on memorization of the *Qur'an* and its higher levels, were geared towards teaching Arabic language, Islamic jurisprudence *Malamat,* Sufism and the interpretation of the *Qur'an* and *Hadith.* Early years of memorization of the *Qur'an,* in the widely spread Qur'anic Schools known in Somalia as *Dugsi* had become part of Somali culture observable in almost every populated area of Somalia.

Circles of Islamic education in the mosques and ancient Islamic propagation centres such as *Zayla, Harar, Warsheikh, Banadir* and *Merca* were well established in a sustainable system for higher education and depositors and reservoirs of the Arabic language-based education. Many leaders of the anti-colonial movements had graduated from these schools, which had produced protectors of the community from the attempted conversion to Christianity by missionaries. Moreover, modern anti-colonial movements had been connected directly to these schools and groups. Religious leaders and clan elders exercised legitimate authority over their communities and had been working in a networked system, united and harmonious in every locality in accordance with a set of rules and regulations called *Heer*, which blended with Islamic *Shari'a.* The role of the elders and religious scholars were complementary whereas job divisions were clear for both types of leaderships. Moreover, they've always cooperated with one another, although it was observed that clan elders were taking the leading role in the nomadic areas where the frequency of outbreaks of warfare was high whilst religious scholars took prominence in the agricultural and settled communities[28].

During colonial rule, the authority of these traditional community leaders became greatly weakened. Often, state authorities intervened in the selection of clan elders and since they became salaried employees of the state, their autonomous authority in their constituencies had been weakened. This did not change in the post-colonial state of Somalia, though Islam was officially recognized as the religion of the state and Islamic *Shari'a* was made the main source of the legal system. However, the modern understanding of Islam in 1960 was not well developed and thus, all legal matters based on the inherited colonial legal system remained intact[29]. The only aspect of law respected all along was the family law, which was based totally on the *Shari'a* until the military regime tried to intervene in 1975. Generally, the Somali state was, on the one hand, trying to show its firm commitment to Islamic symbolism by exploiting it to fit into the state objectives and, on the other hand, taking quasi-secular approach in all its practical actions.

Nevertheless, it was only in the early 1970s, when the basic Islamic canon, the family law, was questioned openly by the military regime under the disguise of implementing socialist ideals of equaling men and women in inheritance[30]. The reaction to that attempt was that Islamic scholars protested peacefully but the uncompromising revolutionary regime opted for public execution of 10 leading Islamic scholars in unprecedented arrogance and savagery in 1975. This execution had shaken the emotions of Somali people profoundly and gave impetus for the revival of Islam. Moreover, indiscriminate state repression had caused mayhem and the emigration of Islamic activists in search peaceful havens, opportunity of work and education. The new migration abode had become Saudi Arabia, Egypt and Sudan, the centres of the modern Islamic movements. Furthermore, the cruelty of the revolutionary regime was felt extensively and a large number of the population was gradually expressing its peaceful resistance by disengaging from the programs of the regime, and taking refuge in mosques. Thus, in the mosques[31], underground Islamic groups were gaining new recruits and establishing networks to counter the socialist ideology with more organized grass roots of Islamic work in 1970s. The military regime had alienated both Islamic and clan-based oppositions; whereas clan-based opposition developed into armed factions and established bases in Ethiopia, Islamic opposition opted for grass roots strategy based on intensification of the call for Islamic laws and ways of life, and strengthening their underground organizational base. It is believed that the voice of an organized Islamic challenge was first heard loud in Somalia in 1989 during the black Friday massacre.

After the collapse of the state and the outbreak of the civil war, religious groups took the initiative of reconciling warring groups, but in vain. During the civil war, Islamic groups took different approaches. *Al-Itihad* became more radical and took up arms as a way of political participation, while *Al-Islah* opted for peaceful means of propagating Islam, reconciling communities and providing social services. On the other hand, traditional Sufi leaders were either neutral in the conflict or aligned themselves along clan lines. During the civil war, Islam became a way out for many Somalis inside Somalia and in the Diaspora communities, flocking in the mosques and around the centres of Islamic studies. In these mosques, modern Islamic scholars offered Islamic perspectives of the calamity befalling the Somalis. Besides that, hundreds of schools were opened throughout the country with strong Islamic inclinations, recreating traditional Islamic education coupled with modernity in a sustainable system supported by the communities. Moreover, Somalis looking for a unifying factor found Islam the only available indigenous ideology capable of uniting them. During the civil war, the Somali society was being transformed, with a better understanding of Islam and an improvement in the people's religious outlook alongside the consistent violations of the basic values of Islam by militia and warlords. Finally, it is important to point out "Somalis, for the most part, don't by and large apply Islamic values for the interest of their lives, but they always protect Islam and guard it from abuses by others". Here comes the Somali wisdom that "two things are inviolable in Somalia: the clan culture and Islam". Most Somalis are ready to sacrifice their lives in defending these two.

Currently, in the absence of strong central authority, traditional elders and the religious scholars play pivotal role in managing the affairs of their communities, reviving their original role in resolving conflicts and mediating disputes. Moreover, all the successful conferences for re-establishing local and national state institutions in Somalia were based on the decisions of the traditional leaders[32]. Furthermore, modernity had influenced both traditional elders and Islamic scholars and many of them became highly educated elite, integrating the best of tradition and modernity. At last, modern Islamic revivalist groups have modernized traditional ways of propagating Islam in the mosques and teaching Islamic sciences in public arenas. As a result, traditional ways of education improved the opportunity of the Somalis for education in the absence of national institutions bringing forth sustainable system of education.

Moderate Islamic Movement: Its nature and role

> "Islam is the supreme guidance and reference for all aspects of life of the Muslim communities and therefore, the prospective Somali state should promote and protect Islamic values within the community and follow the guidelines of Islamic Shari'a law in all its legislative procedures".
> (*The core ideology of the Islamic movements in Somalia*).

Islamic groups in Somalia in general should be understood in the context of modernist comprehension of Islam as a complete way of life, an understanding that does not go well with the secular tendencies of the post-colonial state. In fact, these secular tendencies were embodied in the way of life of the ruling elite and were enshrined in the colonial legal heritage and ethos. On the other hand, Islamic groups disagree with compartmentalising Islam and likening it to the Christian way, by pushing it to the corner of mere spiritual sphere and individual responsibility. Islam being a comprehensive religion, personal as well communal, is not and can't be apolitical. Its *"nature of completeness"*, logically provides guidelines for the political, social and economic life of Muslim communities and states. In accordance with these lines of thought, Islamic activists belonging to different schools of thought have been questioning the legitimacy of state policies, particularly those regarding the role of Islam in the state and society. These activists had in the mean-time formed organizations addressing their way of understanding of Islam, lately called "political Islam"[33]. The reaction of the post-colonial states to activities of these organizations was undemocratic, brutal and violent. It was a denial of the right to freedom in all its forms such as physical, cultural, economic, and political. As a result, Islamic activists were pushed to the unavoidable option of underground activities like all other decedent political organizations in the early 1970s in Somalia[34].

In the wider understanding of Islamic revivalism, many groups and organizations could be categorized in Somalia. However, the most prominent of these organizations are considered to be *Islah, Itihaad* and *Tablig*. All the other organizations largely fall under the ideology of one of these three organizations. These organizations were formed back in the late sixties and early seventies. These organizations are local and Somali by birth, however, their methodology for advocating the harmonization of the indigenous culture and laws of the communities and the state with the Islamic legal system and values, had its roots in the wider Islamic world. Muslim Brotherhood in Egypt, the Wahabi School or "Salafiya" in Saudi Arabia and neo-Sufis in India could be considered their ideological affiliates respectively. Though, these movements share aspirations of bringing Islamic values into the lives of their communities, nevertheless, their strategies sprawls a very wide spectrum, from peaceful evolutionists to armed revolutionaries[35]. Also, their visions, strategies, organizational structures are so diverse, that it could be said that the only thing they share in common are only activism and aspirations. These organizations, obviously, take in their practical application, the colour of the societal peculiarities, and in this context, Somali flavour. It is even so within Somalia, where it reflects the cultural setting: pastoral, agricultural, urban and so on[36]. Moderate Islamic movements (*al-Wasadiyah wa al-Ictidal*) are all those peaceful organizations believing in evolutionary reformation of the society through an educational process and the reviving of Islamic values. In this category falls *Islah* and *Tabliq*. Extreme groups (*al-Tadaruf wal-Guluwu*) include *Al-Itihad* and *Takfir* that are revolutionaries and armed and believe exclusivity and absolutism[37].

Moderate components of the Islamic movements are not isolated from their cultural heritage; in fact, they believe that their historical roots could be traced back to the early struggle of the Islamic scholars *Ulama* to confront British, Italian and Ethiopian colonial invasions and their policies geared towards political domination in addition to the cultural influence of Somali Muslim society. The Dervish Movement of Mohamed Abdullah Hasan, the Sheikh Hassan Barsane resistance, the *Biyamaal* Revolt and other anti-colonial movements led by Islamic scholars could be considered as early Islamic revivalist movements[38]. In that sense, modern revivalism of Islam is a continuous process, progressive and anti-colonial resistance movements standing for the protection of cultural Islamic heritage against the cultural hegemony of the colonial powers. Indeed, early Islamic scholars had at least succeeded in protecting and maintaining Islamic faith in front of the torrent invasion of the privileged Christian missionaries poised to create Christian minorities in Somalia. As documented in the colonial archives, these missionaries had enjoyed financial, political and moral support provided by the colonial powers as part of the overall colonial scheme for conquering and pacifying other weaker nations. Islamic movements strongly believe that their task is to continue the resistance of their forefathers in the new ways corresponding to the magnitude of the threat that is facing Somali society. This new generation of Islamic activists is in the position, and destined to deal with the growing external and internal threats and challenges facing Somalia.

Moderate Islamic movements consider themselves as embodiments and the continuation of the aspiration of the Somali national movement, which had succeeded to bring about political independence[39] in 1960, but fell short of completing the expectations of the people in gaining economic and cultural independence. The national movements, using nationalistic ideology rhetoric alone, also failed to maintain the unity of the Somalis. Therefore, Islamic movements' position is that political independence alone was not sufficient enough to realize national goals in the post-independence period, and in addition to that, it had been focusing primarily on the cultural aspect. This is because it is the belief of Islam that reviving Islamic culture and safeguarding its values will create a conductive environment for societal peace and economic development and will also strengthen national cohesion. Islam is also an effective element in curbing clannish alignment in the society by creating trans-clan affiliations and groupings, the goal of which the ideology of nationalism alone had failed to achieve. Therefore, according to the belief of the Islamic movements, the ideology of nationalism used during the struggle for national independence was not a stand-alone ideology. Rather, it was coupled with the Islamic injunctions calling its devotees to wage inexhaustible resistance *(Jihad)* against infidels, particularly if they are transgressors and occupiers. However, the new ruling elite, trained in the colonial schools, underestimated the Islamic factor in their nation-building programs after gaining independence. In the Somali situation, immoral state policies, including not putting sufficient emphasis on the Islamic factor in governance, had finally produced the collapse of the state institutions. It is absolutely proven that after 30 years of independence, only Islamic organizations and clan militia remained functional as organized groups in Somalia. As a result, Islamic movements envisage that nation building in Somalia requires appealing to their rich Islamic heritage and tolerant and community-oriented values in addition to the revival of national consciousness and awareness. Appealing and sewing these two elements - Islamic values and nationalism- will generate enough innate strength to dislodge and weaken destructive political clanism and separatist tendencies from the psyche of the Somali society.

Islamic movements also represent the *reawakening of the faith* due to the improved understanding of Islamic teachings by modern Somali scholars trained not only in Islamic education centres and Islamic universities, but also in the modern universities[40]. Traditional Islamic education, which is centred on the spiritual aspects of Islam, was short in explaining the totality of Islam and was divorced from being a supreme guidance to the modern state institutions. In fact, the new, revived understanding of Islam is that Islam is a complete way of life, which is not confined to personal creed. Islam is the supreme guide and reference for all aspects of life of the Muslim communities and therefore, Somali state should apply and abide by the Islamic *Shari'a* law and protect Islamic values. Obviously, this concept is contrary to the understanding of religion by the former Christian colonial powers, which founded the collapsed Somali state, and most of the former educated elite in the highest echelon of the political spectrum. The understanding of religion by colonial powers was, and remains that religion, every religion, and state, every state, must be totally separated from each other since modern state, according to their view, should be secular. Moreover, religion is made the private domain of non-governmental organizations. Reawakening of faith *Tajdid al-Iman* is a phenomenon that occurs whenever Muslims suffer external threat such as colonialism and invasion, and Islam is employed as ideology of liberation *(Jihad)*. Also, that reawakening and moral rearmament take place whenever new charismatic preachers, organizations and brotherhoods, appear and intensify the call for the renewal of the faith[41]. In the history of Islam, this cyclical reawakening of the faith had been occurring since the initial revelation before the 6th century AD. In Somalia, waves of reawakening of the faith had occurred during the anti-colonial struggle and in confrontation with the Marxist military regime (1969-1991). The new cycle of reawakening of the faith created new hopes for the desperate and disenfranchised young generations of Somalis who had rightly responded to the call that Islam provides salvation in this world and hereafter.

Moderate Islamic movements are neither anti-western sentiment having the tendency of idealistic nostalgia for the past, nor blind imitators of other nations' culture and way of life. Therefore, in international affairs, moderate Islamic movements in Somalia are neither directed against any foreign states, nor were they established to achieve such sinister objectives. Their main task is focused on internal

Somali affairs, which requires enormous reformation of the collapsed state institutions. In fact, Somalia needs massive international support in all aspects of life in order to reassert itself as a sovereign state among other nations. Somalia also needs understanding and the support of its neighbours in order to reconstruct its statehood. Without achieving the above state requirements, regional peace and common security may be difficult to achieve among nations in the Horn of Africa. Preconditions for peace are that all states of the region should adhere to the principle of *"non- interference"* and cease their subversive activities and hegemonic strategies. Instead, regional cooperation should take its course in the region to foster economic and social development. Contrary to what some writers may want to believe as a "clash of civilizations"[42] ; genuine Islamic revivalism is in the interest of peace and security in the Horn of Africa. Good neighbourliness, particularly between Muslims and Christians, greatly enhances mutual cooperation[43].

During the last three decades, moderate Islamic movements had been working either under the dictatorial rule, where all organizations were not only duly banned as dissidents and harshly persecuted, or in the civil war situation, where law and order was totally lost and the law of the jungle became the rule of life. Surviving within these two stages of Somali history, Islamic Movements are more mature and experienced and play a vital role in Somali affairs. Today, the influence of Islamic movements could be seen in every aspect of life of the Somali people. In business, education, the civil society movement, mass media and in political life, the values and ideals of Islamic movements are taking roots in the social fabric of the nation. Islamic activists are taking important roles in the Diaspora communities and established organizations that propagated Islam, teach children *Qur'an* and urge communities to frequent mosques and Islamic centres. This is simply because Islamic values are deeply rooted in the society, its modern revival, according to the modernist understanding, is just the continuation and revival of faith, not creating innovations and discordance with the available and known doctrines of Islam.

The objectives of moderate Islamic Movements during the civil war were focused on forsaking internecine wars, focusing on internal reconstruction and reorganizations after the fall of the reign of tyranny, improving their image in the community by cooperating with other organizations and making local and national reconciliation as one of their major priorities. Moreover, promotion of education and establishing institutions for that purpose were given priorities. Furthermore, intensification of the Islamic call and education in all regions, promotion of civil society organizations and improving images at the international level were among the main objectives. In the field of national reconciliation, Arta Peace Process in Djibouti in the year 2000 had been the culmination of all reconciliation efforts since 1995.

Moderate Islamic movements strongly believe that they have a vital role to play in reviving Somali consciousness in the society. In addition to their roles of reconciliation, education and social service, they are convinced that any viable national political organizations need active participation of their members. Ironically, Islamic movements on their own are not political organizations, nor do they plan to convert themselves into such. Really, the Somali society of today should be interacting with conventional political parties based on ideology, not clan affiliations. Islamic groups are movements for common good working very hard to bring about social reform that will pave the way for the appearance of national political entities. However, members of Islamic groups may participate in every organization of their own choice, which they believe may bring good for Somalia. The rationales are that national organizations need people with national vision and members of Islamic groups had been coached and trained to uphold the ideals of nationalism and to belong to all segments of society. Therefore, they are ready elements for reconstructing organizations of national character. These members may play the role of "cement" in the segmented clans, where each clan had formed its own militia, political entity and social organization.

Conclusion

This paper has focused on one of the shared values of all Somalis, which has hitherto been undermined in the nation-building process, that is, the role of the Islamic factor in recovering the collapsed state in Somalia. It discussed the role of Islam in the society and state formation, and how the post-colonial state diminished its role and undermined its values. It also traced the reality of the modern Islamic movements as the most active trans-clan and ideologically motivated groups of the society. The paper argued that among the three components of the state, namely, the idea of the state, the physical base of the state and the Institutional expression of the state that only the institutional expression had collapsed. It also argued that recovering the Somali state would require a re-engineering, including reviewing shared core values, appropriate state structures, and considering human capacities required to run institutions of the state.

The paper also argued that ideological reconciliation should be worked out prior to actual political reconciliation in Somalia because whatever hypothesis is projected, the fact remains that Somalia is a

Muslim, clan-based society striving to reestablish its nation-state institutions. It is posited that because clanism is accepted as a political reality in Somalia - partly due to the encouragement of external actors and the absence of strong nationalistic forces - Islamic movements are still despised by the clan-based political forces satisfying the wishes of the external actors.

Any success of the future Somali state will depend on the skilful reconciliation between nationalism and Islam on one hand and accommodating clan attachments on the other. However, the romantic attempts to deny clanism by the early Somali nationalists and the opposition to an increased role for Islam in the state building have been huge obstacles to the efforts at recovering the Somali state.(4)

References

Abdullahi Abdullahi, Abdurahman, *Tribalism, Nationalism and Islam: the crisis of political Loyalty in Somalia.* MA thesis submitted to the faculty of graduate Studies and Research in partial fulfilment of the requirements for the degree of MA, Institute of Islamic Studies, Montreal, Canada, 1992.

Adan, Abdulqadir (2000) "Djibouti Peace Process: a non-clan approach of distributing MPs". a paper presented to the Somali Intellectual symposium held in Djibouti in the preparation for the Somali Peace Conference in 2000 Al-Qardawi, Yusuf (1992) Al-*Sahwa al-Islamiya Beyna al-Tadaruf wa al-Juhud,* Dar al-Wafa, Egypt)

Al-Qardawi, Yusuf (1992) *Awlawiyat al-Haraka al-Islamiya.* Maktabat Wahbah, Qahira, Masr, 1992),

Brons, Maria. (2001) *Society, Security, Sovereignty and the State in Somalia: from Statelessness to Statelessness?* International Books, Utrecht. Nederland.

Hagi Awes Osman & Abdiwahid Hagi Osman (1998) *Clan, Sub-clan and Regional Representation in the Somali Government Organization 1960-1990: Statistical Data and Findings* (Washington DC).

Huntington Samuel P. (Summer 1993) "the clash of civilizations", *Foreign Affairs.*

Hussein Adam and Richard Ford (eds.) (1998) *From Removing Barricades in Somalia: Options for Peace and Rehabilitation,* United Status Institute of Peace.

Laitin, David and Said S. Samatar (1987) *Somalia: a Nation in Search of a State (* Westview Press, Boulder, Colorado)

Mansur, Abdalla (1995) " Contrary to a Nation: The Cancer of Somali State", in *The Invention of Somalia* Ahmed, Ali Jimale (eds.). Lawrenceville, NJ, Red Sea Press.

Medhane, Tadesse. (2002) *Al-Ittihaad.* Addis Ababa.

Mukhtar, Mohamed (1995) " Islam in Somali History: fact and fiction", in Ahmed, Ali Jimale (eds.) *The Invention of Somalia.* Lawrenceville: Red Sea Press.

Rosenthal, Franz (1967). Trans. Ibnu Khaldun, *The Muqadimah,* Princeton.

Tauval Saadia (1963) *Somali Nationalism_.* Cambridge University Press

----

[1]Global war on terrorism was co- related with Islam and the Islamic movements, particularly Al-Qa'ida and other armed groups.

[2]Most of the Muslim countries are ruled by dictatorial regimes that violate human rights. This creates conductive environment for growing underground radical organizations in reaction to the repressive state apparatus.

[3]Examples are Kashmir, Afghanistan, Chechnya, and Palestine.

[4]Examples are Kuwait, Bahrain, Malaysia, Yemen, Jordan, Turkey, Morocco, Algeria and so on.

[5]Under this category falls al-Qa'ida, al-Jihad, al-Takfir and Armed groups in Algeria and so on.

[6]IGAD and the International community under Ethiopian pressure adopted "Building Block" approach in 1998. This approach was further encouraged with "peace dividend" Aid package. Proponents of this approach had been hoping that these blocks will eventually unite to form a new Somali state.

[7]This terminology of "Reviving Religion" is taken from the Hadith of the Prophet related by Abu-Hureyra "Indeed, God sends for this nation on top of every 100 years, some one (a person, an organization, a movement) who revives its religion".

[8]See writings of Ken Menkhaus, Matt Bryden, Ronald Marchal, Medhane Tadesse and Andre Le Sage revolving around counter terrorism perspectives. Mostly, western media and its scholars prefer, for their own reason, to call modern Islamic revivalist movements; fundamentalism, radicalism, extremism and terrorism, while members of these movements prefer to be called Islamic resistance, revivalists, awakening, Islamism and call for Islam etc.

[9]Reconciling tribalism, nationalism and Islam is not an easy undertaking and departs from the conventional perception of their irreconcilability dominated both by political and intellectual discourses.

See Ibid; p.6

[10]Regional administrations: Borama and Growe conferences,. National Reconciliations: Arta peace process in Djibouti and Mbigathi in Kenya (4.5 formula dividing Somalis into 4 equal clans and congregation of other clans represented as 1/2 clan share).

[11]The reason simply is that pastoral segments of the society, privileged under the military rule, had dominated the government; and thus, in accordance with the law that the weak imitates the strong formula, urban elites were conditioning themselves with this new situation.

[12]Creating dominance of specific clans over the political arenas, where others were under represented, systematically ruined this strategy. See

[13]Three important laws were passed prior to 1969. The first was intended to reduce the authority of the tribal chiefs, second to lessen tribal solidarity and third resulted in banning political parties that utilize tribal names. Military regime enacted laws to liquidate " dabar-goynta" tribalism abolishing Diya system (blood money), renaming clan chiefs in the rural areas; and introducing compulsory auto insurance, local government's responsibilities of the funeral expenses. Above all, massive propaganda against tribalism was conducted under the program of socialist transformation of the society. See Abdullahi, Tribalim, Nationalisn and Islam, MA Thesis, p. (78-82)

[14]Actual programs for state formation began after UN Trusteeship of 1950 after which limited modern schools were opened. Also, Somalis were gradually employed in the higher echelons of the state institutions.

[15]This is a right expression for the situations of Somali people past and present. See David Laitin and Said S. Samatar, Somalia: a Nation in Search of a State (Westview Press, Boulder, Colorado), 1987

[16]Tauval, Saadia, Somali Nationalism (Cambridge University Press, 1963), 76-78.

[17]Ibid., 62.

[18]Ibid., 62.

[19]The state was described as a favorite she-camel called" maandeeq" which gives abundant milk to the people looted by the thieves (colonial powers) but later retrieved by the owners (Somalis). But did the owners know how to care for their new camel (the state) as they were in caring their actual camels? See Mansur, Abdalla, "Contrary to a Nation", 112.

[20]Both SYL and Revolutionary Socialist Party,which ruled Somalia (1960-1969) and (1976-1990) respectively had disappeared organizationally. Moreover, Somalis lack national political institutions advocating for the ideals of Somali nationalism. However, recently, in the post civil war period, emerging and active nationalistic tendencies have been observed both inside Somalia and in the Diaspora communities.

[21]The concept of citizenship in Islam could be traced in the text of the Covenant of Medina laid down by Prophet Mohamed (PBUH) after his migration from Mecca to Medina in order to create a unified community from the Muslims, Jews and non-Muslims who were residing in the city of Madina and its environs.

[22]This one nation may be applied to the ideal Muslin nation or in a narrow sense of a particular people like the Somalis. See the glorious Qur'an, verses (92:21, 52:23).

[23]No one should pass the blame onto someone else " no bearer of burden will bear the burden of another in the hereafter, see Glorious Qur, an: (6:164; 17:15; 35:18; 39:7; 53:38).

[24]As related from the prophet "A believer is one from whom people feel secure as regards their lives and property" Al-termedi Hadith. 2551).

[25]See verses from the Qur'an "O people, be conscious of your Lord, who created you from one soul and from it created its mate and from them twin scattered many men and women. Be conscious of God and remember the rights of the wombs, surely god is always watching you" (4:1).

[26]See Qur'anic verse " O you who believe, obey Allah and obey the Messenger and those charged with authority among you. If ye differ in anything among your selves, refer it to Allah and His Messenger, if ye do believe in Allah and the last day…" (4:59)

[27]During the rule of Abdilmalik Ibn Marwan (685-705), a Syrian general Musa Ibn-Umar Al-khatha'mi was sent to conquer both Mogadishu and the neighbouring East African city-state Kilwa. Mukhtar, " Islam in Somali History: fact and Fiction", 3.

[28]It was observed that in the real pastoral areas, clan elders are more powerful than the religious leaders. However, this phenomenon changes in the settled agricultural regions along the banks of the rivers where religious leaders become top leaders of the communities.

[29]See Constitution of Somali Republic, 1961.

[30]Men and women are equal in Islam, but the meaning of equality

is highly contentious all over the world. See Qur'anic verse (49:13)

[31]Military regime had established orientation centres in every district to indoctrinate populations about Marxism and to build popular support for the regime. Participation in the programs of these centres had been considered as evaluation criteria for the loyalty to the regime.

[32]All successful reconciliation conferences in Somalia like Borama, Growe and Arta conferences were based on the empowerment of the traditional leaders as legitimate leaders of the communities.

[33]The word "Political Islam" is coined by non-Muslims in believing that Islam is apolitical and modern Islamic revivalists are using Islam only for political purpose. They don't understand that Islam is a complete religion as stated in the following verse from the holy Qur'an " Indeed, today, we have perfected your religion and completed my bestow on you" (5:3)

[34]Because of the decision of the military government to ban the existence of other political parties or social organizations, all dissidents went either underground or to exile.

[35]For instance, Islah movement is considered evolutionary while al-Itihad was considered during 1992-95 as revolutionary. As widely observed, al-Itihad had been shifting towards being more moderations afterwards.

[36]It was observed that extremism (religious and political) is more entrenched in the culture of pastoralists or that strong nomadic culture. Moderation is, on the other hand, mostly detected in the agricultural and urban locations.

[37]See Al-Qardawi, Yusuf, al-Sahwa al-Islamiya Beyna al-Tadaruf wa al-Juhud (Dar al-Wafa, 1992), 27-60.

[38]These scholars were the intellectuals and leaders of the communities. They understood the dangers of these colonial powers and therefore called for armed resistance. There is no contradiction between being Islamists and being nationalists. This is the best intermarriage for mobilizing internal forces and effectively repelling enemies.

[39]Of courses, extremists consider the founders of the Somali state as the source of the Somali debacle because they were secular and followers of the colonial ways.

[40]Most Islamic activists are graduates from modern universities. The reason may be that modern education offers Muslims better freedom to question and learn their identity and the world than the so-called Islamic universities with state employees controlling its curriculum and activities.

[41]See Al-Qardawi, Yusuf, Awlawiyat al-Haraka al-Islamiya (Maktabat Wahbah, Qahira, Masr, 1992),13-15; see also related Hadith by Abu-Huraira: Allah sent to this nation in eve of every 100 years someone who revives its religion. Reviving Islam means, according to al-Qardawi, establishing organized Islamic movements with clear visions, mission and programs and creating supportive public opinion in addition to accepting international environment for the transformation of the societies in accordance with Islamic values.

[42]See Samuel P. Huntington, "the clash of civilizations", Foreign Affairs. Summer 1993, v72, n3, p22 (28)

[43]See the Article of Medhane Tadesse: "Islamic fundamentalism in Somalia: Its nature and implications", published in www. Somaliawatch.org. This Ethiopian scholar uses the words "terrorism, radicals, and extremists" to explain Islamic revivalism in Somalia. He also wrote a propaganda book entitled, "Global War on Terrorism" labeling most of the Somali Islamic scholars and political activists as terrorists, and excluding only few pro-Ethiopian faction leaders. See Medhane Tadesse, Al-Ittihaad, Addis Ababa, 2002.

Chapter 13

Somaliland's Elections: Transition without transformation

Mohamed Hassan Ibrahim

Between 2001 and 2003 Somaliland was able to accomplish a political transition within a two-year period which it wasn't able to achieve during the previous ten years. On May 2001, a new constitution was ratified, paving the way for local elections to be held in December 2002 and presidential elections in April 2003. This was a remarkable achievement for the self-declared and still internationally unrecognized country. For one thing, the political transition was a complex and vast undertaking, involving a shift to a multiparty electoral system from a clan-based one. Owing to non-recognition by the international community, the process has largely been a local affair. So, with limited outside assistance, expertise and electoral infrastructure, the people of Somaliland were able to successfully and peacefully manage the first election in more than thirty years.

However, the transition to constitutional democracy consists of more than the ratification of a constitution and the holding of elections. In Somaliland, the process can be characterized as a transition without transformation, because it did not entail significant societal change or political, legal and institutional reform. There were time constraints and other internal and external political factors that made the process necessary and expedient. In turn, this meant that the constitutional reform became a hasty and government-driven exercise with limited participation from the public, civil society or the opposition. Further, there was insufficient time to educate voters and to nurture political parties. The resulting transition, therefore, became simply a shift from a system of inter-clan national conference (*shir Baleed)*[1] to one of popular voting to select the leadership. Hence, the shift did not constitute a more profound political transformation, which is unfortunate because it risks discrediting Somaliland's constitutional democracy, and cast a shadow over its greatest achievement: enduring peace.

This chapter will, based on a brief description of Somaliland's political transition, first show how the transition, comprising a constitutional referendum and two rounds of elections, was achieved without significant political transformation, and secondly seek to offers explanations for the absence of more profound changes and what factors made the elections possible.

The political transition[2]

Somaliland's political shift began in May 1991 as an ostensible two-year period of transition. A decade later, the country was still in transition and ruled by a government based on the *Clan* power sharing. Most troubling, as the government term drew to a close, was the uncertainty of Somaliland's political course and its peaceful political transition, as the political reform needed to set the stage for multiparty elections was not accomplished.

This political uncertainty has led to unprecedented vigorous public debate on the future political direction of the country, and public held diverse opinions on the issue of the country's political course (APD, 2002).

Some advocated for a continuation of the existing clan-system of governance, with gradual changes and improvements. Proponents of this arrangement attributed to it the prevailing peace and stability and argued that hasty steps toward constitutional democracy would put the country at undue risk. To them, Somaliland was still unprepared[3] for multi-party elections and they were sceptical about whether elections would actually occur. Opponents of *clan-* system held the view that this system has lost currency and that another *shir-beeleed* (national conference) would negate the gains and the progress of that period. The majority of the country supported neither the holding of another *shir-beeleed* nor western-style multiple party elections, but proposed instead something in between. They considered *shir-beeleed* as regressive and multipartyism impractical. To all intents and purposes, no one was able to come up with a formula for that compromise. Another view stressed the importance of getting the transition right, which entailed being realistic and pragmatic. Proponents of this view posited that any political transition to constitutional democracy required not only constitutional reform but also political and social transformation. Elections may be necessary for democracy but these are far from sufficient; there is a need to develop institutions that can uphold pluralist ideals, civic ideologies and constitutional faith.

In the midst of these public debates, the government took the first crucial step to move the long over due transitional process forward, by scheduling a referendum on the provisional constitution on May 31, 2001, which took the country by surprise[4]. The government's scheduled referendum met stiff opposition form the oppositions particularly *Dib-u-Habaynta* SNM (the reform SNM members), on the ground that there was no public and opposition consultation as promised before putting the constitution for popular endorsement. Both sides were unable to come to terms with each other and a crisis was in the making. The crisis was averted when the two sides the government and the opposition publicly debate the referendum issue in a forum, hosted and organised by the Academy for Peace and Development (APD). The new constitution was public endorsed on May 31, 2001, with an overwhelming majority of 97.7%[5]. The approval of the constitution set in motion the implementation of the electoral process. On August 6 2001, Law No 14 was passed legalizing the formation of political organizations and by September eight political organisations[6] were announced. An electoral law was passed in November 2001, and the National Electoral Commission (NEC) was formed in February 2002.

The administration's second term expired without elections being held. On January 12, the *Guurti* invoked Article 83.1[7], and extended the government one more year within which to complete the transition. The extension eased the political tensions that embroiled the country during the second half of 2001. This was a result of controversy about the invoking of Article 83 and the possibility of free and fair elections under Egal. The opposition was able to galvanize support from some members of Parliament and clan leaders. In August 2001, President Egal survived parliamentary impeachment by one vote. In the same month, a group of clan sultans led by sultans from eastern Somaliland particularly-easy of *Burco* challenged the president's authority, calling for UDUB to be dismantled within 45 days and for a national conference to be held to chart the country's political future. When the government arrested several Sultans from this group in Hargeysa, the country was taken to the brink of another civil conflict. This was averted through mediation of religious, business, and civil society leaders. In May 2002 Egal died suddenly while on a private visit to South Africa. In accordance with the newly approved Constitution, the vice president, Dahir Rayaale Kahin, was named successor. The absence of Egal from the scene provided a more open playing field. On December 15, Somalilanders went to the polls for the first time in more than thirty years to participate in local council elections. Six political organizations (ASAD, *Hormood, Kumises, Sahan*, UDUB and UCID contested the local elections, and on December 23, 2002 the NEC declared UDUB, *Kumises* and UCID as the three national political parties to contest Presidential and parliamentary elections.

The local elections were a prerequisite for presidential and parliamentary elections. According to the constitution both elections should take place a month prior to the end of either term. This meant holding the presidential elections before February 2003 and parliamentary ones before May 2003. The original intention was to have both elections concurrently. However, it was not technically, financially or politically feasible to have back-to-back elections within two months. Furthermore, electoral law pertaining to parliament remained controversial and potentially divisive. Disagreement on such issues as the allocation of parliamentary seats and district demarcation remained unresolved. The government insisted on holding the presidential election as scheduled, whereas the other two parties *Kumises* and UCID wanted the election to take place on May 30. After consulting the government and political parties, the commission opted to hold the presidential election on March 31, citing technical and financial issues. The move was seen as a violation of the constitution by the *Guurti* (the House of Elders), which has sole constitutional right to extend the government's mandate. In the end the commission backed downed and in February 2003, the *Guurti* extended the mandate of the government for three months to hold the Presidential election in 2004.

On April 14, 2003, nearly half a million Somalilanders went to the polls to select a new president. International and domestic observers confirmed the free and transparent way in which polling was conducted (ICG, 2003 & De Wit and Rip 2003). *UDUB* won in very narrow margin over *Kumises*. The preliminary results, announced by the NEC (National Electoral Commission) on April 19, gave UDUB a narrow victory over *Kumises,* by a margin of 80 votes. *Kumises* contested the results and presented evidence of a tabulation error by the NEC in the final tally. UDUB also contested the election results, in the hopes of increasing its margin of victory. The NEC refused to review either side's complaints and referred the matter to the Supreme Court. On May 11, after listening to the arguments of both sides as well as the NEC, the Supreme Court ruled in UDUB's favour. *Kulimye* rejected this verdict and questioned the competence of the court. Dahir Rayale was sworn in on May 16 as Somaliland's president. Shortly after, Kulmiye's leadership conceded the election, bowing to increasing public pressure to do so.

A one-dimensional process

Somaliland was able to ratify a constitution and successfully hold two rounds of elections, in the hope of moving the country towards democratic rule. The transition to constitutional democracy is a complex political challenge. It involves multidimensional and multiple tracks. It is also an undertaking of institutional reform and institution building and diffusion of power in and between government and society (Haas, 2003). But these elections, however, did not alter the distribution of power and the character of the political system. It is one thing to hold elections, but to establish enduring democratic rule requires multidimensional or multiple tracks of political reforms and promoting other elements that foster democratic culture, something the Somaliland's transitional process lacked.

To all intents and purposes, Somaliland's transition program was a one-dimensional process, based solely on constitutional/ legal reform with minimal commitment to institutional reform and broad political participation. President Egal, a man not known for his democratic credentials (Bryden, 2003), suddenly began to advance his newfound mission, which he described as a democratisation program but which was actually purely an electoral reform process. With the help of the Parliament he was able to enact a host of new electoral laws that would put the country legislatively on the path to multi-party elections.

Besides being one-dimensional, the constitutional reform was a one-sided political exercise or government-driven process in which the government excluded the public, civic groups, and the opposition from the debate. There has not been significant multilevel discussion and consultation during the electoral reform. In fact, there has not been a single public hearing or debate on the draft constitutions. The government failed to give the public, civic groups and the opposition sufficient time to grasp and debate the draft constitutions so that their concerns and misgivings can be addressed[8], before the referendum. This lack of wider participation and public awareness certainly deprived the process of a much-needed legitimacy. And it denied the public and the opposition a chance to better understand the ongoing constitutional or electoral reform process, and to articulate their preferences[9]. As result, very few Somalilanders including leading opposition leaders knew or understood the approved documents or bills (ICG, 2003)[10]. Hence, the new constitution is a compromise between two draft constitutions[11]. Many issues remain unresolved and the constitution itself contains numerous omissions and contradictions. None of these were subject to the scrutiny of the public, civic groups and the opposition. The electoral law adopted by the government was similarly a product of the two constitutions, and had its ambiguities and gaps. This was highlighted by the closely contested presidential elections, in which neither party won fifty percent of the popular vote in the first round of the election. A carefully planned electoral law would have taken such a scenario into consideration and would have stipulated a second-round election to spare the country post-election uncertainty.

Finally, the elections were widely perceived as an end not a means to constitutional democracy, in which the whole transition process essentially came down to holding elections. And to serve that purpose, the process comprised election procedures, regulations rather than electoral democracy[12]. Wide ranges of mechanisms were employed to ensure the management of election procedures. A national election commission (NEC) was formed to manage the elections, and some activities, such as limited voter and civic education, domestic observers and party liaison training and publicity about the mechanics occurred only shortly before elections

What was missing from the transitional process was a far reaching political reform that involved steps to truly curb the power of the executive by strengthening checks and balances, allowing unfettered political participation, supporting devolution of power, increasing the protection of human rights, broadening personal liberties and bolstering civic organisations. These aspects of the reform process are proving to be the most challenging, as the country is still struggling to break free from the legacy of decades of dictatorship and strike a balance between national and clan interests.

Apart from constitutional/electoral reform, which is the legal part of the process, another critical aspect of the transition to a functional democracy is the reform of government and the state and the development of other elements that foster democratic culture such as (Carother, 2003):

- Strengthening the rule of law, especially through judicial reform;
- Strengthening parliament, through efforts to build better internal capacity and bolster constituency
- Reducing state corruption, through anticorruption commissions, legislative rationalization, and advocacy campaigns; and
- Promoting decentralization, through training for local government officials and legislative actions to increase the authority of local governments.

Programs to expand civil society should encompass:

- The formation and expansion of NGOs devoted to public-interest advocacy, such human rights, the environment, and anticorruption
- Support for women's and minority rights organisations;
- Strengthening independent media; and
- Underwriting formal and informal efforts to advance democratic and civic education.
- Strengthening political parties in order to help parties and politicians develop basic organizational skills improve their constituency relations, improve coalition building, and the like.

These aspects of the reform process are proving to be the most challenging, and the country's report card has been decidedly mixed. That the transition took place without a simultaneous political transformation is an indication that reform has not gone far enough. Though the country is still struggling to emerge from the legacy of decades of dictatorship and strike a balance between national and clan interests, it has made solid progress in establishing stable peace, a functional administration and a reasonably representative government.

The impediments

There are various plausible explanations and good reasons why Somaliland's democratic reform was not multidimensional, including the following: Generally speaking, a nation's political history and current social and economic condition largely determine its political future. Somaliland, like many subs–Saharan counties, has emerged from a history of colonisation, democratic misrule, one-partyism, and protracted civil and political instability. As result of that, the country has become prone to strong executive with weak countervailing institutions: Parliament and Independent Judiciary, that lacked the backing of broad-based and developed political and social organisations: political parties, social movements, independent media, professional associations, and large civic organisations.

Though there is a strong desire for meaningful political reforms on the part of the public and to break free from the legacy of decade-long dictatorial rules and preservative clanism that still embodied in the culture and social fabric of Somali society, what was lacking is the development of organised citizens demanding political rights, participation and government accountability. For that, political reform became a government-driven process because government critics were unable to put forward alternatives and existing civic organisations were unable to set the standards for good governance, facilitate public participation or educate the populace about the process and democratic participation. The government had a little choice, except to make the rules and set the pace without any meaningful consultation (Bryden, 2003).

The institutionalisation of clan in the country's political system, which made possible the prevailing peace, has also undermined the development of functional institutions in Somaliland[13]. Kinship politics became a source of patronage, corruption, nepotism, and clientelism, while preventing the development of meritocracy and professionalism (SCPD/WSP, 1999). Its adverse effects are manifest at all levels of government institutions, civic organisations, policies, laws and procedures. It multiplied the number of ministerial portfolios and other senior positions in the central government to satisfy clan balance without thought for necessity[14]. Thus making institutional reform very difficult and leaving the government with little option and leeway except to perform the way it did: these underdeveloped or informal institutions are simply a reflection of the society they govern[15].

In the final analysis, there are several factors that arguably made the two elections possible under these extreme challenges and allowed the reluctant parties to join the process. The first one was the sudden death of President Egal, which generated an outpouring of nationalist sentiment and also served to level the political "playing field". The second reason was the passing of electoral laws for the local and presidential elections, and the omission of controversial sections pertaining to the parliamentary elections, an issue still unresolved[16]. Another factor was "voter enthusiasm" and probably this was the key factor. The massive enthusiasm witnessed during the polling was not about democratic rights or choosing their leaders: People did not care about who was going win the elections or what was in the constitution, but it was rather voting against "Mogadishu. Many Somalilanders hope that the elusive recognition will follow soon after, knowing the increasing premium on democracy, and adding an international dimension to the process. While holding the elections were seen by many voters as strengthening Somaliland's independence claim, in term of participatory democracy, but the lack of participation by most Warsangali and Dhulbahante in the elections, made the elections to effectively served to shrink the Somaliland polity and to make Somaliland politics exclusive(Bradbury, Abokor, and Yousuf, 2003).

Conclusion

Somalia's previous experience with democracy in the 1960s had been discredited by increasing level of political patronage. So once again many are questioning whether democracy was appropriate given the lack of institutional development, broad-based constituencies and political awareness. Unless such elements develop, the Somaliland experience so far does give cause for alarm. The country is stuck in a political state several steps away from authoritarianism but still very far away from democracy, but drifting towards one-man rule and rampant corruption.

Since, the democratic institutions of Somaliland are still weak and ill-prepared for upholding democratic rules they have left the whole system to be at the mercy of whoever is in charge, elite manipulation, consequently discrediting multi-party democracy and leading to gradual disillusionment and disengagement. As result of that, people may simply blame it on democracy, rather than on faulty process.

References

Academy for Peace and Development (APD) (2000), *'A Self-Portrait of Somaliland: Rebuilding from the Ruins,* Hargeysa, Somaliland

Academy for Peace and Development (APD) (2002), *'The Judicial system in Somaliland,* Workshop report, Hargeysa , Somaliland

Academy for Peace and Development (APD) (2002), *'Consolidation and Decentralisation of Government Institutions,* Hargeysa (Draft), Somaliland

Academy for Peace and Development (APD) (2002), *'The Role of the Media in the Political Reconstruction,* Hargeysa (Draft), Somaliland

Annemieke de Wit and Riemke Rip (2003): *Voting for Democracy: Presidential Elections in Somaliland.* Netherlands

Bryden, Matt (2003), 'The Banana Test: Is Somaliland Ready for Recognition? *Les Annales de 'Ethipoie,* vol. 19 Addis Ababa: Centre Francais des Etudes Ethiopiannes

Bradbury, Abokor, and Yusuf, 'Somaliland: Choosing Politics over Violence *Review of African Political Economy No.97:455-478*

Carothers, Thomas (2003) 'Is Gradualism Possible? Choosing a Strategy for Promoting Democracy in the Middle East' *working Papers, Number 39 Carnegie Endowment for International Peace*

ICG Africa Report N0 66 (2003),'Somaliland: Democratisation and its Discontents' Nairobi/Brussels

ICG Middle East Report N0 8 (2003), 'Yemen: Coping with Terrorism and Violence in a Fragile State' Amman/Brussels

Initiative and Referendum Institute (2001), 'Somaliland National Referendum May 31,2001' Final Report of the initiative & Referendum Institute's Election Monitoring Team, Washington, D.C. USA.

Haas, Richard (2003), 'Towards Greater Democracy in the Muslim World' *The Washington Quarterl 26:3 pp. 137-148*

Ottaway, Marina and Chung, Theresa, "Debating Democracy Assistance: Toward a New Paradigm,"*Journal of Democracy, 10:4, October 1999,*

Pottie, David and Lodge, Tom "Electoral Management in Southern Africa" www.idea.net

Windsor, Jennifer (2003), 'Promoting Democratization Can Combat Terrorism' *The Washington Quarterly 26:3 pp. 43-58*

----

[1]The Shir Baleed is an inter-clan national conference, in which clan

elders and clan representative/delegation approved by the clan leaders have voting right to elect the President and its vice.

[2]For more detailed information and analyses on the Somaliland transition see ICG "Somaliland: Democratisation and its Discontents" ICG Africa Report NO.66, Nairobi/Brussels and Bradbury, Abokor, and Yousuf "Somaliland: Choosing Politics over Violence" Review of African Political Economy No.97: 455-478 pp474

3 obstacles included: clan still remains pervasive force, little awareness of constitutional democracy, functional literacy is very low, and civil society institutions are undeveloped cited in "Consolidation and Decentralisation of Government Institutions", WSP/the Academy for Peace and Development, 2002, pp. 43

[4]President Egal in 1991, linked international recognition to the adaptation of Multi-party elections

[5]There was however limited voter turnout in Eastern Sanag and Sool regions, where the inhabitants in these areas (Dhulbahante and Warsangeli) are ambivalent to Somaliland's claim to a separate state, a territory that is also claimed by the neighbouring Puntland Administration. Nevertheless, outside observers concluded that the process adhered to internationally accepted standards and estimated that approximately 66% of Somaliland's eligible voters endorsed the new constitution.

[6]Somaliland constitution allows three national parties, numerous registered political organisations have to compete in the local election the top three organisations in terms of the vote they get become the three national parties that can compete in the national elections: President and Parliament elections.

[7]Article 83.1: "If on the expiry of the office of the President and vice-president is not possible, because of security consideration, to hold the election of the President and Vice President, the House Elders (Guurti) shall extend their term of office whilst taking into consideration the period in which the problems can be overcome and election can be held".

[8]Opposition views were not included in the referendum process, contrary to government claims. In Public debate organised by APD in March 15, 2001, some opposition figures stated that, also in public rallies before the referendum.

[9]Whether they prefer no limitation on the number of political parties, Presidential or Parliamentary system etc,

[10]Some leading elements of the opposition that voted "yes" on the constitution realised after the fact, that its article 83.1: "If on the expiry

of the office of the President and vice-president is not possible, because of security consideration, to hold the election of the President and Vice President, the House Elders (Guurti) shall extend their term of office whilst taking into consideration the period in which the problems can be overcome and election can be held". The opposition saw this as an automatic trigger to extend the term of the President.

[11]One was drafted by the president and the other was drafted by the Parliament and current electoral law is a compromise between the two, for instance, the one drafted by the president resembled more like the American Electoral College.

[12]Broad understanding of their political and civil rights and what is free and fair elections.

[13]Some may consider clan itself is an antithesis to modern or formal governmental institutions.

[14]The number of cabinets has been increasing since 1993, in 2001 the total numbers of ministers 42 and now after the election Rayaale broke his promise to create small cabinet when he appointed a record 47 ministers.

[15]Critics accuse the government of manipulating kinship politics to its own advantage and an excuse for not acting. Only one Minister was able to hold compulsory examination for employee under the auspices of the Civil Services Commission

[16]These issues were resolved in April 2005, the Parliamentary elections took place in September 29, 2005, after the author finalised this manuscript. The conduct of the Parliamentary elections was once again a success, and was held in a generally constructive and peaceful atmosphere. As of this writing, the result has yet to be publicised.

Chapter 14

Political identity and the state: Reflections on emerging state structures and conflict in Northern Somalia[1]

Markus V. Höhne

In the Somali civil war the state as an institution collapsed. It was led by the dictatorial government of Siyad Barre for more than two decades before 1991 and provided at least certain services[2]. Over the last thirteen years every attempt to rebuild it failed[3]. This, among a legion of other problems, led to a crisis of the political identity of many Somali. The question is: What should people's orientations be with regard to the state?[4] This question is not about parties or ideologies within a state or an international framework, but very elementary: about the existence of a state within clear boundaries, governed by a more or less effective administration. A closer look at the developments in Northern Somalia reveals that the issue of political identity is connected to a crisis of the national identity. With Somaliland in North Western Somalia and Puntland in North Eastern Somalia two administrations have been set up which partly fill the state vacuum. Their self understanding and their politics towards the future of the greater region and its inhabitants are incompatible.

Somaliland is presented by the government in Hargeysa as an independent state which seceded from the rest of Somalia in the borders of the former British Protectorate. As Isaaq, Dir and Darood/Harti its inhabitants belong to different clan families. The Somaliland government claims international recognition for its country on the basis of territoriality complemented by a notion of a Somaliland national identity. In the context of politics the term "Somalilander" is used by local politicians and by other people pointing at the viability of Somaliland as a nation state. Puntland is according to its constitution part of the Somali state and works for rebuilding the Somali government. The government in Garowe is based on an alliance of different Daarood/Harti clans, such as Majeerteen, Dhulbahante and Warsangeeli[5]. Apart from this genealogical identity the Somali national identity is adhered to. People supporting Puntland very rarely refer to themselves as "Puntlanders". Mostly they use the term "Somali" when talking about their nationality.

These different positions collide most severely with regard to and in the Harti inhabited regions in Eastern Somaliland respectively Western Puntland, which are claimed by each of the two governments in Northern Somalia. The propaganda issued in the political centres, but also discussions about and manifestations of political identity in daily life reflect the tensions between the Somaliland and the Darood/Harti respectively Puntlander/Somali identity in the study area.

The theoretical focus of the research is on identity and conflict. The identity of individuals and groups is not only a construct put in place and manipulated by different "actors" according to various contexts, as constructivists have been arguing since the 1970s. Recent thinking and research underline that an identity, self imposed or imposed from outside, has to be plausible in order to work (Schlee 2004: 148). Plausibility is reached when the different aspects on which an identity is based, are rooted in the every day and historical experiences of the people concerned (Zenker 2005: 2f). Research in the last few years has made it clear that different ethnic identity of people sharing a common environment and joint resources not necessarily lead to conflict. Integration across ethnic boundaries is a relatively common phenomenon (Schlee 2001: 20ff). This study is interested in the logic of political identification of individuals and groups in the context of re-emerging state structures in Northern Somalia and how these identifications are related to conflict. The main focus lies on historical events and social and cultural practices, and how certain aspects of them are used for identification.

Methodologically the research is based on open interviews and participant observation. The largest number of the interviews has been conducted with males residing in villages and towns. I argue that as a result of the civil war and the following developments in the study area new identities have formed on the ground. These identities are not ethnic identities in the sense that anyone in or outside Northern Somalia would seriously argue that the carriers of these identities would belong to different ethnic groups. They rather can be understood as political identities which are based on features resembling ethnic identities such as descent, history, individual experiences and collective memory. These identities are also significantly connected with certain territories. On the local level they are expressed in symbols, practice, newspapers and other media, in poems, songs, individual life-histories and heroic tales. Of course these identities are not new in the sense that they are invented from scratch. But they combine existing identity markers in a particular way and are meaningful in the current political context of the area.

Some of the analytical tools developed in the social-anthropological research on ethnic identities can be used to approach the political identities in Northern Somalia. Two insights presented by Fredrik Barth in his discussion of ethnic groups and boundaries are especially relevant in this respect: identities are most clearly displayed at the boundaries and they are flexible, to a certain extent (Barth 1969: 14-15). The relevant boundaries in the study area are territorially and mentally constituted. The territorial boundaries run through the whole of Northern Somalia, through the countryside as well as through towns and villages. They separate the core resident areas (degaan) of different clans, sub-clans and smaller family groups. This separation is at first invisible; it becomes clear only if one asks about the descent of the people inhabiting certain regions or quarters. The mental boundaries become obvious when political positions are displayed in discussions or in events such as public ceremonies. Flexibility comes in because for each identity certain aspects of Somali history, clan relations and culture are highlighted, others are completely neglected. This allows individuals to manoeuvre when it serves their interest. It also causes contradictions when it comes to individual life histories and to the experience of different generations. It becomes clear that the identities under discussion are internally fragmented. Nevertheless, when the question of the political future is at stake – the secession of Somaliland or the rebuilding of Somalia for which Puntland stands - the relevance of these internal fragmentations diminishes and the identities form relatively clear clusters which divide the social, political and territorial landscape of Northern Somalia today.

In the following I will present two identity clusters in Northern Somalia. The term "identity cluster" refers to a corpus of historical, cultural, social and political features which are clustered together when it comes to an argument about politics in Northern Somalia. It draws from discussions among politicians and ordinary people within the greater region, complemented by observations during the presentation of political positions towards non-Somali visitors and the manifestations of political identities in conflict situations. The two clusters introduced here are not exhaustive for the study area. Nevertheless, they have been chosen because 1) they are most relevant in the political conflict between Somaliland and Puntland/Somalia, and 2) they reveal clear contradictions in themselves which open space for manoeuvres of individuals and groups. In my conclusion I will discuss the dividing and cross-cutting aspects of these clusters and how they are related to state formation and conflict.

Identity clusters

In the following each identity cluster will be presented briefly. I will set out the basis of each cluster, referring to descent, history, individual experience and collective memories; then examples will be given for how these identities are expressed and which contradictions arise within each cluster.

Hargeysa/Central West of Somaliland

General setting:

Mostly Isaaq live in the Central West of Somaliland. The Isaaq are the majority clan in Somaliland and in colonial times they were closely linked to the British. When Somaliland gained its independence on 26th June 1960, political power was in the hands of the Isaaq. After the unification with the South on 1st July 1960 however, the Isaaq became politically marginalized; also most social and economic developments took place in the South. This resulted in a large scale migration of "Northerners"[6] to the South to obtain higher education and find jobs.

The uneasy relationship with the government in the South, especially under the military dictator Siyad Barre, finally led to the foundation of the Somali National Movement (SNM) in 1981. This guerrilla organization was mostly Isaaq based. After the SNM had taken control of the Northwest in the context of a general collapse of the state in early 1991, the independence of Somaliland was proclaimed on a conference of all clans living in the area held in Burco. In the last 13 years peace has been restored and a government with seat in Hargeysa established; since 2001 serious steps have been undertaken to transform the clan based system of governance into a more democratic system[7].

Expression of identity:

One day in early February 2004 a delegation of British Parliamentarians arrived at Hargeysa for a 24-hours visit to Somaliland. A splendid welcome was staged at the airport. Approximately two hundred persons filled the margins of the airstrip at nine in the morning. Until the arrival of the plane about two hours later Edna Aaden, the Foreign Minister and Cabdullahi Maxamed Du'aale, the Minister for Information assisted by some policemen and –women organized the show. Girls wearing dresses resembling the traditional Somali women's wear were put in line to the right and left of the estimated landing place. The traditional white of the dress was replaced by the green, white and red of the Somaliland flag. The girls started singing and dancing to the monotonous beat of their drums long before the arrival of the delegation.

In the centre a group of men was positioned. They were mostly members of the bicameral Somaliland Parliament in which elders and representatives sit to represent the clans and regions of Somaliland. Also a handful of World–War-II veterans decorated with British medals took their positions. The show was made complete by the presence of John Dry dale, the oldest British resident of Somaliland, who has been involved in Somali affairs since colonial times.

Among the participants masses of posters with the Somaliland flag and a picture of Queen Elisabeth II were distributed. The headline on the Queen's poster was: "The Queen, our mother". Some people held large banners with messages referring to the long standing British-Somaliland friendship and to the recent history of Somaliland. Journalists swept all over the place busy with photographing and filming the parade. In the background an armada of new four wheel drives was waiting to take the V.I.Ps to the city.

When the Parliamentarians arrived they were first received by Edna Aaden and the Minister for Information. Some girls stepped forward and decorated the guests with wreaths of flowers. Afterwards Edna Aaden led the group along the masses. The girls danced and sang and the men greeted the guests. Brief conversations were held with the members of the Somaliland parliament, the war veterans and of course, with John Drysdale. After fifteen minutes of shaking hands and posing for the cameras of the journalists the guests together with the more important participants of the event climbed into the cars and drove off. Along the way to the city spectators had gathered shouting and gesticulating at every car that came from the airport. The main roads in the centre of Hargeysa were blocked up by the police and were only open for the government vehicles.

The event was interesting with regard to which aspects of the Somaliland identity were presented and which were neglected. It was striking how openly the memory of the colonial past was revived. Looking at the scene one could almost think that Somaliland was still a British Protectorate, and indeed, British protection was strived after. Not in the sense that the British government should take control of Somaliland once again, but in the sense that London should protect and facilitate Somaliland's way to international recognition. An amusing example for the direct relation of the "airport choreography" and this political agenda could be read in the papers on the following day: it was reported that the war veterans had asked the visitors for their pensions as former British soldiers; but, as the news continued, the veterans assured that they would happily renounce their claims if the British government would recognize Somaliland.

The second theme of the event was the achievements of the Republic of Somaliland since its establishment. Peace and stability of the country were represented by the masses of girls dancing and singing and the absence of a great number of security forces. The Ministers and the Members of the Somaliland parliament discussed what has been accomplished politically so far, almost without external help.

The idea behind this is simple: the only thing Somaliland is renowned for internationally is its peacefulness and the innovative way in which a new political system has been established. This distinguishes it from the rest of Somalia, where up to now heavy fighting flares up occasionally[8].

Equally important to what was presented at the airport is what was omitted. The 30 years in which the North and the South of Somalia were one country were hidden. The logic behind this huge historical gap is that any relationship with the South except economic cooperation is an obstacle to Somaliland's claim to be an independent country deserving international recognition. But this historical omission leads to contradictions with regard to the experiences of the older generation. Especially the above 40-years old remember Somalia as it was in the 1960s and '70s, with a strong national army and widespread international relations. Some of these older Somali, even some of the active SNM fighters, prefer a future reunion with the South to the independence of Somaliland. They argue that the economy of Somaliland is weak and the number of its people is too low to defend itself against potential enemies such as Ethiopia. In their view economic development and independence based on military power can only be reached together with the Somalis in the South, who are their brothers and sisters, even if split by civil war.

Furthermore, at the airport no reference was made to the SNM and its long and bloody war against the former Somali regime. This is consistent with the current political line of the Somaliland government. The SNM has had its role in the past, but now civilians have succeeded to the rule of the guerrillas, which have been almost exclusively Isaaq. Somaliland today is eager to presents itself as a multi clan state where peace reigns[9]. Intra- and inter-clan warfare which dominated the guerrilla war and the first years after secession from Somalia shall be forgotten. But in fact some of the old inter-clan and political tensions prevail. When politics are discussed in the market of Hargeysa members of the Darood clan family (including the Harti clans) are called "faqash". The same term is used for people who had a position in the former Somali government in general, including Isaaq. Many of the latter have high ranking positions in the current Somaliland government. "Faqash" is translated by Hashi in his "Essential Somali English Dictionary" as "a dirty or corrupt person; filth" (Hashi 1998: 170).

Laascaanod/Eastern Somaliland – Western Puntland

General Setting:

Laascaanod is the capital of the Sool region. Sool is almost exclusively inhabited by Dhulbahante, a branch of the Harti clan. In the early 20th century the area was the setting of an anti-colonial uprising led by the Ogadeen Sheikh, poet and politician Maxamed Cabdille Xassan. His followers were called Dervishes; the majority of them were Dhulbahante. They fought mostly against the British, aided by Isaaq troops. After the defeat of the Dervishes in 1921 the Dhulbahante area was effectively incorporated in the British Protectorate. In the 1970s and '80s, most Dhulbahante, being Darood supported the regime of Siyad Barre, who belonged to the Marexaan clan of the Darood clan family. A further factor strengthening this alliance was that with Axmed Suleban "Daffle" a Dhulbahante was head of the National Security Service (NSS) and one of the most powerful men in the state. Up to 1991 they fought on the side of the government against the guerrillas. When the SNM had taken over Somaliland the representatives of the Dhulbahante agreed on peace with the Isaaq. But the political program agreed upon in Burco - to secede from Somalia - has never been accepted by the majority of the clan. The social and political progress of Somaliland was reached outside of the Sool region and largely without the participation of the Dhulbahante. In opposition to Hargeysa the Dhulbahante played a prominent role in the establishment of Puntland as a Harti state in North-East Somalia in 1998[10]. Here a member of this clan obtained the position of the Vice President and therefore the Dhulbahante became the second power after the Majeerten, the "big" Harti brother[11]. Since then the inhabitants of the Sool region are split between Somaliland and Puntland. Some work for the government in Hargeysa, some for the government in Garowe. If one asks about this the answer is mostly that this is a pragmatic arrangement; what matters is to generate some income in a poor region; politically one does not want to get involved in any trouble.

Expression of identity:

I first met Axmed[12] in Laascaanod in November 2003. He was Dhulbahante, but at the time of our meeting he had come only for a visit to Laascaanod. He came from Garowe, the capital of Puntland, where he worked as a high-ranking member of the government. Axmed invited me to visit him in Garowe. I followed his invitation and spent about a week with him. We talked among other things about the Dervish history. Axmed told me that his family, Bixi Drays, has had a conflict with Maxamed Cabdille Xassan during which the Dervishes massacred several Bixi Drays men. In reaction to that this family had allied with the British and become involved in one of the most devastating defeats of the Dervishes in a place called Jidbaley in the Western Sool region. Axmed verbally said: "we defeated him [Maxamed Cabdille Xassan] in Jidbaley". According to Axmed a man called Awke "Jabane" (Awke Cabdi Aaden), the leader of Bixi Drays in those days advised the British how to deal with the Dervishes and taught them the tactics that led to the defeat. Some days later Axmed and I walked in the streets. Axmed was in a very good mood and started to sing poems composed by Maxamed Cabille Xassan. I asked him about that and he answered: "I am a Dervish!"

I heard that Axmed was one of the men who had organized the attack against the Somaliland President Dahir Rayaale Kahin in Laascaanod in December 2002. This attack is one of the recent heroic tales told by Puntland hardliners in Laascaanod and I was very interested to learn more about it. Axmed confirmed that he had been involved in this event and gave me an outline of what had happened[13]. Dahir Rayaale Kahin visited Laascaanod on 7th December 2002; hardly anyone in Somaliland or Puntland was informed about this. The president was accompanied by more than a dozen technicals and about 200 soldiers. In the town several Somaliland followers had organized a number of local forces. The visit was an unprecedented event; no Somaliland president had ever dared to come to Sool.

Puntland had to react, even if totally unprepared. Axmed together with some other Dhulbahante politicians collected a force of three technicals and led them from Garowe to Laascaanod. In the early afternoon they passed the Eastern checkpoint of Laascaanod without being stopped by the local forces posted to guard the place for Somaliland; the soldiers at the checkpoint and Axmed were genealogically closely related. After they had entered the town the Puntland forces immediately started to open fire at the surprised Somaliland troops. After about fifteen minutes of fierce fighting the Somaliland president ordered his troops to retreat. He feared a general uprising of the Puntland followers in town and wanted to avoid bloodshed among the civilians. The president left Laascaanod hastily and retreated to Caynabo, a district town in Western Sool, where Isaaq live.

On the side of Puntland this rather chaotic operation had turned into a great victory. Shocked by the event Daahir Raayale Kahin ordered his local shadow administration in the following months to leave Laascaanod. This paved the way for the effective occupation of the regional capital by Puntland one year later, in December 2003.

The next time I saw Axmed was in Laascaanod in late January 2004. He told me that he would stay in town now for the next months as a member of the new Puntland administration. I was extremely surprised when I heard three weeks later that Axmed had deserted the Puntland camp and come to Hargeysa, where he had been received well. That a high-ranking member of the administration of the "enemy" had switched sides was celebrated as a kind of victory for Somaliland in the papers in Hargeysa. In March I had a chance to meet Axmed in the capital of Somaliland. When I asked him about his change of mind he said that he had had an argument with the Puntland leadership about the politics regarding Sool. In Axmed's view Puntland just pushed more and more soldiers into the region, which burdened the already low economy of the state (Puntland) and provoked a military confrontation with Somaliland. An escalation of violence in Laascaanod and Sool would only cause mayhem to the local population which was already suffering from the severe drought in the region. Some more personal reasons have also been involved in Axmed's decision to leave Puntland. He had not received his salary for about six months, and neither had most of the members of the administration and the army. Furthermore he felt depressed under the dictatorial rule of the president Cabdullahi Yusuf.

This is admittedly an extreme episode; also it plays only partly in Laascaanod and the Sool region. Nevertheless, it reveals some important aspects of the political identity of many inhabitants of the region, including some contradictions. To call oneself "Dervish" has two meanings in the current political context of the Sool region, both of which can be located in history: 1) in the postcolonial years Maxamed Cabdille Xassan was styled as a national hero who fought with his troops for the political unity of all Somalis[14]. To be a Dervish today refers to the vision of building up a strong Somali state again, against the secessionism of the Isaaq, as many Dhulbahante see it. 2) Maxamed Cabdille Xassan did not only lead an anti-colonial rebellion. As oral accounts of history point out, he also fought for power in Northern Somalia against traditional rulers and their clans, such as Boqor

Cusman, the "king" of the Majeerteen, which is the clan dominating the current Puntland politics. Today the term "Dervish" gives an identity to the Dhulbahante in Sool who are still neither Somaliland nor Puntland. Due to this indefinite position Sool is one of the least developed regions in Northern Somalia. Only one international organization has a permanent presence there and not much is coming from Hargeysa and Garowe. Apart from the heroic tale of the Dervish fighting the cultural heritage left by Maxamed Cabdille Xassan as a poet is a source of pride for the impoverished Dervishes of today.

Dhulbahante today monopolize the Dervish history and use it for political reasons, to differentiate between the "British" Isaaq and the "Somali" Dhulbahante. This aspect of the political identity, condensed to "every day propaganda" can be summarized: while the Isaaq clans have been allies of the British in the colonial past and today call upon them to back their ambitions of splitting up Somalia, the Dhulbahante have always been proper Somali "nationalists". This contradicts the more realistic and well known accounts of the history of some individuals and whole families. A good number of Dhulbahante have in fact left Maxamed Cabdille Xassan's camp and joined the British, while some Isaaq, especially in the first years of the uprising, have joined the Dervishes.

Axmed's story also reveals the double loyalty of many Dhulbahante as long as it helps to gain something (a salary, an aid project etc.) from the Somaliland or the Puntland side; but when it comes to the threat or the escalation of a military conflict between Somaliland and Puntland, most Dhulbahante ally with their Harti brothers. This is clearly shown by the history of the defeat of the Somaliland president in Laascaanod[15].

Harti politicians try to create a "natural" division between Isaaq on the one side and the different Harti clans on the other. Therefore they have to neglect the cultural and social closeness which has developed under British rule among Dhulbahante and Isaaq. They learned in school together and they served together as clerks, soldiers or policemen under the British administration. They internalized the "British system", which was distinct from the "Italian system", which the Majeerteen and the other "Southerners" internalized. On a more local level intermarriage patterns reveal the intensive relations between Dhulbahante and Isaaq clans who have lived for decades as neighbours in the central and North-Eastern regions of Somaliland. Intermarriage with the Majeerteen is not so strong, as many Dhulbahante admit freely. Dhulbahante elders, asked about what relates their clan to the Isaaq, quite often said: "Waa isku degaan, waa isku dhaqan; waanu is dhalnay." ("We live in the same area, we have the same culture; we gave birth to each other.").

The final desertion of Axmed from Puntland to Somaliland is only partly representative. Many Dhulbahante are indeed suspicious of the dictatorial ruling style of the old soldier and warlord Cabdullahi Yusuf. They need him to defend them against the complete incorporation into Somaliland. But they don't want him to take full control of their affairs. The massive presence of Puntland forces that entered Laascaanod in a police operation in December 2003 and have stayed since then, supported by additional military troops, which together with the government in Garowe established a military administration in the place, was criticized by civilians who dared to speak out against the new rulers. Nevertheless, this uneasiness with domination does not lead the majority of the Dhulbahante to switch sides and to fully support Somaliland. The main reason for this is the widespread vision to establish Somalia again. Puntland represents this political aim, and is therefore supported when the question of the political future of the region and Somalia as a whole is at stake.

Conclusion

Both quasi-state administrations in Northern Somalia exploit the variety of different identity markers, based on the every day or collectively remembered experience of the people living in the greater region, for their political purposes. Hargeysa stresses the common history, the cultural closeness of the Northerners and the inclusive peace process in the 1990s to incorporate non-Isaaq. Those arguments are made more convincing by the granting of influential positions in the government and generous financial donations to key members of clans and by the release of international aid organizations to the clan territory. While this policy worked well in the West of Somaliland, where Gadabuursi and Ciise live, who belong to the Dir clan family, the Harti in the Sool region are still distant to Hargeysa. This distance has its roots in political mistakes made by the leadership of Somaliland, the last of which was the ill-prepared visit of President Dahir Rayale Kahin to Laascaanod in December 2002, but also in a genuine, historically and culturally based reluctance to fully integrate on the side of the Harti clans. Over the years this caused the comparatively lower political profile of the Harti in Hargeysa as well as the absence of an effective Somaliland administration and the stagnation of development in their regions.

Garowe is eager to attract the Dhulbahante and Warsangeeli as Harti brothers by granting them a clan-balanced share in the government and by adhering to the vision of a united (but federal)

Somalia. With the exception of a few individuals all inhabitants of Sool with whom I spoke about the political future of the Somali shared this vision. By sabotaging the full integration of Somaliland in its colonial borders the Harti politicians hope to prevent its definitive split from Somalia. Nevertheless, historical events as well as social and cultural practices divide the Harti along the former colonial division. Furthermore two internal political problems of Puntland restrict its political success: 1) despite its "clan-democratic" constitution Puntland still resembles a military dictatorship, in which not much can be done against the will of Col. Cabdullahi Yusuf and his close family; 2) Due to severe corruption inside the government and the very costly Somalia policy of the Puntland delegation to the Somali peace conference in Mbagathi/Nairobi the administration is chronically short of money; where even members of the government, the armed forces and the civil administration do not or only very irregularly get their salaries, not much can be given to the communities in the contested Harti regions to firmly link them to Puntland[16].

As long as these two administrations in Northern Somalia and their followers play their political games without reaching a definitive political conclusion, individuals and groups can manoeuvre. Thus a clash of political identities can be avoided due to the inconsistencies and contradictions inside the identity clusters providing cross-cutting ties between them. The peace can be kept in normal life, even if in the discussions between "Somalilanders" and the adherents of Puntland/Somalia incompatible positions come to the fore. But when either the Somaliland or the Puntland side tries to enforce its policy on the ground, the territorial and mental borders of the identity clusters are closed and serious tensions up to a level close to military confrontation arise[17].

Up to now the process of state formation in Northern Somalia is basically limited to the core regions of each of the two political entities in the study area. Further endeavours to set up a fully effective state (be it Somaliland and/or Puntland/Somalia) recognized under international law will possibly produce a large-scale armed conflict. A way out of this conflict scenario would be to limit the sovereignty of the Mbagathi government to the South (including Puntland). After peaceful and stable state structures would be established there, broad based negotiations between Somaliland and Somalia could start.

References

Barth, Fredrik (1969) Introduction, in: F. Barth (eds.): *Ethnic groups and boundaries: The social organization of culture difference*, London, 9-38

Cawl, Faarax M.J. 1974 (1984): Ignorance *is the enemy of love (Aqoondarro waa u nacab jacayl)*, transl. by B.W. Andrzejewski, London.

Farah, Axmed Yusuf (2001) Somalia: Modern History and the End of the 1990s in: WSP international: *Rebuilding Somalia. Issues and possibilities for Puntland*. London, 7-30.

Ferguson, Yale H. (2003) The state concept and a world of polities under perpetual siege, in: R. Brian Ferguson (eds.) *The state, identity and violence. Political disintegration in the post cold war period.*, London, 83-95.

Hashi, Abdirahman A. (1998) *Essential Somali English Dictionary*. Addis Abeba.

Höhne, Markus V. (2002) Somalia zwischen Krieg und Frieden. *Strategien der friedlichen Konfliktaustragung auf internationaler und lokaler Ebene*. Hamburg.

Lewis, Ioan M. (2002) A *Modern History of the Somali*. Oxford.

Schlee, Günther (2004) Taking sides and constructing identities: reflections on conflict theory, *The Journal of the Royal Anthropological Institute*, Vol. 10 No. 1, 135-156.

Schlee, Günther (2001) Einleitung, in: Alexander Horstmann, Günther Schlee (Hg.): Integration *durch Verschiedenheit*. Lokale und globale Formen interkultureller Kommunikation, Bielefeld, 17-46.

WSP international (2005) *Rebuilding Somaliland. Issues and Possibilities*. Lawrenceville.

Vortrag

Zenker, Olaf (2005) "Irish is all around us" Irish identity and the Irish language in discourse and practiceamong Gaeilgeoirí in Catholic West Belfast, unpublished paper (lecture given at the Max Planck Institute for social anthropology in Halle/Saale, Germany, 11.01.2005)

Used internet resource: - www.allpuntland.com.

----

[1]This article is based on 16 months of fieldwork in Northern Somalia which were completed in December 2004. It is a first attempt to make sense of some of my findings. The argumentation and the presentation are by far not complete. Any critisism is welcome to the author (contact: virgil12@gmx.de).

[2]The best general overview of the history of Somali politics is provided by Lewis, Ioan M. 2002: A modern history of the Somali, Oxford.

[3]For a discussion of some international and local strategies of conflict settlement see Höhne, Markus V. 2002: Somalia zwischen Krieg und Frieden. Strategien der friedlichen Konfliktaustragung auf internationaler und lokaler Ebene, Hamburg.

[4]The "state" as a concept for analysis has been under discussion for decades. There are scholars correctly pointing out that the term refers to many different polities in history but also at present. This leads to a host of "[...] different, competing and loaded meanings [...]". The concept becomes almost useless. Nevertheless, in a certain more positive perspective "[...] the state is a legal-normative ideal, a modern symbol and institutional expression of the ‚common good' [...]" (Ferguson 2003: 86). In my experience among urban dwellers and semi-sedentarized nomads in Northern Somalia most people long for a state in this sense, as a symbol of unity on the one hand and of a better life for every individual in the broadest sense on the other.

[5]There are also some smaller clans and minority groups, such as Madiban, Tumal, Yibir living in Somaliland and Puntland. They have not been very prominent in the political developments in the 1990s and are still hardly represented in one of the two governments in Northern Somalia. Therefore I will not deal with these groups in this paper.

[6]The former British part of Somalia in the North West is generally called "North" (waqooyi); the former Italian part is known as "South" (koonfur), even if it includes the geographical North East of the Somali peninsula. For details of the colonial partition of the Somali inhabited territories see Lewis 2002: 40-62.

[7]For details and an analysis of the developments in Somaliland up to the present see WSP international 2005: Rebuilding Somaliland. Issues and Possibilities, Lawrenceville.

[8]Especially Mogadishu is known for its instability. As a consequence the newly established Transitional Federal Government (TFG) sits in Nairobi. It does not dare to resume its political business in the capital of Somalia which is controlled by different factions of warlords, businessmen and religious groups, most of which have some militias at their disposal. Even if most of the warlords have been included in the new government, the situation in the city is still unforeseeable. The leaders of the strict religious community in Mogadishu openly announced their dissatisfaction with the new Somali President, Col. Cabdullahi Yusuf Axmed, who has a reputation as a fighter against militant religious groups such as Al Ittihad. Demonstrations in the city against the new government have been organized shortly after its inauguration in October 2004.

[9]This government perspective is reflected in some journalistic and academic accounts of Somaliland, not based on in depth-field research. This has a somewhat contradictory effect: on the one hand, it is necessary to highlight Somaliland as a positive "African example" with regard to ending the civil war and establishing a well developed

democratic culture in the political center, with free press and a political system shifting from clan representation to democratic elections over the last years, without massive external assistance. On the other hand, not to address the remaining severe problems, especially the long standing conflict between Harti and Isaaq clans within the territory claimed by the government in Hargeysa as Somaliland territory, means to ignore a potential hotspot for civil war in the region.

[10]For the recent history of and developments in Puntland see Farah, Axmed Yusuf 2001: Somalia: Modern History and the End of the 1990s, in: WSP international: Rebuilding Somalia. Issues and possibilities for Puntland, London.

[11]The Majeerteen are numerically the biggest of the Harti clans. Also according to genealogy, Maxamed "Majeerteen" is the eldest son of Harti.

[12]Name changed.

[13]This is very much a personal account. I only crosschecked it with some other people in Lasscaanod. It may be hat the course of events as described here is very biased and that people in Hargeysa would present a different version of what has happened. Nevertheless I use this narrative because it was an important topic among many Dhulbahante in the region and reflects some aspects of their political position.

[14]For example in the novel "Aqoondarro waa u nacab jacayl" (Ignorance is the enemy of love), the first major literary publication in the Somali language, the hero of the story who is a Dervish explains: "The Dervishes are an organization which was created for the Somali people and their country, and their aim is to protect the independence of Somalis and their Muslim faith." (Cawl, Faarax M.J. 1984 [1974]: 20).

[15]No matter how biased the narrative above is, the fact that Dahir Rayaale Kahin has been attacked and had to retreat in a rush is not contested.

[16]On 10th October 2004 Cabdullahi Yusuf was elected President of Somalia. This led to a change in the Puntland politics. In early January 2005 Gen. Cadde Muuse won the presidential elections in Puntland. If this will lead to a new approach towards the Puntland-Somaliland conflict and towards the corruption problems inside Puntland remains to be seen. For more information see: www.allpuntland.com.

[17]On 29th October 2004 the Somaliland and Puntland military troops clashed in the countryside near the village of Adhiadeye, about 30 km Northeast of Lasscaanod. On each side about 15 soldiers were killed and several dozen wounded. Immediately after this event the

political climate on the ground worsened. Even people who had had a tolerant political position before, were now increasingly becoming extremist in their support for either Somaliland or Puntland. Staying in Hargeysa in October and November 2004 I could observe that the borders of the identity clusters closed: during several nights Isaaq neighbours threw stones at the houses of a Dhulbahante member of the House of Representatives of Somaliland, who had lived with his family in the city for years. In reaction to this the family left Hargeysa to Lasscaanod, which was safe according to the genealogical logic. This was not an isolated case. To be a Dhulbahante became an accusation in Hargeysa in those days, regardless of people's personal background. I do not have any information on whether similar escalations happened on the Puntland side.

Chapter 15

The Role of Civil Society in Rebuilding Somalia

Fowsia Abdulkadir

The purpose of this paper is to present an overview of the notion of civil society, examine its role in rebuilding the collapsed state structures in Somalia, and underline some challenges facing civil society in Somalia. Focusing on Somalia makes for an interesting case study; in so far as the Somali dilemma is the product of a world history laced with the scramble for Africa, colonialism, and the ever dynamic and evolving global economy, globalization. I will argue that, given the evolution of the world political economy, the instabilities in Africa, and particularly the upheavals in Somalia are mere manifestations of globally unequal economic power relations.

This paper commences with a glance at some of the major changes in the globalization processes, which have indirectly set the stage for the current mayhem in the Horn of Africa and still continues to set the continental context for the turmoil in Africa. It looks at the current environments, which face civil society in Somalia, highlighting major barriers and concludes with some suggestions for the road ahead.

Global Political Economy:

As a background information, let's take a glimpse at the historical context of today's globally integrated economy and its influences on Africa's political trends. Dealing with the current trends in Somalia, one needs to consider the evolution of the global political economy. In 1884/1885, at the Berlin Conference, colonial powers divided up Africa's geographical space. A century later, in the Uruguay talks, the G – 7 divided up Africa's economic space. What this history underlines for the destiny of Africa, in the context of the complex and dramatic transformation in global dynamic, is the challenges that lie ahead for Africans in general and civil society in particular, throughout the transition to the 21 century, pertaining to the need to steer the continent towards a direction that will ensure its substantive engagement in the global system (Haroub Othman & M. Halfani 2000). With regards to the political turmoil in Somalia, I would contend that the prolonged civil war and destructive clan conflicts are manifestations of the external global factors, which heavily influenced the internally hostile environments that led the current state of affairs. In the next section I will situate the Somali question within the larger context of the African continent by looking at two concepts, which dominate the debate on civil society, democracy and democratization processes in Africa and the 'good governance' discourse.

Democracy and Democratizing Africa:

Setting the context for democracy and the process of democratization in Africa, George Nzongola-Ntalaja (1998) examines major current difficulties facing African countries pursuing democracy. Studying democracy from different aspects such as historical, and as a universal principle of governance, he posits that it is a moral imperative, a social process, and a specific kind of political system which can apply to all societies, including Somalia. He dismisses the perception that democracy is something imported to Africa from abroad. According to this author, the important question today is not *"Africanizing democracy, but rather considering the necessity of democratizing Africa"*.

Further in the analysis, the author considers the internal environments, which I believe to be consequences of external global factors that hinder democracy in Africa, underlining the fact that postcolonial states and governments in Africa are for the most part hostile to democratizing their countries. The author further argues that African leader of the postcolonial era have exploited resources at their disposal to weaken democratic processes, an example, par excellence, is the collapsed state of Somalia.

I would submit that internal weak leadership in the continent has succeeded in slowing down democratic process on the one had, because of how independence was brought about in African countries. European colonizers realizing that they were no longer able to hold complete control over these lands and their resources engaged in negotiating freedom talks with the sole intent of safeguarding their trade interests. And, on the other hand, as posited by Issa G. Shivji (1991), postcolonial consensus in Africa was based on narrowly defined anti-colonialism and non-alignment in a world controlled by the two super-powers. During the cold-war era the Horn of Africa was hot geopolitical spot, which had ramifications for its societies, such as Somalia.

At the dawn of independence, African countries pursued nation-building ideologies, which, according to Wamba's formula as cited by Shivji, can be summarized as: *"one people, one nation, one political party and one supreme leader"* (Shivji, 2000, p.30). And as it is evident from history and the analysis of authors like Wamba (1991a), Shivji (1986), in the context of postcolonial nation-building ideologies, the state itself was replica of the colonial tyrannical state. The main common characteristic of post-independence African states was the concentration of power in the executive arm of the state.

According to Shivji, during the economic crisis in the late seventies, many African states lost their political legitimacy leading to a breakdown of broad consensus. He further argues that democracy, as a way of resistance and as a method of organizing and constituting a new consensus, is very much on the agenda. However, Shivji analyzing the little impact or change, that hasty conversion to political multi-partyism and economic liberalization have had on improving the difficult conditions of life in the continent, calls for a deeper interrogation of the process of democratization. Shivji emphasizes the fact that narrowly defined ideologies have fallen short of building a new consensus that can hold Third World societies together, unless they are solidly linked to the local realities of the people of these societies.

Governance and the 'good governance agenda':

According to Rita Abrahamsen, the 'good governance agenda' has emerged when the Cold-War era ended and it is a fundamental part of methods of power utilized in global politics in manners that allow the North to continue its hegemony in the South(Abrahamsen 2000). Abrahamsen argues strongly that in addition to the collapse of communism and the failure of World Bank and IMF structural adjustment policies created the conditions that resulted in the emergence of the 'good governance agenda'. This agenda, posits Abrahamsen, is intimately linked to the development discourse and existing global structures and relations of power. Furthermore, the author cautions against the claim, of the good governance agenda, 'empowering ordinary people'. Abrahamsen argues that a critical analysis on the agenda's claim uncovers that the discourse removes from the term 'empowerment' its radical political subtext and instead gives it an instrumental meaning.

Abrahamsen further articulates warnings against how seductive the suggestions put forth by the World Bank in its promotion of the 'good governance agenda' can be as it rejects the development models of the past. *"The 'postindependence development efforts failed, 'because the strategy was misconceived" (World Bank 1989: 3, as cited by Abrahamsen, 2000: 48).* According to the World Bank report, (*Governance: The World Bank's Experience, 1994b), as* analyzed by Abrahamsen, 'the misconceived' old development initiatives relied heavily on state-led hasty modernization efforts that were imitating Western notions of development. In blaming the state-led development failures, World Bank driven 'good governance agenda' claims to be culturally sensitive to traditional societies ensuring high level of 'appropriateness' since there are closer connections between cultural appropriateness, good governance, and parts of civil society. Further in her critical analysis, Abrahamsen highlights the way in which the good governance discourse depicts African societies as full of concealed capitalist energy and entrepreneurial spirit. In this regard the good governance discourse creates opposing sides, one which is the rejected state intervention closely associated with past development failures, and 'indigenous capitalism' which creates the favourable conditions for future successful development models.

Abrahamsen states: *"In the good governance discourse, civil society emerges as the key link between the economic liberalization and democratization; it is both the locus of economic growth and vitality and the seedbed of democracy"*(Abrahamsen:2000:p. 52*)*.

It is this kind of conceptualizing civil society and the role it occupies in African societies that we need to be weary of, because this conception re-enforces and perpetuates 'neo-colonial' power relations. While there is no denying the mushrooming literature on the emergence of civil society, the good governance discourse depicting it as essentially democratic is problematic, and needs to be scrutinized. As Abrahamsen points out, civil society should neither be seen as automatically democratic nor undemocratic, but rather, its characteristics being contextual to particular time and place.

Civil Society:

According to Robert Fatton Jr., Lewin's definition of civil society speaks to the African landscape:

> "Civil society is the aggregate of networks and institutions that either exist and act independently of the state or are official organizations capable of their own, spontaneous views on national or local issues and then impressing these views on their members, on small group and, finally on authorities" (cited in R. Fatton Jr., 1992: 73).

In this regard, Fatton suggests that civil society function as the mechanism that allows Africans to withdraw from, in order to escape from, the reach of authoritarian states. Fatton further posits that the mechanisms that allow the emergence of civil society are not ideologically neutral, but rather dependent on the prevailing political and cultural processes, which define the state domain (Fattton 1992). According to Fatton, the emergence of civil society in Africa originated from two major processes. The first is African societies tackling limited resources and the rising cost of obligation of collective welfare. The second is facing authoritarian state governments, so subordinate classes are retreating into private spaces of survival where they help themselves. In this regards, the discourse is permeated by the shrinking role of the state and economic liberalization.

According to Célestin Monga, to define civil society is an ambitious task particularly because of the extensiveness of the recent literature on the concept. In his book, Monga defines it as *"…new spaces for communication and discussion over which the state has no control"* (Célestin Monga 1996)

Although this narrow definition does not capture the reality of the whole of the continent's civil society, and certainly not the Somali situation, I appreciate some of the complexities and confusion around defining this concept in the context of the serious threats to the future stability and viability of each African state which can be posed by the anarchic emergence of an ill-defined civil society. Whether it fits within the various definitions, some narrow and some general in the literature, the fact still remains that there is a vibrant civil society in Africa. In the Horn of Africa, civil society includes traditional as well as non-traditional groups. Traditional groups are organized at the community level as clans, sub-clans with their elders, these traditional communities' social relations are formed geographically and on the basis of clan lineages. Non-traditional groups are organized also at the community but are based more on professional and personal interests and might share common ideology about development.

The Role of Civil Society in Somalia

Definition

According to Dr. M. Abdi Mohamed (Gandhi), civil society as it is currently being defined in the context of Somalia encompasses two streams of Somali society: 1) traditional civil society which consists of clan-based community leaders/elders; 2) urban-based, non-traditional, civil society which consists of academics, professionals, peace building organizations, human rights activist organizations, community development NGOS, community groups.

Historically, civil society has had strong role in Somalia after independence, it was members of the traditional elders who brokered the process that brought together the former British and Italian

Somaliland, which formed the Somali Republic. After independence, the role of civil society faded as the country embarked on hasty multi-party system, which was based on clan politics. In other words, once civil society established the republic of Somalia its role faded into the margins. In the two decades of experimentations with scientific socialism, needless to say, the political environment in Somalia was not conducive civil society to self-organize.

After the collapse of the state in Somalia, the elders have played a key role in negotiating peace processes in different parts of the country. The traditional leaders and urban members of Somali civil society have been instrumental in relatively stabilizing the country for the last decade.

Challenges for Somali civil society:

Since 1993 when the international community left Somalis to their own devices; the need for civil society to take a central role in this abandoned country has emerged. Civil societies have grown stronger and stronger in the face of anarchy and lawlessness in Somalia. For instance, clan elders, (Gurti), have accomplished cease fire and voluntary disarmament which brought relative peace that resulted the creation of regional administrations like the Republic of Somaliland in the North-Western part of Somalia and Puntland in the North-East. The scale of the voluntary disarmament negotiated by Somali clan elders in Somaliland is a remarkable achievement in the history of the continent.

Clan Representation and Gender Representation:

Both the traditional and urban civil society groups in Somalia have been active in all the meetings and peace negotiating initiatives in the country. One might question the importance of the role of civil society in Somali peace negotiations, when warlords have been hogging the peace discussions. Granted that the role civil society played in the earlier negotiations was not strong, but as time went on their role has grown and their credibility has risen. In Arta, Djibouti, civil society actively participated and was instrumental in securing some gender representation in the composition of the former TNG. It negotiated for 25% parliamentary representation for women, though this was unfortunately reduced to 12% at the Kenyan conference.

So, one major challenge facing Somali civil society is the inherent contradiction between the chosen path of sharing political power along clan lines and the fundamental rights of women to political representation. As Somalis grapple with finding the right path to democratic process, and the incorporation of solid conflict resolution principles, in the context of a society stratified along clan lines, peace negotiations inevitably are debated and negotiated through the process of sharing power along clan lines. One might wonder if this is the only way out of this anarchic situation or whether are there other paths open for Somalis? May be there are, but right now, the distribution of political power along clan lines is the option being pursued.

Although all Somalis, women, men and children, will reap the benefits of peace, stability and effective conflict resolution processes, the danger is, in my opinion, gender inequity in the balance of the political power. And moreover, "gender dimensions" to peace building processes will not be central to these peace deals. Members of civil society, particularly the urban folk, need to seriously address the limitations of clan representations and the serious consequences of the impact it can have on Somali women. All Somalis and civil society in particular, need to embark on setting in motion mechanisms that will facilitate a paradigm shift, which underline the shortcomings of clan representation in the political arena. Even though, in the short term it looks like clan blood line are the chosen method of power sharing, we, Somalis need to proceed with a mindset that will eventually bring about 'substantive gender equity' and transform the clan dominated context today. There is a contradiction in sharing-power along clan lines and cautioning against the negatives consequences for gender equality, reality is unfolding in a complex way in Somalia. Somalis are struggling with construction of basic societal institutions, and it seems that focusing on gender equity is not a major concern in the bigger scheme of things right now.

Having said that, Somalis are for the most part proud of being Somali and continue to carry the badge of their heritage; my optimism lies in this fact: I have confidence that the contradiction of mixing blood lines and political ideologies will be resolved by resilient Somali scholars and members of civil society.

Somali women have always been the backbone of Somali society. The author Nurudin Farah, who has written about Somali women, suggests that given the current events in Somalia and the essential role women have played in peace negotiation, rebuilding the society, and supporting individual families survive; the leadership of Somalia ought to be placed in the hands of women and /or supporters to the cause of women[1]. Although, in theory this sounds far-fetched, the fact remains that women's lives crisscross clans. As Nurudin posited, a Somali woman could be married to one clan and have the children of a different clan while she herself could belong to yet another clan[2]. Hence they can be instrumental in implementing and enduring and last peace.

Gender issues are not the only challenges facing Somali civil society. Because of the protracted civil war, there are serious security problems. Members of civil society can look at this challenge as an opportunity, because post-conflict situations can provide opportunities to develop new norms, write new rules, reach out to new progressive leaders, and build new institutions. Civil society can start from the stand point of rights-based approach, which ensures that women are included and given the right to participate in a meaningful way in the decision making processes, and benefit from resources and services.

In the current prevailing conditions, civil society is weak and its role is not well defined. According to Dr. Mohamed Abdi Mohamed, of Somali Peace Line, civil society members are subjected to constant harassment and bullying by the warlords and their thugs while the international community has taken the role of a distant observer. Nonetheless, civil society efforts are non-stop, and they are involved in numerous activities that range from participation in the ongoing peace negotiations, leading disarmament initiatives to sponsoring tours of famous Somali poets, like Hadrawi, and scholars to crisscross the country in peace building and civic education initiatives.

Diaspora Civil Society

As a result of the civil war, for Somalis, this is the age of refugees and mass exodus, and consequently, there is a large number of Somalis in the Diaspora. Equally important, in the peace building processes, is the role of Diaspora civil society. Somalis in the Diaspora continue to provide substantial economic support. Through associations such as the International Somali Studies Congress, they tirelessly debate the issues and analyze the barriers that face all Somalis and civil society particularly. According to Lee Cassanelli, during the Fifth Congress of Somali Studies, for instance, there was a well attended panel, which debated, whether the future leadership of Somalia should come from those being schooled in Islamic schools, or from the children of those who are currently in the Diaspora.

Recommendation for the road ahead

Having underlined some of the difficulties facing the civil society in the Somali situation let me attempt to make some suggestions and recommendations for the future. First, there ought to be to endeavours searching for ways to build new consensus for Somalia and entire continent of Africa. According to I.G. Shivji, there are important issues that need to be addressed for the pursuit f building new consensus.

These are: *"popular livelihoods, popular participation and popular power or sovereignty"*. In this analysis, the author uses the term *'popular'* a) in a way that rejects the narrow definition of the postcolonial nation building in Africa; b) the term is to capture the broad based masses, which constitute the social core of the new consensus; c) the term should encompass culture and tradition as the most important aspects of ideological forms.

For these 'critical elements', as Shivji puts it, to be realized the tasks ahead are indeed challenging, but not impossible to achieve. Civil society and a new leadership in Somalia, with substantial support from the international community, need to engage in and implement 'Trans-formative Education' and the strengthening of civil society. Trans-formative education is an opportunity to educate the masses, in and outside of classrooms, providing them with a process of learning through historical reflections and challenging the customary dichotomies between the personal and the public. A critical aspect of trans-formative education is the fact that it builds on people's strength as well as their previous knowledge.

Somali civil society can participate in processes that can realize:

- Good governance, that is not driven by mainstream (i.e. World Bank) popular agenda, but rather good governance which is rooted in local realities and attempts to deal with the unique complexities of the Somali situation.
- Poverty alleviation programs which are sustainable and long term oriented as oppose to one-time projects that provide band-aid solutions.
- Closely linked to sustainable development are disarmament and conflict resolution initiatives that provide the opportunity for lasting peace.
- Substantive gender equity, which can be the most difficult to achieve in the short term given that the Somalis are resolving and rebuilding societal trust on the bases of clan lineages.

References

Abrahamsen, Rita. (2000) *Disciplining Democracy: Development Discourse and Good Governance in Africa*. Zed Books Ltd.

Fatton, Robert Jr (1992) *Predatory Rule: State and Civil Society in Africa.* Lynne Rienner Publishers, Inc; Boulder and London.

George Nzongola-Ntalaja & Margaret C. Lee (1998). (eds.) *The State and Democracy in Africa* World Press Inc.

Haroub Othman & M. Halfani (2000) (eds.)*"Reflections on Leadership in Africa: Forty Years After Independence"*. VUB University Press.

Mills Landel (1992: p. 567), as cited in Abrahamsen 2000)

Monga Célestin (1996) The *Anthropology f Anger: Civil Society and Democracy in Africa* translated by Linda L. Flec & Célestin Monga. Lynne Rienner Publishers, 1996, chap.1

Shivji Issa G. (1986). *Law, the state and working class in Tanzania. Dar es Salaam.*

Shivji Issa G. (2000). Critical Elements of New Democratic Consensus in Africa. In (eds.)_Haroub Othman & M. Halfani *"Reflections On Leadership in Africa: Forty Years After Independence".*

Shivji Issa G. (Spring 1991) The Democracy Debate in Africa: Tanzania Article from Vol.18 No.50 *of the Review of African Political Economy* (pp79-91)

----

[1]Bildhaan: An International Journal of Somali Studies", vol. 1, 2001; published by Macalester College International Studies and Programming; "Interview with Nurturing Farah" by Ahmed I. Samater; p.92

[2]Ibid

Chapter 16

Linkages between International Aid and Identity Creation in Somalia

Valeria Saggiomo

The involvement of international support in the Somali identity creation process can be analysed by taking into consideration two different aspects:

- The first is the contribution of international aid for development to the reconstruction of social sectors, such as education;
- The second is the contribution of the international community to the political processes leading to the reconstruction of the state structure.

The two levels of analysis are different since the actors involved and the final aim are different. However, the two aspects of international aid are inter-related and influence each other. Both of them influence identity creation processes, in terms of state identity creation on the one side and people identity modification on the other.

This paper describes how international aid for state formation and for development, in the education sector in particular, contribute to shape Somali identity creation processes. It will also highlight the lack of ownership by Somali population of both the aspects of identity creation processes, the state formation identity and the Somali identity in terms of history, traditions and customs.

The first part of this paper will analyse the importance of the education sector in the identity creation process of Somali people, in terms of transmission of local culture to the new generations, and it will describe the external interferences (colonisation and international aid) to the development of this pivotal social sector in Somalia.

The second part of the paper will address the concepts of nation-building and nationhood related to the Somali clan identity concept, as a methodological premise, before going into details about the state creation processes supported by international community in Somalia. The theory that the clan, due to its internal rigidity, constitutes an obstacle to the nation-state creation process shall be contested and its limits demonstrated.

The paper concludes by outlining the similarities in the international community approach regarding the two aspects of aid: aid to development, and aid to state creation. The lack of true participation by Somali civil society in the two mentioned processes is here seen as the major attempt to undermine an endogenous identity creation process in Somalia.

Education and Nationhood

According to Ernest Gellner, one of the main theorists on nationalism, the pivotal element of national self-consciousness is the alphabetisation of the people[1].

Alphabetisation however is only the first step. The education sector, as a whole, is considered pivotal to promoting the transmission of local culture, values and beliefs with the long-term perspective of consolidating a national identity and local patterns of governance.

In Somalia, British and Italians introduced modern formal education. However, colonial education was restricted to some settled population centres and had a very low coverage. At independence, in 1960, Somalia inherited 233 primary schools and 12 secondary schools. During the first period of Siad Barre regime (1969-77) until the early 1980s, the formal education system expanded considerably[2].

The 1973-74 literacy campaign, promoted by Siad Barre, considerably improved the alphabetisation of the Somali people. Secondary schools were temporarily closed and students were sent to the remote areas to teach. During 1970s the Somali National University of Mogadishu was established with the support of the Italian Government. By 1981 the University had 9 faculties, 490 teaching staff and an enrolment of 3,700 students.

The situation started declining during 1980s, due to the Ogaden war engagement of Siad Barre regime who critically reduced the budget allocated to education from 14% in 1961 to 1.5% in 1990. As a result, many schools were closed and abandoned, the enrolment sharply declined and most of the qualified teachers and administrators left in search of better incentives elsewhere.

Following the breakout of the civil war in 1991 the situation of the education sector worsened tremendously. Many students and teachers were displaced, school buildings were either completely or partially destroyed and all the educational materials looted. All the formal education sectors were affected, the secondary schools and the University ceased to operate. For almost two years (1991-92) no formal education took place, until 1993 when the interventions of the donors' community, United Nations Agencies and Non Governmental Organizations started operating in the education sector. Until now, the international aid interventions in the education sector in Somalia have been mainly focused on the emergency/relief approach by rehabilitating the former educational structures destroyed during the civil war[3].

The major donor strategy for the education sector in 1998 identifies policy options according to the different level of political stability in three identified zones (Somaliland, Puntland and Central-South Somalia). In areas that could guarantee reasonable levels of security the main sectors of intervention included teacher training, improvement of learning conditions (i.e. rehabilitation and construction of school facilities) institutional capacity building and strengthening of the resource base (i.e. cost sharing mechanism for sustainability). The document outlined the need to develop a suitable curriculum for primary school, a guiding school syllabus, a quality control system for examination and certification, a harmonized school calendar, and educational materials for schools.

At the time, primary school enrolment was estimated at less than 20%. In 1997, 91% of the pupils were enrolled in lower primary (grades 1 to 4) with only 1% in upper primary (grades 5-8). An estimated three quarters of the primary schools did not provide children with the opportunity to acquire essential educational competences. Also qualified teachers and supervisory cadre that virtually disappeared as a result of the civil war needed to be re-injected into the system. The perception by many parents of lack of relevance of secular primary education was highlighted as the main factor hindering the development of the secular educational system in Somalia. Parents, in fact, do not see opportunities for their children to complete primary education or to gain better employment opportunities after completion of school.

In 2004, this perception became stronger than ever. From 2000 to 2003, a total of almost 70 million dollars[4] was spent in Somalia in the education sector. During the last years, considerable efforts have been focused on rehabilitating existing infrastructure, enhancing management capacity, providing incentives for teachers, and distributing school materials (books).

However, many of the core problems identified in 1998 still need to be properly addressed. These need to be approached with due consideration of Somali culture and lifestyle and with the full involvement of Somali stakeholders at all decision making levels. I am referring for example to the school calendar, which has been set but which does not reflect the seasonal movements of nomadic people, with the consequent risk of having perfectly functioning schools in rural areas, but empty for a large part of the school year. I am also referring to the development of the primary school curriculum, which only exists in the form of textbooks, whose content scarcely addresses the thousands of aspects of Somali culture, starting from the Somali literary production to the Somali history or, better, histories. Finally, I refer to the lack of a comprehensive coherent donor strategy for the education sector in Somalia drawn with the contribution of Somali stakeholders.

The pertinence of the secular education model, in terms of contents and methodologies, and the issue of scarce opportunities for Somali pupils to continue the educational career, still need to be seriously addressed in the near future, possibly, with the contribution of Somali experts from Diaspora community and surely, with the involvement of Somali civil society.

In fact, the participation of Somali civil society and Somali intellectuals in the curriculum development process has been scarce. When involved, Somali experts were in charge of translation jobs and, at best, of contributing to the editing of books for Islamic studies. The rest of the books have been mostly edited by European consultants. Not being in the position of writing about Somali history, as Abdi Kusow rightly points out, choosing a people's history is not merely a matter of fact, but of power[5]. UN agencies that were in charge of the Curriculum development process chose to abide by the standards of the current humanitarian policies, giving emphasis to issues like basic sanitary rules and HIV-Aids knowledge. While the importance of these messages is generally recognized, they scarcely contribute to local Somali culture transmission to the new generations.

The risk is concrete: when the support to the education sector is based on external approaches or patterns of knowledge, the impact of international aid risks being non-pertinent to the local environment, and the process of local identity creation will be adversely affected. Education therefore risks splintering local cultures when it is based on external approaches rather than promoting local identity creation.

Thirty years ago, Paulo Freire in his dialogic theory, pointed out how programmatic content of education in developing countries can not be elaborated starting from the objectives of the educators, but from the elaboration and systematisation of what local knowledge is. The result would be otherwise to deliver knowledge in the same way as people deposit money in a bank. Planning education in developing countries based on exogenous models, Freire explains, is like continuing in colonising them instead of freeing them from the vicious circle of oppressed-oppressors[6].

According to K. Salia Bao, the education system in African countries has to be *integrated* to children's life, so to be perceived as part of human activities inside the community, not as a separate component of daily community life; it has to be *pertinent* to local needs, it has to be *functional* to social activities of the community, meaning that notions taught in school need to be directly applicable in daily life; and finally, it has to be *community oriented* and therefore shall promote the values that enhance the unity of the community for its survival[7]. By respecting these principles, education shall have a long term impact on community life and shall contribute to the development of the individuals within their environment.[8]

Teaching local mythology, proverbs, local contemporary literature as well as the cultural heritage of a given African community within the school means to create and enhance a sense of pride of being African. This pride is needed to resist the myth of western culture that since colonialism has penetrated African cultures. At the same time, the curriculum in African countries shall be integrated with the modern western knowledge because it is not possible to use the tools of forefathers for developing the society today, and result in a modern society tomorrow[9].

The balance between African traditional culture and western knowledge is very delicate and difficult to achieve and implies the active involvement of African intellectuals and members of the civil society in the development of the school curriculum for a given African country. According to the works of many educationists that have analysed the curriculum development process in several African countries[10], this is not yet the case in Somalia, where such an effort has been tried only for the development of upper primary school curriculum. It is not yet even the case in Eastern Africa in general. Identity creation processes are strictly tied to what is taught to the new generations in and outside the school, to the transmission of knowledge, skills and habits belonging to the past, interwoven with those belonging to the present. A stronger interaction between western inputs and local outputs needs be sought in order to achieve that balance and to sustain an endogenous identity creation process in Somalia.

Nationhood and clan identity

What is Nationhood and Nation Building

The concept of Nation state refers to the establishment of a group of individuals united by a natural tie on which basis they build up the organisation of political power in the form of a Nation State. Originally, in the 19th century, this tie was strongly related to the concept of race, therefore the original group was intended to share certain specific characteristics like the language, customs, religion, territory. Nation-building processes were seen as something spontaneous for groups sharing the same ethnic origin.

Modern examples of Nation States, however, include different ethnic groups, with different languages and customs, and, vice-versa, a common language is spoken in different Countries. Therefore the relation of Nation State to the concept of ethnicity sounds erroneous already in the 20th century. It is thus questionable whether Nation-building processes are directly related to the issue of ethnicity anymore

A modern definition of nationalism relates this concept to an ideology, i.e. to a feeling of membership to a given territorial entity (the State), thus determining a feeling of loyalty by the individuals towards it. The concept of Nationalism is therefore a shared idea, an ideology to apply to a given territorial state. Nation-building processes seem to follow more cultural patterns of aggregation rather than genetic ones.

What is interesting to note here is that:

- The rationale behind the concept of nationalism is to create and maintain loyal behaviour of the citizens towards the state.
- Nation-building process is more related to cultural patterns of aggregation rather than ethnic ones.

Clan identity and nationalism.

Following I.M. Lewis (2002), ethnically and culturally the Somali belong to the Hamitic ethnic group. The six clan families into which Somali nation is divided are generally too large and widely scattered to act as a corporate political unit. Therefore, clans are divided into sub-clans and into extended families. Genealogy defines the basic political and social status of the individual within Somali society[11]. According to I.M. Lewis, Somali social organisation is based on two reference axis: descendents in male lineage and a form of political contract (*Xeer*) that includes the most binding loyalty to a "*diya*-paying group"[12], although these segmentations, when externally attacked , unite to protect their interests. The structure suggested by I.M. Lewis indicates certain rigidity in the relationships within the clan where alliances and divisions are determined by blood ties and customs. This approach was determinant in the development of Somali studies and led many scholars to adopt what Abdi Ismail Samatar calls a static vision of Somali society, that does not consider the effects that social transformations, such as colonialism, might have had in the transformation dynamics of Somali social fabric[13].

In analysing the causes of the failure of the nation-state building process in Somalia, Abdalla Omar Mansur suggests that Somali society, being based on the concept of clan with its segmentation logic, does not adapt itself to the concept of state and to its power hierarchy. Clan identity together with the negative impact of foreign aid, are therefore the impedimental elements that prevent Somalia from being a united nation-state[14]. However, Mansur himself, later clarifies that the need to fully examine the nature of the Somali clan system is apparent, since Somali clan structure is not based on blood relationships but rather it is the consequences of nomadic pastoral life, with its necessity of defence of natural resources, that results, over time, in the formation of new alliances and, later, in new clan identities[15].

The Somali saying *"Tol waa tolane"* ("Clan is something joined together") is illustrative of the fluidity that characterises Somali clan identity which is a changing phenomenon where alliances and divisions are determined by a number of factors and where economic considerations are often stronger than blood relationships. To maintain this segmentation as a pillar of all the social analysis of Somali-related issues means to proceed in a sort of stigmatisation of Somali identity, which might be a limitation in the current analysis of Somalia nowadays.

One of the most recent examples of how clan identity can be manipulated, destroyed and re-built is offered by Siad Barre's policy of nation-building. During the first period of its regime (up to the Ogaden war) Siad Barre utilises the western imported banner of scientific socialism, which in the Somali version was translated as 'the sharing of the wealth based on wisdom' for legitimating its power and gaining external support. We are in an historical context where the western division of the world policies imposed the 'two blocks' lining up of the international scenario.

The propaganda was to overcome the internal tribal divisions in order to unify the nation and work together towards development. Tribal or clanic behaviours became a serious crime, *diya* payment was forbidden and marriage was emptied of its lineage significance. The socialist terminology was imposed upon the traditional clan terminology and the identification by clan lineage was banished in favour of the socialist rhetoric[16]. By these means, tribal loyalty had to be replaced by national loyalty and tribal identity had to be replaced by national identity.

Even though these identity destruction and re-creation mechanism may sound unrealistic, they had a great impact on the Somalis during the first period of Siad Barre's regime. One of these impacts could be found on its effects on the international aid flow of funds in the state coffers, that enabled Siad Barre to "provide resources" to Somali people, and probably in the fruitful results of a well planned propaganda. Soon after the Ogaden war, the myth of Somalia as a nation-state started showing its internal fractures and subsequently collapsed in the early 1990s.

What happened, in fact, was that Siad Barre did not practice what he preached: while he preached self-reliance he accepted foreign aid money as a tribute to his power and to the relationship he managed to build overseas; while he preached (and imposed) a ban on the clan approach, he nonetheless pursued the interests of his clan of origin (Marrehan clan). After the Ogaden war, the credibility of Siad Barre as a victorious leader of the nation began to show evident signs of decline: the political opposition reflected the same tribal pattern that Barre followed in pursuing his personal clan interest and rule[17].

Siad Barre's attempt to build a nation is the evidence that clan logic is not unbreakable in principle.

Bearing in mind this consideration, the theory that clan identity prevents Somalia from being a nation-state is not valid. In fact, while the rationale of clan cohesion is to maintain loyalty of individuals towards the group, for the defence of resources, the rationale behind the concept of nationalism is to create and maintain loyalty of the citizens towards the state; therefore, the shift from loyalty towards the clan to a loyalty towards the state is not impossible if the common denominator is the fulfilment of the concrete needs of the population.

Somali social identity must be seen as fluid, and adaptable to the ideal containers that from time to time host it, being the extended family, the clan, or the state. The approach that should be considered when dealing with issues of clan identities in the nation building process is deeply tied to the analysis of that container, together with the identities that move inside it, the reasons that cause their alliances, and the fulfilment of their needs.

Internatioal community and political support to state creation

In order to analyse the involvement of international community aid in the support to Somali state creation, we have to shift our attention from international aid for humanitarian assistance and development to a higher political level, and compare external support with internal state creation processes. The analysis shall start from early 1990s when the first endogenous attempts to restore peace and security in the country were made, starting from Somaliland to Puntland and then moving down the country to Central South situation. The analysis will underline the process for achieving stability against the outcome both taking into account the endogenous models and the external driven attempts of the peace processes[18].

The Somaliland model of reconciliation

Somaliland has been the first territorial entity to achieve a relative stability in the North eastern part of the country even during the first months of the civil war that was blooding the Southern part of Somalia.

In 1991 the Isaaq-based guerrilla that led Somaliland out of the Barre area of control, invited non-Isaaq clan to a traditional authority meeting (*shir beeleed*) in an effort at building a common political agenda for restoring Somaliland after the fighting instead of turning the guerrilla also against them for gaining power. This approach helped a lot to build a climate of confidence among the different clans in Somaliland and was the first step towards reconciliation.

The key strategic element used to restore peace was the *Guurti*, the supreme council of lineage leaders, who organised two clan peace conferences in Burao (1992) and Borama (1993), where *Guurti* gained an active political role becoming a wing of the Parliament. These can be considered the first peace conferences whose aim was to smoothen over clan rivalries and achieve a political stability in the region. The outcome was a peace charter that was endorsed by all the clans of Somaliland territory, Isaaq, Harti, Dir and other smaller clans. The process, which can undoubtedly be labelled endogenous, has been extensively participatory and locally based. Moreover, it led to a system of governance, which is strongly anchored on the clan based political culture of the nomadic northern Somalian society. This was probably the key for the success of the peace initiative, despite the internal power struggles of 1994-95 and the evident tendency of President Egal towards hegemony.

In March 2001 Somaliland managed to conduct a referendum for the approval of the new constitution and indirectly for its auto-declared independence from the rest of Somali territory. This is perhaps the first democratic process in Somalia over the last thirty years or more that brought together over one million votes out of an estimated 1.6 million voters. UNOPS (United Nations Political Office for Somalia) chose not to observe the referendum. In effect it must be said that all the political achievements of Somaliland have been gained without the external support of the International Community who has never legitimated Somaliland's claim for independence.

The Puntland model of reconciliation

Puntland later achieved a certain measure of stability on its territory, but what is worth noting is that the process was based on the emulation of Somaliland model. Puntland *Isimo* (the traditional institution comparable to *Guurti* in Somaliland) played a central role in securing internal stability among the different clans (Majeerteen, Harti, small Darod allied groups) after 1991, even if it did not become a political actor as the *Guurti* in Somaliland.

The traditional leaders (*Isimo*) and the major political party in the Northeast Somalia, the Somali Salvation Democratic Front – SSDF, informally administered the area up to 1998, when the, even slow, political process culminated in the clan based Conference in Garowe, where the Puntland State of Somalia was declared. Behind the relative stability in terms of security, however, an intense political rivalry for the control of the administration continued between two strong men, Colonel Abdullahi Yusuf (a military man) and Abshir Muusa (Former Somali Police chief). Despite the fact that Abdullahi Yusuf imposed his presidency by force in 2001, relative stability was achieved in the region, even if the major challenge of ensuring social services to the local communities was far from achieved.

What is important to note in these two models of governance is that they, firstly, are spontaneous and endogenous models, and secondly that the key to their success has been the involvement of traditional structures of power who, on the basis of a recognised legitimacy, have jointly worked to overcome inter clan hostilities and pave the way for political stability. Once the state is constituted, a feeling of loyalty of its citizens towards it was gradually emerging and would probably take roots if it could meet the immediate needs of the population.

The Central South situation

Central South regions did not enjoy the same internal capacity of restoring peace and the stability, probably due to the wider coexistence of many clans and the higher availability of resources in the area. Mogadishu, the epicentre of the conflicts, is at the time of writing in 2004, still an open battle-field where the two Hawiya sub clans, Abgal and Habar Gidir, are engaged in a power struggle and competition for the control of the city and of the future Somali state. From 1991 to now, a total of 14 peace conferences have been held under the sponsorship of various international bodies.

The Arta Peace Process and the Transitional National Government

The initial emergence of clan based political entities on the base of the Northern experience, especially in Bay and Bakool Regions, has been overshadowed by the Arta Peace process, the third peace process led by Djibouti in 2000. Over 700 delegates and 1000 participants, including faction leaders, traditional leaders, civil society representatives, professionals, Diaspora people, gathered at Arta for almost 3 months.

The result was a centralised and united political setting led by the Transitional National Government (TNG) whose mandate was to search for national reconciliation and dialogue with political actors outside the Arta framework, within three-year period from August 2000. The TNG immediately gained international recognition and was hailed as a political actor by the international community.

Despite the wide participation of stakeholders at Arta, probably scarcely representative of the civil society part, the TNG showed its internal fractures from the first months of its mandate. Many of the leaders who joined the Government later boycotted it, including a wing of Ali Mahdi Abgal sub clan and factions of the Rahanweiyn Resistance Army.

Due to internal divisions and the hostility of some of the fighting factions who wanted to show to the international community that TNG had no control over Mogadishu and had failed in gaining political legitimacy all over the territory, TNG progressively lost international support, especially UN support, after the kidnapping of some aid workers in March 2001.

In May 2001 TNG tried to enhance its credibility by appointing a Peace and Reconciliation Committee with the task of "completing" the peace process and addressing the property issues, but this attempt failed after only three months due to the lack of political will of the chairman who did not endorse the second mandate and the process of selection of the members of the committee.

At the beginning of 2001, opposition leaders started to gather in order to discuss alternative ways of restoring peace. In January 2001 the first meeting was held in Ceel Berde village, in Bakool Region. Rahanweiyn Resistance Army (RRA) hosted the meeting with the participation of Puntland authorities, which saw in the TNG, an attempt on their independence and a possible claim on some of the territories that were unilaterally included in the Puntland state of Somalia - the Somali Patriotic Movement (SPM) of the Ogaden sub-clan of the Darod and the Southern Somali National Movement (SSNM) based on a sub clan of the Dir.

The Ceel Berde meeting led to a new political grouping known as the National Restoration Council (NRC) whose approach was directed towards the formation of a federal system of government where the southern part of Somalia was divided in two blocks, the Hawiya-dominated one, composed of the central regions and Benadir, and the non-Hawiya entity in South and Southwest Somalia, dominated by Rahanweiyn, Dir, Darod and other smaller groups. The Ceel Berde meeting however failed to agree on the distribution of power over the proposed self-governing regions of South and Southwest Somalia. A consensus opposition political proposal did not emerge from the Ceel Berde meeting.

Soon after, in March 2001, Ethiopia sponsored a follow-up to Ceel Berde in Awassa where, in addition to the Ceel Berde participants, Mogadishu-based faction leaders opposed to TNG, were also invited. This new political alliance was called Somali Reconciliation and Restoration Council (SRRC) and produced an interim charted signed by 16 faction leaders from South Somalia and a draft transition charter. Unfortunately, this seemed to replicate the TNG structure and once again, the issue of leadership failed to be resolved. Out of the eight major factions, four managed to group under one leadership, and the other four failed to find a common denominator.

The National Reconciliation Conference - IGAD

Before the expiration of the TNG mandate (August 2003), another conference was organised. The Conference was hosted by Kenya and was led by the Intergovernmental Authority on Development in Eastern Africa (IGAD), starting in October 2002 and ending in August 2004, with a Transitional Federal Charter[19], which defined the Somali territory as a Federation of three or more States under the guidance of a transitional Government.

The final endorsement of the Charter in September 2003 led to an impasse of the Conference; some leaders, including the President of the TNG, rejected the adoption the Charter and abandoned the Conference. An agreement was later achieved, though with some dissatisfactions: some of the nominated members of the Parliament were opposed by Hussein Mohamed Farah Aideed, who initially refused to be sworn in, as a mark of protest. The agreed 12% of women participation to the Parliament was not achieved and there were allegations of fraud in the selection process.

The need for the neighbouring countries to sort out the disruption of the Somali state so as to limit its negative consequences probably led to a forced acceleration of the peace process, not just in terms of time since the IGAD peace process lasted almost two years, but in terms of modalities. Despite the aforementioned frictions, a Parliament and a President were elected, but failed to move to Mogadishu due to low security levels. The temporary duty station as at the time of writing in

2004 is Jowhar.

The analysis of the efforts made to achieve political stability in Somalia showed the predominance of international support-led peace processes, and their outcome models of reconciliation over the endogenous models such as the Somaliland one. The consequent lack of ownership by Somali population of the state formation process in terms of stability-building modalities and political representation could represent a risk in the coming attempt of the Transitional Federal Government to gain legitimacy all over the territory.

Conclusion

In conclusion, the impression is that the international approach at macro political level seems to be more interested in state-oriented outcomes than people-oriented solutions[20]. The Nairobi Peace Conference emphasizes a federative outcome while what was probably needed was a federative process. This would have implied that the already existing autonomous states joined together in the formation of a national government where the powers and responsibilities would have originated from the federative states in a bottom-up approach, not from a central transitional government, in a top-down approach.

The same modalities of international aid to state creation can be outlined when addressing the issue of aid policy for development, and the case of the education sector drawn before is an example. Both approaches result in a top-down outcomes and both failed to involve the civil society in the definition of national objectives and needs. This is valid for education that contributes to shape the identity in terms of history, customs and traditions of Somali people, and it is valid for the state formation process that contributes to shape national identity. In this sense, the approach of the international aid for development, used for the education sector, reflects the macro-level policies of sustaining political processes of nation building in Somalia.

The attempt to rehabilitate the state structure in Somalia through the process of reconciliation and peace conferences supported by the international community, probably lacks the fundamental principle that generates and leads to the endogenous state formation in Somalia, i.e. the empowerment of local structures of power, beyond the guns, and their recognition of their leading role in the process of state formation. The same goes for international aid support to the education sector. It is generally recognised that strong intervention to ensure basic rights to education is needed. However, neither the principle of wide participation in the decision making process nor the issue of the pertinence, in terms of content and of continuity, of the model proposed, seems to be duly addressed. The obvious wish is that this peace conference will produce effective mechanisms to reverse the actual situation, and that a restored peace context shall facilitate international community in a more productive interaction with Somali people for their development as people and as nation.

References

Abidi S.A.H. (1987) *The Future of Education in Eastern Africa" Sasamoto Publishing Group*. Nairobi,.

Ahmed, Ali Jimale (1995) (eds.) *The Invention of Somalia*. The Red Sea Press.

EC Strategy for the Education Sector in Somalia (1998)

Fafunwa, A. Babs and Aisiku J.U. (1982) *Education in Africa. A comparative survey*. George Allen &Unwin Publishers, London.

Ford, Richard,. Hussein M. Adam and Edna Adan Ismail (2004) *War Destroys Peace Nurtures. Reconciliation and Development in Somalia*. The Red Sea Press.

Freire, Paulo. (2004) *La Pedagogia degli Oppressi*. EGA.

Hinzen, H. and V.H. Hundsdoerfer. (1979) *Education for Liberalisation and Development: the Tanzanian experience*. UNESCO Institute for Education, Hamburg.

Lewis, I.M. (2002). *A Modern History of the Somali. Nation and State in the horn of Africa*. James Currey Ltd, Fourth edition.

Lewis, I.M. (1992) Nazionalismo frammentato e collasso del regime somalo in *Politica Internazionale*,4, 1992, pp. 35-51.

Mansur, Abdalla Omar. (1995) The Cancer of the Somali State in Ahmed, Ali Jimale (eds.) *The Invention of Somalia*. The Red Sea Press.

Salia Bao, K. (1989) *Curriculum Development and African Culture*, Edward Arnold, London.

Samatar, Abdi Ismail (1992) Destruction of State and Society in Somalia: beyond the tribal convention, *Journal of Modern African Studies*, 30, 4, 1992, pp. 625-41.

Semali, Ladislaus (1999) Community as a Classroom: dilemmas of valuing African Indigenous literacy in Education, *International Review of Education*, vol. 45, n. 3-4, 1999, pp. 305-319.

Somalia Aid Coordination Body (2000, 2001, 2002, 2003) Donor Report.

UNICEF-UNDP-UNESCO (2000) Year 2000 Education for All. Assessment Report. Somalia.

----

[2]Quoted by I.M. Lewis in "Nazionalismo frammentato e collasso del regime somalo" Politica Internazionale,4, 1992, pp. 35-51.

[3]Cfr. UNICEF-UNDP-UNESCO, "Year 2000 Education for All. Assessment Report. Somalia".

[4]Cfr. EC Strategy for the Education Sector in Somalia, 1998.

[5]Donor Report, Somalia Aid Coordination Body, 2000, 2001, 2002, 2003. The breakdown donors' contribution for the education sector in Somalia by year is the follow: 2000 ($10.974.400); 2001 ($10.786.900); 2002 ($12.180.186); 2003 ($ 35.596.929).

[6]Quoted by Irvin Leonard Markovitz in Ali Jimale Ahmed, "The Invention of Somalia", 1995.

[7]Paulo Freire, "La Pedagogia degli Oppressi" EGA, 2004.

[8]K. Salia Bao, "Curriculum Developmental African Culture", Edward Arnold, London, 1989, Cfr. p. 86.

[9]A. Babs Fafunwa and J.U. Aisiku, "Education in Africa. A comparative survey" George Allen &Unwin Publishers, London, 1982.

[10]Ibid. p. 256. Cfr also M. Bray, P.B. Clarke, D. Stephens, "Education and Society in Africa, Edward Arnold Ltd, London, 1986, p. 108-110.

[11]M.L. Mbilinyi, "History of Formal Schooling in Tanzania" in H. Hinzen and V.H. Hundsdoerfer, "Education for Liberalisation and Development: the Tanzanian experience" UNESCO Institute for Education, Hamburg, 1979.Sorobea N. Bokongo, "Indigenous Education in East Africa: the Present and the Future" in Abidi S.A.H., "The Future of Education in Eastern Africa" Sasamoto Publishing Group, Nairobi, 1987. Ladislaus Semali, "Community as a Classroom: dilemmas of valuing African Indigenous literacy in Education", International Review of Education, vol. 45, n. 3-4, 1999, pp. 305-319. Jan Kaayk, "Education, Estrangement and Adjustment. A Study among the Pupils and School Leavers in Bukumbi, a Rural Community in Tanzania" The Hague, 1976. See also other authors, K.Salia Bao,1989; Ababs Fafunwa and Aisiku J.U, 1982.

[12]I.M. Lewis, "A Modern History of the Somali. Nation and State in the horn of Africa", James Currey Ltd, Fourth edition, 2002.

[13]A group composed by few hundreds of men united by a contractual alliance whose terms stipulate that, in case of heavy offence such as a murder, the group should pay compensation to the deceased's people.

[14]Abdi Ismail Samatar, "Destruction of State and Society in

Somalia: beyond the tribal convention" Journal of Modern African Studies, 30, 4, 1992, pp. 625-41.

[14]Abdalla Omar Mansur, "The Cancer of the Somali State in Ahmed, Ali Jimale (eds.) The Invention of Somalia. The Red Sea Press.

[15]Abdalla Omar Mansur, "The Nature of the Somali Clan System" in Ali Jimale Ahmed "The Invention of Somalia", The Red Sea Press, 1995, pp.107-122.

[16]I.M. Lewis, "Nazionalismo frammentato e collasso del regime somalo" in Politica Internazionale,4, 1992, pp. 35-51.

[17] ibid.

[18]Information about this section have been taken by Ahmed Yusuf Farah, "Assessing Reconciliation Initiatives by the Transitional National Government (TNG) after the Arta process" in Richard Ford, Hussein M. Adam and Edna Adan Ismail, "War Destroys Peace Nurtures. Reconciliation and Development in Somalia" The Red Sea Press, 2004.

[19]The Transitional Federal Charter of the Somali Republic" February 2004, Nairobi.

[20]See also Matt Bryden, "Choosing Democracy: Institutional Alternatives for Somalia" in Richard Ford, Hussein M. Adam and Edna Adan Ismail, "War Destroys Peace Nurtures. Reconciliation and Development in Somalia" The Red Sea Press, 2004.

Chapter 17

A Gap from Relief to Development - Returning Back 'Home'[1]

Tiina Salmio

The UNHCR is promoting voluntary repatriation and is trying to guarantee safe return for refugees to their home areas in collaboration with local actors[2]. However, in post-conflict societies, such as Somaliland, repatriation processes have faced many obstacles due to lack of infrastructure and poor living conditions in general. For example, in Somaliland a part of returnees and internally displaced people (IDPs)[3] have concentrated in areas where environmental problems are similar to those in refugee camps[4]. However, one should not forget that the whole country and its people face environmental challenges as most of Somalia is desert or semi-desert. It is year-round hot and there is irregular rainfall with chronic droughts.

Refugees are often blamed for causing environmental problems such as deforestation, loss of grazing land and ground cover, depletion of fall-back resources, degradation of agricultural lands, water consumption and pollution, solid waste and threats to protected areas (see e.g Hoerz, 1995: 32-41; UNHCR, 1991:2). Nevertheless, environmental problems often depend on such things as geographical circumstances, size and population of a camp, as well as on the location of a camp and distances between camps.

These vulnerable groups, refugees and returnees without property, do not have any other alternative than, for example, cut firewood for cooking and for constructing a shelter. Thus, problems should also be looked from their perspective; environmental problems threaten the well-being of refugees.

Black and Koser (1999: 3) question whether return is "the end of the cycle" or "the beginning of a new cycle". They (1999:11) point out that several studies indicate how "vulnerability can effectively be created after return". For example, in some cases returnees are allocated inappropriate land to settle down. Therefore, there is a need to pay attention to the situation and condition after return. (Ibid: 3, 11.) 'Governing' environmental problems in refugee operations has not been studied to great extent, even less in returnee areas.

Short-term planning, lack of resources and incapability of taking into account environmental risks in returnee operations may generate new conflicts in a society. Understanding refugee related environmental issues as one root cause of conflicts, is assumed to facilitate conflict prevention and peace building. Thus, the general aim of this chapter is to pay attention to the environment-refugee relationship and the possibility of environmental problems causing new conflicts.

This chapter therefore looks at the following issues: First, I will shed light on the complex relationship between refugees and the environment in Somalia. Secondly, I will explore what kind of environmental problems arise in Northwest Somalia's/Somaliland's returnee locations[5]. Thirdly, I will look at attempts to govern returnee related environmental problems[6] in Somaliland in order to see what kind of 'governance' has emerged to solve these problems. On the basis of the research done so far, I will finally present some ideas concerning repatriation operations and environmental challenges.

On Global Problems: Links between Refugees and the Environment in Somalia

In 2003, the UNHCR was taking care of about 17.1 million people fleeing either war or persecution. About 9.7 million of these people were considered to be refugees according to the Geneva Convention[7]. Though refugee problems and migration in general is widely shared and truly global, refugee and migration studies are still on the margins of International Relations studies. There is a need in refugee studies to look at refugee issues from a holistic point of view, in a problem-oriented way[8] as well as concentrating on refugee policies and governance of this issue.

Global problems might be classified as follows: 1) violence-related security problems; 2) economic and development problems; 3) problems of resource depletion; 4) environmental problems; 5) human rights and refugee problems; 6) global danger of viral or bacterial epidemics; and 7) other world-scale problems such as international crime. Population growth is not included because it is seen as a background cause (Hakovirta, 2000: 8.)

These different global problems are often interwoven with one another in complex ways, forming system-like sets of interdependencies, especially in developing countries. One way to shed light on the relationship between refugees and the environment is to build a model.

The one below (see Model 1) is a simplified way of looking at the complex relationship between refugees, environmental problems and conflicts in the case of Somalia and Somali refugees. The logic of the model resembles circular reasoning, but it can help to understand the relationships. However, in "real life" there are no straightforward causal relationships, but several intervening factors.

Model 1: On Relationship of Refugees and the Environment

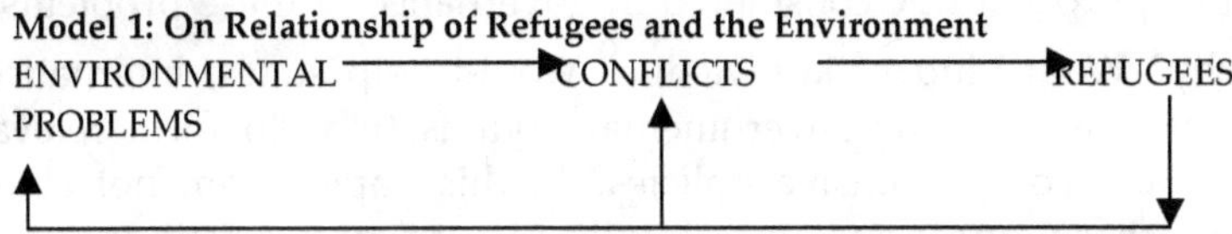

Explanations of the causes of Somali conflict have so far overemphasised the role of the clans. In fact, scarcity of natural resources has caused disputes, fighting and conflicts between different clans in Somalia. Therefore, a root cause of the conflict was probably partly an environmental one. One should not underestimate the significance of famines, droughts and forced migration movements as a cause of disputes and conflicts, not only in Somalia but in the whole Horn of Africa.

In recent studies it has been argued that the struggle for land was a central theme in the recent history of Somalia (see e.g. Besteman and Cassanelli, 2000), which is also connected to the large number of Ogaden refugees and their impact on the environment such as deforestation (see e.g. Waldron and Haschi, 1995; Young, 1985; Actionaid Evolution Report 1988; Christensen, 1982; Maren, 1987; Africa Watch, 1990). In 1982 there were 41 refugee centres in the Democratic Republic of Somalia. In North West Region there were nine camps (Agabar, Adi Addeys, Arabsio, Daray Ma'An, Dam, Darbi Hore, Las Dhure, Saba'ad and Tug Wajale. (UNHCR 1982, 7). The population/refugee pressure and environmental problems were probably factors increasing the likelihood of conflict. Some sources indicate that the military regime of Siad Barre used refugee camps as a recruiting ground for soldiers as these refugees belonged mainly to the same clan as him, General Siad Barre (See e.g. Maren, 1997; Africa Watch, 1990). In some cases refugees were forced to become soldiers and join the government forces (Field notes and interviews in Somaliland, 2002). It was probably the only way to guarantee livelihood. However, there is not much documented information on these accusations though several sources mentioned it.

On the basis of a few socio-historical studies concerning Somalia (see e.g. Hutchinson, 1991; Markakis, 1998; Prendergast, 1991; Sorenson, 1991; Thrupp and Megateli, 1999) one could ask: To what extent are conflicts caused by environmental problems in the Horn of Africa? How have the coping strategies of people in these areas changed during the last 50 years for instance? What are the ways of getting out of this vicious circle? How should interdependencies of refugees/returnees and environmental problems be taken into account in humanitarian and development aid policies in the context of Somalia? Should more holistic approaches be considered in governance of these problems? If so, why? What kind of knowledge[9] would help states, international organisations and non-governmental organisations to form relevant, holistic and comprehensive policies? In this paper, I am not able to answer these questions, but I will like to pay attention to the complicated relationship between refugees and the environment. This relationship is not always the same but depends on such factors as place and time .

Somali Refugees Escaping Fighting and Persecution[10]

The civil war in Somalia started from the north-western part of the country in 1988. Almost all the people in Somaliland had to seek refuge either inside or outside the country. Approximately 600,000 residents of that area sought refuge in Ethiopia (see e.g. UNDP, 2001: 58)[11]. Later on there were massive flows of refugees from central and southern parts of Somalia as well. Since the fall of the Siyad Barre regime in January 1991, the situation became severe. As a result of state collapse, inter-clan fighting, banditry and famine about 240,000-280,000 Somalis lost their lives between 1991-1992. There were over 800,000 Somali refugees from different parts of the country displaced mainly in Kenya, Ethiopia, Djibouti and Yemen in 1992[12]. In addition, in 1992 there were approximately 2 million IDPs (See e.g. Ibid, 2001: 58-59; UNHCR; USCR, 2001: 5).

As Somaliland in Northwest Somalia declared its independence, more than 400,000 refugees were repatriated to that area during the late 1991. However, about 90,000 Somalis fled again in 1994[13] as new strife erupted in Hargeisa and Burao (USCR, 2001: 5.) Many Somalis have returned, especially from Ethiopia, mostly to safe areas in north-western Somalia. According to UNHCR statistics (2004) about 244,000 Somali refugees have returned back from Ethiopia to Somalia since 1997. By the end of 2002 there were still 230,000 Somali refugees in other African countries (UNHCR, 2004). Majority of the Somali refugees remaining in exile are in Kenya, Ethiopia and Yemen. According to UNHCR since 1991 an estimated one million Somalis have returned home, 467,000 of them were assisted by UNHCR (Ibid, 2003).

The Ethiopian refugee camp called Hartisheik was closed in July

2004 and the remaining two camps host some 24,400 Somali refugees (Ibid, 2004.) In addition to massive refugee flows, there are a great number of IDP camps in different parts of Somalia. The UN estimates that between 372,880 and 376,630 people out of a total of seven million Somalis are internally displaced. Approximately 280,000 IDPs live in Mogadishu only, which also is the city recording the highest concentration of displaced people (Global IDP database 2004.) In these areas occur environmental problems similar to refugee camps. These undermine the well-being of IDPs and may lead to disputes between IDPs and local people over natural resources in the long-term (Salmio and Essak 2002).

According to the UNHCR (2003) the main obstacles to further repatriations in Somalia were the absence of basic social services and the lack of economic prospects. Furthermore, severe drought in the north and insecurity in the south worsened the complex situation (UNHCR, 2003: 199.) The reconstruction has started in some areas of Somalia, especially in Somaliland and Puntland, with the help of generous remittances from the Diaspora and migrant workers (see for instance Gundel, 2002).

Environmental Problems – Caused by Voluntary Repatriation?

In Somaliland, returnee locations sprung up during the 1990s and the population of these settlement areas increased especially since 1997 with mass repatriation from Ethiopia. In 2002, there were eight returnee locations in and outside Hargeisa, the capital of Somaliland and other camps near Burao, Berbera and Boroma cities[14].

Similar environmental problems as in refugee camps, such as deforestation and lack of water, occur in returnee areas. Environmental problems associated with refugee camps and returnee settlements could be listed as follows: 1) natural resource deterioration e.g. degradation of renewable natural resources such as forests, soils and water, 2) irreversible impacts on natural resources e.g. serious negative impacts on areas with high environmental value that may be related to the area's high biodiversity level, 3) impacts on health e.g. contamination of drinking water, 4) impacts on social conditions e.g. women and girls have to walk long distances to gather firewood and 5) social impacts on local populations e.g. competition for scarce resources can lead to conflicts between refugees/returnees and locals and 6) economic impact (ibid, 1996). The first two refer to problems of using natural resources and the latter two to their social and economical impacts.

Returnee movements create the same kind of environmental

problems in locations as refugees in camps. However, there is no known research published on the long-term impacts of refugees and returnees. It is important to think of the ways to avoid these problems because the returnees and the local community rely on the same resources in their immediate environment. The table next page presents some of the views of different actors on the environmental problems in Somaliland's returnee locations.

Table 1: SOME VIEWS ON ENVIRONMENTAL PROBLEMS IN RETURNEE LOCATIONS
<u>People living in returnee locations:</u> ✓ Returnees were not given firewood. The wood, gathered from the surrounding areas, was needed for shelter and fencing. Returnees use mostly firewood because they are advised not to use charcoal for environmental reasons. Deforestation is a problem, because returnees gather firewood from the surroundings (interview 41, The Chairman of Kossar camp, 2002.) ✓ Nowadays it is hard to find firewood in Sheikh Nur location. When returnees arrived, they found firewood in the nearby location (interview 46, returnee women in Sheikh Mubarak, 2002.) ✓ People have to travel long distances to fetch firewood (interview 44, a returnee woman in Mohammed Mogge location, 2002). ✓ Returnees get water for free every second day from Burao town, but it is not enough. However, there is no fighting because of the water (interview 41, the Chairman of Kossar camp, 2002). ✓ Sometimes 'problems' occur when there is not enough water (interview 50, Returnees in Kossar location, 2002). ✓ Water is a big problem and people have to fetch it from remote areas (interview 51, Returnees in Ayaha location, 2002). ✓ Water is a serious problem in Sheikh Nur, but there is no fighting over it. Women fetch water once a day (interview 45, women's general committee in Sheikh Nur, 2002).
<u>Workers of local NGOs and INGOs</u>: ✓ The worker of one organisation noted that returnees are cutting down trees in Kossar which is causing soil erosion and deforestation. They are cutting trees for firewood because charcoal for cooking is expensive (interview 49, NGO worker, 2002.) ✓ Other workers viewed that before the arrival of returnees from Ethiopia, the land of the Kossar location was arid, now it is a desert. This has impact on the environment and the life of returnees and surrounding communities (interview 38, NGO worker, 2002.). ✓ Returnees do not have anything and they have to find firewood and fencing material. (interview 38, NGO worker, 2002.) ✓ According to one organisation worker there are at least three kinds of problems in the returnee locations: 1) the most serious one is cutting trees for fencing; 2) sanitation and garbage; and 3) education. People/returnees are not aware of sanitation issues. Thus, there is a need for environmental awareness programmes (interview 47, NGO worker, 2002.) ✓ One NGO worker viewed that the environmental aspect is disastrous in Somaliland. You can see the negative impact of returnees cutting trees in locations (interview 35, INGO worker, 2002.)
<u>Somaliland authorities on different levels:</u> ✓ The Kossar village was a 'forest' before but now it is a desert (interview 52, Local authority, 2002). ✓ In Kossar returnees cut trees for fencing and building *tukuls,* which is causing deforestation (interview 39, Local authority, 2002). ✓ There is no conflict but there is competition over natural resources, sometimes returnees invade the land (interview 53, Local authority, 2002). ✓ Previously there were lots of trees in the locations, but now it is a bare area. Returnees cut all the trees (interview 54, Local authority. 2002.)

To illustrate the point, I took a closer look at a settlement called Kossar outside the city of Burao, Somaliland. The UNHCR brought returnees from Daror camp in Ethiopia to the city of Burao in January 2002. In the beginning, there was no firm plan where these people were supposed to be settled. There were even disputes over the land before the returnees were settled in Kossar[15]. According to several respondents, the immediate area surrounding the location has been deforested as a consequence of the arrival of returnees. *Tukuls* (traditional huts) were built very near to each other. The areas around *tukuls* and blocks were fenced. The environment was very harsh; it was dusty and there was little vegetation as most of the trees was cut (Field notes in Somaliland, 2002.)

International Rescue Committee (IRC) carried out a study on Hargeisa's resettlement areas. It estimates that there are approximately 57,000 people living in eight locations in Hargeisa area. On the basis of IRC's household survey, the population in these areas consists as follows: about 60 % were in Ethiopian refugee camps before arriving in the location, 8% were from Southern Somalia, 16% moved from other parts of Hargeisa, 9% had been in Ethiopia but not in the camps, 4% in other parts of Somaliland and 2% elsewhere abroad (Clark, 2002: 6.) There are no such studies carried out on other locations in the cities of Boroma, Berbera and Burao.

The IRC report, carried out in close collaboration with different international organisations as well as Somaliland authorities, is a pioneering work on returnee settlements. The report gives important information on what kind of conditions people live in these areas. It studies in detail the demographics, household backgrounds, landownership, economic status, children's education and work, adult work and employment, water and sanitation, general and maternal health, vaccination coverage and security. However, it does not cover information on such things as the kinds of cooking/household fuels used?

How do returnees get shelter materials? Do returnees face any risks when gathering firewood? One may argue that environmental problems are not a problem only in the returnee locations of Somaliland, but have also occurred, and are taking place all around the country due to issues such as overgrazing because of enclosures, livestock export ban imposed by Saudi-Arabia, charcoal production as well as the lack of a strong government and an environmental legislation and its implementation (Cf. Little, 2003). To sum up, it is necessary to study the relationship between refugees and the environment in order to understand its complexity, which is also a prerequisite for sound 'effective governance'[16].

Is There a Gap From Emergency Aid to Humanitarian Aid?

Developmental approach in refugee operations and the notion of 'from relief to development continuum' are not new as their origins could be traced back to discussions in conferences such as the ICARA II (Second International Conference on Aid to Refugees in Africa) in 1984 (Black, 1998: 174; see also Crisp, 2001).

Since the 1980s the UNHCR has paid increasing attention to the environment in its refugee operations and a more holistic view on refugee operations has been called for, due to the concern that refugee movements and camps cause environmental damage. However, until the 1990s the UNHCR did not have any comprehensive long-term policy on environment. Only after the UN Conference on Environment and Development (UNCED) in Rio de Janeiro in 1992, were the basic principles of UNHCR's environmental policy presented.

Repatriation from Ethiopia has been organised by the UNHCR in collaboration with the Administration for Refugee and Returnee Affairs (ARRA) of the Ethiopian Government and the Ministry of Resettlement, Rehabilitation and Reconstruction (MRRR) of Somaliland. The UNHCR is working together with a kind of "state-within-state", which has weak capacities and resources (Salmio, 2003)[17]. Furthermore, development agencies have faced funding constraints (UNHCR, 2003). Some authorities on Somaliland and NGO representatives pointed out that the UNHCR should have involved other organisations in the repatriation programmes in order to avoid a gap from relief to development (interviews and field notes in Somaliland, 2001 and 2002). In addition, it seems that the coordination of repatriation activities is not very efficient (Salmio, 2003). The workers of NGOs also noted that policy makers are not aware of environmental problems being a root cause. They do not see environmental sustainability as a priority and they are not aware of links between ecological, economic, social and cultural dimensions (interviews and field notes, 2001 and 2002). In fact, returnees end up in similar or even worse conditions as where they were in Ethiopian camps. It is not very clear who, and to what extent, is responsible for monitoring the returnees' situation. However, the UNHCR's mandate is limited to taking care of the returnees and funding constraints make the work extremely difficult in a post-conflict society.

Numerous workers from the NGOs, INGOs and Somaliland authorities noted that it is important to link up different organisations because the UNHCR has limited mandate to support returnees in the settlements. It is unlikely that the UNHCR would prefer to assist returnees in locations if there is a risk of creating new "refugee camps". Rather they aim at supporting returnees' integration to the local communities. The UNHCR tries to facilitate the integration of returnees through, for example, Quick Impact Projects (QIPs). These are small-scale projects that try to improve living conditions in the areas of return. One aim is to "promote the complimentary and smooth interface between short-term humanitarian assistance and longer term development programmes and thereby contribute to sustainability of projects results and effectiveness in meeting the needs of the community" (Olatokunbo, 2000).

In Somaliland the UNHCR is modifying its policies to work in a special situation in collaboration with 'governmental actors', international organisations and a number of local NGOs. Due to the politically vague status of Somaliland, the active and involving role of NGOs and civil actors has been important (Salmio, 2003). On the base of discussions, interviews and observations, one could say that the repatriation and environmental activities have been carried out, in general, in a rather 'top-down governance' manner. However, it seems that on the local level, there is will for more active participation, but the lack of resources makes the local actors dependent on the international community.

Breaking the 'Vicious Circle'

The vicious circle of dependencies between two problems, refugees and the environment has so far been presented. With different kinds of policies and governance attempts, certain tendencies could be prevented. Thus, governance attempts could be seen as interventions to break the vicious circle. The way out of this vicious circle is to create innovative policy alternatives. The most important prerequisite for effective governance is good knowledge and basic understanding of the complex nature of the problems.

It might be helpful to identify some tendencies on the governance attempts at different levels; *international, national and local*. On the *international* level, there is at least a wide awareness of the seriousness of global problems as well as the interdependencies between different global problems. The governance of these interlinked global problems, such as refugees and the environment, would demand a holistic approach to problem solving. There is a need, in the case of Somalia, for co-ordinated long-term plans and co-operation between various international actors working on both humanitarian and development aid. The lack of resources may be seen as an immediate problem, but the holistic approach, taking into account the problem of dependencies, and focusing on early action prevention in problem solving, would be cost-effective in the long term. Environmental issues should be mainstreamed in all policy sectors.

At the *international* level, the UNHCR could enforce its institutional memory on environmental management through such activities as collecting information on the experiences and good practices of the governing environmental problems in refugee operations around the world. In that way, the UNHCR's knowledge and expertise on environmental management could also be utilised more effectively in voluntary repatriation. Furthermore, it should co-operate with the environmental organisations and the environmental authorities from the beginning of the refugee and repatriation operations. For instance, environmental ministries of the host countries should be included in the discussions of returnees such as where to settle or how to facilitate the integration process. Nevertheless, some of these issues have been raised also by the UNHCR itself. Therefore, these may have to be raised and noticed by the UN system itself to give them more influence and authority (Cf. Salmio, 2004b).

At the *national* level the refugee issue is often securitised (see e.g. Salmio, 1999). The way refugees and returnees are assisted may create local conflicts related to such issues as water, firewood, ethnicity, religion and grazing lands. Therefore, in some cases, the security problem is created by certain types of policies of host states and international organisations. For example, returnees may be settled in remote areas without resources. Securitising 'the problem' of refugees and returnees may hinder moving towards 'sustainable development'. When returnees or refugees live in vulnerable conditions and are blamed of causing environmental problems, they are likely to fall into 'second class citizens' in the hosting society. As a consequence conflicts may arise between different groups in the society. Thus, there should be clear plans to integrate returnees into the receiving societies.

At the *local* level the voice of returnees and host communities should be taken into account. The options of refugees/returnees for taking part in the decision-making processes concerning issues directly affecting their lives are still limited. Refugees or returnees should not only be seen as passive vulnerable targets of the measures taken. The limited role of refugees in decision-making may be understandable in the beginning of refugee operations as it is hard to form decision-making bodies in chaotic situations. In the long term however, participation of returnees in planning and decision-making may guarantee sustainability (Salmio, 2004a; 2004b; Ford and Abokor 2004).

The receiving local host communities and organisations should also take part in the planning of voluntary repatriation operations. This may be cost-effective in the long-term as the locals may have valuable information and knowledge on the environment. Furthermore, environmental awareness campaigns should be promoted through the leaders of refugee and local communities. This way, the new environmental methods and tools can easily be promoted. It requires, however, a good relationship and trust between these two communities and the UNHCR (Salmio, 2004b). International actors should also closely co-operate with local actors, identify problems together and form rational strategies to avoid further conflicts, which would be beneficial for the international community as well.

In so far as the situation is expected to be stabilised as a consequence of the IGAD mediated peace process in Central and Southern Somalia, large numbers of Somali refugees in Kenya and other countries are likely to return back to their home country within the next years. To prevent the creation of new, problem-prone settlement areas, the UNHCR, NGOs or other INGOs should carry out surveys of socio-economic status and situation of the refugees. Would they like to return? To which areas: countryside or a city? How would they like to make a living? Do they have animals? These are just some examples of important questions that should be studied. Nevertheless, if returnee settlements are likely to occur, good models and experience on local environmental governance systems such as Environmental Working Group in Dadaab refugee camps, Kenya as well as environmental programmes promoting sustainable development could be copied from refugee camps (See more Salmio, 2003, 2004a and 2004b).

References

Actionaid Evaluation Report December (1988) Malka Hidda Refugee Programme. Members of the Evaluation team: A. Bariir, Mohamed, A. Bah, Mamadou, R Bunbury, Andrew and Warsame, Shuaib. Received from Refugee Studies Documentation Centre, University of Oxford.

Africa Watch (1990) *Somalia: a Government at War with Its Own People*: Testimonies About the Killings and the Conflict in the North. Africa Watch report. Africa Watch Committee, New York.

Besteman, Catherine and Cassanelli Lee V. (ed.) (2000) *The Struggle for Land in Southern Somalia.* The War behind the War. Haan, London.

Black, Richard and Koser, Khalid (eds.) (1999) *The End of the Refugee Cycle?: Refugee Repatriation and Reconstruction.* Berghahn, New York.

Christensen, Hanne (1982) *Survival Strategies for and by Camp Refugees*. Report on a Six-Week Exploratory Sociological Field Study into the Food Situation of Refugees in Camps in Somalia. UNRISD, Geneva.

Clark, Damon (2002) *Interagency Returnee Settlement Area Assessment.* Information Report. IRC, Somaliland.

Crisp, Jeff (2001) *Mind the Gap! UNHCR, Humanitarian Assistance and the Development Process.* New Issues in Refugee Research. Working Paper No. 43. [www.unhcr.ch]

Ford, Richard and Abokor, Adan (2004) Participatory Tools for Peace Building, in Ford, Richard, Adam, Hussein M. and Ismail, Edna Adan (eds.), *War Destroys: Peace Nurtures.* Somali Reconciliation and Development, pp. 341-366. The Red Sea Press, Inc., Lawrenceville and Asmara.

Global IDP Database (2004). Somalia. *An estimated 375,000 persons remain displaced in Somalia* (April 2004). [URL: www.idpproject.org] Taken 5.8.2004.

Gundel, Joakim (2002) 'The Migration-Development Nexus: Somalia Case Study', in *International Migration,* Vol. 40 (5), pp. 255-281.

Hakovirta, Harto (2000) 'Editor's Introduction: At the Crossroads', in: Hakovirta, Harto (ed) *Globalism at the Crossroads.* Wedges into Global Theory and Policy, pp. 5-14. The Finnish Political Science Association. Kopijyvä, Jyväskylä.

Hakovirta, Harto, Kaisa Herne, Minna Jokela, Kaisa Lähteenmäki-Smith and Tiina Salmio (2002) 'Global Problems and Their Governance: The Contribution by the Figare/Safir Project', in: Käyhkö, Jukka and Talve, Linda (eds.) *Understanding the Global System:* The Finnish Perspective, pp. 167-175. FIGARE. Painosalama, Turku.

Hoerz, Thomas (1995) *Refugees and Host Environments.* A Review of Current and Related Literature. For Deutsche Gesellschaft für Technische Zusammenarbeit (GTZ). Unpublished paper. Refugee Studies Programme, University of Oxford.

Hutchison, Robert A. (ed.) (1991) *Fighting For Survival: Insecurity, People and the Environment in the Horn of Africa.* IUCN, Gland.

IRC (2001) *Refugee Returnee & IDP Situation and Needs 2001. A Study by IRC Somaliland.* Draft Report. April 2001. Given by Peter Muthgiani, IRC, Hargeisa. 14.7.2001.

Korn, David A. (1999) *Exodus Within Borders.* An Introduction to the Crisis of Internal Displacement. Brooking Institution Press, Washington, D.C.

Little, Peter D. (2003) *Somalia: Economy Without State.* African Issues. The International African Institute. James Currey, Oxford.

Maren, Michael (1997) *The Road to Hell.* The Ravaging Effects of Foreign Aid and International Charity. The Free Press, New York.

Markakis, John (1998) *Resource Conflict in the Horn of Africa.* Sage

Publications, London.

Prendergast, John (1997) *Crisis Response.* Humanitarian Band-Aids in Sudan and Somalia. Pluto Press, London.

Salmio, (Tiina 1999) *Suomen maahanmuutto- ja pakolaispolitiikka 1990-luvulla - maahanmuutto ja pakolaisuus turvallisuusuhkana valtion politiikassa.* (Finnish Immigration and Refugee Policy in the 1990s - Immigration and Refugeeism as a Security Threat in the State Policy) University of Turku, Department of Political Science. Studies of Political Science 54. Digipaino, Turku (Master's Thesis), 78 pp.

Salmio, Tiina (2003) *Governing Environmental Problems Related to the Refugee and Repatriation Operations.* Nordic Africa Days 3-5 October, 2003. The Nordic Africa Institute, Uppsala.

Salmio, Tiina (2004a) Two Interdependent Global Problems: Refugees and Environment – The Case of Dadaab Refugee Camps in Kenya, in Ford, Richard, Adam, Hussein M. and Ismail, Edna Adan (eds.), *War Destroys: Peace Nurtures.* Somali Reconciliation and Development, pp.239-250. The Red Sea Press, Inc., Lawrenceville and Asmara.

Salmio, Tiina (2004b) An Attempt to Govern Environmental Problems in Refugee Operations - the Environmental Working Group as an Example of Local-international Co-operation in Kenya. In: Jokela, Minna and Herne, Kaisa (eds.) *Fairness Environment and Multilateralism.* Valtio-opin laitos, Turun Yliopisto, Turku. (forthcoming)

Salmio, Tiina and Essak, Batulo (2002) *Maternal and Child Health Care in Somalia - Fact Finding Mission Report.* Fact Finding Mission by Finland-Somalia Association to Mogadishu and Afgoi in July, 2002. Unpublished.

Schmidt, Anna (2003) *Campus Versus Settlements.* FMO thematic guide. [URL:http: //www.forcedmigration.org/guides/fmo021/fmo021.pdf] Taken 28.7.2004.

Sorenson, John (ed.) (1995) *Disaster and Development in the Horn of Africa.* Macmillan Press Ltd, Great Britain.

Thrupp, L.A. with Megateli, N (1999) *Critical Links: Food Security and the Environment in the Greater Horn of Africa.* WPI Project Report. WPI (World Resources Institute) and ILRI (International Livestock Research), Nairobi.

UNDP (2001*) Human Development Report Somalia 2001*. UNDP, Somalia Country Office, Nairobi, Kenya.

UNHCR (1982*) Refugee Situation in Somalia.* UNHCR Branch Office Somalia. Mogadishu. March 1982. (Received from Oxford Refugee Studies Centre)

UNHCR (1991) *Refugees and the Environment.* Discussion paper for internal use. October 22,1991. Prepared by Stephan Gurman. Acquired from Oxford Refugee Studies Centre Library 2000.

UNHCR (1996) *Environmental Guidelines*. UNHCR, Geneva.

UNHCR (2003) Global Report 2003. Achievements and Impact. UNHCR, Geneva.

UNHCR (2004) *Voluntary Repatriation in Africa: Levels and Trends 1993-2002.* Population Data Unit/PGDS. Division of Operational Support. UNHCR Geneva. March 2004. [www.unhcr.ch/statistics]

USCR (2001) *Somaliland. Wellcome home to Nothing:* Refugees Repatriate to a Forgotten Somaliland. U.S. Committee for refugees.

Waldron, Sidney and Hasci, Naima A. (1995) *Somali Refugees in the Horn of Africa.* State of the Art Literature Review. Refugee Studies Programme. Queen Elisabeth House, University of Oxford. The Nordic Africa Institute, Uppsala, Sweden.

Young, Lincoln (1985) A General Assessment of the Environmental Impact of Refugees in Somalia with Attention to the Refugee Agricultural Programme. *Disasters* 9 (2), 122-133.

Young, Oran R. (1994) *International Governance, Protecting the Environment in a Stateless Society.* Cornell University Press, Ithaca and London.

Interviews conducted by the author

Interview 35 (2002) with the worker of Danish Refugee Council, INGO. Hargeisa, Somaliland. 4.4.2002.

Interview 38 (2002) with the worker of Candlelight, NGO. Hargeisa, Somaliland. 30.3.2002.

Interview 39 (2002) with the Governer of Burao. Burao, Somaliland. 26.3.2002.

Interview 41 (2002) with the chairman of the Kossar returnee location. Burao, Somaliland. 25.3.2002.

Interview 44 (2002) with returnee woman. Mohammed Mogge settlement. Hargeisa, Somaliland. 30.3.2002.

Interview 45 (2002) with the women's general committee. Sheikh Nur settlement, Hargeisa, Somaliland. 2.4.2002.

Interview 46 (2002) with returnee women. Sheikh Mubarak settlement. Hargeisa, Somaliland. 24.3.2002.

Interview 47 (2002) with the worker of Candlelight, NGO. Hargeisa, Somaliland. 30.3.2003.

Interview 49 (2002) with a member the Representative of Agricultural Development Organisation (ADO). Burao, Somaliland.

Interview 50 (2002) with returnees. Kossar location. Burao, Somaliland. 25.3. 2002.

Interview 51 (2002) with returnees. Ayaha settlement. Hargeisa,

Somaliland. 26.3.2002.

Interview 52 (2002) with the Regional Labour Officer. Burao, Somaliland. 25.3.2002.

Interview 53 (2002) with the Major of Burao. Burao, Somaliland. 26.3.2002.

Interview 54 (2002) with the worker from the Minister of Pastoral Development and Environment, Hargeisa, Somaliland. 30.3.2002.

Other Material

Field notes in Dadaab refugee camps, Kenya. January-February 2002.

Field notes in Somaliland. June 2001.

Field notes in Somaliland. March 2002.

---

[1]This chapter is a preliminary part of my PhD study: "The International Refugee Regime Governing Environmental Problems" The study is a case study of Dadaab refugee camps in Kenya and returnee locations in Somaliland. I thank warmly all those people who helped me to carry out my research in Somaliland 2001-2002 and in Dadaab, Kenya 2000-2002 as well as the Nordic Africa Institute and Oscar Öflund Stiftelse for their economical support.

[2] Here local refers to both civil and official actors at the local level.

[3]IDPs are "persons or groups of persons who have been forced or obliged to flee or to leave their homes or places of habitual residence, in particular, as a result of, or in order to avoid the effects of armed conflict, situations of generalized violence, violations of human rights or natural or human-made disasters, and who have not crossed an internationally recognized state border" (Korn, 1999: 127).

[4]At this point it is important to note that one could compare environmental impact of refugees in different situations. The UNHCR distinguishes three types of locations where its population of concern is assisted; 1) camps, 2) urban settings and 3) dispersed/various. See also Schmidt, 2003.

[5]Somalia refers to the territory recognised by the international community. The Republic of Somaliland in Northwest Somalia declared its independence in 1991 but it remains unrecognised by the international community.

[6]In a broad sense, governance means the establishment of social institutions for solving conflicts and facilitating co-operation through

collective action on a larger scale (Young, 1994: 15, 26). Furthermore, governance refers to not only participation of state actors but also sub- and trans-national actors. By this I refer to the policies and actions taken by states, international organisations, local organisations and authorities.

[7]The UNHCR defines refugees as those who are outside their countries and who are unable or unwilling to return because of a well-founded fear of being persecuted for reasons of their race, religion, nationality, political opinion or membership in a particular social group. There is all together about 45-50 million people who have been forced to leave their homeland.

[8]My PhD study falls into so called problem-based globalism approach in International Relations, global problems being at the core of the study. (See e.g. Hakovirta et al. 2002.) Problem-oriented way does not necessary refer to refugees being a problem rather refugee movements being a problem caused by conflicts and human rights violations.

[9]By 'knowledge', I do not refer only to scientific knowledge produced by epistemic communities, transnational groups of scientists and public officials (Young, 1994: 40). but also to the 'knowledge' produced by different actors on local level.

[10]In June, 2001 and March-April, 2002, I interviewed local authorities and ministers, discussed with returnees and local community elders as well as several NGO and UN workers in Somaliland. I also made observations and photographed. I visited returnee locations in Hargeisa and Burao as well as the old refugee camp areas from 1980s.

[11]Furthermore, the refugees from Ogaden war returned back to Ethiopia. Therefore, it was hard to distinguish refugees from returnees and local population in eight Ethiopian camps located in Ethiopian Somali region.

[12]However, Somali refugees also sought refuge in USA, Canada, Great Britain, Netherlands and many other countries.

[13]Hartisheik was once world's largest refugee camp hosting more than 250,000 refugees (UNHCR, 2004).

[14]There are not such returnee areas in Boroma like in Hargeisa and Burao where the returnees are more scattered. (Field notes and discussions in Somaliland 2002).

[15]The other name for the location is Kandahaar, named after the camp in Afghanistan by the locals.

[16]See more on different dimensions of effectiveness e.g. Young

(1994); see also Salmio (2004b) on effectiveness of refugee regime solving environmental problems in Kenya.

[17]The majority of the Somaliland's government's budget goes on security. According to the UNDP's Human Development Report (2001, 55) some 55 % of the Somaliland administration's expenditure was allocated to the military and security services (UNDP, 2001: 55).

Chapter 18

Post-Script: Studying the state formation processes in Somalia

Abdulkadir Osman Farah and Joakim Gundel

> "Our main request for the so-called Somali political and warlord elites is that they stop the constant internal meaningless disagreement among themselves, and at the same time refrain from manipulating us Somali people, and particularly youth, to fight their useless wars" (*Statement by a youth group in Somalia, July 2005, in response to the question of their expectations to the current Somali leadership.*)

In ancient times the Eastern part of the Horn of Africa, which today is inhabited by Somalis, was known as the land of 'Punt.' The people who inhabited this area were at all times connected to other great civilisations. For instance, the great Egyptian Queen and ruler, Ma'at-ka-Ra Hatshepsut (1473-1458 BC)[1], sent senior envoys to the land of Punt. The ancient Egyptians, Greeks and Romans all came to the Northern coastline of the land of Punt to obtain the much cherished Frankincense, which only grew in the mountains there. From the east, merchant ships came from ancient China and India to trade with the people along the Somali coastline. From the 9th century onwards, Arabic people established commercial city states from Mogadishu and all the way past Zanzibar on the Eastern African Coastline, which from the 12th century eventually became known as the city state empire of Zinj. More importantly, also during the 9th century, Arabs expanding into Northern Somalia introduced the camel and met and intermarried with the '*Maxay*' speaking people who expanded northwards from central Somalia (Ehret 1995). It was in this cauldron that the present people known as the 'Somalis' have their myth of origin evidenced in their lineage-based clan system, which makes reference to a descent from cousins of the prophet Mohammed (Lewis 1961: 12). This contact was also believed to have led to the introduction of Islam into Somalia.

The point of this historical background is that the inhabitants of present-day Somalia were engaged in commercial and diplomatic exchanges and undertakings long before the Europeans started to establish a foothold there some two hundred years ago. This indicates a deep historical thrust which should be taken into consideration when the current processes of state formation in this part of the Horn of Africa are considered. Hence, the Somalis have interacted dynamically with other distant cultures for centuries, and migration, trade and Diaspora settlements formed a natural force in their struggle to escape the modern human tragedies in terms of extreme poverty, warlordism and underdevelopment, which Somalia unfortunately has become renown for.[2] It is to this nexus between Diaspora, migration, trade, identity, religion, intervention and modern political concepts influencing the transboundary Somali state formation processes that the chapters of this book focus on.

It is common to find the view that the division of the Somalis by the colonization process followed by decades of cold war militarism and domination not only humiliated and subordinated the Somalis but transformed their character and identity. Some observers refer to the absence of an internal unified Somali political leadership that could operate beyond the ethnic convention in rising to the task of imagining and eventually constructing a progressive nation-state as a main problem. However, the colonial reasoning appears rather vague as in fact the country never experienced a strong colonization in practice. For instance, the powerful British Empire did not succeed in totally bringing the Somalis under its rule as they met fierce resistance from a coalition of religious and pastoral Somalis.[3] Instead, they were subjected to a loose domination based on indirect rule arrangements with the traditional Somali clan leaders. Whatever historical explanations for the recent socio-political debacle, the question of imagining a viable Somali state is getting ever more interesting and complex, and raises both empirical questions about the desired form of state as well as theoretical ones questioning the very concept of the state.

The various contributions in this book address these big questions, from various angles. Indeed, that the state-formation processes in the Somali-inhabited regions of the Horn of Africa are taking a trans-boundary character is evidenced by the contributions in this book and include the following factors:

- The aspirations and entrepreneurships of the globally and regionally dispersed Somali Diaspora (Gundel 2003, and Cassanelli and Kleist & Hansen in this volume);
- The changing identities of the Somali Diaspora, resulting from their struggles for survival and belonging abroad, on values, identity and ideas in their places of origin (Part One of this volume);
- The internationalisation of the Somali conflicts leading to a displacement of the natural power structures beyond the boundaries

of the Somali state, following external involvement from regional and international powers and the donor community, the influence of international peace mediations led by the Inter-Governmental Authority on Development (IGAD) and UN representatives, the external ideological impact of human rights organisations (Farah, Saggiomo, Salmio and Hill in this volume);

- The ideological impact of Islamic movements in Somalia in the context of global Islamic radicalisation and the US- led war on terrorism (Abdullahi in this volume);
- The impact of civic efforts and civil society on the development of Somalia, which itself is strongly influenced by the international civil society and International NGOs (Yahya and Jabril and Abdulkadir in this volume);
- The idea of nation-hood and fragmented identities within the Somali society (Ibrahim, Hihne, Bereketeab and Kleist & Hansen).

Furthermore, the processes of state-formation in the Somali-inhabited part of the Horn of Africa are trans-boundary in another sense, as the Somalis continue to apply their traditional customary laws, Islamic Sharia and their own ways of building trust and reconciliation in an effort to create social structures with relative peace and coexistence. For instance, Somaliland and Puntland were successful in their systematic application of a social and political contract based on traditional consensus and bottom-up approach. The traditional conflict resolution mechanisms are applied by Somalis across the physical boundaries that originally were carved by the colonial powers, between present-day Kenya, Ethiopia, Somalia, Somaliland and Djibouti. The application of customary practices by the traditional and religious leaders is also crossing the conceptual boundary between the state and civil society, and raises some very interesting theoretical questions about the relevance of the modern capitalist-based political structure, also known as the modern state, for the Somali society (Brons 2001). The recent take over (June 2006) of Mogadishu and most parts of Southern and Central Somalia by the Union of Somali Courts (UIC) is further evidence of the significance of the theme of this book, and especially the contribution by Abdurahman Abdullahi (in this volume) which focuses on the Islamic factor in recovering the Somali state.

Hence, the chapters in this book contribute to the debates about the complex socio-political processes in contemporary Somalia in terms of the importance of the Somali Diaspora on the political, social, religious, cultural and economic development of Somalis 'away' as well as at 'home', and in terms of state formation in a regional context, which is not necessarily confined to the existing structure of so-called 'nation-states', but which also opens for investigation of the processes that may result in the formation of political structures or states, even if transgressing both the physical (regional, trans-boundary or non-territorial) and conceptual boundaries of our contemporary understanding of the state (Callaghy 2001).

This concluding chapter will attempt to frame the significant points of the contributions to the central theme of *Diaspora and state formation processes in the Horn of Africa,* and bring them up to date with observations of the recent developments inside Somalia since the 9th Somali Studies International Congress was held in Aalborg, Denmark, in 2004, made by the authors of this chapter during their travels throughout Somalia.[4] First, the contributions and observations on the prospects for reconfiguring the Somali state will be set in perspective by some reflections on the key theoretical concepts about the state, civil society and Diaspora.

Reflecting on the state and civil society concepts

Recent studies on the political sources of intra-state conflict, in places with more or less state collapse such as Somalia, suggest that the core problem is a question of unresolved statehood (Holsti 2000). These studies are often state-centered, and find that the weak position of African states in the international system are related to their failure in establishing strong links between the communities within their territorial jurisdiction, and between the communities and the political center of power, the state (Clapham 1996).

While being relevant for the view where state failure in Africa is seen as a failure of the expected modern post-colonial state formation, such approaches may not be sufficient explanations because state failure also can be viewed as the result of very intense processes of state formation linked to other traits such as pre-colonial history, ethnicity, culture and globalisation (Kaldor and Luckham 2001). Furthermore, the internal integrity of the state should not be taken for granted, which analyses of failed states and the breakdown of neo-patrimonial relations between the central state and client networks in Africa demonstrate (Allen 1999).

Departing from the ideal-type definitions of the state by Max Weber, we will in the following introduce a different approach to state-formation, to which the chapters in this book, in various ways contribute to an understanding of. In short, this approach regards states as entities that are caught up in a constant and precarious process of formation resulting from shifting images and practices, and where the emergence of socio-political structures should be understood holistically as a process in which the forms of political power develops and changes (Migdal 2001: 15-23).

Defining the state

The state is most often portrayed as an abstract umbrella that includes the entire range of offices and institutions, which enforce collective decisions for society. According to this understanding, the state benefits from, and threatens the society, and its presumed neutral state institutions have the monopoly on coercion. Apart from monopolising power, the state enjoys internal sovereignty, referring to its authority to formulate and enforce laws and create and control institutional structures, and external sovereignty, referring to its right to international conduct, diplomacy and exercising judiciary over its territory. This general description originates from the works of Max Weber who described the modern state as a compulsory association which organizes domination. Hence, he defined the state as a human community that successfully claims the monopoly of the legitimate use of physical force within a given territory (Weber 1958: 78). Most definitions of the state take a point of departure from this notion of Max Weber, but they emphasize different aspects: some emphasize the institutional character of the state, which sees it as an organization or set of organizations. Others emphasize its functions in terms of making of rules. Finally, some emphasize its recourse to coercion, which is the monopoly of the legitimate use of physical force.

Combining these elements, a widely used definition considers the state to be a set of organizations invested with the authority to make juridically binding decisions for people and organizations located within the particular given territory and to implement these decisions, if necessary, by force (Reuschemeyer & Evans 1985: 46-7). A weaker, but wider version sees the state as a power organization that engages in centralized, institutionalized and territorialized regulation of many aspects of social relations. Power is here understood as the capacity of the state to penetrate civil society by implementing political decisions throughout the realm (Migdal 2001: 111). Regardless of emphasis, at the core of all the definitions lies the question of domination or authority over the state's claimed territory and people, and the degree to which the state can expect voluntary compliance with their rulers (legitimacy) or need to resort to coercion (Migdal 2001: 110).

The strength, but also weakness, of Max Weber's definition is that he defines the state in terms of an ideal type state. While contributing to a clear image of the state, this is also unfortunate because on the one hand, it limits the possible imaginary forms of the modern state, and on the other hand, also limits the ways we can discuss real life states. According to Migdal, the implication is that as long as the idea of the state remains uniform and constant, the variation of states can only be expressed in terms of deviation from the standard (Migdal 2001: 15-17). For instance, the assumption that only the state can create rules and maintain the violent means to make people obey them effectively limits the ways we can discuss the state, because the notion of the ideal state becomes perceived as the normal state and thereby obscures as much as it illuminates by continually measuring actual states against an ideal version of what states are, or should be.

Another important weakness in Max Weber's formulation of the state is related to the boundaries of the state, because the state is portrayed as a reified entity that can be identified separately from society. However, to talk of the relations between state and society as if both always had firm boundaries misses some of the most important dynamics of state formation processes. Furthermore, the emphasis on monopoly on coercion masks situations where authorities fragment and the power of the state becomes contended, just as the notion of legitimacy diverts attention from contending forms of authority.

The state-in-society approach

To overcome these limitations, Migdal suggests a state-in-society approach to the study of the state. He approaches the state as a field of power in society, but not separated from it, marked by the use and threat of violence and shaped by the image of a coherent, controlling organisation in a territory (or space), which is a representation of the people bounded by that territory, and the actual practices of its multiple parts (Migdal 2001: 16).

Accordingly, the *image of the modern state*, which during the 20th century essentially is equivalent to the Western state, melts all the institutions of authority into one single center of authority in society. In this image the state is an autonomous dominant integrated entity that controls, in a given territory (geographic), all rulemaking, either directly through its own agencies/institutions, or indirectly by sanctioning other authorized organizations such as businesses, families, clubs, non-governmental organizations (NGOs) trade unions etc. to make and perform certain rules. Hence, the image refers to the very idea of the state, and as such implies perception both by those inside a claimed territory of the state and by those outside it. Thus, the image posits an entity with two sorts of boundaries (Migdal 2001: 17):

- Territorial boundaries between the state and other states;
- Social boundaries between the state (its public actors and agencies) and those who are subject to its rules (private actors and agencies).

However, in this chapter we argue that these two boundaries are blurred and needs to be debated when the state formation processes in Somalia are considered.

Firstly, some groups such as nomadic tribes, *territorial boundaries* may be seen as a hindrance and, hence they may seek a polity that has relevance to them and their understanding of territory and belonging. Thus, territory is often used to set the criteria of belonging of a 'people' to a given state. This raises the question of the identity of people inside a given territory as belonging to the given state, and not always the other way around, making the question of people and identity in relation to the territory of a state a highly relevant issue in the Somali context, because some would define the 'nation' of Somalis beyond the territorial borders of the Somali Republic. The question is, should the identity of a 'Somali people' determine the territory of a 'Somali state' or should the presently given territory of the Somali Republic define the 'nation of the Somali people? Thus, the image of a 'nation' becomes relevant in terms of the 'belonging' of a people to a sudden territory of a state. However, if there is no correspondence between the two, or if there is a huge Diaspora outside the given state, but which nevertheless are seen to belong to that 'nation' of that 'state', the clarity in defining the state – at least as a 'nation-state' becomes problematic. Hence, we may, for instance, have to question whether state-authority is always related to a given territory, and whether the territorial state necessarily is the only type of politico-legal organisation that we can conceive of. Indeed, we may even find 'boundary-less' societies with non-territorial polities, which nevertheless functions as states, and there may be 'stateless' societies (Brons 2001).

Secondly, especially in the African (and Somali) context, the other kind of boundary - the social boundary - separating the state from all other non-state or private actors and social forces, needs to be contested as well. Again, according to Weber's ideal types, the separation of public and private is a hallmark of the modern bureaucratic states, which implies a conceptual separation of the state as carrier of sovereign prerogatives such as the right to legislation, and from personal authorization of and by individuals. However, we cannot take this notion for granted if we wish to understand both processes and outcomes, because in places like Somalia the fluidity of boundaries, the privatisation of the state and the particular fabric of society do not necessarily correspond to the dominant perception and image of the state (Hibou 2002). Furthermore, as a nearly 100% Islamic society, the Somalis may consider Islam as a potential unifying factor in their fragmented, clan-based society, hence religion may very well be an important driving factor for establishing a unifying 'idea' of a future

Somali state, which may not be secular – that is separating religion from the state.

Practice refers to the performance of state actors and agencies in reinforcing the image of the state or weakening it. For instance, they may bolster the notion of territorial and public-private boundaries, or neutralize them. Furthermore, practices may serve to recognize, reinforce and validate the territorial elements of state control as well as the social separation between the state and other social formations (public-private). There is a close relationship between the image and the practices of the state as they can mutually reinforce each other. But, practice can also prove to be at discrepancy with the image of the state hence revealing any weaknesses in the state construction. For instance, patron-client linkages interpenetrating state and society may in effect weaken the imagined 'emancipation' of the state, and hence the state itself (Chabal & Daloz 1998).

An important implication of the state-in-society approach is that the hitherto given distinctions between territorial states (the external-internal distinction) and between the state and society (public-private) needs to be dissolved as a point of departure (but not necessarily in synthesis), in order to enable 'a step back' from the object (here processes of state-formation in general, and the Somali state in particular) and approach the issue as a question of studying the 'state in society', rather than as one of studying the state as an independent reified entity that exist separately from society.[5]

The territorial boundary of the state, or the internal – external aspect

Within political science, there is traditionally a disciplinary boundary between the field of international relations (between territorially distinguished states) and comparative politics that focuses on the internal or domestic political relations within states. However, with the prevailing economic globalisation and degree of external interventions, the external and internal levels seem to be increasingly intertwined making the notion of a causal relationship between external and internal forces difficult to draw. This is not made easier by real life external interventions and meddling in internal affairs of states, because when external forces enter the internal relations of state formation processes, external forces becomes part of the processes of new emerging structures of power[6].

Nevertheless, an important and powerful aspect in state formation processes is related to the way sovereignty of states is produced and reproduced. In theory, there are two sources of sovereignty. An internal one related to the degree of power and legitimacy in the relationship between the state and the citizens, also known as *de-facto* sovereignty. The external one is sovereignty allocated to a given state though recognition by other sovereign states, and is called *de-jure* sovereignty. Accordingly, one characteristic of a weak state is that its sovereignty is upheld *de-jure* via recognition by other states in the international system, while its internal *de-facto* sovereignty is disputed to such an extent that they cannot provide for their own citizens' security (Holsti 2000). Thus, a weak state is characterized by a major deficit in internal legitimacy, but is prevented from collapsing by the force of external recognition. Somalia is a case in point, where the image of the Republic of Somalia is consistently kept alive by the international community, while the opposite is the case with Somaliland, where you find *de-facto* sovereignty, but no *de-jure* recognition.

The social boundary of the state, and the society – state relation

The state-centred approaches can be misleading our efforts at understanding processes of state-formation, because of their tendency to reify and anthropomorphize the state, which obscures the dynamics and patterns of the struggle for domination in societies (Migdal 2001: 98). While the separation of the state from society provides us with an elegant analytical clarity, it seems that the resulting 'modern' conception of the state predestines our understanding, thus the abstract analytical distinction between state and society is often confused with the Weberian concept of the legal-rational, and ideal-bureaucratic state that is 'emancipated' from society. For instance, some studies assert that one of the main features of African post-colonial states seems to be that the state here has not become emancipated from society.[7] Instead power is managed along personalised, neo-patrimonial lines and in a context of fragmentation of local authorities.

Hence, in order to bring the analyses of 'the state back into society' it may be useful to regard the state as just another organisation in society, which however plays a crucial role in both domination and transformation (Migdal 2001: 128). Whether the state then is the instrument for domination by the ruling classes as argued by Marx, a neutral arena for the unfolding of political struggles as suggested by Poulantzas or a dominating superstructure to society is less important, because in different historical and social contexts all can be true. For our present framework, what is more important is that the state can be seen as a socio-political and organisational outcome of continuous processes and struggles of domination between different social forces in society. Hence, separating the state from society can make sense for analytical purposes – in terms of framing a study object separated from the rest of society. However, that must not divert us from seeing the real state in society, nor must the ideal-type definition of the state become the only benchmark for measuring or understanding the state, and its differentiation from society.

Another prevalent confusion is the tendency to treat society and civil society as synonymous (Migdal 2001: 132). Within society we often identify many 'societies' and social categories such as classes, castes, ethnic groups, clans, religious groups etc., as well as many kinds of more or less related social organisations such as trade unions, sports associations etc. All of these may not be part of civil society, especially not in its most narrow definition where it is composed of interest groups and private voluntary organisations only. Hence, one of the most prominent references to civil society describes it

> "...as encompassing only one portion of what has become a complex and diverse associational scene. What distinguishes those groups incorporated in civil society from other associations is their partial nature: they are separate from but address the state"
> (Chazan 1994: 278).

Indeed, as Migdal emphasises, society includes other organisations, striving at making their own rules and moral codes, than the ones who directly addresses the state (Migdal 2001: 132). Religious groups stand out in this respect.

Nevertheless, the civil society is often defined against the state, and has been framed as a collective entity existing independently from the state. This illuminates the boundary problem between the state and the civil society in particular, because if one entity is defined against the other, it also means that they disappear with each other. Hence, what happens to civil society when the state collapses, as it did in Somalia? And what is the implication of this for the prevalent strategies of International NGOs and for instance the EC in supporting civil society in the Somali context: What is the civil society when there is no state? Are those who actually are being supported as agents engaged in a struggle of domination and transformation, representatives of the state or civil society? How do we distinguish? And where do we place phenomena such as the traditional authorities, religious leaders and business groups who all may be involved in setting up various kinds of polities, including Islamic Sharia Courts? What are they, state or civil society?

It can be argued that patron-client networks in Africa,which extend to the very centre of the state, and penetrate the institutions of civil-society are fundamental to state-society linkages in circumstances of social crisis. An important notion in this context is that when states fail to deliver essential social goods, efforts are made by people to withdraw from the state by relying on other structures in society such as kinship-relations, clan structures within ethnic-groupings and personalised patron-client relations. This is important when the failure and collapses of African states are to considered, because these structures in African societies also form the basis for the alternative structures which non-state actors such as militant factions and revived traditional institutions are based on, which has been profound in post-civil war Somali the last 15 years.

Conflict and state formation processes

Political conflict may be defined as a struggle about the primary function of the political system: who may define and enforce collectively binding decisions about the allocation of values that effectively apply to all members included in the given society, and how these decisions are made, carried into effect and are controlled. Values of interest should not be understood only in terms of material resources (food, water and shelter are primary), but just as much in terms of ideational values such as religious ideas, spiritual needs and normative, ethical and even aesthetic ideas about how inter-human social relations should be formed - not to forget how the human – nature relationship should be (religion often informs us about such values).

Furthermore, modern intra-state conflicts may be understood in terms of combined power and survival strategies that are inextricably linked to the expanding informal sectors in an increasingly globalised economy. Such strategies may lead to politically assertive formations, where violence and coercion may be an integral part of the socio-political processes, and where there is not necessarily any need to establish territorial, bureaucratic or consent-based political authority in any traditional sense, or any need for nation-state competence (Duffield 2001: 161). Accordingly, such strategies may base political mobilization on identity, which can involve deliberate population displacement, starvation and other forms of destabilization of those whose identity is 'different,' while at the same time they may be closely entangled with the dynamics of the political economy of intra state war (Jung 2003). For instance, politico-military factions may plunder the assets of people, the remnants of the state as well as external assistance destined for the victims (Gundel 2003). Thus, anarchy and disorder in 'new wars' provides a 'legitimate' cover for various forms of private aggrandizement, which at the same time are necessary sources of revenue to sustain their warfare (Chabal and Daloz 1998: 77-91). The result is a circular dynamic in which the warring parties may need more or less permanent conflict (chaos) in order to simultaneously reproduce their positions of power and maintain control over resources. While violent conflicts may be fought along communal or ethnic lines in a seemingly primordial manner, the involved identities may rather be the result of processes of social construction than given things (Mamdani 2002).

A state-in-society approach to state-formation in the Horn of Africa

Structuration of power relations involves a process of institutionalisation of politico-legal relations, which may result in 'emerging political complexes' that eventually may form the basis of a state. Hence, the process of state formation may be approached as a question of institutionalisation of political power structures. Christian Lund may in this context provide us with some useful hints as to what we should look for with the processes of state-formation in Somalia (Lund 1996, 2001). Phrased as questions:

- Do the emerging political complexes seem to develop a functional capacity to define and enforce collectively binding decisions?
- Can the observed decision-making processes within emerging political complexes be described in terms of fiat (dictation) or by negotiation (dialogue, voting and/or consensus)?
- Are the observed attempts at establishing forms of institutional regularisation congruent and coherent (centralised, formalised) or incongruent (fragmented, informal)?[8]
- Do the emerging structures enjoy legitimacy in terms of support due to belief in them (trust) or due to expected benefits (provision of security in exchange for accepting domination)?

How violence is distributed and regulated is crucial, as the power to engage in organised violence is one of the most basic forms of any socio-political structure. All other social relations cannot exist unless they are compatible with the relations of violence. All social relations are of course not reducible to the structures of violence, but they depend on how violence is regulated, thus the nature of violence technology, who controls it and its social life, affects all other social relations (Wendt 1999: 8). In the long run the relations of power cannot be based on coercion alone. Hence, the struggle for power within a confined society must show consideration for existing interests and prevailing norms and values. The question of whether an emerging political complex can be described as a 'state' depends on the extent to which authority can be said to be *res public'*, meaning that it is applied to and for all the members of, or the entire population within, the given entity.

Reconstructing the Somali polity

The civil war in Somalia led to a collapse of the institutions of security, law and order, such as judiciary, police etc. This contributed significantly to a situation where, especially in South-Central Somalia, lawlessness could prevail with impunity, and where the lost monopoly on the use of coercion by the state could be picked up by whatever group was able to maintain some sort of limited security institutions. The task of rebuilding the state was tremendous, not at least because an important stumbling factor for building a centralised state in the Somali social fabric is essentially the very notion of government and presidency being centralised, in a society that is socially organised along vertical clan lines, with clearly no long historical tradition of political centralisation. Although Somalis are considered one of the most homogeneous people in the world with a single language and ethnicity, their clan factions and fault lines complicate any endeavour to stabilise the country and introduce and sustain the rule of law. How to solve this feature has been central to many analyses of the Somali polity during the last decade.

Various ideas and suggestions have been presented to find alternatives to the wilderness Somalia is currently undergoing. These ideas vary from the notion of a stateless society, to the creation of hybrid forms of state combining the Somali clan-based political structures and modern democratic governmental institutions. Another idea sees a potential in building a state upon Islamic principles, because it is believed that Islam can unite the disunited Somalis. Two lines of thought, and practice, seem to have emerged. One idea builds upon the incorporation of the elder-institution into the formal political system, where their main role is to ensure political stability and be the ultimate conflict resolution mechanism. The other emphasises the ideationally unifying potentials of Islam, especially Islamic values and law. However, the main limitation to the application of Islamic values and law is that most Somalis in fact rather cherish their traditional Somali practices in their daily life. In addition, practising and implementing Islamic moral code requires that people have a certain knowledge and understanding of the holy scripts.

Rather than building modern political institutions other scholars on Somalia have stressed the primacy of the economy and the significance of regional trade-networks and global markets, hence advocating the potentials of the Somali stateless society. Somalis have in the last decade managed to engage in economic activities that created an environment where private enterprises flourished (Little 2003); they have cooperated and prospered within a stateless setting. However, this is not without negative side effects because this does produce an uncontrolled capitalist structure where the fittest survives and the vulnerable groups are left behind. Nevertheless, evidence shows that a significant number of economic activities increased during 'stateless' Somalia as compared to the previous centralised regime, leading to a discussion of whether the establishment of a viable state that can protect people's properties and investments for the common good is possible or not.

Other major obstacles include the local political culture. Political allegiances are not based on ideology but on group identity, based on the Somali clan structure. Ideas are not valued or debated on their own terms, but only in terms of who is proposing them. Formulas for power-sharing take precedence over formulas for problem-solving (the "legitimacy" of any government depends on the inclusion in it of every sub and sub sub-clan, rather than on its adherence to law and democratic procedures, its efficacy in solving problems, or its fairness in distributing the benefits of its solutions). Somalis tend to identify politics with individuals, not institutions.

Furthermore, the international situation after 9/11 and specifically the "war on terrorism," have also diverted energy and resources away from development and local peace-making initiatives. Additionally, there is the international involvement and interference, which complicates the process of creating peace and a stable state in Somalia. In the reconciliation and peace process, there are layers of external actors who took an interest in the conflict or in its management acting out of security, geopolitical, cultural, economic and humanitarian concerns. The relationship between the conflicting parties and their sponsors abroad, colonial relations, weapons, aid resources, the issue of terrorism are, among other things, identified as some of the factors that internationalised, exacerbated and prolonged the conflict.

While state collapse had serious humanitarian consequences, and the lack of a viable state formation in all of Somalia still has its tolls, the variety, richness as well as failures in the ongoing state formation processes are very interesting. The different post-civil war trajectories of change in Northern versus Southern Somalia resulted in very different security environments, which again varied and changed according to the local conditions and can be described as localized ranging from the relative high level of security and stability in the Northern administrations of Somaliland and Puntland[9] to the mosaic of polities based on varying mixtures of traditional authorities, clan militias, local warlords and Sharia courts. Since June 2006, the security environment in Mogadishu and parts of South-Central Somalia has lately improved radically as a Union of Islamic Courts (UIC) managed to drive out the previously dominant warlords from Mogadishu, while the Transitional

Federal Government (TFG) only maintains a fragile control over Baidoa in Bay region.

Even in South-Central Somalia local efforts to manage and reduce insecurity emerged, first as deals with local militias to provide protection in return for food and other assets, and later increasingly through a revival of the customary practices such as clan-based deterrence strategies (threat of revenge attacks)[10]. These attempts were scattered, but did show that the Somalis tried to build security arrangements on their own. In the North, as well as most places where a minimal level of security has come to function in the South, these arrangements involve combinations of traditional authorities, business interests, religious leaders, and civil leaders applying traditional conflict resolution mechanisms. It should be noted that security in the Somali context is not necessarily contingent upon the reestablishment of 'modern' formal state structures[11].

Somali communities have a long experience in adapting customary sources of law, security, and conflict management to changing political settings created by a weak or predatory state, while the 'modern' state never succeeded in entirely replacing the traditional authorities and their customary laws (Gundel 2006). The evolution of various local security arrangements set up by Somalis themselves, which in some places combine informal systems of security with formal state authority structures are at the heart of the current state formation processes in Somalia.

Hybrid state-formations in Northern Somalia

In Northern Somalia, the collapse of the central Government did not precipitate the kind of warfare and plunder that devastated the South. Somaliland (SL) in Northwest declared independence from the South already in May 1991 (unrecognized internationally), strongly motivated by the desire to improve their security. Inter-clan clashes did occur, including two serious wars in 1994 and 1996. But, the dependency of the *Isaaq*-clan based rebel group, the Somali National Movement (SNM), on their traditional clan elders, greater political cohesion amongst the clans, and support from businesspeople to establish peace, the civil war prevented SL from evolving into anarchy.

Since declaring its sovereignty in 1991 SL has gradually developed a modest capacity to govern, and. succeeded in maintaining what appears to be a durable internal peace. SL maintains all the symbolic attributes of a state, including an executive president, a bicameral parliament, municipal councils and a constitution, which was approved by more than 90% of the population at a referendum in 2001 (Chapter

14). SL's achievements in building a safe and secure environment largely free of crime and a political system which is at present one of the most democratic and constitutional in Africa is very much the result of the country's innovative integration of traditional and modern sources of law and authority. Hence, the political structure in SL is based on a unique homegrown hybrid between a western type democracy and the traditional Somali 'pastoral democracy' incorporating non-state social institutions such as the traditional clan elders into political institutions such as the Upper House of elders (Guurti) (Lewis 1961, Drysdale 2000). This system ensures that all clans feel represented, because the seats in the Guurti are proportionally allocated by clan. This increased the legitimacy of the state by incorporating the most respected source of authority in the society: the conflict management role of the traditional elders. Though the allocation of power, patronage, and resources within the SL state is the subject of endless grievances, the SL state has not been the source of violent clan or factional competition for control since 1996, a major achievement given the stakes involved. The significant force behind SL's high level of security remains the robust application of customary law and blood compensation, administered by clan elders[12]. Today, SL enjoys a relatively high level of political stability, despite terrorist attacks in 2003/2004, and the country managed to carry through its democratization process in 2005, and held parliamentary elections in September 2005, which international observers regarded as fair (Hansen 2006, Abokor 2006). In effect, politics in SL are more representative than has been the case for decades, and local security arrangements rooted in the non-state social sphere, provides better security than was previously provided by the Somali state (Bradbury 2003).

In North-eastern Somalia, the regional administration called Puntland State of Somalia (PSS), was established in 1998. PSS is ethnically unique as it is comprised almost entirely of members of the Harti clans (Majerteen, Dhulbahante and Warsangeli) with Majerteen dominance, and its self-declared borders are drawn on the basis of their territorial claims.

The impetus to create a regional state was the result of civic efforts to improve security and rule of law, despite the area already enjoying a relatively high degree of security and stability. PSS has since its establishment developed a range of security forces, including an army, police forces, and a rapid response force, as well as a court and prison system to deal with crime. Traditional clan elders were instrumental in founding the PSS and together with their customary laws, they stand for local security and rule of law, and they play a crucial role as gatekeepers between the state and society. Puntland authorities rarely pursue and arrest a suspect directly. Clan elders are contacted and they negotiate terms of surrender. The clan elders also represent their constituencies in the selection of leadership in Puntland. When Puntland President Abdullahi Yusuf's term expired in 2001, it was an assembly of clan elders who selected Jama Ali Jama as his successor because Abdullahi Yusuf did not follow the Constitution of the PSS. Abullahi Yusuf challenged this decision by force, leading to the armed stand-off from 2001 to 2002. There has since been a tenuous peace between the PSS administration and opposition groups.

There is a territorial conflict between SL and PSS, because SL bases their territorial sovereignty on the colonial borders of British Somaliland, which includes large chunks of Dhulbahante and Warsangeli territory, which are claimed by PSS. Hence we here have a dispute where one state uses territory to define the identity of its people (citizens), and the other uses its identity as a people to define its territory.

Competing state-formation processes in South-Central Somalia

After the failure of the UN- led intervention (UNOSOM II), and the withdrawal of the international community from Somalia in 1995, South-Central Somalia did not return to outright civil-war, but to a stateless state-of-affairs, of 'no war and no peace', with some military conquests, and re-conquests by armed clan-factions, continued armed confrontations, fierce political rivalry and intense competition for the scarce resources. The ensuing political confusion in South-Central Somali was characterized by widespread insecurity, recurring famine and a mosaic of polities mixing warlord-rule, self-imposed governors, district-and regional authorities and a widespread return to traditional clan-based governance. However, it was not all anarchy as the Somalis continuously struggled at creating local order by forming local governance systems, often based on combinations of the traditional customary (*xeer*) and Islamic Sharia laws, humanitarian agencies (Islamic as well as Western) as social welfare providers, and all largely financed by new business people from the revitalized local economies, which previously suffered as the 'informal economy' (Little 2003: 154).

Many of these local governance systems can best be described as security arrangements based on protection rackets and warlord fiefdoms. They could provide some degree of security to households and communities, and in at least a few instances appeared to be capable of making the transition from predatory expropriation of resources to taxation of resources in return for services to the local community. What is significant about the warlord fiefdoms is not their poor disguise of their occupation of someone else's land by appointing governors etc., but that they in fact both find a need and advantage in providing a minimal level of security and other services in exchange for popular support (legitimacy based on benefit). However, this may not be sustainable in the long-term due to their status as dictating occupiers who base their rule on fear rather than positive legitimacy based on belief and trust.

A variety of local administrations based on 'formal' sources of governance replicating structures and functions of conventional state-based administrative units did develop over the past fifteen years. Some of them developed modest administrations providing public security, and other governance functions as well as basic services. Luuq (Gedo region) and Beledweyne (Hiiran region) are among a number of towns where formal municipalities have played active and constructive roles in local governance and in security. But their most important contribution to local security is indirect: by serving as a fixed venue for political and clan representatives' conflict solving efforts, and as such approximate state at the local level as these local administrations most often established systems for allocation (usually by clan elders) of whatever resources that enter the community, including resources from international aid agencies such as car and land rental contracts, procurement, and employment.

Mogadishu was until recently controlled by more than a dozen factional leaders (warlords) who had divided the city. But their control was limited to the 'benefit' kind of legitimacy only, and often only provided some protection and benefits to their sub-sub clan. Hence, they became increasingly marginalized from 1999 and onwards, not the least due to the emergence of a new class of businessmen who, dissatisfied with the poor security conditions, created their own clan militias, and refused to pay protection moneys. Instead, they bought up gunmen from the warlords, formed their own security forces or passed them on to the new local Sharia courts. The result was the spread of Islamic Sharia Courts, who were able to enforce law and order. Originally, the Sharia courts in Mogadishu were established in the mid-1990s by traditional clan elders, businessmen, and religious leaders who all sought to improve basic law and order in their towns and neighbourhoods. Hence, the Sharia courts were instruments of law and order, under the control of clan elders and the businessmen who were their paymasters, and administered by local sheikhs who more often than not were committed to the traditional moderate Sufi Islam practiced in Somalia. Initially, they practiced the traditional custom of letting relatives of a victim choose between a customary solution, involving *diya* payment (blood compensation), or Sharia punishment. While the Sharia courts were 'illiberal' in the sense that they occasionally violated international human rights norms, they were not formed with the objective of establishing a radical Islamic State in Somalia. When they did try to impose the severe Islamic punishments (*xudud*), such as amputations, they were often strongly opposed by the public and the clan-elders because they were in contradiction with traditional customary laws the *xeer* (ICG 2005a). In fact, more than often, when radical Islamists tried to use the courts as political platforms, they would be constrained by their founding businessmen and traditional elders.

The initial weakness of the Sharia courts was their lack of law-enforcement capacity to effectively face the well-armed freelance gangs. This was exploited by former members of the now defunct radical Islamic movement Al-Ittihad[13]. Hence, former Al-Ittihad militants were able to gain influence by providing the courts with the needed military expertise to enforce the implementation of Sharia - thanks to their provision of trained and disciplined militias. This 'trade-off' gave the radical Islamic wahabbist elements an opportunity to build an influential political platform within the Courts. Considering the Somali Islamist groups, a report from the International Crisis Group (ICG) states that

> '...the behaviour of Somali Islamist groups is characterized by competition and disaccord hardly less severe than that which plagues the political factions. They are neither uniformly anti-Western, nor hostile to Somalia's neighbours, and only a tiny minority has been associated with terrorist violence' (ICG 2005a).

Nevertheless, because the Courts rally wide popular support due to their ability to provide the highest level of public security since the civil war broke out, they also provide a platform that can be exploited by the radical Islamist groups. In that case a new fault line in the Somali state formation process may break out between the moderate Islamic forces such as Al Islah and the fundamentalist Wahabist Islamists (Chapter 13).

In 2004, the most significant attempt at reviving the collapsed Somali state emerged as a result of the latest and longest running peace and reconciliation conference on Somalia undertaken by the Inter-Governmental Authority on Development (IGAD).[14] It resulted in a transitional charter and the formation of a Transitional Federal Parliament (TFP) in August 2004. The expectation was that an effective Transitional Federal Government (TFG) would improve the security situation dramatically.[15] However, this has yet to materialize as a rift on the location of the Government, and international peacekeepers first kept the TFG away from Somalia, then to be located in the small town of Jowhar, and since January 2006 in the town of Baidoa in Bay Region.

In February 2006, a war in Mogadishu broke out between a new alliance of anti-Islamic Court Warlords on one side and the Islamic Courts on the other. This Alliance for Peace and Fight against Terrorism (APFT) claimed to fight for peace and anti-terrorism, prompting a reaction from the Islamic Courts which in response formed the Union of Islamic Courts (UIC). While never confirmed by the US Government, the APFT apparently received funding from the US, which contributed to Mogadishu residents rallying behind it. Hence, the fighting took the outlook of a proxy-war between the US- led war against global terrorism, and elements in support of Al-Qaeda.

However, the actual conflict is more complicated and comprises a violent dispute between former warlord allies over control of the main infrastructural assets in Mogadishu[16] (such as ports and airports), and between the Warlords (now armed Ministers of the TFG) and the Sharia Courts (Islamic but also clan-based) for the control of Mogadishu. The UIC commanded popular support because the Islamic Courts did provide security, law and order as well as welfare through their Islamic charity work. With the recent success of the UIC in Mogadishu in defeating the APFT (June 2006), the question of radical Islamism and terrorism linked to the Sharia Courts has re-surfaced significantly, and has indeed changed both the political and security fault lines especially in South-Central Somalia, where the UIC maintains control of not only Mogadishu, but most of the *Hawiye* dominated territory from Galkacyo to Kismayo[17]. This has produced a window of opportunity because the UIC potentially can create the secure space for both the TFG and international aid operations in Mogadishu and South Central Somalia. However, the often overriding dynamics of clan-politics and the alleged connections of leaders of UIC to international terrorism, as well as the agendas of the TFG President, regional powers such as Ethiopia, and finally US anti-terror policies, may run counter to this opening. If the TFG and the UIC, in this new situation, are unable to keep a dialogue aimed at preparing the ground for the TFG to be established in Mogadishu, a new national armed conflict may very well erupt between the 'secular' TFG, and the 'Islamic' UIC.

Societal forces and state formation in Somalia

The following is an attempt to identify and frame some of the most important societal forces at play in the Somali context. The societal forces cannot necessarily be described as being civil society, as mentioned earlier. If civil society is defined against the existence of a state, the most important societal forces defy the definition as they, in the context of state collapse, can best be described as social groups or categories which are engaged in either a) filling the gap left by the collapsed state; b) being the very social forces representing the new emerging, even if fragmented, state structures; c) and finally being agents for a full reconstruction of the state, either being towards a modern and secular one, or non-secular, Islamic or in other ways which does not conform with the Western Weberian notion of a modern 'ideal bureaucratic' state.

The traditional structures and Islam

The first group combines the traditional pastoralists and the Islamic components of Somali society, because these, together, represent the historical and cultural continuity and identity of the Somali people. Hence, both the traditional and the religious leaders enjoy relatively large popular legitimacy as they are endogenously rooted and capable of organising Somalis through clan and religious lines. They attract support from the majority of the Somalis, except the educated elites (including many former officials from the Siad Barre regime), and Westernised elites (including Westernised Somalis among the Diasporas) and parts of the urbanised-secularised communities.

The clan is the primary social base for the individual Somali, and therefore also the most important base for protection and insurance. The clan is therefore, historically, also the most important political constituency, political dividing factor, and hence fault-line in conflicts in Somali society. At the same time, the traditional elders' performance of conflict resolution mechanisms has since the state collapsed proved to be most effective in reconciling clans and solving conflicts, perhaps because their application of the Somali *xeer* and practices are well adapted and integrated with the logics of the segmentary social clan system. Hence, the Somalis maintain centuries old traditional pre-Islamic customary practices of governance, which exercises authority and mediates inter-personal and intercommunity conflicts. The traditional governance and mechanisms for conflict management are based on clan elders, who negotiate and manage their customary laws (*xeer*), which serve as oral and memorized codes governing relations between clans, and blood payment (*diya*) groups who are collectively responsible for crimes committed by their members. The risk of paying *diya* (traditionally 100 camels) in case of killings, functions in principle as a deterrence mechanism that prevents killings. The *Xeer* are oral codes of conduct and rules that regulate inter- as well as intra-clan behaviour. They are usually developed as specific bilateral clan laws between neighbouring clans who have a historical relationship with each other. However, under the impact of the civil war and as clans have been uprooted and cast around by conquest and persecution by stronger clans, new *xeers* between clans such as multilateral arrangements had to be entered to prevent new cycles of revenge killings and to establish peace between clans (Gundel 2006). The *xeers* are crucial for peace because a) they can constrain powerful clans from completely overriding weaker clans, b) the strong clans have an interest in maintaining the basic rules of the game because they have long-term interests in predictable security and in not being perceived as unreliable and untrustworthy by the other clans.

The role of the clan elders is first of all to intervene in conflicts, create ceasefire, represent their clan lineage in negotiations with other clans, as well as to resolve internal disputes within the clans. They also serve as third party mediators when called upon by other clans who are in conflict with each other. Since the state collapsed, they have also importantly served as interlocutors between the clan and external actors, especially international aid agencies. The role of elders in establishing local security arrangements are vital, and they play a crucial role in the establishment of operational security in Somalia because they are key actors for any security strategy in Somalia, evidenced by the fact that whenever an international agency experiences a security problem, it is the clan elders who most often ultimately resolves the issue. Some elders, especially in South Central, however, lost legitimacy over the post civil-war years because they became infamous for being 'warmongers', also called *bac madoobe* (black plastic bag) allegedly fighting for the rights of their sub-clan, rather than *nabadoon* 'peace-makers' as their customs say they should be. Women were normally excluded from direct participation in this type of decision making process, though women are said to exercise influence through their husbands, brothers or sons. However, democratic the Somali 'pastoral democracy' may be, and efficiency of the traditional conflict resolution mechanisms, one of the main challenges to the traditional system, as shown by Jabril and Yahya in Chapter 10, will be the role of women in the emerging state formation in Somalia.

With the introduction of Islam in Somalia, the traditional approach was modified and supplemented with aspects of providing justice and well-being for minority groups and an obligatory charity for all who are in need. Although Somalis are overwhelmingly attributed Muslims, their proper knowledge of the religion and its content is a recent development. As the modern written word is a recent breakthrough in a predominantly oral culture, the Somalis still hang on with cultural and traditional performances and lifestyles that predate Islam. For instance the clan system which is the prime source of identity for most Somalis predates Islam. No doubt that there is and will be a convergence between groups that see Islam as a unifying factor in the present state formation process and the Pan-Somalist nationalist ideology of the initial nationalist independence movement, the Somali Youth League (SYL).

Thus, Islamic groups represent a significant social and political strength. With mosques and religious gatherings as their staging ground, religious communities are interconnected with pastoral constituencies and their vast properties consisting of livestock and land in rural areas. This is the oldest surviving political alliance structure in Somalia. Nomads and their clans provide the economic and manpower strength and religious preachers provide the ideology and the working framework. Tensions nonetheless occur when ordinary people, in challenging conflict situations, have to choose allegiance between clan and ideology (religion). Another clashing point emerges in connection with the diverse interpretation of competing schools of Islamic thought that occasionally suggest and promote highly controversial subjective ideas (Chapter 13).

It is still too early to say whether the UIC uniformly seeks this, but parts of the group definitely does: the vision of large parts of the Islamic pastoralists is to one day witness an effective Somali Islamic state that can rule the country in accordance with Islamic principles. In this context there can be found many references to the past resistance against the Christian colonizers, especially in Puntland and the areas where Sheikh Mohammed Abdille Hassan (which the British called the 'Mad Mullah') led his religious movement and Dervish forces against the British (and to some extent the Italians), which have many religious Islamic connotations. In addition, they believe that Islamic teachings and ordinary traditional Somali life do not necessarily contradict but complement each other (Chapter 17). In practical terms, the group undertakes numerous social, charity and political activities. They often oppose any debate or proposal of introducing western democratic styles of governance into Somalia. They appear self-confident in their beliefs and predestination. For similar reasons, they categorically reject the requesting and depending on external aid from the West. They believe the country is rich enough to feed itself, if resources are managed and distributed properly.

The business communities

Another powerful group is the Somali business community, especially the merchant sector. They are primarily based in urban areas, many have strong links, often via their Diaspora, to the global economy, and their members are the prime financiers of all major economic and political conducts in the country. In periods they appear to be in alliance with traditional Islamic groups. In times of political manoeuvring and speculation, they prefer to finance warlords and mafia-style adventures. They have access to both Western and Asian financial markets. Some of them educate their children in Asian and Western universities and in times of sickness and medical checkups they immediately fly to exclusive private hospitals in the West, or Dubai.

There are two main groupings: The first are the trans-national merchants. They have commercial and trade ties with most of the world and their money is saved in big commercial cities like Dubai. They fly frequently and make major trade deals occasionally with sovereign countries. The second are the national traders. As local entrepreneurs, they take over diverse goods imported by trans-national merchants and resell to ordinary Somalis. They are local merchants who make deals and transfers within the country. Local merchants are less involved in high politics and due to economic restrictions they have limited chances of influencing other powerful groupings.

An example of the vibrant local, Diaspora and global business links in Somalia today is the newly constructed Las Qoray Tuna factory in Puntland. The factory is a modern facility, built by a returnee, with financial support from his clan-Diaspora in the USA and UAE. The factory produces tuna fish for both the national and international markets, and employs about 400 people. No doubt, this is of great significance for the local and regional economy. At the same time the factory is a standing proof of the productive cooperation between Diaspora groups and merchants that invest in development back home.

Somali business men such as Mr. Tuna Factory, often engage in local politics. They do this to further their own business, as well as political ambitions. The problem is that they often use corruption as their way to accumulate power. In addition they import more than they export, thereby damaging the country's economic balance. Furthermore, while the investments they bring in contribute positively to the economy, they also contribute to the importation of foreign goods such as pasta, Japanese cars and building materials that affect the Somali balance of payments negatively. Due to the lack of a banking system, they deposit the money extracted from the country in foreign bank accounts in the Arabian Gulf and in the West.

The Warlord Politicians

An influential category when it comes to the formal state formation processes are the predatory political actors (Somalis call them 'politicians') and the primarily military warlords (who most often also, or primarily, are politicians too). Their main aim is to enrich themselves, even if at the expense of other organised groups and the Somali people at large.

Many of the Somali warlords are responsible for the destruction of the Somali state and economy. They nevertheless consider themselves to be legitimate leaders that fight for justice and prosperity. However, none of them have consistently been engaged in ensuring the rights of people, or in pursuing justice, real reconciliation and peace. Initially, they were the leaders of the political clan factions known by abbreviations such as USC, SNA, SNF etc. In principle they learned to build their fortunes, especially in Mogadishu, on protection scams, which is a way to extract extra profits from trade and 'security provision' in a context of continuous insecurity and instability. In other words, the warlords had a shared interest in maintaining insecurity and instability because they based their limited power and legitimacy on the provision of security to their sub-clans (benefit type of legitimacy), and their income on road-blocks and the extra profits that can be generated in the context of insecurity. They also often control the *khat* trade.

One of the reasons behind the 13 to 14 failed attempts at international peace mediation in Somalia, is that the warlords consistently managed to place themselves as the key actors (primarily through show of 'de-fact' military control on the ground) to be given a place in peace conferences (often held abroad in Addis Ababa, Cairo or Nairobi), and that the international community consistently accepted or insisted on their presence. These peace conferences often fail because the involved warlords often had no interest in their success, unless they, as winners, could reap the entire benefit from an agreement. Even more tragic is that these warlords, more or less, enjoy indirect international support.

In parallel with the intimidation, threat and victimization of ordinary civilians by armed warlords, there are warlord politicians that are not armed. They are found among all regions in Somalia (among the leadership in Puntland, Somaliland and the newly formed trans-national government). They are Somali politicians that are the remnants of the state collapse. Some of them have been in politics since the country obtained its independence in 1960, others have been in the opposition for generations, and some are self-appointed politicians who saw political and economic opportunity in the current uncertain situation. These different groups often share no long-term visions or consistent political approach, but the sole aim seems to be an attempt to personally gain from the insufficient external aid to Somalia. An insider in the current Transitional Federal Government, who participated in several so-called ministerial meetings, said that the sole agenda of the government meetings concentrated on how much money the government received from Arabian and Western donors and how much the president of the transitional government and his prime minister acquired while touring abroad, and if distributed how much should each minister get in cash.

NGOs and Civil Society Groups?

The remaining, but less powerful groups could be categorised as Somali professional NGOs that increased considerably in numbers after the state collapse (Abdillahi 1998: 73-84). The NGO group is a rather recent development in Somalia. After the collapse of the Somali state, many humanitarian NGOs, inspired by the West, emerged and filled the gap of providing relief assistance for needy and vulnerable Somalis. Many Somali NGOs are financed through UN agencies and international NGOs. Normally NGOs are organised within the dominant international system of state framework, however, except for Somaliland and Puntland, Somali NGOs do not have this state reference and therefore need to acquire recognition and respect from the local communities within which they work. Local communities may on the one hand see the NGOs as 'theirs' if they belong to the local clan – which they often do. Sometimes they may, however, consider the NGOs to be Western inventions, maybe extension of foreign government programs aimed at changing the Somali culture. As the sources of their economic and moral backings primarily are in the west, they confront declining legitimacy among their people. This might probably explain why various NGOs that focus on human rights and gender issues are failing in the country, while those that work with employment, environmental and practical livelihood issues sometimes succeed. Indeed, at the local level, most of the local NGOs are not really separate from the state (at the local level of operation), but in fact, as social welfare provision organisations functioning in extension and interest of the local dominant clans, are 'state institutions'. To some extent the same may be the case with locally operating International NGOs which has the support, and work in partnership with local authorities, which often are based on the traditional elders. However, here we may see a 'displacement of the power structures' as governance, and government, is not characterized by being in the structure of Centralised vs. Local Government in a national state, but in a trans-boundary structure being Donor Government vs. UN agency/International NGO vs. Local Authorities. In this latter case, the process of state formation is suddenly very complex, and the loci of power can be displaced to an extent where it may be difficult for a local natural power structure to emerge. Within the group of NGOs, there are two major societal forces that are worth mentioning. The first is women's groups or associations. They may not always be organised professionally (with institutional managerial set-ups), but often function as activist and interest groups, advocating for women's rights and interests, for peace, for health, in support of children and poor vulnerable groups, and some have no qualms using means such as public demonstrations or awareness campaigns. They may also unite to help each other in setting up businesses. The importance of women in keeping the post civil-war social fabric together in Somalia cannot be underestimated, and they may very well play a vital role in the ongoing and future state formation processes (Chapter 10). However, what is more difficult to see is a united political women's movement with a clear idea about women's place in a future state, and also in terms of how a future state should look like, which is independent of the agendas set by the international agencies (UN and INGOs). Urban based youth groups are another very interesting societal factor, which will increase rapidly in importance over the coming years.

External forces and state formation in Somalia

Another complicating factor in the persistence of violence in Somalia is the ongoing involvement of external actors in support of local Somali clients. Regional states have intermittently engaged in proxy wars in Somalia and have the potential to both create and worsen tensions and violence inside Somalia in pursuit of their own goals. These states have also shown the capacity to support peace-building efforts. It is alleged that some regional powers, including Ethiopia and Yemen and a 'third country' believed to be the US via its new base in Djibouti set up in connection with its global war against terrorism, had fuelled the situation by supplying arms and ammunition to the warring factions in the country, thereby violating the longstanding UN arms embargo imposed in 1994. The recent development, where the US supported the APFT group of warlords in Mogadishu to intercept individuals on the US list of wanted international terrorists prompted a strong unification of the courts in the Union of Islamic Courts (UIC), and popular support to the UIC, has effectively played into the hands of the hard-line islamists. What most Somalis probably desire is that the international community should refrain from interfering in Somali's internal affairs. One of the most productive, purely internal, Somali endeavours and negotiations resulted in the creation of the autonomous and relatively peaceful regions, Puntland and Somaliland. Khalif Farah (in this volume) shows how the so-called peace processes organised, and financed by external regional and international powers tend to reinvent the top-down centralised Somali state that failed so woefully on each occasions.

The Somali Diaspora and state-formation

The legendary Somali poet and educator, Mohamed Ibrahim Hadrawi, visiting Denmark in November 2003 in connection with his International Peace Journey, told a gathering of Danish public officials that Somalis were learning to act as refugees in the Diaspora. They could be described as nomads but to be a refugee in a large scale is relatively new experience for them. Never in the history of this nation, he added, had so many ordinary Somali people moved and settled in far away places where their cultures were estranged and subordinated.

With regard to the role of the Somali Diaspora, rather than focusing on their patterns and processes of adopting or assimilating into their host societies, the debate increasingly stresses trans-nationalism and trans-border communities where immigrants and refugees are considered global factors. For instance, Kusow (this volume) searches for a new methodology which on the one hand can grasp the diversity and fragmentation of the Diaspora, shed light on the social and spatial boundaries between Somalia as a geographical entity and the multiple centres that Somali Diaspora populations are constituted, including their evolving identities, and on the other hand the impact of this on the state formation process in the Somalilands.

The possible impact of the experiences of the Somali Diaspora with Western social and political structures and governance systems on the ideas and systems that Somalis may want to bring back to Somalia, and which potentially can have a profound effect on the development of state-institutions, but even more so on the very idea of the state, needs to be given more attention in future studies of the Diaspora. Similarly, the meeting of Somali women with Western family structures and women's rights there will most likely have a more significant effect on the evolution of similar structures in Somalia, than what International NGOs seek to achieve through their aid work in Somalia. A contrary effect leading to dissolution of the traditional Somali family networks, may be the result of the identity crises, which especially the young Somalis in the Diaspora experience, and which may confuse their sense of belonging and eventually also their links to Somalia. One of the consequences of this will be that the Diaspora links and influence on the state-formation process will diminish.

An interesting and direct impact on the state-formation processes in Somalia, by the Diaspora, is evidenced by Nauja Kleist and Peter Hansen (this volume), who show how a new nationalist Somaliland identity has emerged, and how the practices of this 'Somaliland Diaspora' influence the nationalist sentiment and identity in Somaliland itself.

Somalis dispersed in most parts of the world remit money to their families and relatives on monthly or quarterly bases. This financial input is, through Hawaala (the traditional Somali transfer system), immediately felt in the many towns and villages in Somalia. The remittances are crucial for the survival of numerous Somalis in the face of lacking public social welfare services. Families with relatives residing in more prosperous parts of the world receive on average 100- 200 USD per month. Most of this money is spent on consumption by families and relatives. The greater share of it might go to the chewing of Khat. Some of the families who receive remittances from abroad try their utmost to manage their income properly by, for instance, investing in the education of their children. The majority of Somalis spend remittance income on daily consumption and do not speculate on the future. These remittances of money has vital effects on development and state formation processes in Somalia, and may, apart from feeding relatives in need, be used for marriage ceremonies, to pay for *diya* compensation, for education, to buy land, construct housing, to fund political campaigns, and during civil conflict also for waging war.

If the Somalis in the Diaspora organize themselves in development associations or the like, they could increase the impact of the remittances into the development of their country considerably. For instance, remittances can be used for development and sustainable reconstruction projects that benefit not only the individual community but also the country as a whole. They can also support peace and reconciliation efforts such as the Swedish Diaspora community when they collected and transferred funds aimed at assisting national reconciliation in removing roadblocks in the Capital Mogadishu in 2005. Other communities in the UK and the US started financing hospitals and successful higher education institutions such as Amoud University in Somaliland. One of the major challenges facing Diaspora assistance and involvement in Somalia, apart from the fragmentation and local orientation, is the lack of viable state institutions that can accommodate their efforts.

References

Abdillahi, M.S. (1998). The emergence of local NGOs in the recovery and development process of Somaliland (Northwest Somalia), in *Conflict, Peacekeeping and Reconstruction,* Voices from Africa, Issue No.8, United Nations Non-Governmental Liaison Service

Abokor et.al. (2006). Further Steps to Democracy, The Somaliland Parliamentary Elections, September 2005, Adan Abokor et.al., Progression Report, January

Allen, C. (1999). Warfare, Endemic Violence & State Collapse in Africa. *Review of African Political Economy* (81): 367-384.

Beachey, Ray (1990). *The Warrior Mullah: The Horn Aflame 1892-1920.* London: Bellew Publishing

Bradbury, Mark (2003). Living with Statelessness: The Somali Road to Development, *Conflict, Security & Development 3:1* April

Brons, Maria (2001). *Society, Security, Sovereignty, and the State: Somalia, from Statelessness to Statelessness.* Utrecht: International Books

Bryden, Matt (2003). No Quick Fixes: Coming to terms with terrorism, Islam and statelessness in Somalia, Journal of Conflict Studies, Vol.XXIII, No.2

Callaghy, T., Kassimir, R., and Latham, R., Eds. (2001). *Intervention and Transnationalism in Africa: Global-Local Networks of Power.* Cambridge: Cambridge University Press.

Chabal, P., and Daloz, J.-P. (1998). *Africa Works Disorder as Political Instrument.* Oxford/Bloomington: James Currey/Indiana University Press.

Chazan, Naomi (1994). Engaging the state: associational life in sub-Saharan Africa. In Migdal, Kohli and Shue (eds.) *State Power and Social Forces: Domination and Social Transformation in The Third World,* New York: Cambridge University Press

Clapham, C. (1996). *Africa and the International System: The Politics of State Survival.* Cambridge: Cambridge University Press.

Drysdale, John (2000), *Stoics Without Pillows,* London: Haan

Duffield, M. (2001). *Global Governance and the New Wars: The Merging of Security and Development.* London: Zed Books.

Ehret, C. (1995), The Eastern Horn of Africa, 1000 BC to 1400 AD: The Historical Roots, pp.233-256 in Ali Jimale Ahmed (Ed.), *The Invention of Somalia,* Lawrenceville: Red Sea Press

Gundel, J. (2003). Assisting Structures of Violence? Humanitarian Assistance in the Somali Conflict. In D. Jung (Ed.), *Shadow Globalization, Ethnic Conflicts, and New Wars: A Political Economy of Intra-State Wars.* London: Routledge.

Gundel, Joakim (2006), *Exploring the old in the new, or the new in the old? Somali traditional structures in contemporary security, State building and development,* Paper presented at the Nordic Network on Horn of Africa Studies' Workshop, Helsinki University, May 11-14, 2006

Hansen, Stig J., R. Hollekim & G.M. Sørensen, Somaliland: Elections for the Lower House of Parliament, September 2005, Nordem Report 03/2006

Hibou, B. (2002). *Fluidity of boundaries and the privatisation of the state in Africa.* Leipzig: University of Leipzig.

Holsti, K.J. (2000). Political Causes of Humanitarian Emergencies. In E.W. Nafziger, and F. Stewart (Eds.), *War, Hunger, and Displacement*. Vol. 1. 239-281. New York: Oxford University Press.

ICG 2005a, Somalia's Islamists, International Crisis Group, Africa Report No.100, December 2005

ICG 2005b, Counter-Terrorism in Somalia: Loosing Hearts and Minds?, Africa Report No.95, July 2005

Jung, D. (2003). A Political Economy of Intra-State War: Confronting a Paradox. In D. Jung (Ed.), *Shadow Globalization, Ethnic Conflicts, and New Wars: A Political Economy of Intra-State Wars*. 9-26. London: Routledge.

Kaldor, M., and Luckham, R. (2001). Global Transformations and New Conflicts. *IDS Bulletin*. 32(2): 48-69.

Lemarchand, R. (1992). Uncivil States and Civil Societies: How Illusion Became Reality. *The Journal of Modern African Studies*. 30(2): 177-191.

Le Sage, A. (2004), Somalia and the War on Terrorism: Political Islamic Movements and US Counter Terrorism Efforts, PhD Dissertation, Cambridge University

Lewis, I.M. (1961). *A Pastoral Democracy. A Study of Pastoralism and Politics among the Northern Somali of the Horn of Africa,* Oxford: IAI/James Currey, Reprint, 1999

Little, P. (2003). *Somalia: Economy Without State,* Oxford: IAI/James Currey

Lund, C. (1996). Approaching Twilight Institutions. Analytical Dimensions of Politico-Legal Institutions and Disputes. *Forum for Development Studies*(2): 353-375.

Lund, C. (2001). Precarious Democratization and Local Dynamics in Niger: Micro-Politics in Zinder. *Development and Change*. 32: 845-869

Mamdani, M. (2002). African states, citizenship and war: a case study. *International Affairs*. 78(3): 493-506

Marchal, Roland (2004), Islamic political dynamics in the Somali civil war, in Alex de Waal (ed.), Islamism and its enemies in the Horn of Africa, Indiana University Press

Menkhaus, Ken (2004), Somalia: State collapse and the threat of terrorism, IISS Adelphi Paper 364

Migdal, J.S. (2001). *State in Society: Studying How States and Societies Transform and Constitute One Another*. Cambridge: Cambridge

University Press.

Reuschemeyer, D. & P.B. Evans (1985). The State and Economic Transformation: Toward an Analysis of the Conditions Underlying Effective Intervention. In Evans, et.al., *Bringing the State Back In.* New York: Cambridge University Press

Weber, Max (1958). *Essays in Sociology, English translation,* New York: Oxford University Press

Wendt, A. (1999). *Social Theory of International Politics.* Cambridge: Cambridge University Press.

----

[1]http://www.thekeep.org/~kunoichi/kunoichi/themestream/hatshepsut.html

[2]The UN considers Somalia to be the second poorest country on earth.

[3]The most famous resistance was that of Mohammed Abdille Hassan, also infamously called the 'Mad Mullah' by the British. A good account of the wars between Mohammed Abdille Hassan's extreme puritanical religious movement, the Salihiya brotherhood, and the British can be found in 'The Warrior Mullah' by Ray Beachey, London: Bellew Publishing, 1990.

[4]Abdulkadir Osman travelled in Puntland and Somaliland, July 2005, and Joakim Gundel in Somaliland, Puntland and South-Central Somalia from February to June 2006

[5]However, the analytical dissolution of these boundaries is not necessarily in contradiction to an end result that may confirm or even define the existence of classic demarcations and boundaries of the state.

[6]External intervention may even involve non-state actors acting on behalf of states, who in partnerships with local states or other non-state actors in conjunction acts as authorities.

[7]In Africa, the introduction of the state-society distinction by colonialism did not penetrate the African societies to such a degree that the concept can be considered internalised by them. To paraphrase Lemarchand (Lemarchand 1992: 178), there is no clear line of demarcation between state and society in Africa. Rather they seem to interpenetrate each other in more or less complex ways and at different levels (symbolic, normative, or structural).

[8]If institutionalisation alone entails the formalisation of practices into state institutions, then we will miss very important aspects of the

processes of power structuration because the exercise of power may pursue strategies that avoid formalisation, build on clientelist networks, use coercion, work disorder as a political instrument etc. We therefore need a concept of institutionalization that covers informal practices and structures, such as oral based traditional authorities and practices, the workings of informal clientelist politics and clandestine economic networks (Lund 1996: 353).

[9]Note that these Northern state authorities were established without external assistance.

[10]The most important source of individual protection in Somalia is the threat of retaliation by entire sub-clans in response to an assault on a clan member. While, individuals from powerful clans enjoy this kind of protection, those from weak clans and low caste groups can be preyed upon with impunity unless they seek protection from a stronger clan. Retaliatory actions can however also lead to fatal cycles of revenge killings, and hence cause instability.

[11]Historically, most of the rural Somali communities were largely 'stateless' pastoral or agro-pastoral societies organized by lineage or clan. They did not rely on, nor need state structures as sources of security and rule of law. To them the modern State was either seen as weak and marginally present, or as predatory and oppressive. Hence, they retained their customary laws to manage and resolve their inter-clan disputes.

[12]In cases of crimes, such as killings, elders will prompt investigate work and negotiate with the kin of the accused for his or her handover. The police are requested to assist with arresting suspects and take them to custody. Hereafter, the crime is the subject of inter-clan negotiations and is usually solved according to the customary practices of blood compensation. Customary law exists as a complement to, not a contradiction with, formal police and judicial systems and resolves more than 80% of all cases (Gundel 2006).

[13]See the ICG Report on 'Somalia's Islamists' for an elaborate account of Al-Ittihad (ICG 2005a).

[14]Somaliland opted out of this peace process as they claim their sovereignty. Puntland takes part under the condition that they will form an autonomous administration in a future federal state system for Somalia.

[15]The TFG may eventually develop into a functional central government, but as of June 2006 South-Central Somalia remains a de facto zone of state collapse.

[16]The fighting actually started as struggle between two formerly

allied Warlords, Bashir Raghe and Abokar Aden (both from the from same sub-sub clan, Hawiye/Abgal/Warsangeli) about the El Maan beachlanding facility North of Mogadishu.

[17]For comprehensive discussions of Islamic activity and terrorism in Somalia refer to Abdullahi Chapter 13 above, and the ICG reports (2005a & 2005b), as wells as the publications by Andre Le Sage 2004, Ken Menkhaus 2004 and Roland Marchal 2004).

Charpter 19

General Conclusion: Options for the Future?

Mammo Muchie and Abdulkadir Osman Farah

In the midst of the Horn of Africa lies a collapsed state. The real challenge is to use our moral, intellectual, humane and political resources to rise up to the challenge and at least avoid being an obstacle to the Somali people to get out of the morass.

Paradoxically the elites of the region continue to apply a perspective of playing politics by privileging first and foremost what they perceive to be their interest without contextualising and aligning their specific interest in relation to the collective welfare and interest of the region. The relevant questions then become: is there a regional interest that is more than the sum of the countries constituting what is known as the Horn of Africa? If Somalia is burning, can the other countries in the Horn be safe? If Somalia is open game, can the others feel secure? It seems that the political elites at the helm of the states of the region behave and act with a logic of a zero or negative sum game. If a neighbouring regime decides that unless those friendly to its rule and interests are in charge in Somalia, the prevailing chaos there is to be preferred to any other Somali political elite rule or government, then we will have a protracted Hobbesian situation in the region for as long as this type of selfish thinking defines the political rule of the game.

Regimes come and go. Countries stay on. Nations endure. Even if it is in chaos, Somalia as a nation and the Somalis as a people live on and will do so in the flowing river of time. People, even when they pass away, live through their progeny. Regimes too, unless they are like monarchies that are able to reproduce them, often come and go. In our region there are no ruling monarchies. It is thus fallacious to say only those friendly to a current regime of a neighbour of say of Eritrea or Ethiopia, Sudan or Djibouti must rule or else. This thinking lacks vision and foresight. Unfortunately, it is the prevailing paradigm in the politics of the Horn of Africa. It lacks any long term conception and political imagination to bring collective security, stability, democracy and prosperity.

How can a regional strategic framework evolve by going beyond the selfish concerns of selfish political elites? How can inspired leadership and leaders become capable of not only seeing their own political interests, but also the collective security of the wider region as a whole? Can an Eritrean put herself as a Somali, or Ethiopian, or Sudanese or Djiboutian? Conversely can a Somali do like wise? Can an Ethiopian do that? And so on…

Until we all learn to show concern and regard to the interest of not only ourselves but also our neighbours, we will continue to suffer the humiliation of conflict, war, drought, floods, poverty, ecological breakdown and many other ills.

There is a need to develop a regional perspective for the security and well-being of all the people in the region. The questions then become: given the bewildering variety of our identities, our differences, what shared bases can provide the opportunities to transcend the selfish concerns of selfish elites? Can religion do it? For Somalia, which is racked by inter clan rivalry and conflict, some Somali scholars look to Islam to provide a constitutive foundation for bringing Somalis together. The Islamic Union Courts appear to promote a Somali version of Shari'a Law to re-establish a Somali nation. But even if this were to work for Somalia, and many who wish Somali to attain a semblance of stability and security were open to the IUC and welcomed them, it remains doubtful whether the region would emerge as an oasis of peace and stability with an imposed Islamic state in the Horn of Africa. For example the imposition of Shari'a law in Sudan has contributed to the crises in Darfur and the Southern Sudanese conflict.

It may be wise to use Islamic principles and appropriate the virtues in Islam for local government purposes and, if possible, it may be desirable to hybridise and combine tradition with modern ideas of rule of law, human rights, and democratic governance. But it may be unwise to make it the defining logo for bringing together the region simply because there are other religions which may feel excluded and thus it may not help to damn conflict but potentially exacerbate it.

At the general level of state building it may be prudent to use enlightenment values of reason and statecraft to permit the clarity of shared purposes and bring out common challenges and problems to work and solve them. In local areas in each country of the region it may be useful to build on the values people hold dearly and which fulfil their existential security and moral development. This can be left to the various states to tolerate and encourage local communities to self-recognise, and self-define their values and choices. Societies that thrive are also those that attain moral reasoning and become moral communities.

If religion may not be able in the long run to be the constitutive foundation for the region to get closer, can nationalism do it? That is to say, can nationalism provide the constitutive foundation to form a Horn of African collective identity? Nationalism too can be destructive or constructive. In our region, it has been very destructive and has not produced anything we can consider is progressive and welfare enhancing to date. The record shows that it has stimulated inter- state war, and prolonged animosity that has not subsided after the formal end of the conflict. Elites have used either ethnic nationalism or the nationalism of colonial freedom to fight long wars, and after the end of the long war, other wars have been fought. It looks like the national project, which is not inclusive of all the peoples of the region, is also fraught with major difficulties.

.We can go on listing and fishing for a number of constitutive foundations to bring us together. None will do other than universal ideas of shared sense of justice, a determination to root out our sources of humiliation together as a shared project, a commitment to democracy, rule of law, human rights and democratic governance. Without submission to these values, our region will not be able to come together. The overriding role of the elite not aligned to those who have turned the region into conflict, depravation and suffering, is to find new trajectories to mobilise and energise a democratic movement, communicate, converse and link together across the region to found a new covenant for the region to work and live together.

The regional perspective for solving the major problems of the region must also confront who the main agency can be to try to stimulate the effort. Can the post- colonial state provide the impetus to bring the region together as it is constituted today? It looks certainly not. The key problem of the states as they are now is the fact that they have been imposed by force or as relics of post- colonial hangovers. The main weakness of the states in the region is that they have a tenuous link with society. They seem to have better links with external actors than their own people owing to the fact that their domestic base is often limited and their capability to comply and respond with priorities and needs of the population is woefully inadequate. Often their repressive machinery is fat whilst their capacity to link with civilised relations with the people is often absent.

What needs stimulating is people to people, society to society, intellectual to intellectual linkages and work towards restructuring and reconstituting a people- friendly, knowledge- friendly and society friendly state that can, in the course of its insertion in society, people and knowledge, sheds its repressive and donor- addicted crippled status.

The Diaspora can play a catalytic role and can engage either constructively or destructively as well. When it is engaged in promoting conflict by supporting the conflicting parties in the region it can play a destructive role. When it tries to promote peace and stability by using its knowledge, its resources and capabilities to promote democratic dialogue amongst each community and across communities, its role can be constructive.

In Scandinavia we are trying to promote this spirit by establishing a Horn of Africa research community that will primarily engage all the intellectuals of the region to work together and create knowledge and share experience. At Lund University, there have been, over the last five years,

This work opens the debate and will contribute to the democratic dialogue that is necessary to foster in the region. Let the conversation for bringing the region together continue.

Notes on Contributors

Abdi M. Kusow: Dr. Kusow is an associate professor of Sociology at the University of Auckland, USA

Abdulkadir Osman Farah: is attached to the Centre for development and International Relations Aalborg University. He is in process of presenting a PhD thesis to the same University. Mr. Farah is also employed as consultant for the municipality of Aarhus, Denmark. He is the co-founder of the Centre for Research and Integration, Aarhus, Denmark.

Abdulkadir Yahye Ali: was one of Somalia's most respected peace activists. He was Co-Director and Founder of Centre for Research and Dialogue. July 12 2005 he was assassinated at his home in Mogadishu by unknown assailants. Mr. Yahya has been active in Somalia peace efforts for a long time. He was a prominent peace activist, an active member of the Somali civil society and intellectuals who decided to work for and live with their people in the face of all odds.

Abdurahman M. Abdullahi: Dr. Abdurahman Badio is researcher at the University of Mogadishu, Somalia and attached to McGill University, Canada.

Cindy Horst: Dr. Horst is a senior researcher at the International Peace Research Institute, Oslo, Norway.

Fowsia Abdulkadir: Ms. Abdulkadir is a Somali women activist, researcher and Head of Somali Human Rights Association, Canada.

Jabril Ibrahim Abdule: Mr. Abdule is a Researcher and co-chair of the Centre for Dialogue and reconciliation (CDR), Mogadishu, Somalia.

Joakim Gundel: is a PhD candidate at the University of Copenhagen. He is specialist in humanitarian emergencies and the consequences of civil wars in Somalia and Liberia. He is currently working as a consultant in Somalia and Somaliland. Mr. Gundel conducted studies of the humanitarian security environment for the Humanitarian Policy Group/ODI, London and of the traditional structures in Somalia for the Danish Refugee Council.

Katrine Fangen: Dr. Fangen is researcher at the department of Sociology at the University of Oslo, Norway.

Khalif Farah: Mr. Farah is Governance Officer at UNDP, Nairobi, Kenya and attached to the Institute of Diplomacy and International Studies, at the University of Nairobi, Kenya.

Lee Cassanelli: Dr. Cassanelli is a Professor of history and Director of the Centre for African Studies at the University of Pennsylvania, USA.

Mammo Muchie: is a Professor and Director of Research Centre on Development & International Relations, Aalborg University, Denmark. Professor Muchie has taught and researched at various Universities including Cambridge University, and Amsterdam University in The Netherlands

Markus Hoehne: Mr. Hoehne is a Researcher at Max Planck Institute for Social Anthropology, Halle/Saale, Germany.

Martin Hill: Dr. Hill is a senior researcher at Amnesty International, UK.

Mohamed Hassan Ibrahim (Gani): Mr. Gani is a senior researcher at The Academy for Peace & Development, Hargaisa, Somaliland.

Nauja Kleist: Dr. Kleist is researcher at DIIS (Danish Institute for International Studies), Copenhagen, Denmark.

Peter Hansen: Mr. Hansen is a researcher at DIIS (Danish Institute for International Studies), Copenhagen, Denmark.

Richard Ford: Dr. Ford is Professor at Clark University, USA.

Stephanie R. Bjork: Mrs. Bjork is a researcher at the University Auckland, USA.

Tiina Salmio: Ms. Salmio is a researcher on Somalia and Coordinator at Plan Finland, Finland.

Valeria Saggiomo: Ms. Saggiomo is a Researcher and formerly with CISP (an Italian International NGO) where she was an education coordinator for Somalia & Sudan.

Virginia Luling: Dr. Luling is a researcher and one of the profiles at Somali Studies International Association, UK.

Index

A

B

C

H

I

J

K

L

M

www.ingramcontent.com/pod-product-compliance
Lightning Source LLC
Chambersburg PA
CBHW070552270326
41926CB00013B/2291

9781905068838